Music and Literary Modernism

Music and Literary Modernism: Critical Essays and Comparative Studies 2nd Edition

Edited by

Robert P. McParland

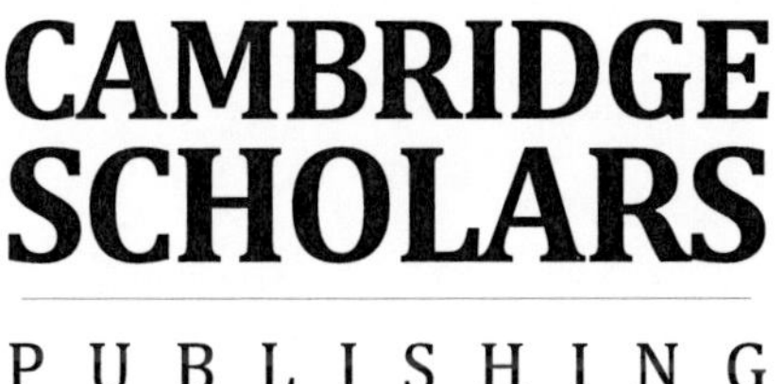

Music and Literary Modernism: Critical Essays and Comparative Studies 2nd Edition,
Edited by Robert P. McParland

This book first published 2009

Cambridge Scholars Publishing

12 Back Chapman Street, Newcastle upon Tyne, NE6 2XX, UK

British Library Cataloguing in Publication Data
A catalogue record for this book is available from the British Library

ISBN (10): 1-4438-1402-4, ISBN (13): 978-1-4438-1402-7

TABLE OF CONTENTS

INTRODUCTION

Modernism, as an event in contemporary culture, continues to resonate among us today. Some have called our own period post-modernist – suggesting something after or beyond modernism or counter to it. Perhaps we ask how we are to not be modernist, or how to be something else. Yet, we remain in a conversation with modernism. This collection intends to continue that conversation with an international dialogue that moves between music, literary history, and theory.

To literary modernism, we attach the names of Joyce and Pound, Woolf and Eliot. A transformation in fiction, poetry, and music emerged in their work, in that cultural space of Anglo-American and French literary modernism that is investigated here. For each of these writers discussed here, from Proust to Hemingway, or from Yeats to Stevens, music was intertwined with their language. By exploring the interaction of these literary artists with music we develop another means by which to engage in a reevaluation of modernism.

The contributors to this collection take up in their essays many of the issues that we are presented with today by modernism. In doing so, they not only cross time and space, they dissolve the boundaries of isolation between academic disciplines while seeking a common cultural legacy. These writers promote interdisciplinary dialogue as they probe a space between the linguistic and the musical that has sometimes been called intermediality, or 'melopoetics.'

The contributors to this collection, in various ways, underscore how the writers and composers we refer to as modernists sought to "make it new" and were initiators shaping a new narrative. This was a period in which literary and musical artists were fascinated with technique, a time in which poets, writers, and composers developed a variety of strategies, new forms, and artistic breakthroughs. As we have entered the twenty-first century, we also, with our perhaps different insights and approaches, likewise seek re-formulations and breakthroughs. Perhaps critical reevaluations, like those in the following essays, will suggest ways by which to continue this process.

Essays on music and language and on the intersections of the French and Anglo-American strands of modernism have been placed together in the first section, "Criticism, Music and Literature." We begin, in a sense, with post-modernism so that we might work our way back from it. Here the approaches are first focused upon music and center on theory. In section two, "Musical and Literary Interactions," we meet with a variety of perspectives on modernist writers, such as Virginia Woolf, Ezra Pound, Mina Loy, Gertrude Stein, Ernest

Hemingway, William Butler Yeats, James Weldon Johnson, and Wallace Stevens, in which their relationships with music are explored. In section three, the generally materialist poetics of the first section are offset by alternative transcendental probings of works by Marcel Proust, and James Joyce respectively. In our final section, we look at the music and literature of high modernism, such as that of T.S. Eliot, in its argument with and relation to popular culture. The collection concludes with a reflection on The Beatles in relation to modernism.

For readers who would like to investigate the sources mentioned here, bibliographic references follow each essay. A brief essay noting additional material for further reading is appended to the text. Notes to the essays by the contributors to this volume appear as endnotes, prior to the Index. We are grateful to the family and estate of George Antheil, for permission to quote from the composer's correspondence. The editor also wishes to extend thanks to Robert Ingoglia for his computer assistance and to all of the writers of these essays for their insights and contributions.

I

Criticism, Music and Literature

THE SONORITY OF LANGUAGE IN LITERARY AND MUSICAL MODERNITY

MARC DERVEAUX

In my work on the sonority of language[1] I defined nineteen different sound figures of language—needless to say this list is not exhaustive.

The idea of the sound of speech might evoke for many the emotional charge of the voice, the theatrical play of the affects. However, this is not the focus of this text.

The expression "music and language" is often associated with the narrative aspect of a composition; for example, we often make reference to the musical syntax or to the discursivity of music. Again, this is not what semiophony is about.

When we say "music and literature", we mostly refer to the use of texts by composers, the borrowing of musical forms by writers or even to music-related themes in fiction. This is not addressed in my work either—or not specifically.

Finally, when we associate music with poetry, we perhaps think first and foremost of prosody, of the melody of speech and of the rhythm of words. But once again, prosody—at least in its traditional acceptation—is only a minor phenomenon in the field I am interested in.

So, what do I mean by sonority of language?

In my research, the key question has been all along: what do we hear in language when it does not mean anything? How can we describe the unusual experience resulting from the peculiar entwining of our linguistic faculties and our auditive sense? Moreover, by coming close to this singular experience, can we learn something about the relationship we have to our language, about the history of western music and poetry and about what these arts mean to us moderns? It seemed to me that some answers to these very questions lay in the hypothesis of there being a common root between the two arts as revealed (or created…) by modernity, of an autonomous aesthetic material that is neither song nor verse; it is some of these answers that I would like to present in the following.

Sound poetry, contemporary music, the experimental novel, the hoerspiel are all forms or genres where the particular phenomenon of sonorous speech occurs—that is to say, *speech perceived as a sound and yet recognizable as language*. It is therefore in the works by, among others, John Cage, Bernard Heidsieck, Hans G. Helms, Franz Mon, James Joyce, Steve Reich or Kurt Schwitters that we are able to find such objects. (A list of recordings can be found at the end of the text.)

As stated earlier, these figures are not emotional modes of voice; neither are they rhetorical figures; they are, rather, aesthetic figures, a play with patterns of perception and with artistic forms. Some of them, for example, are specific aspects of language—sometimes essential characteristics—that are revealed through the erasing of meaning (an erasing that can either take place by means of the techniques used by the artist or simply through the listener's apperception). To a certain degree, we could consider meaning here to be a veil masking these features of speech which in turn usually serve to convey the sense of the words.

Other figures can be subsumed under the common theme of the syncretism between music and poetry, an expression used by Roman Jakobson (1974). This idea refers both to the *Verfransung der Künste* (or an eroding of the arts), a concept Adorno uses to describe the evolution of modern art as of the end of the 19th century (1967)—and to the hypothesis of the common origin of the two arts that we for example find expounded in Rousseau's work (1968). It is on these figures that I would like to focus here.

Semiophonic objects belonging to the *spoken-sung* figure hesitate indefinitely between vocal art and simple speech. They find their paradigm in the Schoenbergian *Sprechgesang*, a technique developed by the Austrian composer to obtain a "speaking voice which has to transform the indicated pitch into a spoken melody" (Scheitler, 1998, p. 89). By asking the performer to leave the sung tone immediately after the attack and to carry on in a speaking manner, he brought about a fusion between song and language: with the *Sprechgesang*, the almost physiological border that separated song from word was indicated—if not erased—and the vocal, corporal origin of speech was emphasized. It was a reaffirmation of the phonatory system being a meeting place for musical and poetic gestures. From a more aesthetic perspective, it could be claimed that spoken-sung objects produce a distanciation by bringing a way of listening to awareness, by creating a sensory experience that unveils essential patterns of our auditory perception. In this sense, *Sprechgesang*—and similar vocal objects that may appear in sound poetry and contemporary music—realizes the dissolution of the "mechanized formulae" of *bel canto*, thus exemplifying the very movement of new music as identified by Adorno in his short essay about music and language (1978, p. 252). The spoken-sung figure creates a place where the "melodious voice" and the "spoken voice" can be one, incarnating the myth of an aesthetic or historical space where music and poetry find their common origin. Indeed, for Jean-Jacques Rousseau, "the first speeches were the first songs: the periodical and measured return of the rhythms, the melodious inflexions of the accents gave birth to poetry and music together with language, or rather, all of this was language (…)." (1968, p. 139) And Heidegger once described day-to-day language as a "forgotten and therefore worn poem." (1959, p. 31)

In fact it is undoubtedly possible to regard modern poetry as a constant effort to refresh language, to make a living word out of the poem. By way of example, T. S. Eliot saw in free verse "a revolt against dead form." (1957, p. 37) From that point of view, the sound figures of language present themselves on the one hand as a break in tradition through which the dynamism of forms is preserved and on the other, as the continuation of this tradition—with tradition defined here as the constant awakening of language through poetry [2]. Other semiophonic objects provide further proof of the waning of poetic and musical forms. Among these, the *somatic* and *phonetic* figures hold a prominent role.

Many of the aforementioned works make extensive use of buccal, laryngeal, labial or breathing sounds that are usually pushed back or erased in ordinary verbal communication. I chose to call these semiophonic occurrences "somatic" owing to their being productions and signs of the body.

An archaic, raw, previous form of language is evoked through such sounds; they are produced by the phonatory system and yet seem anterior to linguistic phonems. One could say that they represent a kind of acoustic frontier of language, an origin of speech that is a physical production of the body. In fact, rather than being a primary stadium of linguistic activity, this expelled air, these throat, mouth, lip and tongue sounds point to the body as being first and foremost a "noisy" and pneumatic device where language as a raw material is kneaded and grinded.

Furthermore, the apparition of breathing and buccal sounds in modern works of art is a way of reproducing the elementary gesture of poetry, of refreshing it. For Gaston Bachelard, "poetry in its simple, natural, primitive form (…) is a joy of wind, the obvious pleasure of breathing. (…) All poetry is dependant of this primitive economy of breathing." (1943, pp. 271-272) But the somatic figure is also an indication of the end of traditional poetry as we know it or at least of an interrogation regarding its future: after all, what is left of the poetic space when the boundaries between the sounds of language and the mere sounds of the body crumble or when the resources of the literally exhausted language are reduced to a "primitive economy of breathing"? In this sense, the somatic objects in contemporary music or sound poetry can certainly be seen as signs of the erosion of language which Mallarmé once described as an "overworked tool." (1945, p. 644)

The understanding of language as an eroded means of communication, of words as mechanised patterns, is very much at the origin of dadaist poetry. During an evening at the Cabaret Voltaire in Zürich in 1916, Hugo Ball described his work as follows: "with poems of this kind, we renounce to a language distorted and rendered impossible by journalism. We withdraw into the most secrete alchemy of the word, we even give up the word itself and we keep what is most sacred for poetry, its last refuge." (1992, p. 70) Objects of the phonetic figure are good examples of what experimental poetry and modern vocal music have become following such a radical attitude.

Within the field of semiophony, what I describe as phonetic occurrences are simply elementary sound of language that can appear in the flow of a text, be it musical or literary. One of the most striking characteristics of such auditive objects is their constitutive ambiguity: it is often impossible to determine which particular sphere of meaning they belong to. Are these elongated vowels phonems or melody? Is this very short utterance a word or a mere phonatory noise? The phonetic figure defines itself in three ways: firstly, by indicating isolated segments of the linguistic string—thus causing language to lose its transparency; by dismantling the structure of the word despite it seeming necessary as an elementary poetical unit; and finally, by evoking a fused origin of speech and song through the voice insisting on a particular phonem—thus producing the impression of a sung tone. The semiophonic material establishes here its identity in a negative way: its poetic meaning grows on the ruins of poetry; as a musical object, it abolishes the distinction between vocal art and language, and furthermore it is a questioning of the value of speech as an instrument of exchange and information.

From this point of view, semiophonic objects represent one of the most vigorous critiques of language by modern art—this at a time when the unquestioned understanding of language as an obvious part of social communication was progressively challenged. It is no doubt possible to explain this mistrust from historical and sociological perspectives and to find, with Hans G. Helms (1968) and Yves Kobry (1981), the main reasons behind the gradual reification of linguistic forms in the rationalisation of administrative structures, in the development of specialised idioms and in the expansion of the media.

This loss of meaning, a consequence of the waning of artistic forms and of the erosion of language, is exemplified by among other figures the *prosodic* one. Originally, the term "prosody" referred to the rules concerning metrics; today prosody as a branch of linguistics ("a subcomponent of phonology and/or phonetics") concerns itself with the study of "all sorts of phenomena like stress, intonation, noise, pauses, flow, rhythm." (1979, p. 299) Within the frame of the semiophonic enquiry, I defined as prosodic objects occurrences where phrastic elements, expressive features, acoustical characteristics of speech make sense in themselves by abandoning verbal meaning. In this sense, we can see in them the results of distanciation [3]; it is possible to describe the particular effect of the semiophonic distanciation by means of semiotics, saying that the level of expression—in this case the acoustic level of speech—becomes its own level of content. According to Roman Jakobson, this way of producing meaning is called "introversive semiosis" which he associates with music, abstract painting and sound poetry, since they are all self-indicating artistic forms (1974, p. 171).

In the view of Eero Tarasti, distanciation as antinarrativity is the common denominator of modern art (1994, p. 68); this is easy to understand in the case of semiophony and especially in the case of prosodic objects: it is namely by erasing the meaning and what contributes to the building of a narrative discourse that these objects come into being. Again, "the old distinction between music and literature" (Mallarmé, 1945, 649) is abolished through this very movement: semiophony brings "pure" musical discursivity that is bare of lexical elements back to the poem—thus restoring the once abandoned *melos*, as Helms puts it, to poetry (1966, p. 143); and in suggesting verbal meaning through the use of vocal sonority it confers to song the aspect of speech—thus imparting music with a narrativity that is progressively getting lost.

The concise works of Webern, the formalist pieces of the serial school and the conceptual productions of John Cage are proof enough of the loss of meaning and the exhaustion of musical material in the 20th century. In this context, it is possible to see the interweaving of language fragments with sound texture as a way of saving musical narrativity in contemporary pieces. The fact that music only takes the acoustical envelope of words and thereby discards the verbal meaning prevents it from becoming just poetry: music has to stay within the realm of sound to keeps its identity. Once again, semiophony emerges here as a negative form: unwilling to become poetry, unable to remain purely music; this aesthetic figure is an attempt by the two arts to overcome the historical crisis of modernity.

Another figure exemplifiying the antinarrative, "meaningless" movement of semiophony is the *gestural* figure. In these objects, the voice presents itself in one block, like a simple statement, an object that is thrown—in other words an act and not a verbal message or piece of information. This act is always by hypothesis inherent to the voice and confers to speech a gestural meaning that is immanent to it according to Maurice Merleau-Ponty (1945, p. 209). For Greimasian semiotics, "the language act has to be seen first and foremost as a signifying gestural doing that can be related to similar vocal gestures (like singing, whistling, burping, stuttering…) (…), without the actual content of what is said necessarily playing a role. The designation of the speech act should be limited to this 'signifying somatic activity'." (1979, pp. 5-6) It is when speech is reduced to this "signifying somatic activity" and gives up its verbal, meaningful component that it becomes a gestural object in the semiophonic sense of the word—otherwise put when through its gesture it reveals the core of language that is essential to signification but which signifies nothing in itself, that is to say it expresses no verbal sense. It is because semiophonic objects present themselves stripped of verbal meaning that they momentarily become speech as an act, a movement of the body which according to Nelson Goodman exemplifies rather than denotes. "The label a movement exemplifies may be itself." (1968, p. 65) If the dance gesture "expresses" the body through the body, then the semiophonic gesture expresses speech through speech. Such vocal objects are emblematic of the speech act that "like every other gesture draws its own meaning" (1945, p. 217), they are almost like the quiddity of spoken language, equal, perhaps, to a coin being silently passed from hand to hand—an image in which Mallarmé could see all linguistic activity (1945, p. 857). And if we wanted to take as a starting point of semiophony the Mallarmean works—in which "the word comes close to a brief and singular act through being freed from usual clichés and technical reflexes of the writer" (1953, p. 55)—we could say that the gestural objects as elementary speech acts represent a true "degré zéro" of the poetic material, an ultimate boundary that poetry can't cross lest it vanishes.

Ultimately, the attempt to reach the very essence of language through poetry leads to the idea of a prelapsarian language. According to Genesis II, 19, the words Adam used to name things with in the garden of Eden were one with these things: "and whatsoever Adam called every living creature, that was the name thereof". As Walter Benjamin puts it, "the paradisal language of human beings had to be the language of perfect knowledge." (1977, p. 152) The sonorous gesture of language in modernity seems to tend towards such biblical reunion of words and things, towards the original identity between the sign and what it denotes. Like music that "reaches the absolute in an immediate way but at the same time loses its clarity" (1978, p. 255), semiophony aims at the utopia of immediacy and in order to do so has to paradoxically give up semanticism.

To conclude: loss of meaning in modern art, antinarrativity, syncretism between music and poetry, understanding of form as a critique in modern art work, renewal of artistic forms through distanciation and finally the search for the immediacy of edenic language, for the utopian idea of an "absolute language" constitute the key words to this approach. In my view, semiophony as a theoretical concept provides a platform for exploring modernity in art under a number of different perspectives, be they historical, sociological, aesthetical or linguistical. Only some of the questions raised by this concept have been exposed in this paper.

Works Cited

Adorno, T.W. "Die Kunst und die Kunste," *Oh ne Leitbild, Parva Aesthetica.* Frankfurt am Main: Suhrkamp Verlag, 1967.

—. Fragment uber Musik und Sprache," *Quasi una fantasia.* Musikalische Schriften II. Frankfurt am Main: Suhrkamp Verlag, 1978.

Bachelard, Gaston. *L'air et les songes.* Paris: Librarie Jose Corti, 1943.

Baronnet, Jean / Dufrêne, François. *U 47*. Paris : Studio Apsonne, LP Philips 835 485/86 AY, 1960.

Barthes, Roland. *Le degree zero de l'ecriture*. Paris: Editions du Seuil, 1953.

Benjamin, Walter. "Uber Sprache uberhaupt und uber die Sprache des Menschen," *Gesammelte Schriften. Band II,1*. Herausgegeben von Rolf Tiedemann und Hermann Schweppenhauser. Frankfurt am Main: Surkamp Verlag, 1977.

Berio, Luciano. *A-Ronne*. Swingle II. CD Decca Head 15. Partition : London - Wien –Zürich : Universal Edition 15988, 1975.

Cage, John. *Second writing through Finnegans Wake*. Hrsg. von Klaus Schöning. Königstein/Ts : Athenäum Verlag GmbH, 1985.

Courtes, J. and Griemas, A.J.. *Dictionaire raisonne de la theorie du language*. Paris: Classiques Hachette, 1979.

Eliot, T.S.. "The Music of Poetry" (1942), *On Poetry and Poets*. London: Faber and Faber, 1957.

Goodman, Nelson. *Languages of Art*. Indianapolis, New York and Kansas City: Bobbs Merrill Company, 1968.

Hausmann, Raoul. *Poèmes Phonetiques Complètes*. München : S Press Tonbandverlag (S Press Tonband Nr. 2), 1972.

Heidsieck, Bernard. *Derviche/Le Robert: lettre H (1984)*. LP Lautpoesie. Eine Anthologie. Hrsg. von Christian Scholz. Obermichelbach : Gertraud Scholz Verlag, 1987. ISBN 3-925599-09-5

—. *Poème-partition J*. Hattingen : S Press Tonbandverlag (S Press Tonband Nr. 18), 1973.

Heidegger, Martin. *Unterwegs zur Sprache*. Stuttgart: Verlag Gunther Neske, 1959.

Helms, Hans G. "Uber die Entwicklung mit sprachlichem Material," *Melos* 33. Jahrgang, Heft 10. Mainz: Schott, 1968.

—. and Yves Kobry. "Walter Benjamin et la langage," *Walter Benjamin. Revue d'esthetique* n.1. Paris: Privat, 1981.

—. *Fa:m' Ahniesgwow*. LP DuMont Nr. 6001/1, 6046/6047. Köln: Verlag M. DuMont-Schauberg, 1959.

Jakobson, Ramon. "Die Sprache in ihrem Verhaltnis zu anderen Kommunikationssystemenin," *Form und Sinn*. Munchen: Whilhelm Fink Verlag.

Jandl, Ernst. *Das Röcheln der Mona Lisa. Lesung im Tip*. Berlin : VEB Deutsche.

Joyce, James *Finnegans Wake*. Siobhan Mc Kenna lit *Anna Livia Plurabelle*. 1961. Réédité par Caedmon, 1985. ISBN 089845039X

Kriwet, Ferdinand. *Hörtext I*. SFB, 1963.

Mallarme, Stephen. "Avant-dire au Traite du Verbe," *Oeuvres complete*. Edition etablie par Henri Mondor et G. Jean-Aubrey. Paris: Gallimard,

Biblioteche de la Pleiade, 1945.

Merleau-Ponty, Maurice. *Phenomenologie de la perception.* Paris: Librarie Gallimard, Biblioteche des Idees, 1945.

Mon, Franz. D*as gras wies wächst.* München: *Akzente.* Carl Hanser Verlag, Heft 1, Februar 1969. Production : SR Saarbrücken/Studio Akustische Kunst WDR Köln/BR München, 1969. LP Luchterhand-Verlag, 1972.

Pastior, Oskar. *Mein Chlebnikov.* Obermichelbach : Gertraud Scholz Verlag GSV CD 003, 1989.

Reich, Steve. *It's gonna rain (1966).* CD Elektra - Nonesuch 979 169-2, 1987.

Rousseau, Jean-Jacques. *Essai sur l'origine des langues.* (1781) Texte establi et annote par Charles Porset. Bordeaux: Guy Ducros Editeur, 1968.

Scherstjanoi, Valeri. *KCH (1986).* LP Lautpoesie, eine Anthologie. Obermichelbach: Gertraud Scholz Verlag LP, 1987.

Schleiter, Imgard. "Musik als Thema und Struktur in der deutschen Gegenwartsprosa," *Euphorion* 92. Band. Heidelberg: Universitatsverlag C. Winter, 1998.

Scholz, Christian. "Zur Geschichte der Lautpoesie zwischen Sprache und Musik," *Sprach Ton Art.* Hrsg. Von de Berliner Gesellschaft fur Neue Musik in Zusammenarbeit mit Podewil und dem literarischen Colloquium. Berlin, 1992.

Schwitters, Kurt. *Die Sonate in Urlauten.* Original performance by Kurt Schwitters. CD WER 6304-2, 1993.

Streidter, Jurij. "Zur formnalischen Theorie der Prosa und der literischen Evolution." *Russischer Formalismus.* Munchen: Whilhelm Fink Verlag, 1971.

Terasti, Eero. *A Theory of Musical Semiotics.* Bloomington and Indianapolis: Indiana University Press, 1994.

Sounds Like Now: Music, Avant-Gardism, and The Post-Modern Sublime

Kiene Brillenburg Wurth

I. Introduction

In the later eighteenth- and nineteenth centuries, instrumental music became a privileged vehicle of the sublime because it (presumably) lacked any empirical content. In those days, the idea of the sublime referred to supersensible ideas, such as the infinite or the eternal, which our minds cannot picture or imagine but fill them with awe and stupefaction. Though those days are over now, and the supersensible has become another dirty word, both the idea of the sublime and its special connection to the idea of the 'musical' has survived like a remnant of Romanticism that the postmodern age cannot bear to part with.

Significantly, however, this remnant has been invoked by the French philosopher Jean-François Lyotard as marking an end to nostalgia. As I will show in this essay, Lyotard has revived the sublime to at once dismantle it in its traditional, transcendental aspect. The sublime no longer features a far and beyond, an 'over there' that our souls can pine after endlessly and just as fruitlessly, but has become an 'over here': a material happening that takes place completely on the level of sensibility. For Lyotard, as Renée van de Vall has put it, the sublime has to do with 'an awareness, or feeling, or idea that does not hover above ordinary reality as some sort of thing or quasi-positive entity, but is rather present *within* that reality as an anxiety or limit'.[1]

Strikingly, this so-called postmodern sublime has been modeled on a very modernist conception of twentieth-century avant-garde art as breaking free from the bounds of realist representation. More specifically, Lyotard's argument recalls the formalist dictum of Clement Greenberg that avant-garde poetry and painting undermined their own (traditional) presuppositions in adopting the 'method' of music as a so called strictly sensuous, non-imitative art. Poetry and painting no longer figured 'something', but disfigured and reinvented themselves by withdrawing into the flat surface of their own, material make-up. Knowingly or unknowingly, Lyotard took up this idea of the musicalization of poetry and painting and reworked it into his central statement that the postmodern sublime no longer announces itself in the subject matter of an artwork but in its very matter, in the 'presentation itself'. As I will argue, however, this 'presentation' does not refer to formal design but to an amorphous substance that, precisely, undoes the consolation of recognizable forms.

II. Music and Modernism: Purification Through Contamination

In a recent article on culture, multimodality, and intermediality, Mikko Lehtonen has claimed that intermediality conceived of as an expanded form of intertextuality epitomizes modern, technology-controlled popular cultures.[2] For Lehthonen, intermediality refers to the interactions and cross-pollinations between different media, each medium functioning as a junction or intersection in a network of other media. Popular culture, which Lehtonen puts on a par with mass culture, is intermedial in so far as it feeds on combined media technologies that (endlessly) recycle texts in multiple media.[3] Thus, a novel can be recycled in a movie, a television series, or on a compact disc, while different media forms often converge in mass-mediated products of popular culture, such as advertisements and commercials. According to Lehtonen, this indicates that 'the mixing of media borders is characteristic above all of popular culture, whereas high culture has traditionally been characterized by media purism'.[4]

Though Lehtonen contends that this rift between popular or 'low' culture and artistic or 'high' culture is increasingly subverted in the era of late modernism and postmodernism, his thesis that traditional high culture shuns criss-crossings in-between media is highly questionable.[5] Indeed, in spite of traditional artistic hierarchies strictly categorizing and compartmentalizing different media (as in Lessing's distinction between the spatial and temporal modes), later nineteenth- and twentieth-century 'high' art displays a media purism that, paradoxically, draws on *inter*medial processes and techniques.

Media purism in this essay refers to the manner in which especially later nineteenth- and earlier twentieth-century avant-garde texts (whether they be verbal, visual, or aural) increasingly retreated into the materiality of their own master medium: poetry retreating into the materiality of the verbal signifier (as in much symbolist and concrete poetry), music retreating into an apparently amorphous sound world (John Cage), or painting retreating into figureless fields of color and paint (Barnett Newman). This story of (communal) self-retreat has been told repeatedly in formalist theories intent on screening out 'content' (the level of the signified) in modern art and literature: the subject-matter of art was to be art itself, its very matter, rather than anything external or accidental to it. As Wallace Stevens phrased it in 'The Man with the Blue Guitar':

> Poetry is the subject of the poem.
> From this the poem issues and
> To this returns. Between the two.
> Between issue and return, there is
> An absence in reality.
> Things as they are.
> Or so we say.[6]

'Things as they are'–in their givenness, apparently autonomous in their self-enclosed referentiality, moving back and forth from themselves to themselves with no detour in-between. This ideal of autonomy dates back to the later eighteenth century, when philosophers like Adam Smith already proclaimed that poetry was to be its own subject, self-sufficient, rather than representing something 'outside' of itself–and depending on that 'outside' for its content and significance.[7] In the twentieth century, Clement Greenberg reiterated the issue in 'Towards a Newer Laocoön', which represented the history of avant-garde painting as a history of self-purification: a history of painting becoming ever more 'itself' in its sensuous self-sufficiency.

Interestingly enough, however, in Greenberg's discourse this process of purification is at once a process of contamination. For the method that avant-garde painting employed to achieve its self-validating ends was, according to Greenberg, a method gleaned and adopted from instrumental music: the method of an ' 'abstract' art, an art of 'pure form' '.[8] It is this adoption that I would like to call intermedial. Instead of being just an expanded form of intertextuality, intermediality refers to the process whereby medium *x* absorbs the 'method' or semiotic system of medium *y*. In this way, medium *x* turns into something (slightly) other from its own, no longer its familiar or traditional self, but not (yet) quite the medium it mimics either. Thus, it falls in-between *x* an *y*, between traditionally demarcated medial categories.[9]

Such intermedial mimicry ('the same but not quite') becomes an issue in 'Towards a Newer Laocoön' when Greenberg claims that the abstract currents of twentieth-century avant-garde art grew out of a fascination with, even a jealousy of, the allegedly suggestive, sensuous, and non-representational ways of instrumental music as 'an art in itself'. As Greenberg observes, due to 'its 'absolute' nature, its remoteness from imitation, its almost complete absorption in the very physical quality of its medium, as well as because of its resources of suggestion, music had come to replace poetry as the paragon art. It was the art which the other arts envied most, and whose effects they tried hardest to imitate'.[10] This envy of music as an autonomous art in the literary and pictorial arts had already been diagnosed by Walter Pater in the nineteenth century, who had suggested in Hegelian fashion that all arts constantly tended towards the 'musical'. This was not a tendency to verily *become* music, but to incorporate what Pater considered to be the abstract qualities of music–and I will presently show what those abstract qualities would amount to–in painting and poetry.[11]

According to Greenberg, in twentieth-century painting and poetry this *Anders-streben* (or: intermedial mimicry) only succeeded when the avant-garde's focus on music changed from a focus on musical *effects* into one on 'music as a *method* of art': from an imitation of the kind of vague impressionism associated with instrumental music since the later eighteenth century, into a mimicking of its mode of functioning as an art of 'pure form'.[12] What was this mode of functioning? First, this entailed an emptying of empirical content: in its formalist conception the sign of instrumental music lacked–as we would now say–a stable signified. It was signifier-only, which is to say that this sign was made up of forms (sounds) that did not carry any meaning, be they emotional or conceptual. A verbal sound like 'mtrakloijye' which (within the codes and conventions of the English language) does not carry any sense, would equal such a signifier: it is a sound without meaning.

Secondly, though the musical sign was without empirical content it was nevertheless not empty. Rather, the sounds of instrumental music constituted their own content: their own world of tonally moving forms. Music, as the nineteenth-century theorist Eduard Hanslick claimed, was about music. It lacked imitative and referential potential, because there would be 'nothing in nature for music to copy'. Music, according to Hanslick, 'reiterates no subject matter already known and given a name; therefore it has no nameable content for our thinking in definite concepts'.[13] What it figures, is but its own substance. (This is, of course, a highly debatable issue, for music is still a cultural practice participating inevitably in the (unconscious) circulation of cultural meanings).

Greenberg infers from this the paradox that music was 'abstract because almost nothing else except sensuous'.[14] Abstract here denotes an absence of concrete references to or figurations of individual objects and actual instances that is achieved through a predominance of the materiality of the signifier: through an almost exclusive focus on the substance or materiality of a medium (sound, color, etc.) as an end in itself rather than a means for an end. Thus, the abstract is here not so much opposed to as inscribed in the 'concrete', in so far as the latter functions as the matter of presentation instead of representation.

What the avant-gardes subsequently discovered was that the splendid self-absorption of music could also be made to apply to painting and poetry. That, more specifically, the effects of these arts could be no longer accidental to their 'formal natures'–that the content or subject matter of, for instance, painting could be its own substance, color, paint, and nothing else, operating only on the sense of sight *as* color, paint: an objectless world in itself. To become abstract, the emphasis in avant-garde art 'was to be on the physical, sensorial'.[15]

The result of this abstraction was an increasing self-reflexivity. Painting renounced representation, image-making, formation (to the extent that, say, colors or brush strokes 'defined for their own sake' embody matter not transformed into a recognizable figure), and became one-dimensional, leaving a shallow 'material plane which is the actual surface of the canvas'. Painting represented its own medium. In this way, it at once progressively surrendered 'to the resistance of its medium; which resistance consists chiefly in the flat picture plane's denial of efforts to 'hole through' it for realistic perspectival space', along with the destruction of the 'realistic' pictorial object.[16] Avant-garde painting thus undermined its viewer's expectations in so far as it blocked the possibility to see through, to see *as*, or to see *in*. What you saw was what you got–or at least, what you got was a painting that was about painting.

Similarly, nineteenth- and twentieth-century avant-garde poetry withdrew into its own materiality in so far as it expressed not ideas or emotions, but written and spoken language as an artistic instead of communicative medium. Thus, Stéphane Mallarmé experimented with this 'musical method' in his project of a poetic language without a referent. Poetry, he declared, was about words rather than ideas and about de-familiarizing the function of words as vehicles of (arbitrarily) fixed meanings. Such de-familiarization could be achieved through an ambiguous play with word sounds and their (apparently haphazard) interactions, triggering a chain of unpredictable (and uncontrollable) associations. Language here became a mechanism, if not an organism, functioning on its own in which verbal meanings were never stable but rather grew rife in an endless sonorous interplay. At their strongest points, as Jacques Derrida has observed, Mallarmé's texts remain semantically *undecidable*:

> from then on, the signifier no longer lets itself be traversed, it remains, resists, exists and draws attention to itself. The labor of writing is no longer a transparent ether. It catches our attention and forces us, since we are unable to go beyond it with a simple gesture in the direction of what it 'means', to stop short in front of it or to work with it.[17]

As with abstract painting, poetry here displays its face value, indeed refuses to be more than a surface–a surface which, Derrida never ceases to point out, *should* be taken for its face value rather than being penetrated for deeper meanings. In this abstract (because almost nothing else except sensuous) game of language, '[t]he 'subject' of the text would be, if we could still talk of a subject here, this word, this letter this syllable, the text which they already form in the tissue of their relations': the text is about writing, its own becoming.[18] Thus, Mallarmé's poetry ceases to double a recognizable reality 'that went before'. It departs from traditional rules of literary mimesis by undermining the presence of a stable pre-given (a center of meaning) anterior to literary texts and sabotages the notion of signifiers as unequivocal and 'transparent vehicles of signification'.[19] The latter instead gain pride of place in their opaque materiality.

In this way, medial purism in avant-garde painting and poetry was motivated by intermedial envy and realized through intermedial mimicry: through the adoption of the so called 'empty sign' of music in the medial field of the visual and the verbal. This process could also be called remediation (in the sense that Bolter and Grusin have defined the term), in so far as poetry and painting here import (the method of) another medium to refashion it in their own environment.[20] As we have seen, this remediation revolved around the subversion of media transparency and resulted in a 'hyperconscious recognition or acknowledgement of the medium'–instead of concealing it in strategies of immersion and make-belief typical of realist painting and literature.[21] For Greenberg, this is what typifies modernism to its core: 'to use art to call attention to art', to its mode (and limits) of presentation, rather than using art to create a willing suspension of disbelief, to suppress its mediating materiality in the staging of gripping and convincing reality effects.[22]

To define this modernist remediation exclusively as a refashioning of the musical empty sign is, no doubt, reductive. Greenberg's story of the birth of the avant-garde out of the spirit of music has, for that matter, often been criticized as being all too simplifying and schematic. Thus, it does not take stock of the rise of mass media (film, photography, etc.) that took over the mimetic function of the traditional arts, allowing the latter to retreat more and more into their 'abstract sensuousness'. To claim, moreover, that thenceforth, these arts referred only to themselves, rather than participating in the circulation of cultural meanings is problematic at least: even their alleged purity was inscribed in a network of cultural significations (such as the meaning of 'music') that one can hardly ignore. Finally, and in relation to this, Greenberg's conception of music is severely limited in its heavy dependence on the formalist view that has, by now, grown obsolete–even if it was, indeed, this view that poets like Mallarmé and painters like Kandinsky embraced in the reworking of their respective arts.

In spite of this, however, Greenberg's essay on music and the avant-garde remains of interest, because it at once prefigures and illuminates one of the main concerns in more recent, *post*modern reflections on art and aesthetic theory. This is the concern with materiality and the shock of the new as elaborated extensively in Jean-François Lyotard's critical essays on the aesthetic category of the sublime. In these essays, I will show below, Lyotard proposes a rewriting of the eighteenth-century notion of the sublime that is fashioned on avant-garde strategies of medial foregrounding and self-reflexivity. Lyotard uses these strategies to his own ends, yet like Greenberg he conceives of avant-garde arts as surface-only 'events' which–significantly–are for him always already aural events: they are like sounds coming out of nowhere, not meaning anything but just 'being there'. Before, however, showing how Greenberg's idea of modernism and Lyotard's notion of the postmodern sublime intersect in a common concern with matter and the 'musical', it is necessary to sketch the outlines of the sublime as it has been analyzed traditionally in aesthetic theory.

III. The Traditional Sublime Feeling: Pleasure through Pain

In the eighteenth century, the idea of the sublime revolved quite prominently around the idea of a mental (cognitive) excess: a 'too much' that the mind could not seize and process in a normal, unproblematic way. Thus, as a mental excess, the sublime figured in Kant's *Critique of Judgement* [*Kritik der Urteilskraft*] as the idea of the infinite transcending the bounds of imaginative grasp: the bounds of our mental capacity for image-making (*einbilden*: literally to build or mould into one image).[23] Logically, the infinite cannot be framed in a picture without at once being disowned in its open-endedness or fundamental unaccomplishedness–in its being a process that can go on and on, extending indefinitely without ever reaching a limit or end-point. Operating on the level of sensibility, on the level of forms and figures that organize the manifold data of experience into (re)cognizable units, the imagination fails, so to speak, to take this process together in its totality and subject it to the forms of sensibility.

Try, for instance, to imagine (to picture) the indefinite extension of the universe: a movement without end or finality. Almost automatically, your imaginative mind will try to *form* this movement, to fix a boundary around it because that is the way in which it normally digests and appropriates the world. Differently said, you cannot imagine an ever-extending universe without–and in direct contradiction to the idea of extension without end–at once trying to enclose it within the finite forms that facilitate the perception of sense data: you cannot imagine limitlessness because forming, limiting is (at least in Kant's philosophical system) precisely what imagining is about. So now you have reached a deadlock: on the one hand, your imaginings (always limited and limiting) cannot keep up with the indefinite extension marking the infinite; something is always escaping from view, making it impossible to integrate this extension into a bounded form. On the other hand, once you have tried to give shape to the idea of the infinite, you will have lost it inevitably: finished, finite, rounded off, it is, precisely, reduced to being just that. You can, therefore, at best try to present this idea negatively, or at least indeterminately: the infinite requires an *incomplete* form, since the synthesis (here: the bringing together as one entity, an endless succession becoming an 'all in one') of an endless progression remains necessarily unaccomplished, *unvollendet*.

As Kant suggested in the *Critique of Judgement*, this failure of imagination to accomplish a synthesis is experienced as painfully frustrating. Imagination feels its own limits, no matter how strenuously it tries to stretch them. However, for Kant this is not the end of the matter. With a cunning dialectical move he argues, as Andrew Bowie has put it, that to become aware of a limit in ourselves–a limit to what we can figure, to what we can grasp on the sensuous level–is *also* to become aware 'of what is *not* limited in ourselves, otherwise we would have no way of being aware of a limit'.[24] We must have some 'higher' capacity in our minds, a capacity transcending the bounds of sense that enables us *at all* to judge that the sensuous capacity can only carry us up to a certain point. This higher capacity is the supersensuous faculty of reason that, lifted far above the world of sensuous phenomena, lacks the restrictions of the imagination: it can *think* the infinite which imagination cannot form.[25]

Now, this realization of a de-limitation in oneself, this realization that one is not merely a being of sense but also a being of reason, marks a transition from pain to pleasure. *In* the pain experienced on the level of imagination, the Kantian subject is awakened to the superior capacities of the supersensuous faculty of reason–superior because, in Kant's view, everything that we can see and imagine dwindles into insignificance before the ideas that reason can think. Once this has fully hit the mark, the subject is elevated to a higher plane, standing in awe before the limitless extent of its own reason.

This sense of elevation makes up the feeling of delight that, since Edmund Burke's *Philosophical Enquiry Into the Origin of our Ideas of the Sublime and Beautiful*, has been the trade mark of the sublime: the painful sense of frustration is removed, making way for a joyful sense of transcendence, as the subject moves from the perspective of the imagination to that of reason. Thus, one could also say, the delight of the sublime offers itself as a pleasure (elevation) that is mediated through a displeasure (frustration), the former at once arising out of and resolving the latter. Just as 'the supersensuous becomes available in a negative way'–namely through the frustrating sense of an imaginative limit that 'entails the sense of its opposite'–so the delight of the sublime is a pleasure realized negatively through pain.[26]

IV. The Postmodern Sublime and the Avant-Garde

Seen in this light, the traditional sublime feeling can be epitomized as a breaking through to the other side: a felt transition from sensuous limitedness to supersensuous limitlessness, from immanence to transcendence. For Lyotard (who brought the sublime back into fashion in the domain of philosophy during the 1980's and 1990's) it was precisely this transition from the immanent to the transcendent that required revision. On the one hand, he was positively intrigued by Kant's idea of the sublime as something that resisted formation, and could at best be evoked in a negative presentation: an image-degree zero that attested to the fact *that* something cannot be figured or represented (I will return to this below). On the other hand, however, Lyotard rejected the ultimate triumph of reason–and the concomitant sense of elevation–in the Kantian sublime. He considered this triumph repressive to the senses and the work of imagination which, in the end, must bow down before the (totalizing) force of reason.

Lyotard therefore wanted to refashion the sublime into a critical concept that could retain its legitimacy in a later twentieth-century cultural setting. To this end, he pointed to an artistic practice rather than a philosophical system: the subversive practices of the avant-garde in late-nineteenth- and twentieth-century literature, painting, music, drama, film, and other art forms. As we have seen, these subversive practices revolved around an undermining of traditional, recognizable forms, a rejection of the dominance of subject matter, and a foregrounding of undetermined matter–of matter 'in itself' not (yet) subjected to familiar figures: around an adoption of the 'musical' method. Lyotard took up two aspects of these avant-garde strategies to rewrite the idea of the sublime as a break *within the bounds of the realm of the sensuous, rather than a break between the sensuous and the supersensuous.* The first was the idea of experimentation as a general 'current' in avant-garde art: its tendency toward the new and indeterminate. The second was the particular way in which avant-garde art would pay tribute to the unpresentable as a material instead of transcendental presence exceeding the grasp of imagination. I will briefly outline these respective aspects of avant-garde art below, indicating how they have informed Lyotard's rereading of the sublime as a postmodern sublime.

To start with the idea of experimentation. In 'Response to the Question: What is Postmodernism?' Lyotard circumscribed artistic experimentation as a search for new presentations that are 'not in principle governed by pre-established rules, and...cannot be judged according to a determining judgment, by applying familiar categories... Those rules and categories are what the work of art itself is looking for'.[27] Experimental art works are thus governed by indeterminacy. They do not fit existing rules and categories, but are rather in the process of formulating new rules that are, as yet, unnamed and unknown. Lyotard called this process of indeterminacy *postmodern*: instead of a historical period 'after' the modern, the postmodern is rather present within the idea of the modern (the idea, one could say, of the new) 'in the nascent state'. Postmodern is what, as a suspicion of what 'has been received' from the past, 'if only yesterday', accelerates the modern in its search for 'new rules of the game'.[28]

According to Lyotard, this postmodern 'state' of modernism announced itself in the exchange of the aesthetic question 'What is beautiful?' for the critical question 'What can be said to be art?'.[29] The fact that Lyotard reserved the latter exclusively for modernist art is debatable (as if pre-modernist art never posed itself this question), but the point is that it is postmodern in being at once and already a self-questioning: a questioning of grounds and essentials. What, for Lyotard, made up the postmodern in the modern was an interrogation and undermining of the presumed conditions of any given art form. Should painting be figurative, music be organized sound, literature be representational and communicative? Painters like Kasimir Malevich, composers like John Cage, and poets like Hugo Ball showed that such 'elementary criteria' of any given art form were subject to doubt. This doubt is at the heart of the postmodern as a 'nascent' presence within the modern. It epitomizes the uncertain feeling occasioned by a questioning of artistic restrictions and prescriptions in the full awareness that ultimate artistic grounds or foundations are no longer valid.

This doubt, in turn, informs a specifically postmodern sublime feeling revolving around the shock of the new. In the absence of 'essentials' or absolute foundations something new and unforeseen by artistic rules and traditions may suddenly happen. And what for Lyotard is sublime, is that something happens after all, when all well-known conditions of possibility of a given art form have been subverted–when, in the absence of such conditions, the certainty of a next work automatically following this or that work created in this or that tradition, is undermined:

> What is sublime is the feeling that something will happen, despite everything, within this threatening void, that something will take 'place' and will announce that everything is not over. That place is mere 'here', the most minimal occurrence.

Without the consolation of tradition, an infinite space ahead is opened up in which just anything might occur without warning–or not. It is this tension caused by the suspension of the known, safe, and familiar that avant-garde art stages, and it is this particular tension that sums up the postmodern sublime feeling: a pain of imaginative disorientation that comes with dead certainties, yet also, and at once, a delight of open, possibly infinite experimenting.

Thus, the postmodern sublime refashions the idea of the infinite into a plastic infinity, directed as it is 'towards the infinity of plastic essays to be made rather than towards the representation of some lost absolute'.[30] For Lyotard, this was a crucial issue: attuned to the here and now, the postmodern sublime lacks the nostalgia–the pining after a lost absolute–still haunting the Romantic sublime. It does not look back, or beyond the horizon of sensuous perception, but rather immerses itself in a present that is not yet determined by the goals, (artistic) purposes and programs of a predefined future: it manifests itself as a break or rupture within the continuity of traditional ways of world-making. (This is, however, not a romantic-heroic break–a manifestation of original genius unburdening itself of its artistic past and heritage–but rather one attesting to the multiplicity and heterogeneity of *different* ways of world-making.)

The absence of nostalgia as a distinguishing trait brings me to the second aspect of avant-garde practices relevant to the postmodern sublime: the idea that avant-garde art stages the unpresentable as a material instead of transcendental excess. As Lyotard argues, '[t]he postmodern would be that which, in the modern, puts forward the unpresentable in presentation itself; that which denies itself the solace of good forms'.[31] To 'put forward the unpresentable in presentation itself'–this enigmatic project coincides, to a considerable degree, with Greenberg's idea of the avant-garde as having released itself from the dominance of 'subject matter'. For the sublime here signals a disruption of art in its representational, realist aspect, a doing away with the buffer of the figurative.

Thus, what separates the postmodern from the Romantic sublime (in a rather schematic way) is that the former resides in the 'very matter of the artistic work', its mode of presentation, indeed its self-presentation, while the latter manifests itself through the subject matter of an artistic work: the spectacles of vast oceans, high mountains, starry heavens that have been *re*-presented.[32] Postmodern is what wrecks and breaks the familiar forms that have been used to *suggest* the unpresentable as an 'over there', something residing beyond the horizon of sensuous grasp. It is the breaking *itself* of such familiar forms, the disintegration of figuration, that attests to the sublime as a negative presentation. The sublime announces itself, precisely, in matter not forged in 'good forms'.[33]

Theodor Adorno, of course, already remarked something similar in his *Philosophy of New Music* with respect to Arnold Schönberg's free atonal music. This was an expressionist music without (subjective) expression: a music that had emptied itself out of its expressiveness (in the Romantic sense of the term) by reducing the very subjectivity of that expressiveness to a protocol. 'Music as a protocol of expression', Adorno argued, 'is no longer 'expressive'. The expressed no longer hovers above the music in an undefined yonder and no longer grants it the reflection of the infinite [as Romantic theorists such as E.T.A. Hoffmann had claimed]'. Such music not only breaks apart conventions conforming to public taste, it also explodes in this very way 'the dream of subjectivity' informing the Romantic (ab)use of musical expressiveness.[34]

Lyotard (whose writings on the sublime critically elaborate on Adorno in more than one way) likewise emphasized that avant-garde works of art 'do not call for the 'common sense' of a shared pleasure. These works appear to the public taste to be 'monsters', 'formless' objects, purely 'negative' entities'. The 'social community no longer recognizes itself' in these objects as they no longer communicate a content (a figure, a story, a feeling) that fits the parameters for (a shared) subjective experience. If, once, art had staged the sublime through vicarious thrills of the infinite and excessive relative to mimetic spectacles in painting, literature, and music, avant-garde art would at once embody and radicalize the aesthetics of the sublime by making 'presentation suffer': by making the idea of negative presentation into its very mode of construction.

Lyotard recognized this *locus* of negative presentation in art-objects like Malevich's white square on a white canvas: paintings, as Lyotard put it somewhat pompously, 'that will enable us to see by making it impossible to see'. It was, however, particularly the abstract-expressionist paintings of Barnett Newman that figured as happenings of the sublime in its postmodern aspect. In these paintings, Lyotard recognized both the idea of experimentation and negative presentation that he made into the *nexus* of the postmodern sublime. Significantly, he approached these paintings not so much as pictorial artifacts but as sonorous events: as sounds that happen and can be 'heard'.

V. Paintings as Soundings

What Lyotard liked about Newman's huge color field paintings such as *Vir Heroicus Sublimis* or *Stations of the Cross*, was the way in which they would short-circuit the beholder's imaginative ability to see and grasp containable, self-subsistent forms. Imageless, figureless, and to that extent 'vacant', they would resist one's effort to form or picture something, overwhelming the beholder instead with their excessive 'chromatic matter'.[35]

Yet there is more to Newman's paintings–and more to the postmodern sublime–than this explosion of the visible conceived of as a 'material whose function it would be to fill a form and actualize it'.[36] As Van de Vall explains, Newman's paintings do not represent a sublime event (as, say, the nineteenth-century spectacle-paintings of John Martin do), but *perform* a sublime event. For Newman, she writes, 'the sublime in painting is not so much to be portrayed or depicted, such as the portrayal of a sublime landscape or the depiction of a sublime literary theme, or…merely alluded to, as to something outside the painting…Instead of being *about* a sublime event, the painting had to *become* a sublime event'.[37] It does not show, it *does*–precisely by casting off the bounds of figurative form and the laws of illusory, visible reality-making.

Lyotard presented this performative aspect of Newman's paintings in Greenbergian formalist terms of self-reference and self-presentation. A painting by Newman, he argued, 'announces nothing, it is itself the annunciation… Newman is not representing a non-representable annunciation; he allows it to present itself'.[38] *What* such a painting presents is *that* it presents itself in its shallow but somehow 'instant' materiality. Instant, in this respect, refers to the way in which such a painting would not divert the viewer's gaze with figures and stories represented, but catches this gaze immediately in a moment not (yet) fully informed by interpretation: it does 'not 'recount' any event' that the viewer might recognize or 'reconstitute', and it is in fact so open as to hide 'no technical secrets, no cleverness that might delay the understanding [the physical understanding, that is] of the gaze… No one, and especially not Newman, makes *me* see it in the sense of recounting or interpreting what I see.'[39]

Instead, Lyotard continued, 'I (the viewer) am no more than an ear open to the sound which comes to it from out of the silence; the painting is that sound, an accord'.[40] It is not the commonplace, and incorrect, distinction between vision and hearing as a distinction between active appropriation and passive subjectedness (as if sound always passes through you in its entirety, whether you want it to or not; as if the ear cannot filter or shut itself off, choosing not to hear–playing deaf–or choosing to hear selectively) that I want to address here. Obviously, Lyotard used the ear as a *metaphor* for a way of looking that has the characteristics of listening–a listening, more particularly, that a composer like John Cage would have had in mind for what he called experimental music. This is a listening to 'sounds in themselves', as they occur apparently randomly and singularly without a predetermined structure or narrative outline.[41] It is a listening–as Cage put it with respect to Morton Feldman's music–with an 'immediately' open ear that hears a sound 'suddenly before one's thinking has a chance to turn it into something logical, abstract, or symbolical'.[42] It is *this* indeterminate listening that comes to represent listening *as such* for Lyotard, conceived as *dresser son oreille*, 'pricking up one's ears'.[43]

What is so striking about this sonification of Newman's art is that it presents the artistic sublime in terms of a media 'purism'–a painting offering itself as nothing but 'chromatic matter', completely reduced to its own surface, sending no messages, portraying no narrative, suspending interpretation–that is subsequently revealed as *intermedial mimicry.*[44] Echoing Greenberg's representation of avant-garde paintings as self-reflexive yet, as such, musically informed, Lyotard renders Newman's sublime paintings as instant 'occurrences' that refer *only* to their own material occurring as paintings–performatives rather than depictions–yet become, as such, (like) sonorous happenings. Their 'method', if you will, is no longer traditionally pictorial: as embodiments of the postmodern sublime, these paintings mimic the sonic materiality of music in so far as they would contain nothing but their own, bare chromaticism.

VI. The Now Here Happening

I would like to suggest that in this way, Lyotard's reading of the postmodern sublime (and his reading of Newman) is itself informed by a modernist, formalist reading of the avant-garde such as Greenberg's analysis exemplifies. Both point to the way in which avant-garde painting withdraws into its own superficial materiality, while both relate this withdrawal to an anti-representational shift that is epitomized by musical (and for Lyotard more generally sonorous) processes: abstract because almost nothing else except sensuous. For Lyotard, however, it was not just the making abstract of the visible, but the temporalization of painting that was of prime concern in this respect: Newman's art approached the way in which sounds can occur instantly, out of nowhere, affecting the mind before it can begin to organize a response. They embodied, within certain limits, the instantaneousness of the instant.[45]

Again, this is a rather enigmatic quality: the instantaneousness of the instant. It can perhaps best be illustrated by a concrete poem of the 1960's by Gerhard

Rühm that features a performative display of the word *jetzt* [now] through a fusion of the temporal with the visual:

Gerhard Rühm, 'Jetzt' (1963)

Hovering in-between the verbal, the musical and the pictorial, this poem emphasizes 'poetry' as process: the coming into being, or rather into view, of letters and words on a page. As Wendy Steiner has remarked, here 'each token of the word 'now' marks a unique moment in time, the time of the reading of the word 'now', and each token is physically different from the others both in its typographic rendering and disposition in space'.[46] The typography, moreover, suggests a movement of becoming or 'arising' to the extent that the smaller letters in the background and the largest 'jetzt' in the foreground mimic a temporal dynamic, whereby the latter seem to flash out of the direction of the former. In this way, it creates the illusion of a sudden arrival, bursting into view.

Most interesting, however, is the way in which 'Jetzt' openly contradicts itself, or testifies to its own impossibility. As Lyotard observes in *The Inhuman*, the occurrence of 'now' is a sublime occurrence in so far as it cannot be appropriated and represented by consciousness. To capture the now, consciousness is always a fraction too late: even to say 'now' is to have lost it already–it is an instant that either 'is', outside the schemata of consciousness, or can no longer be *as such*. Thus, we experience 'now' always after the fact, so that we really know nothing about it. 'Now' is threatening and frightening: it floats away while we try to think of it and *when* we think of it, which mostly we want to avoid, it seems eternity and high-speed temporality at the same time.

It is this evanescence of the 'now' that Lyotard recognized in the elusiveness of sonorous materiality, more in particular its most indeterminate aspect: its timbre or, as Lyotard called it, its nuance. This timbre is what 'takes place' uniquely, once-only. Even when it can be recorded or remembered, it changes into 'a nuance reported, retained, deferred, so that it becomes a different nuance'.[47] As we have seen, Rühm's 'Jetzt' exemplifies this radical fleetingness of the 'now', each 'now' being typographically different from the other, thus undermining the repeatability of verbal signifiers as they usually appear on the printed page and infusing them with the instability of once-only, sonorous occurrences. Yet at the same time, all these different instances of 'now' are undeniably fixed on the printed page. They can be seen, re-seen, and overseen all at once and all together, rather than disappearing the very instant when they appear. Seen in this perspective, Rühm's collage-like construction emphasizes, precisely, the impossibility of capturing the 'now' *as such*. It registers the now at best as a trace–a residue, left-behind of the instant that is itself unrepresentable within the conditions of time and space: 'now' is what eludes these conditions.

In *The Inhuman*, this ungraspability of the 'now', the most minimal occurrence, epitomizes the idea of a material excess that the mind cannot digest and appropriate. In this context, Lyotard used the concept of matter in an ontological sense as the matter 'given' to perception: the matter of data that in Kantian philosophy 'is represented as what is *par excellence* diverse, unstable, and evanescent'.[48] This matter is difficult, if not impossible to capture in its 'raw' state–a logical problem pertaining to the (Kantian) fact that the mind can only process objects that conform to the mental forms and categories regulating perception and cognition, whereas matter 'in itself', not-yet subjected to these forms and categories will bypass or resist perception and cognition: it cannot (yet) be made into an object.

'Raw' matter, matter 'in itself', is thus what exceeds or resists the active powers of mind that produce and rework the data of experience into a (re)cognizable, unifying whole. Conversely, one could also say: as an 'in itself', untouched and unshaped by the formative and cognitive faculties, this matter can only 'exist' when these faculties are (momentarily) suspended:

> …forms and concepts are constitutive of objects, they pro-duce data that can be grasped by sensibility and that are intelligible to the understanding, things over there which fit the faculties or capacities of the mind. The matter I'm talking about is 'immaterial', an-objectable, because it can only 'take place' or find its occasion at the price of suspending these active powers of the mind.[49]

This is an obvious variation on the well-known theme 'death is where the mind is not'. In *Heidegger and 'the jews'* Lyotard indeed proclaims that when 'the sublime is 'there'…the mind is not there. As long as the mind is there, there is no sublime. This is a feeling that is incompatible with time, as is death'.[50] The mind must somehow be 'mindless' to be touched by an *il-y-a*, a material event that *is*, on its own, rather than just being material for perception and cognition. For Lyotard, the sublime is this event that happens outside the reach of mental grasp, withdrawing 'itself from every relationship': 'singular, incomparable'.[51] Thus, it could be suggested, the difficulty of grasping this occurrence of matter in 'itself', its 'raw' form, is what replaces the Kantian difficulty of grasping ideas of reason in Lyotard's reflections on the sublime. Indeed, to make matters very simple, I would say that in Lyotard's rewriting of the sublime matter is what comes 'before' the forms of sensibility, just as ideas of reason come 'after' or are 'above' these forms in Kant's analytic of the sublime–matter here is the bare fact (and wonder) *that there is*, before a *what is* has been determined.[52]

VII. Sounding Words: Acoustic Poetry and the Postmodern Sublime

In 'Avant-Garde and Kitsch' Clement Greenberg wrote:

> It has been in search for the absolute that avant-garde art has arrived at 'abstract' or 'nonobjective' art–and poetry, too. The avant-garde poet or artist tries in effect to imitate God by creating something valid solely on its own terms, in the way nature is itself valid, in the way a landscape–not its picture–is aesthetically valid; something *given*, increate, independent of meanings, similars or originals. Content is to be dissolved so completely into form that the work of art or literature cannot be reduced in whole or in part to anything not itself.[53]

Echoing Greenberg's account of the European and American avant-garde, Lyotard's writings in *The Inhuman* also radicalize it: Lyotard no longer speaks of a coinciding of content and form, or a dissolving of the latter into the former, but points to the possibility of a disconnection between matter and form. This disconnection would break with a dominant tradition in Western art that can be traced all the way to Aristotle: 'Matter is put on the side of power, but of power conceived of as potential, as an indeterminate state of reality, whereas form…is thought of as the act of giving a figure to material power'.[54] Form finishes off what matter promises to be: the latter becomes what the former decides.

For Lyotard, the reverse was at stake in the more experimental assays of the avant-garde: the fit between matter and form was here undone. In literature, Peter Conrad has pointed out, this manifested itself in the disintegration of language as a rational, communicative instrument.[55] In the work of the Russian Futurists, the Dadaists, or the Italian Futurists, language was stripped of its meaningfulness, functionality and (presumed) transparency to end up as nothing but sound: primitive sounds, babbling sounds, infant sounds, cries, moans. Thus, the 'Zaum' of the Russian Futurists refers to a word which, 'if it means anything at all, means that words have no necessary, inherent meaning; its coinage sums up the crisis of confidence suffered by language when confronting a modern world which its inherited implements could no longer describe'. Like the word Dada, coined in 1916, Zaum is 'sound not sense: a rudimentary, elementary syllabic stammer' that defies linguistic signification.[56]

It would lead me too far to consider the cultural changes relative to this demise of language–one can think of the abuse of language in World War I propaganda that led to a distrust of words, the 'discovery' of the language of the unconscious, or the philosophical 'discovery' of the disjointedness of words and the reality they are supposed to represent–but what it gave rise to was a growing ascendancy of matter, the vocal matter of words over their grammatical functioning and syntactic parameters. The Dadaist Jean Arp, for instance, practiced a so called 'automatic poetry' that according to him 'springs directly from the poet's bowels or other organs, which have stored up reserves of usable material. The poet crows, curses, sighs, stutters, yodels, as he pleases. His poems are like Nature'. His poems are, to recall Greenberg, something increate instead of compositions that determine matter according to 'good' form.[57]

One may, of course, question the reality of this absence of the determining factor of form, yet it can hardly be denied that the acoustic poetry of Dadaists such as Hugo Ball or the work of Kurt Schwitters defamiliarized traditional aspects and uses of language as a carrier of thoughts and ideas. Consider, for instance, Hugo Ball's 'Totenklage':

Totenklage (1916)

Ombula
take
bitdli
solunkola
tabla tokta tokta takabla
taka tak
Babula m'balam
tak tru-ü
wo-um
biba bimbel
o kla o auw
kla o auwa
la-auma
o kla o ü
la o auma
klinga-o-e-auwa
ome o-auwa
klinga inga M ao-Auwa
omba dij omuff pomo-auwa
tru-ü
tro-u ü o-a-o-ü
mo-auwa
gomun guma zangaga gago blagaga
szagaglugi m ba-o-auma

szaga szago
szaga la m'blama
bschigi bschigo
bschigi bschigi
bschiggo bschiggo
goggo goggo
ogoggo
a-o-auma

Not quite the pure meaninglessness that Dada purports to imply, 'Totenklage' appears as an outcry of pain, the sound 'au' that expresses this outcry dominating the poem throughout. Moreover, one can hear in these apparently disjointed sounds a moaning that, as has been frequently suggested, invokes the moaning of mothers who lost their sons in World War I. (Sonorously, this even comes to the surface in the last line: 'a-o-auma' that combines the 'au' outcry of pain with the moaning 'o' sound and the faint trace of 'mama' encapsulated in the first). Yet while signification can never quite be erased from these 'vocables' arranged according to a specific rhythmic pattern, it is not the signified but the materiality of the signifier that gains pride of place. Whatever meaning the poem might communicate, it does so through is sonorous potential that becomes so potent precisely because it remains without conventional determination: it does not depict pain and the moaning of the dead, but performs this pain and moaning instantaneously through its 'raw' outcries.

To be sure, one can recognize in this ascendancy of the signifier a move or *Anders-Streben* towards the musical, even though at the same time sound poetry of the earlier twentieth century already started to incorporate sonorous matter that had always been discarded in music: noise, cries, howls. Most interesting, however, is the fact that such poems as 'Totenklage' depend on their performance to come into being, and in that sense mimic the quality of music as a temporal art in the most literal sense of the word: an art that is never the same, that manifests itself differently in every performance, in so far as its timbre, the matter of sound, cannot be repeated without being irretrievably lost *as such*. This is how the postmodern sublime, the musical and the poetic converge in Ball's 'Totenklage': not only in the withdrawal of words into their own sonorous materiality, not only even in the predominance of the signifier as an 'empty' material vehicle, but in the instability of this signifier as a sound come into its own that never emerges fully, but always partially and impermanently.

VIII. Conclusion

The postmodern sublime is intimately tied up with the idea of an intermedial process that reorients both the visual and verbal avant-garde arts toward the method of music. This method, we have seen, is the method of an art that is abstract because almost nothing else except sensuous: an art of self-presentation that figures only its own sensuous movements, rather than anything outside of itself. Adopting this method, painting and poetry dissolved their traditional, representational content and filled it with (presumably) non-figuring colours and non-signifying sounds instead. They became surface-only.

Elaborating on (yet at the same time radicalizing) this formalist genesis of the avant-garde, Lyotard connected the material self-withdrawal of the avant-garde to the possibility of an immanent, rather than transcendent sublime. Thus, conceived of as a bare material event that comes 'before' sensibility, 'before' the activity of consciousness that schematizes and categorizes the world, the sublime moment for Lyotard manifested itself in art as a *performative*: not as something depicted or represented through familiar figures and verbal depictions, but as something happening instantaneously that refers strictly to its own happening in the process. As such, this sublime moment would announce itself in art works that figure and refer to nothing but their own material becoming: that imitate, as Greenberg would say, their own imitating. Seen in this light, paintings and poems that aspire to the sublime (or that can be said to be affected by the aesthetics of the sublime) always already aspire to the condition of music as Greenberg described it–and as Lyotard continued to describe it as a momentary occurrence that constitutes the *now* here happening.

In this context, sound poetry, acoustic poetry, concrete poetry (different names that mostly denote a common practice) of the earlier twentieth century are of special significance to Lyotard's theory of the postmodern sublime. On the one hand they exemplify the anti-representational shift, the move towards abstraction and self-reflexivity, that marks the postmodern sublime as inscribed into the very matter (rather than the subject matter) of artistic works. On the other hand, sound poetry foregrounds the evanescence and elusiveness of sonorous matter that Lyotard privileged as a central trope of the sublime happening. This is a poetry that depends on timbre and subtle inflexions: on the plasticity of the word whose function is no longer constative but performative.

Works Cited

Adorno, Theodor. *Filosophie van de nieuwe Muziek* (Philosophy of New Music). Trans. Lisbeth van Hamelen. Nijmegen: Sun, 1988.

Barry, Kevin. *Language, Music and the Sign: A Study In Aesthetics, Poetics and Poetic Practice from Collins to Coleridge.* Cambridge: Cambridge University Press,

Bowie, Andrea. *Aesthetics and Subjectivity from Kant to Nietzsche.* Manchester: Manchester University Press, 1993.

Cage, John. "Lecture on Something," *Silence, Lectures and Writings by John Cage*. London: Marion Boyars, 1991.

Conrad, Peter. *Modern Times, Modern Places: How Life and Art Were Transformed in a Century of Revolution, Innovation and Radical Change.* New York: Alfred Knopf, 1998.

Derrida, Jacques. "Mallarme," Jacques Derrida, Arts of Literature. Ed. Derek Altridge. New York: Routledge, 1992.

Greenberg, Clement. "Toward a Newer Laocoon," *Art and Theory, 1900-1990: An Anthology of Changing Ideas.* Ed. Charles Harrison and Paul Wood. Oxford: Blackwell, 1999.

Hanslick, Eduard. *On the Musically Beautiful.* (1854) Trans, Geoffrey Payzant. Indianapolis: Hackett Publishing Company, 1984.

Higgins, Dick. *Horizons: The Poetics and Theory of Intermediality.* Carbondale and Edwardsville: Southern Illionois University Press, 1984.

Jay, Martin. *Downcast Eyes: The Denigration of Vision in Twentieth Century French Thought.* Berkeley: University of California Press, 1994.

Kant, Immanuel. *Kritik der Urteilschraft.* (1790) Hamburg: Felix Meiner Verlag, 1990.

Lehtonen, Mikko. "On No Man's Land", trans. Aijaleena Ahonen and Kris Clark. www.nordicum.gu.se/review contents/ncomreview/Lehtonen pdf.

Lyotard, Jean Francois. "Heidegger and the Jews" trans, Andreas Michel and Mark S. Roberts. Minneapolis: University of Minnesota Press.

—. "Newman: The Instant," *The Inhuman: Reflections on Time*. Trans. Geoffrey Bennington and Rachel Boudby. Cambridge: Polity Press, 1999. 78-88.

—. "Representation, Presentation, Unrepresentable," *The Inhuman: Reflections on Time.* Trans. Geoffrey Bennington and Rachel Boudby. Cambridge: Polity Press, 1999. 119-129.

McEvilly, Thomas. *Art and Discontent: Theory at the Millennium.* New York: McPherson and Company, 1991.

Nyman, Michael. *Experimental Music: Cage and Beyond.* Cambridge: Cambridge University Press, 1991.

Pater, Walter. "The School of Giorgione," *The Renaissance* in *Art and Theory.* 830-33.

Richter, Hans. *Dada: Art and Anti-Art.* London: Thames and Hudson, 1997.

Sidje, Nico van der. *Het literaire experiment: Jacques Derrida over literatuur (Th Literary Experiment: Jacques Derrida on Literature*). Amsterdam: Boon, 1978.

BOULEZ, JOYCE, MALLARMÉ: MUSIC AS MODERNIST LITERATURE

ZBIGNIEW GRANAT

In a spirited account of contemporary musical quests written in 1954[1], Pierre Boulez noted a significant delay in the field of musical composition in comparison with the advancements found in painting and literature. The attempts of modern painters to find a new concept of perspective or the linguistic explorations of writers such as Mallarmé and Joyce, claimed Boulez, had no equivalents in contemporary music, and he insisted on the most urgent need of renewal in the area of form, "which has not changed since the advent of tonality." What he had in mind was not merely a rejection of classical formal schemes but a total reexamination of the notion of the closed work, to which, he believed, even the most important modern works still succumbed. Such a musical work, according to Boulez,

> consists of a series of separate movements; each is homogeneous in structure and tempo; each forms a closed circuit (a characteristic of western musical thought); the balance of these different movements is achieved through a dynamic distribution of 'tempi'.

Against this old-fashioned concept of the work, he envisioned:

> a musical work in which this division into homogeneous movements would be abandoned in favour of a non-homogeneous distribution of developments. Let us claim for music the right to parentheses and italics...a concept of discontinuous time made up of structures which interlock instead of remaining in airtight compartments; and finally a sort of development where the closed circuit is not the only possible answer.

> Let us hope for a music that is not this series of compartments to be visited willy-nilly one after the other. Let us try to think of it as a domain in which, in some sense, one can choose one's own direction.[2]

Boulez was to realize this unique vision of his very shortly, in 1956-57, by composing a work that has since become one of the most celebrated examples of open form in twentieth-century music: the Third Piano Sonata. Indeed, in this sonata Boulez attempted to break away from what he considered the "closed circuit," compartmentalization, and homogeneity of the closed work, and proposed instead a concept of an open work based on multiplicity and non-homogeneity of its developments.

Much has been said about the overall formal design of the sonata that Boulez had planned but never completed, and the composer's own essay, "Sonate, que me veux-tu?" of 1960[3], remains the fundamental elucidation of the work's structural principles. Based on Boulez's original intention, the general disposition of the work was to involve a symmetrical permutation of movements entitled *Antiphonie*, *Trope*, *Strophe*, and *Séquence* around the central movement, called *Constellation*, (or its double, *Constellation-Miroir*), thus resulting in a mobile arrangement of eight possible trajectories. However, out of the five originally planned "formants," as Boulez calls the sonata's movements, only two were published - *Trope* and *Constellation-Miroir* - and it is in this two-movement form that Boulez's Third Piano Sonata has been usually performed and discussed analytically.[4]

In addition, both published formants of the sonata contain a number of features that may change from performance to performance: Formant 2, paralleling the mobility of the overall form, allows for the circular permutation of its four structural segments, *Texte, Parenthèse, Glose,* and *Commentaire*, and two of them, *Parenthèse* and *Commentaire*, also contain some optional passages; Formant 3 offers multiple possibilities for the linking of fragments within the main sections of the work. It is these mobile features of the work that reveal strong reliance on literary models.

Indeed, the main portion of "Sonate, que me veux-tu," the essay designed to explain the nature of the Third Sonata, is devoted to literary influences that impelled Boulez to write the piece. "It may well be," he writes, "that literary affiliations played a more important part than purely musical considerations. In fact my present mode of thought derives from my reflections on literature rather than on music."[5]

Boulez is quite specific about the nature of these influences and explains that it was mostly the revolutionized organization, "the actual mental structure" of certain literary works that fascinated him the most. He mentions four writers, Mallarmé, Joyce, Kafka, and Butor, as those responsible for the greatest advancements in this area. It was these developments in literature that Boulez saw as the source of renewal and inspiration for the world of music. "It must be our concern in future," he proclaimed, "to follow the examples of Joyce and Mallarmé and to jettison the concept of a work as a simple journey starting with a departure and ending with an arrival."[6] In this way, Boulez defines the true space in which the sonata functions as the one in which two distinct worlds, that of music and that of literature, converge; and he explains elsewhere that his actual realization of this convergence involved "the transmutation of modes of thought that had hitherto seemed to be specific to one or other of these two means of expression."[7]

A look at the overall form of "Constellation-Miroir" gives a clear picture of the application of this idea. The whole formant is based on the alternation of large structural groups labelled as *points* and *blocs*, each consisting of a variable number of fragments which can be linked in a variety of ways. Thus, the actual developments generated in performances will obviously be different in their internal details, though they will all share the general design of alternating textures prescribed by the formant and, as György Ligeti put it, "a constant oscillation of register and density, a wave around a central line, as it were."[8]

This musical conception of the formant originated in a specific literary work, Mallarmé's *Un Coup de Dés*, whose formal, visual, physical, and decorative presentation suggested to the composer, as he put it, "the idea of finding equivalents in music."[9] Indeed, the unique appearance of the score is clearly modelled on the unconventional typographical layout of Mallarmé's poem, and its nonlinear distribution of the musical fragments might perhaps be viewed as an allusion to one of the central images of the poem: that of a constellation. In this way Boulez is imitating the visual device designed to suggest the multi-directionality of thought in Mallarmé's poem.

At the same time, however, the multi-directionality found in Boulez's score brings to mind yet another image: that of a labyrinth, which is clearly implied by the disposition of the formant's main segments, each of them having a variable number of entrances and exits and consisting of individual fragments capable of being linked in multiple "routes." The labyrinth analogy comes from Boulez himself:

> The work is like a town or a labyrinth. A town is often a labyrinth too: when you visit it you choose your own direction and your own route; but it is obvious that to get to know the town you need an accurate map and knowledge of the traffic regulations.[10]

The labyrinthine layout of a segment called "Points 2," together with its "traffic regulations," may be seen in Example 1. The segment allows one entry from the previous one and two exits leading to the next, and consists of eight fragments marked A – H that can be organized in four possible trajectories. There is also a certain hierarchy in the grouping of the fragments: the first, "external" group comprises fragment A, which opens the segment, and two movable fragments B and H, which function as alternate endings. They encircle the second, "internal" group of fragments, C - G, which possesses its own double organization. From the point of view of their mobility, both groups of fragments may be seen as two concentric orbits; a scheme of this segment with its possible trajectories is shown in Example 2.

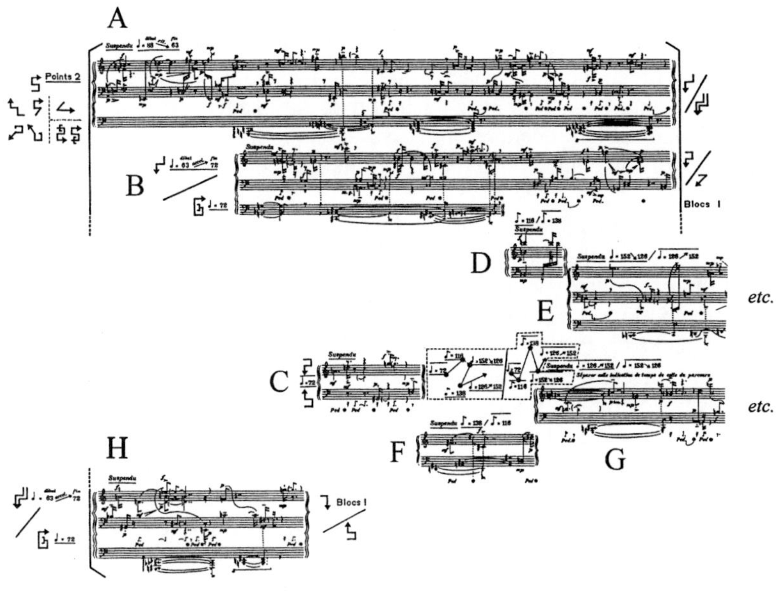

MUSIC EXAMPLE 1. "Points 2."

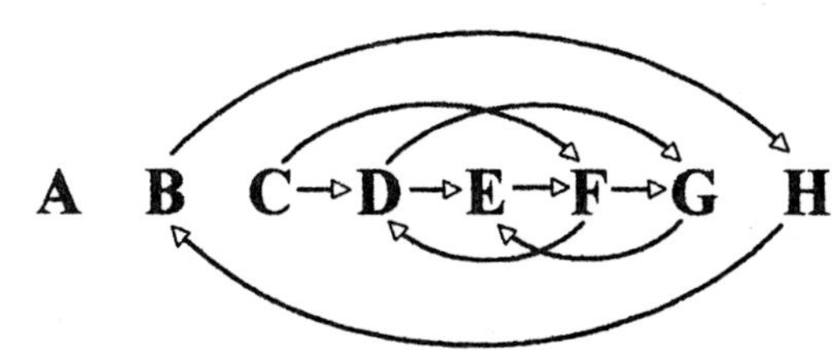

MUSIC EXAMPLE 2. Scheme of "Points 2."

In "Sonate, que me veux-tu," Boulez makes reference to two literary works that served him as models for the labyrinth of Constellation-Miroir: Michel Butor's novel *L'Emploi du temps* and Franz Kafka's short story "The Burrow." In Butor's novel, the main character, Revel, repeatedly wanders through the labyrinth of Bleston's streets until he can form a clear picture of the whole city. Similarly, a visitor to Formant 3 of Boulez's sonata will discover the work's routes one by one until the complex design of the maze's totality will be revealed. And if this visitor is assiduous, he will also notice, paralleling Kafka's precise description of the subterranean animal's burrow, the technical side of the maze: its architectural logic, hierarchy and distribution of passages, multiplicity of structural devices and their functions, elements foreseen and those left to chance. For Boulez, such borrowing of ideas from other artists is a perfectly acceptable procedure; an artist, he explains, may "settle in an already existing maze since any construction he inhabits he cannot help but mould it to himself." [11]

One of the main things that fascinated Boulez about such images as the labyrinth or the constellation is their non-linearity, the emphasis on a seemingly discontinuous course with unpredictable turns and surprises, which the composer contrasted with the "closed cycle" of classical compositions. These surprises reside not in the fragments themselves, but in the "multiple nodal points with different probabilities of triggering," [12] i.e., in the complex system of arrows that allow the linking of the individual fragments together.

But, as the layout of Points 2 in Example 2 shows, the four routes through this segment are composed in such a way as to be "both foreseeable and foreseen," or, in other words, to be structurally complete. Boulez makes this possible by means of a special kind of "phrasing," i.e., a method of combining heterogeneous structures within a segment into coherent courses. This procedure is polyphonic in nature, since it proceeds on two levels: that of fixed structures, i.e. the fragments themselves, and that of "mobile elements," or "enveloping phenomena," such as tempo or timbre, which are capable of adapting to the fixed structures in all possible courses. Both structural levels must be sufficiently independent so as to be detachable from each other and adequately modifiable so that no absurdities, such as an "accelerando on a rest," will result. But they must also be responsible to each other by means of "turntables," or points of intersection, which divide the course of the composition into "phrases" and ensure the global sense of form.[13]

An example of such "phrasing" can be seen in the middle unit of "Points 2" quoted in Example 1 above. As has already been noted, this small unit comprises two possible courses based on two different orders of fragments labelled C-D-E-F-G and their corresponding progressions of tempi. In this particular case, both of these structural levels are very tightly connected in that the order of fragments in a given course is governed by the agogic plan, which Boulez indicates in the score in the form of a diagram that is reproduced in Example 3.

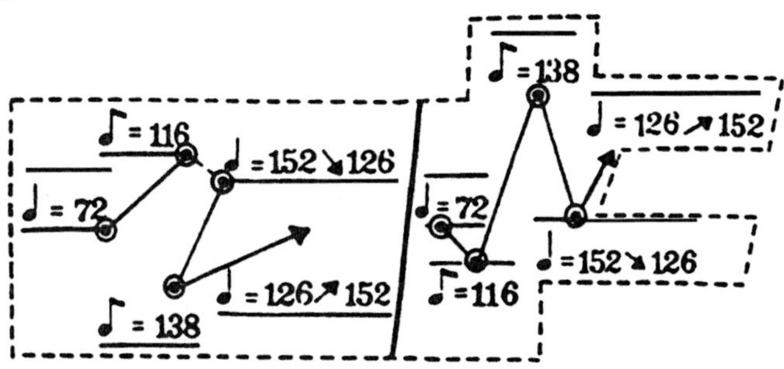

EXAMPLE 3. The agogic "phrasing" in the middle unit of "Points 2."

As can be seen from this diagram, this double phrasing makes it possible for four of the fragments, D, E, F, and G, to acquire different characters thanks to the variable tempo indications assigned to them for each of the two courses. At the same time, this agogic phrasing imposes continuity on the two courses made up of otherwise discontinuous fragments, which proves that Boulez's concept of openness has primarily to do with multiple continuities. As such, this method is comparable with the procedures found in works by both Mallarmé and Joyce, in which various fragments or sections of the work are related to each other in many ways and thus introduce multiple levels of meaning.

Boulez's concept of "phrasing," too, is a way of relating various structures to one another so that they can form a number of sensible arrangements. In Constellation-Miroir, we have seen how this phrasing governs the multiple organizations of individual fragments, all of which must be included in a given course; in Trope, Boulez demonstrates that the same concept can be used to regulate developments in which several structures may be treated as optional.

In two of the four segments of Trope, Parenthèse and Commentaire, we find developments with a number of interpolations notated in smaller notes and enclosed by parentheses. These interpolations represent one of the possible kinds of tropes that Boulez employs in this formant to interrupt, or comment upon, the main serial structure notated in larger type. As can be seen in Example 4 below, which shows the opening of Commentaire, the obligatory sections are to be played in a strict tempo and the parenthetical ones freely. In a fashion similar to that in the previous example, these contrasting tempo indications allow Boulez to "phrase" several possible courses that will result from the inclusion, or exclusion, of the parenthetical comments. In this way, the compositional procedure employed in this example realizes Boulez's vision quoted in the beginning of this chapter, which demanded for music "the right to parentheses and italics...a concept of discontinuous time made up of structures which interlock instead of remaining in airtight compartments; and finally a sort of development where the closed circuit is not the only possible answer."[14]

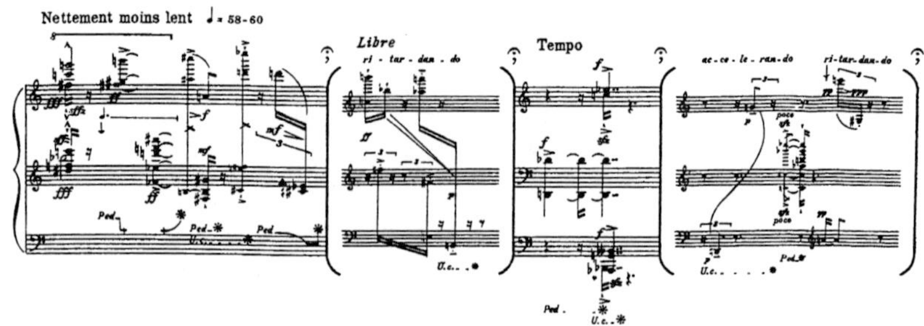

EXAMPLE 4. Opening of Commentaire.

Finally, Boulez's concept of phrasing can be applied to the overall form of the composition. It has been noted earlier that Trope has been conceived as a circular form, in which any one of the four segments, Texte, Parenthèse, Glose, or Commentaire, may serve as beginning or end. And because the last two segments are capable of changing places, this formant with "a direction but no fixed beginning"[15] comprises a total of eight possible courses.

It is obvious that such circularity of form challenges the dramatic trajectory principle associated with the traditional musical work, though it does so in a particular way. For, while it would be impossible to speak of a single "curve" of Boulez's sonata, it is still feasible to describe the individual curves that each arrangement of the segments will produce; indeed, by indicating in the score that all segments should enchaîner sans interruption, Boulez ensures the continuity of each course. The defining characteristics of each curve, however, will depend on different criteria than those associated with tonal pieces. As the composer himself explains, the curve in each individual case will be established "by the registers selected, the density of the texture and the preponderant dynamic. Satisfactory connections between them are ensured by a very strict control of the initial and terminal zones."[16] Thus, Boulez invokes the dramaturgical principle of the closed work only to subvert it, for his imbuing of the work with such multiple curves neutralizes the very idea of the curve understood as an expression of the work's "drama," and replaces it with a relative field of equally viable curves defined by different distributions of their parameters.

Boulez related this circular structure of Trope to the principle of circular permutation that he used in the construction of its series. As he explains in Boulez on Music Today, this principle allowed him to create a chain of serial permutations, in which the last of the four segments of the series becomes the first of the subsequent permutation.[17] This purely technical explanation, however, tells only part of the story, for the concept of circularity in Boulez's sonata may have also resulted from his attempt to transmute a literary device into a musical one. For instance, Boulez's description of Trope as "a work with neither beginning nor end, able to unfold at any given moment," [18] strongly resonates with Stéphane Mallarmé's observation made in reference to his projected Livre: "a book neither begins nor ends: at the very most it pretends to do so."[19] And apart from Mallarmé, Boulez also had another prototype to which he could turn for ideas on circularity: Joyce's *Finnegans Wake*, which, as Eco puts it, "is molded into a curve that bends back on itself, like the Einsteinian universe." [20] Clearly, contemporary literature reveals many devices and modes of thought that probably enriched Boulez's musical language on both its morphological and formal levels.

As has been shown above, the formal devices that Boulez uses in his sonata, such as the labyrinth, parentheses, circularity, or the concept of phrasing in general, govern the multiple courses of the work. As such, they constitute a new dimension, characteristic only of open works, which communicates its own meaning by means of formal procedures themselves, in a manner similar to that found in contemporary literature. "From Joyce onwards," writes Eco, "there are two separate universes of discourse. The first is a communication about the facts of man and his concrete relations. Here it makes sense to speak about the 'content' of a story. The second carries out, at the level of its own technical structures, a type of absolutely formal discourse." [21]

In fact, Eco could have easily started with Mallarmé, whose *Un Coup de Dés*, and especially the most quintessentially mobile though unfinished *Livre*, both exhibit the same kind of formal discourse that the author of Opera aperta discovered in Joyce. In both writers, there is the same tendency to multiply the possible meanings of the work by means of formal innovations and to treat form as "expressive," that is, as one in which, according to Eco, there is a "radical conversion from 'meaning' as content of an expression, to the form of the expression as meaning." [22]

We have seen how Boulez utilizes some literary devices to generate a similar formal discourse in his sonata; we must yet specify how this dimension of the musical work relates to the concept of openness found in literary works. This can be seen most clearly in the concept of reflection.

Marvelling at Joyce's writing technique, the composer noted that in his hands the novel "observes itself *qua* novel, as it were, reflects on itself and is aware that it is a novel." In the same way music, he proclaimed, "is not exclusively concerned with 'expression', but must also be aware of itself and become the object of its own reflection." [23]

To be sure, music's reflection upon itself can take many different forms. One of them is the idea of tropes that could be said to reflect on the main structures of Formant 2's segments. This can be seen, for example, in the opening of *Commentaire*, cited in Example 4 above, where the first parenthetical trope clearly imitates and complements chromatically the full twelve-note series, the three-note serial fragment appearing just before the parenthesis. But tropes can also represent a reflection in a more literal sense, i.e., when their structure reveals mirror-like symmetry, as can be seen in the example below:

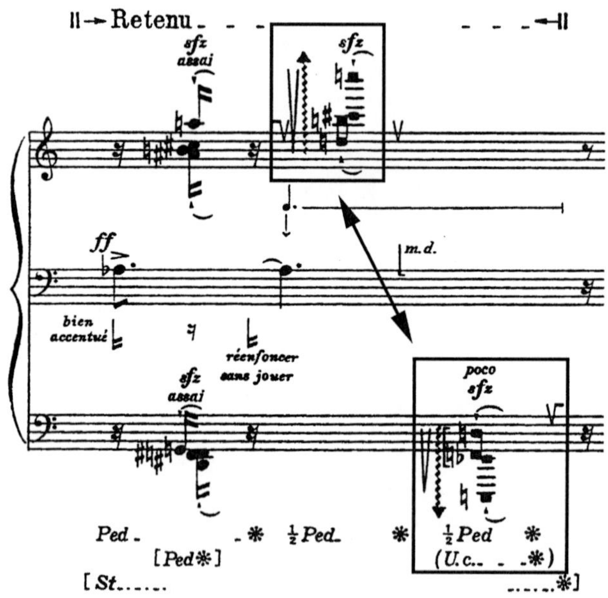

EXAMPLE 5. A symmetrical trope from *Texte*.

Sometimes Boulez combines such mirror-like symmetry with a retrograde, in which case the structure reflects upon itself in both vertical and horizontal dimensions, as can be seen in the following trope from *Glose*:

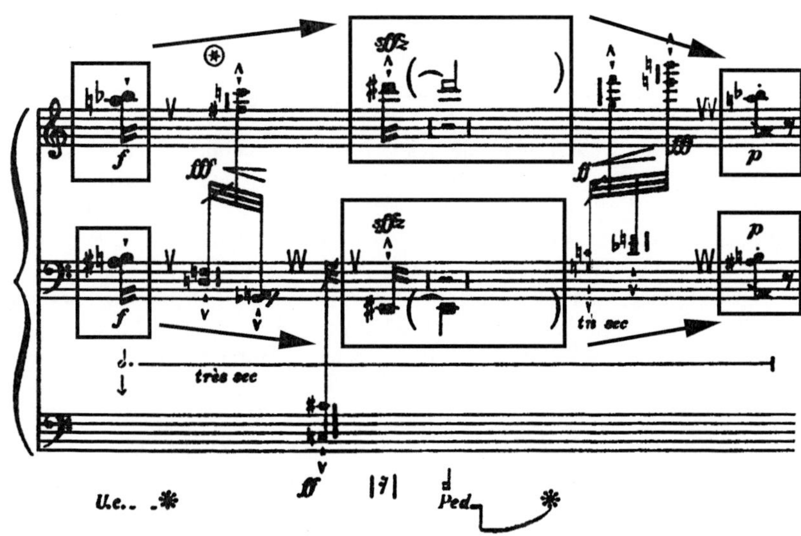

EXAMPLE 6. Trope from *Glose*.

Finally, the concept of reflection can also be used to shape the overall form, as is the case with *Parenthèse*, whose second half represents a free retrograde of the first. Example 7 shows the central parenthesis of the piece, in which the corresponding structures on both sides of the retrograde are connected with arrows.

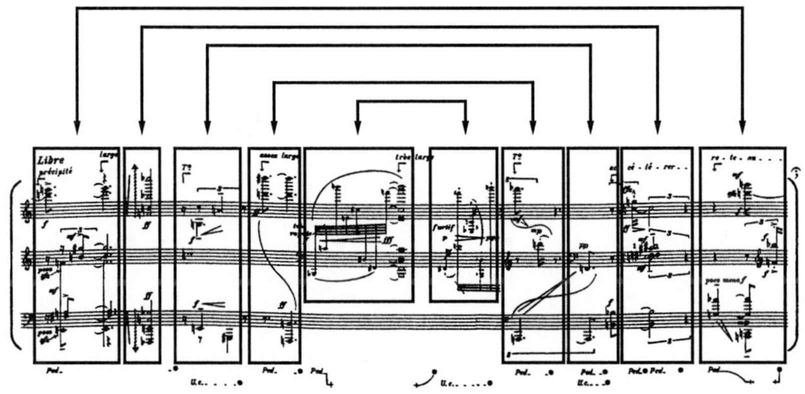

EXAMPLE 7. The central trope from *Parenthèse*

Although such symmetrical patterns had been used by composers for centuries, their employment in Boulez's sonata seems less to suggest a link with tradition than a connection with Mallarmé's ideas for his *Livre*, especially with his notion of "creative symmetries" that arise when the reading direction of syllables, words, pages, and volumes is reversed. Such a process of structuring demands that the reader grasp both versions of a given unit in order to establish their "profound identity" in the intertextual space. [24] Thus, for Mallarmé, symmetry is a formal device that allows him to manipulate linguistic units on all syntactic levels in order to generate meaning of a higher degree. The Boulezian symmetries lend themselves to the same approach in that they also assume the function of meaning-generating devices on all levels of formal discourse, from the smallest unit of musical significance to the total form. The palindromic structure of *Parenthèse* represents one application of this latter idea; but there are also other possibilities that Boulez explores in Formant 3 of his sonata.

According to the composer's original plans, this central formant of the work was to be reversible and could be performed either as *Constellation* or *Constellation-Miroir*, depending on the disposition of the other formants "gravitating" around it. This reversal of the temporal direction is a device that Boulez, again, borrows from Mallarmé's *Livre*, which, according to Jacques Scherer, was designed as "an intelligence capable of mastering a subject by reconstructing it in all directions, including the reverse of temporal succession." Thus, by replicating what Mallarmé calls an "unfolding" and a "folding-up" of the book, this formant would also prove to be a mobile apparatus capable of revealing its two structural identities: the thing itself and its reflection. [25]

There is yet another way in which *Constellation-Miroir* is "aware of itself" and becomes "the object of its own reflection." Its opening segment, called "Mélange," constitutes a miniature image of the whole movement, "a microcosm of the large constellation," as Boulez calls it, in both its content (three "points" and three "blocks") and the spatial disposition on the page. This idea seems to be borrowed directly from Joyce's novels: the mysterious letter of *Finnegans Wake*, with its multiplicity of meanings, is generally interpreted as a direct image of the whole book; similarly, the central episode of *Ulysses*, "Wandering Rocks," represents a tiny universe which, "in its eighteen paragraphs, reproduces the techniques of the eighteen major chapters, in a minor scale." [26] This device constitutes what literary criticism sometimes describes as a *mise en abyme*, a "mirror in the text," which may be inserted at various places in a work to reflect its narrative in a condensed form. According to a typology offered by Lucien Dällenbach, Boulez's "Mélange" might be said to represent a "simple duplication," i.e., a sequence "which is connected by similarity to the work that encloses it." [27] A schematic representation of the last two kinds of reflection on the formal level of *Constellation-Miroir* can be seen in the following diagram provided by Boulez in "Sonate, que me veux-tu?":

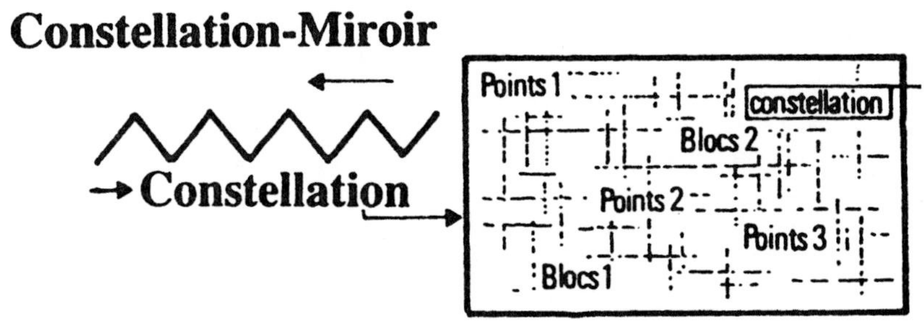

EXAMPLE 8. A diagram of *Constellation - Constellation-Miroir.*

Clearly, the concept of reflection in Boulez's sonata performs a multiplicity of structural functions designed to generate a number of coexisting perspectives from which the work can be viewed. It is thus a formal procedure that illuminates the polyvalent structure of the work. In the same way, the multiple courses of the sonata's formants, determined by such concepts as the labyrinth or circularity that have been discussed earlier, reflect upon each other and, by analogy with Mallarmé's concept of "profound identity," reveal a new, higher level of the work's meaning. They show that the essence of the sonata's openness lies not only in its ability to reveal a different aspect of itself each time it is performed, but also in the total sense derived from the plurality of its formal solutions.

I have already mentioned a few instances of the influence that the writing techniques of Joyce and Mallarmé exerted upon Boulez. It was not my goal to list all such examples, nor would such an attempt make much sense, simply because the presence of both writers in Boulez's Third Sonata is so ubiquitous that it is frequently impossible to distinguish their spheres of influence. The main point that I wish to emphasize, however, is that in his sonata, Boulez attempted to create a new mode of expression based on the synthesis of the literary and the musical; and that the result of this synthesis is a kind of musico-literary entity preserved in the text.

In the preface to *Un Coup de Dés*, Mallarmé used a musical metaphor to describe the formal dimension of his poem: its typography, spacing, relations between words and phrases, and multi-directionality. In his sonata, Boulez does the opposite: he uses literary devices to structure and articulate the musical discourse. We might say, then, that in his work Boulez combines the musical "content" with a literary "form." Obviously, such a statement is not to be taken literally, implying the distinction between form and content in the pre-

Hanslickian sense, but merely as a figure of speech serving to disentangle the truly organic relationship of the literary and the musical in Boulez's work. The perfect symbol of this organic synthesis is a notational device that Boulez uses in Parenthèse and Commentaire to set off the parenthetical sections from the fixed ones: a fermata over a comma. While these two punctuation marks, one musical and one literary, may be distinguished for the purpose of analysis, their true meaning lies in the total effect they produce through fusion into a unity. Thus, the symbol is obviously designed to be enjoyed on the aesthetic plane. But that leads us to the question about the proper mode of perception of such a double entity; in other words, the question of how the musico-literary text of the work relates to its performances and perception.

Commenting on the labyrinthine design of *Constellation-Miroir*, Iwanka Stoianowa considered it a purely visual object and noted the impossibility of translating the complexity of the "digital code" found on the page into the "analogue code" of the sonic flux. [28] Charles Rosen, on the other hand, asserted that "the creation of such a structure would be an uninteresting game if each individual realization or performance did not imply the existence of the total form." [29] Boulez himself resolved this contradiction by stating that "it is not important that the listener should immediately perceive the mobility of a work (...). The interest does not lie in comparing two facets of a work but rather in knowing that it will never have a definitely fixed appearance." [30] In the same way he minimized the role of the work's performances saying that each performance represents merely "a single, specific option, neither better nor worse than any other." [31] In this way, he simply calls our attention to the fact that his concept of the open work centers around the text, the potential of which will never be exhausted. Thus, the best way to answer the question about the proper mode of perception is to give no answer at all, for each experience of the work, whether by the performer, the listener, or the reader of the score, will only reveal some of its aspects. The work is open in that a definitive version simply does not exist.

Thus, the kind of openness that interests Boulez could easily be encapsulated in one word: ambiguity.

> For my own part I always consider a work as something essentially ambiguous – that may be a question of temperament or character, but I know that any picture that I have exhausted after three minutes' inspection I find unsatisfying. (...) What really interests me (...) is a work that contains a strong element of ambiguity and therefore permits a number of different meanings and solutions. This profound ambiguity may be found in a great classical work, though there it is limited by precise length and basic structural data. Even so such a work does contain ambiguities in its deeper meaning than the one revealed at a first hearing or a first performing. [32]

In his Third Sonata, Boulez does a bit more: he introduces ambiguity into each of the links of the traditional aesthetic situation. As a result, the composer does not provide "a single viable" solution for a given context but rather a set of equally viable ones; thus, the compositional process is no longer about selecting but rather about offering multiple possibilities. And while such an approach gives certain liberties to the performer, it does not lessen the role of the composer; on the contrary, it "entails an increase in the composer's powers, since it is far more difficult to build a town than to build a street: a street leads from one point to another, whereas a town has lots of streets and presents many different directions for building." [33]

The resulting work is therefore a totality of these choices and possibilities; whether we view it as a town, a labyrinth, a constellation, or a circle, there are always different "viewpoints and perspectives from which it is seen." [34] But that is why the text of such a work must have this ambiguity "built-in" so to speak. Eco calls it "a rule of ambiguation," by which he means an underlying multi-layered structure of a literary work that makes the free interplay of ambiguities possible. In this way, the freedom of the reader's choices is directed by the text itself. [35] Boulez refers to the same structural rule when he says: "If the player can modify the text at will, such modification must be implied by the text, and not merely supplementary to it. The score must contain this interpretative 'chance' like a watermark." [36]

Thus, the recipient of this ambiguous work is not presented with a single specific message but with a choice among many possibilities; every performance is only a single option, "neither better nor worse than any other," [37] and so is each listening experience only a process of "selecting from it what suits [the listener]." "No two solutions will ever actually be the same; it is a plural solution; a multiple phenomenon in which a path has always to be discovered." In this way Boulez emphasizes an active and intelligent response to the main characteristic of contemporary music, "its lack of determinate form, the fact that it does not oblige you to select it but does oblige you to make your own selection of the form that you wish to give it."[38]

Why is it, then, that such a revolutionary work bears the traditional name of sonata? According to Anne Piret, the term is justified because the work is in several movements; but the comparison with the classical sonata stops there, she concludes, "as the Formants, instead of being played in an unchanged order, can be permutated among themselves based on eight different possibilities proposed by the composer." [39]

But contrary to Piret's sweeping statement, the multi-movement structure of Boulez's work does not suffice to call it a sonata; in fact, its open nature seems rather to contradict most associations that this generic term might bring to mind. But let us not forget that the sonata under discussion in this chapter is his third. This fact alone suggests a certain validity of the genre in Boulez's compositional poetics, and even more than that: it implies the existence of a certain idiom of Boulez's piano writing, analogous to the specific idioms of Mozart or Beethoven. But, while the idioms of these two composers derive their meanings from the forms and rhetoric of the classical style, Boulez's idiom might perhaps be associated with his attempts to destroy classical forms and to construct new ones on their debris. Indeed, this is precisely what he attempted in his Second Sonata, the formal aspects of which the composer himself described in highly negative terms.[40] Since the third sonata follows the second, perhaps it could also be viewed in a similar, "negative" way.

Such an approach would not be highly unusual or limited to the field of musical composition. In 1956, at the time Boulez was composing his Third Sonata, Jean-Paul Sartre noticed a similar trend in contemporary literature:

> One of the most curious features of our literary epoch is the appearance, here and there, of penetrating and entirely negative works that may be called anti-novels. (…) These anti-novels maintain the appearance and outlines of the ordinary novel; they are works of the imagination with fictitious characters, whose story they tell. But this is done only the better to deceive us; their aim is to make use of the novel in order to challenge the novel, to destroy it before our very eyes while seeming to construct it, to write the novel of a novel unwritten and unwritable (…) These curious and hard-to-classify works do not indicate weakness of the novel as a genre; all they show is that we live in a period of reflection and that the novel is reflecting on its own problems.[41]

Sartre's comments on the state of the novel reflect the same concerns that lay at the root of Boulez's Third Piano Sonata. Indeed, as has already been noted, it was the innovations of James Joyce's novels in particular that directly influenced the French composer, who felt that music, like literature, "must also be aware of itself and become the object of its own reflection." By analogy with Sartre's "anti-novel," then, one could risk describing Boulez's work as an "anti-sonata," i.e., a work that "makes use" of the genre in order to "challenge" it. In this way, it is only against the traditional concept of the sonata that the unique characteristics of Boulez's work will become fully apparent.

Thus, Boulez's original conception of the work as consisting of five movements challenges the concept of the sonata cycle in that it preserves the multi-movement structure of a traditional sonata, but introduces relativity into the order of movements. At the same time, the dramaturgical principle associated with the traditional "closed" musical work is called into question, for now the work's curve is also relative and depends on a specific arrangement of movements and their components. Finally, the very concept of movement as a homogeneous entity is replaced with the idea of formant, understood as a cluster of possibilities capable of giving rise to a variety of sonically differentiated developments. All of this amounts to what Boulez described in his article "Alea" as "the need to destroy all immanent structure."[42] For in a relative world in which the "architectural schemes" and thematic development of the closed work are rejected, the sonata too must have "a form that is not fixed, an evolving form which rebels against its own repetition; in short, a relative formal virtuality."

The Third Sonata of Boulez is therefore a sonata for a new age, in which new approaches to the work of art are created; in which new kinds of transmutations of creative modes between the arts are possible; in which, at last, music once again joins the other arts in their universal quest for ambiguity, which is perhaps the chief goal and essence of genuine works. For, as Boulez reminds us, "genuine works are those in which one can never come to an end ("infinite nucleus of the night"); and when all is said, one has still said nothing, and one will never say anything."[43]

Works Cited

Boulez, Pierre. "Current Invesitigations," *Stocktakings from an Apprenticeship.* Trans. Stephen Walsh. Oxford: Clarendon Press, 1991.

—. "Conversations with Celestin Deliege," *Orientations.* Trans. Martin Cooper. Cambridge: Harvard University Press, 1986.

—. "Poetry- Centre and Absence," *Orientations*, 195.

—. "Sonate, que me veux yu?" *Orientations,* 216.

—. "Sound, Word, Synthesis" *Orientations*, 179.

—. "Where Are We Now?" *Orientations*, 461-62.

Dallenbach, Lucien. *The Mirror of the Text.* Trans. Jeremy Whiteley and Emma Hughes. Chicago: The University of Chicago Press, 1989.

Eco, Umberto. *The Aesthetic of Chaosmos: The Middle Ages of James Joyce.* Trans. Ellen Esrach. Cambridge: Harvard University Press, 1989.

Ligeti, Gyorgy. "Some Remarks on Boulez' 3rd Piano Sonata," *Die Reihe* 5

Nattiez, Jean Jacques. *The Boulez-Cage Correspondence.* Trans, Robert Samuels. Cambridge: Cambridge University Press, 1994.

Rosen, Charles. "The Piano Music," *Pierre Boulez: A Symposium.* Ed. William Glock. London: Eulenberg Books, 1986.

Sartre, Jean-Paul. Preface to Nathalie Sarraute, *Portrait of a Man Unknown.* Trans. Maria Jones. Paris, 1956.

Scherer, Jacques. *Le 'Livre' de Mallarme.* Paris: Gallimard, 1977.

II.

Musical and Literary Interactions

'WITHIN A SPACE OF TEARS': MUSIC, WRITING, AND THE MODERN IN VIRGINIA WOOLF'S *THE VOYAGE OUT*

EMMA SUTTON

Virginia Woolf's first novel, *The Voyage Out*, was published in 1915, after more than six years of painful writing and revision.[1] As its pre-War composition might suggest, it is a text that draws on many of the characteristics of Victorian fiction, but which is also alert to its youthful twentieth-century status. The novel explores the lives of young artists, and their relations to their elders' lives and art. Many of its protagonists are amateur artists: the central figure - Rachel Vinrace - is a pianist and a number of her contemporaries, including the man to whom she becomes engaged, are writers. The relationship between literature and music is a central subject of *The Voyage Out*, and I will argue that this relationship was crucial not only to Woolf's understanding of her own writing but also to its modernity. In her determination to differentiate her own fiction from its Victorian precursors, Woolf looked to music as a means of establishing the newness of her own work. She conceived of *The Voyage Out*, that is, not only as a 'musical' text but also as concomitantly 'modern'. The significance of music in Woolf's aesthetic development is a subject that has still been insufficiently explored, and I will argue that music played an important part in her conception of her fiction at the outset of her career as a novelist.[2] Before turning to discuss the novel itself in detail, however, I will consider the ambiguities that inform Woolf's characterization of music as a 'modern' art in the early years of the twentieth century, and the significance of music in her early development as a novelist. My discussion aims to suggest the formative role of music in Woolf's work, but also the broader complexities surrounding music's status as a 'modern' art in the early twentieth century.

Woolf started work on the text that would become *The Voyage Out* in 1907 or 1908.[3] She began writing, then, in the immediate aftermath of a period in which music had enjoyed extraordinary cultural prestige in Britain (buoyed by the English Musical Renaissance) and, more broadly, in Continental Europe. Music had been eulogized in much late nineteenth-century aesthetic theory and literature, and its eminence was apparent too – as has been widely noted - in performance, publishing and consumption practices. From Walter Pater's famous assertion in *The Renaissance* (1873) that '[a]ll art constantly aspires towards the condition of music', to the enormous publicity that surrounded the first Bayreuth festival in 1876, to the massive scale of the Handel festivals in the 1860s, music's idiosyncratic and revered place within late nineteenth-century European culture was apparent.[4] Music was a common subject of poetry and fiction too. Taken up by writers and fine artists associated with the Aesthetic and decadent movements, music became a prominent subject in British literature and art in the *fin de siècle*. By the turn of the century, there was a distinctive and influential corpus of literature in which certain musical genres, and the work of certain composers (notably Richard Wagner), were associated with expressions of musical rapture. In the ecstatic accounts by decadent writers including Baudelaire, Gabriele D'Annunzio and Arthur Symons, music's emotive capacity was celebrated in mannered terms. Varied though these accounts were in their stylistics and their detail, they shared a sense of music as the supreme art, and they were often 'immoderate' or absolute in their language and sentiments; frequently describing their musical experiences in highly subjective terms, these accounts formed a conspicuous and controversial corpus of *fin-de-siècle* writing about music.

As I have argued elsewhere, there was a reaction against such forms of aestheticism in the late 1890s, and in the early years of the twentieth century.[5] Such responses to and accounts of music rapidly began to appear mannered, and 'ninetyish'. There was a reaction against certain genres and composers, and also against certain forms of expression of enthusiasm for music. Rather than evidence of uplifting moments of aesthetic ecstacy, such accounts became an embarrassment to those wishing to differentiate their own art and aestheticism from that of their immediate predecessors. As these comments suggest, music had become a touchstone of one's aesthetic principles, and commentaries on music were often not only self-revealing but also self-conscious. The shift in taste was particularly problematic for writers, faced with the legacy of decadent and Aesthetic literature about music. For writers wishing to establish their own modernity, and their independence from the aesthetic tenets of previous decades, music was a topic to be approached with care.

This awkwardness about 'ninetyish' musical aestheticism is hinted at in the gushing language of the socialite Clarissa Dalloway in *The Voyage Out*. Observing Rachel's copy of the score of *Tristan und Isolde*, Clarissa exclaims:

> 'D'you remember this? Isn't it divine?' She played a bar or two with ringed fingers upon the page.
> 'And then Tristan goes like this, and Isolde – oh! – it's all too thrilling!'

> [...]
> 'I shall never forget my first *Parsifal* – a grilling August day, and those fat old German women, come in their stuffy high frocks, and then the dark theatre, and the music beginning, and one couldn't help sobbing. A kind man went and fetched me water, I remember; and I could only cry on his shoulder!'[6]

Although Clarissa goes on to dismiss 'the kind of attitudes people go into over Wagner' and to judge that music makes young people 'too emotional' (47), her own words hover perilously close to just such mannered emotionalism. Woolf's parody reminds us of her familiarity with this sort of discourse about music: taught by Pater's sister Clara, Woolf had spent her childhood and teens in the *fin de siècle*, and knew at first hand a number of avid Wagnerites among family and friends.[7] And whilst her own writing about music could sound Paterian in moments (referring, in a letter of 1906, to 'a debauch of music' she eulogized the 'pure simple notes – smooth from all passion and frailty, and flawless as gems'), she was also alert to the datedness of certain forms of musical aestheticism.[8] In 'The Opera', an article of 1909, she qualified her enthusiasm with acknowledgement of the antiquated quality of the genre – opera was 'one of the oddest of all worlds – brilliant, beautiful, and absurd'.[9] There is a wary self-protection to this affectionate praise. By May 1913, when *The Voyage Out* had gone to press, she described her disenchantment with Wagner as representative of a wider cultural shift: 'O the noise and the heat, and the bawling sentimentality, which used once to carry me away, and now leaves me sitting perfectly still. Everyone seems to have come to this opinion, though some pretend to believe still'[10] modern aestheticism.

Given the ambiguities that surrounded music's reputation at this date, it is all the more surprising that Woolf should have turned to music as a means of developing the modernity of her own writing. Nonetheless, at the very outset of her career as a novelist, when needing to establish the newness of her writing, she repeatedly alluded to and reflected on music. There is no doubt that she was intently interested in the relationship between music and writing whilst working on *The Voyage Out*. She attended numerous operatic and concert performances in London and on the Continent, and visited the Bayreuth festival in 1909. Her correspondence of this period is scattered with anticipations and reflections on performances, comparisons of opera houses, and reiterations of the amount of time which she was devoting to opera: 'We go almost nightly to the opera', she wrote in May 1908, and complained 'I am so bewildered with operas – we go regularly – that I cant make sensible engagements'.[11] In addition to numerous casual allusions to music in her correspondence, she produced several articles on music before beginning and whilst working on the text ('Street Music' in 1905, and 'The Opera' and 'Impressions at Bayreuth' in 1909). This cluster of essays suggests a concentration on music, and at no other point in her life did the subject resurface so prominently in her non-fiction.[12] Woolf's attendance at performances and her non-fiction writing suggest that her interest in music was considerable and sustained. Her letters and essays, as well as the novel itself, return again and again to the affinities and differences between these art forms, as if Woolf were testing her own writing against the properties of the music in which she was immersed. Furthermore, it appears that she conceived of the evolving novel as an experiment in 'musical' prose. From Bayreuth she wrote that:

> We heard Parsifal yesterday; it was much better done, and I felt within a space of tears. I expect it is the most remarkable of the operas; it slides from music to words almost imperceptibly. However, I have been niggling at the effect all morning, without much success. It is very hard to write in one's bedroom, without any books to look at, or my especial rabbit path, into the next room' (406-7).

At the very point at which Woolf was working on *The Voyage Out*, then, she acknowledged her desire to recreate the qualities of Wagner's work in her own writing. Her 'niggling' at the 'effect' of *Parsifal* implies a determination to produce a form of writing that was modeled on, or in some ways imitative of, Wagnerian music drama.[13] And this interest in producing a 'Wagnerian' text was inseparable from her desire to create distinctly 'modern' fiction.

Woolf's interest in producing fiction that was in some way modeled on music was intrinsically linked to her desire to find a contemporary alternative to Victorian fiction and prose. It is unsurprising – as many critics have noted - that in the early stages of her development as a novelist she looked to her father Leslie Stephen as a figure against whom to define her own work. As eminent biographer, essayist and editor (most famously of the *Dictionary of National Biography*), Stephen was an exemplar of the prodigiously productive late-nineteenth-century professional writer. He was a *Victorian* writer – in all the nuances of the term – *par excellence*. It was necessary for Woolf, both in familial and aesthetic terms, to establish her difference from her father and the period of literary history with which he was associated. What is more unexpected, perhaps, is that her interest in music seems to have gone hand in hand with her reflections on her relationship with Stephen. It was whilst attending the Bayreuth festival that she considered not only the relations between words and music, but also her own literary affinities to and differences from her father. In part, this may have arisen from the fact that Woolf's companions at Bayreuth were her brother Adrian, and their friend Saxon Sydney-Turner, the latter of whom reminded her of Stephen in his temperament and behaviour:

> Saxon is dormant all day, and rather peevish if you interrupt him. He hops along, before or behind, swinging his ugly stick, and humming, like a stridulous

> grasshopper. He reminds me a little of father. He clenches his fists, and scowls in the same way; and stops at once if you look at him (405).

Though her affection and admiration for Saxon are evident in her correspondence, it is apparent too that Woolf was frustrated by Saxon's pedantic knowledge, his factional advocacy of Wagner's work, and the intellectual bullying at the hands of her companions who 'make me read the libretto in German, which troubles me a good deal' (407). During this period of intense musical experience, then, the behavior of her male companions reminded her of Leslie Stephen and echoed some of the dynamics of her relationship with her father. Only a few days after writing the letter quoted above, Woolf confided to her sister Vanessa that:

> I have been thinking a great deal about father too, and discussing him with Adrian. I believe he was really very modest; he was certainly not selfconscious in his work; nor was he an egoist, as I am. He had very few sympathies though; and practically no imagination. You might give your view; this is very much at random (408).

Woolf differentiates herself from Stephen by her implicitly greater 'egoism', 'sympathies' and 'imagination', qualities that speak as much of her writing as her character. It is these criteria by which Woolf distinguishes her writing from that of her father. It is striking that at the very moment when Woolf was prompted to experiment with 'Wagnerian' prose, she was acutely aware of her aesthetic divergence from Leslie Stephen – a man who had, she judged, 'no ear for music'.[14] Despite Woolf's disclaimer that these observations are haphazard and 'random', her concentrated consideration of this subject is clear. What this suggests, of course, is that Woolf recognized that an alternative to Stephen's literary aesthetics lay in a prose that was shaped in some way by music. Her use of terms like 'sympathy' and 'imagination' stresses the importance of the imaginative and the emotional over the prosaic literalism with which she associates Stephen's writing; Woolf's vocabulary associates her own work with qualities conventionally attributed to music and musicians. In perceiving her own writing as 'musical', Woolf had found a means of differentiating her work from the resolutely unmusical Stephen.[15]

The hypothesis that Woolf saw 'musical' prose as an attractively modern form of writing is supported by the earliest of her essays on music, 'Street Music' (1905). In this essay she characterized music not only as an ancient art, but also as the source from which the other arts would draw their modernity. Music was characterized (in the modernist vocabulary of neo-paganism) as instinctual, vigorous and intoxicating: the musician 'is the minister of the wildest of all gods'. Suggesting that 'the art of writing, [...] is nearly allied to the art of music, and is chiefly degenerate because it has forgotten its existence', Woolf argued that modern writing would be invigorated by the influence of music: 'We should invent – or rather remember – the innumerable metres which we have so long outraged, and which would restore both prose and poetry to the harmonies that the ancients heard and observed'. Exhorting writers to remember the musical (and especially the rhythmic) roots of their work, Woolf eulogized music's potential for aesthetic and social reform, anticipating the time in which 'the work of the hand and the thoughts of the mind [will] flow melodiously in obedience to the laws of music'. [16]Although she would undercut this utopian conclusion with the wry observation in an informal letter that '[m]y remarks will revolutionise the whole future of music', it is clear that Woolf was excited by music's potential influence on contemporary writing.[17] Indeed, 'Street Music' argues that this innovative writing will be modern precisely because of its musical qualities.

Woolf's essays, correspondence and memoirs illustrate her knowledgeable sensitivity to music's ambivalent status in the early twentieth-century. These accounts suggest the ambiguities surrounding music's status as a modern art, and the significance of music to Woolf's aesthetic and familial development. The musical allusions in *The Voyage Out*, to which we will now turn, may thus be read both biographically and historically, in terms of Woolf's development as a writer but also as evidence of broader factors in the perception of music at this date. It is evident that Woolf was quick to recognize some expressions of musical enthusiasm and some musical genres and styles (notably nineteenth-century grand opera) as alarmingly mannered and dated for an early twentieth-century writer. Nonetheless, it is clear too that she was excited by the innovations that she expected music to bring to contemporary writing. The relations between music, writing and modernity in *The Voyage Out*, to which we will now turn, further illustrate her alertness to and reflections on these complexities.

With its cast of writers and critics, a painter and a musician, it is unsurprising that the dialogue as well as the narrative of *The Voyage Out* is littered with references to books, music and painting. Through her portraits of a variety of young artists, Woolf explores various definitions of modern art and various models of the early twentieth-century artist. In their conversation and unvoiced reflections, the young artists repeatedly consider their aesthetic aspirations and principles; in addition, many of the older artists, whether amateur painters or respected academic critics like Mr Ambrose, comment on contemporary art. Modern art is thus an explicit subject of the text. The eccentric painter Mrs Flushing, for example, stands as a forthright advocate of not only modern but specifically Modernist art in the novel.[18] She maintains that:

> nothin' that's more than twenty years old interests me [...] Mouldy old pictures, dirty old books, they stick 'em in museums when they're only fit for burnin' [...] There's a clever man in London called [Augustus] John who paints ever so

> much better than the old masters [...] His pictures excite me – nothin' that's old excites me (222-3).

On the river trip to a 'native' village, Mrs Flushing is observed 'dotting and striping her canvas'; her painting, like her speech, is staccato, confident, and provocative (311). Her paintings of hills 'were all marked by something of the jerk and decision of their maker; they were all perfectly untrained onslaughts of the brush upon some half-realized idea suggested by hill or tree; and they were all in some way characteristic of Mrs Flushing' (271-2). Mrs Flushing's examples of modern art appear ludicrous partly because they bear such overt traces of their creator: she has failed to transcend herself and realize any subject impersonally (in contrast, as we shall see, to Rachel's playing). The narrator also satirizes the paintings' imprecision (the 'half-realized' ideas), their aggressive exuberance and their brash disregard for training. Mrs Flushing's contempt for older art, and her amateurism, are clearly satirized by the narrator and regarded with amusement by the other characters. As a female artist, she is a problematic role model for the young musician Rachel, yet her energy and frankness are engaging. She is a marked contrast to the male scholars such as Mr Ambrose, whom his wife Helen describes as 'spend[ing] his life in digging up manuscripts which nobody wants' (223). His opinion of contemporary art could not be more different from that of Mrs Flushing: he exclaims to Rachel, for example, 'what's the use of reading if you don't read Greek? After all, if you read Greek, you need never read anything else, pure waste of time – pure waste of time' (192). His dismissal of all writing since that of the Greeks stands as an alternative, equally extreme, attitude towards contemporary art. Between these poles various conceptions of modern art are considered and discussed.

As we might expect, the novel is particularly alert to the situation of the modern woman artist, principally represented by the protagonist Rachel. Rachel's development as an artist and as an individual is considered in detail, and her experiences illustrate some of the constraints and dilemmas facing a woman artist in the early twentieth century. It is possible, for a number of reasons, to identify Rachel as a fictional representative of Woolf. Certainly, there are parallels between their situations as young women artists: Rachel's age is close to that of Woolf when she started work on the novel;[19] Rachel is the only young female artist in the novel, immediately suggesting a resonance with Woolf's position; similarly, she finds herself in the company of distinguished writers and critics, predominantly men;[20] and, like Woolf, Rachel is ambitious and (intermittently) confident of her own value as an artist but has not entered the public realm of concert performance, or (in Woolf's case) extensive literary publication. Furthermore, a number of phrases in Rachel's dialogue echo the enthusiastic allusions to music in Woolf's correspondence.[21] It is possible, too, that other affinities exist. Rachel's exaggerated insulation from modern life, for instance, may allude to Woolf's frustration with the restrictions placed on her own knowledge and actions (such as her exclusion from a university education). In addition, Rachel's isolation as an artist may suggest Woolf's perception of the absence of female literary ancestors and of writers with shared aesthetic aims. And Rachel's sheltered upbringing and social diffidence may mirror Woolf's caution about addressing ostentatiously topical or contentious subjects in her fiction, her sense that these remained problematic subjects for women writers at the start of the twentieth century (and at the start of their careers). These affinities suggest that Woolf used the character of Rachel as a way of exploring both her own personal and professional circumstances, and those of women artists more broadly. It is striking, then, that in a novel populated with writers and literary critics Woolf seems to have identified with the solitary example of a musician in the text.

These observations might suggest that Woolf identified music as a 'female' or 'feminine' art; certainly, her interest in developing a modern and a 'musical' prose was conceived in opposition to Stephen's 'masculine' Victorian writing. In her account of her childhood in 'A Sketch of the Past' (written 1939-40), Woolf appears to contrast music and literature in gendered terms, associating her mother with music: 'she could play the piano and was musical [...] My mother [...] is of course "a vision" as they used to say [...] [t]he sound of music also comes from those long low rooms'.[22] Jane Marcus has proposed that this and other passages imply that Woolf perceived music as a female art form.[23] It is possible, therefore, that Woolf's musical prose was conceived as a specifically female form of modern writing – what we might retrospectively call a female Modernism. Woolf's gendered representation of the arts, and of modern art, is complex and nuanced, and invites extended attention. Here, I wish primarily to emphasize that – against the grain of 'Street Music' and her correspondence from Bayreuth – *The Voyage Out* repeatedly associates music with the past. In contrast to 'Street Music''s utopian account of music's modernizing powers on literature, *The Voyage Out* emphasizes the weight of (male) aesthetic traditions for the female writer and musician. As a consequence of its insularity from twentieth-century life, music appears to be anti-feminist, or at least removed from contemporary feminism. In this novel, music has an oblique and complex relationship to modernity.

From the very opening of the novel music is associated with the past. All of the music that Rachel plays is pre-twentieth-century, and although we are told that she owns a copy of Wagner's *Tristan und Isolde* (1859) we never hear her play even this mid-nineteenth-century work.[24] Wagner is, in fact, the most modern composer referred to in the novel, though he had died in 1883, and his works had been in vogue in Britain for the last quarter of the nineteenth century. Although Woolf was undoubtedly familiar with a range of more recent - and innovative - music, no such works are alluded to in the text. Her enthusiasm for one example of experimental post-Wagnerian opera is evident in her account of hearing Richard Strauss' *Salome* (1905) in Dresden. She wrote to Vanessa:

> We went to Salome, (Strauss as you may know) last night. I was much excited, and believe that it is a new discovery. He gets great emotion into his music, without any beauty. However, Saxon thought we were encroaching upon Wagner, and we had a long and rather acid discussion.[25]

From Woolf's comments on this performance, which immediately followed her attendance at Bayreuth, it is clear that she was excited by Strauss' work, seeing it as a stimulating development ('a new discovery') on Wagnerian opera. Yet Woolf's association of music with the past seems unequivocal in *The Voyage Out*: although the text alludes to contemporary visual art and literature (such as Terence Hewet's novel about 'Silence') there is no contemporary musical equivalent in the novel. And these differences do not arise simply from the fact that Rachel is a performer or consumer rather than a creative artist: she doesn't play or study contemporary music either. Music appears therefore as aloof from the contemporary world – it appears as anti-realist, and anti-contemporary. Furthermore, the performance and consumption of music are invariably represented as moments of withdrawal from the concerns of contemporary life. For Rachel, music functions as an escape from the frustrations of her life:

> Rachel was indignant with the prosperous matrons, who made her feel outside their world and motherless, and turning back, she left them abruptly. She slammed the door of her room, and pulled out her music. It was all old music - Bach and Beethoven, Mozart and Purcell – the pages yellow, the engraving rough to the finger. In three minutes she was deep in a very difficult, very classical fugue in A and over her face came a queer remote impersonal expression of complete absorption and anxious satisfaction. (58)

In this first account of Rachel's playing, Woolf simultaneously draws attention to Rachel's interest in antiquarian music, and its irrelevance to her contemporary life. Rachel is clearly a child of the nineteenth-century early music revival, her choice of texts reflecting the composers championed by Arnold Dolmetsch and others.[26] Her antiquarian impulses are combined with a retreat from the contemporary world: Rachel's playing is represented as a moment of solipsistic isolation. Rachel's companions share the perception of music's alienation from contemporary subjects, and especially from contemporary social concerns: Rachel's mentor, Helen Ambrose, 'desired that Rachel should think, and for this reason offered books and discouraged too entire a dependence upon Bach and Beethoven and Wagner' (137). Helen's comment may indicate one reason why Woolf places so much emphasis on the 'outdatedness' of music in this novel: by asserting music's alienation from topical subjects, and underlining Rachel's passionate aestheticism and her naivety, Woolf alludes to and undercuts the problematic aspects of *fin-de-siècle* musical aestheticism. Rachel reproduces, in other words, some of the traits of the late nineteenth-century musical aesthete that were most criticized by their successors. In this way, Woolf expresses a Modern's rejection of an art that had become associated with introspective, politically indifferent, aestheticism, whilst presenting a sympathetic portrait of this female musician.

If Woolf suggests that Rachel's interest in the musical past divides her from contemporary concerns, the novel emphasizes too the burden of the literary past. And it is a past which is particularly oppressive for the modern woman artist. Apart from Rachel and Mrs Flushing, Miss Allan is the only other example of a female artist in the novel, and the only example of a professional woman artist. Her life is one of literary drudgery, as she works as a teacher and critic, producing textbooks on a canon of male authors:

> She touched her manuscript. 'Age of Chaucer; Age of Elizabeth; Age of Dryden,' she reflected. 'I'm glad there aren't many more ages. I'm still in the middle of the eighteenth century' (295).

Though kindly and gentle, her face is 'much lined with care and thought' (295), and in contrast to the male scholars such as Mr Ambrose, her relentless work is explicitly the outcome of financial necessity. The literary past – all these 'ages' – is clearly a burden, an impediment to her own intellectual pleasure and creativity. In this context, the literary past is oppressive, something which absorbs Miss Allan's time and energy, and which is essentially aloof from the contemporary world – it is 'aged'. As a professional woman artist, she must have been an unappealing model for Rachel and Woolf. The literary past, in this novel, is unequivocally male (Gibbon, Milton and classical writers dominate the literary allusions), and not one text by a woman author is discussed. Through Miss Allan, Woolf suggests women's fragile foothold not only in the literary canon, but also in modern literary production.

The oppressiveness of the literary past is countered, however, by Rachel's enraptured encounter with the *fin-de-siècle* writing to which she is introduced by Helen Ambrose; Rachel's exposure to relatively recent literature marks the beginning of her development as an artist and as an independent individual. The physical appearance of the recent fiction and drama to which Rachel is introduced is in sharp contrast to her aged musical scores with their yellowed paper:

> Rachel chose modern books, books in shiny yellow covers, books with a great deal of gilding on the back, which were tokens in her aunts' eyes of harsh wrangling and disputes about facts which had no such importance as the moderns claimed for them (137-8).

The contemporary physical appearance of these texts is emphasized even before the modernity of their subject matter is noted; and elsewhere, Rachel's books are described as 'red and yellow volumes', again stressing their vibrant – modern – appearance (340). Their bright colours associate them with the only example of Modernist visual art in the novel: Mrs Flushing's paintings, which are also vulnerable to the charge of gaudiness. Woolf draws further attention to the texts' novelty through the repetition of the word 'modern', and through the criticisms of Rachel's aunts, who disapprove of the apparently strident topicality of these texts. The aunts' disapproval suggests the recent changes in literary production and subject matter, and the differences between the generations in their literary tastes. Rachel's encounter with *fin-de-siècle* literature occurs after Rachel's performance of Bach (above) has been described, and thus after her authority as a musician has been established. It represents a new stage in Rachel's development, when she starts to learn more about the complexities of contemporary life – and, especially, women's lives. It seems, in this early part of the section set at Santa Marina, that literature will enhance Rachel's development as a female – and a feminist – artist. Furthermore, these passages set up an explicit opposition between music and literature.

The descriptions of Rachel's reading in the tenth chapter illustrate a fundamental difference between Rachel's responses to music and to literature. The books that Rachel reads contribute to her development as a young woman; they increase her knowledge of some aspects of contemporary life (particularly sexual relations) and they also enhance her ability to act as a social agent in modern, early twentieth-century society. We are told, for example, that Rachel:

> was sitting alone, sunk in an armchair, reading a brightly-coloured red volume lettered on the back *Works of Henrik Ibsen*. Music was open on the piano, and books of music rose in two jagged pillars on the floor; but for the moment music was deserted.
>
> Far from looking bored or absent-minded, her eyes were concentrated almost sternly upon the page, and from her breathing, which was slow but repressed, it could be seen that her whole body was constrained by the working of her mind. [...]
>
> She acted [Ibsen's plays] for days at a time, greatly to Helen's amusement; and then it would be Meredith's turn and she became Diana of the Crossways. But Helen was aware it was not all acting, and that some sort of change was taking place in the human being [...] (Her mind wandered away from Nora, but she went on thinking of things that the book suggested to her, of women and life) (136-7)

Rachel's reflections on 'women and life' have been prompted by her reading of Ibsen's *Doll's House*, the notorious proto-feminist play of 1879, and of Meredith's New Woman novel *Diana of the Crossways* (1885). These reflections are the outcome of the subject matter of the novels and plays that Rachel reads: they are, in other words, an outcome of literature's representational qualities. Music, frequently perceived as a non-representational art, has no such capacity in the novel. While music may increase Rachel's rigor and interpretative skills as an artist, it does not increase her self-knowledge or knowledge of contemporary life. Indeed, it has been 'deserted' for this very reason. Music, previously depicted in architectural images, now lies in ruins, as the 'jagged pillars' suggest. The urgency of Rachel's need for knowledge of 'women and life' is emphasized (the deceptively simple but capacious phrase sounds like an anticipation of the titles of Woolf's later feminist essays). And Woolf emphasizes that this need can be met more readily by reading than by playing. These literary texts address recent or contemporary topics in a way that the music Rachel studies does not, and they alter her knowledge of and behavior in contemporary society. Her reading makes her more 'modern' as a young woman – more confident, more outspoken and less naive. For Rachel, then, the consumption of these (though not all)[27] literary texts enables her to begin a process of what we might call modernization.

However, Rachel's passionate responses to these texts are qualified by the comments of her fiancé, the young writer Terence Hewet, later in the novel:

> 'God, Rachel, you do read trash! [...] And you're behind the times too, my dear. No one dreams of reading this kind of thing now – antiquated problem plays, harrowing depictions of life in the East End - oh no, we've exploded all that. Read poetry, Rachel, poetry, poetry, poetry!' (341).

Terence's comments sharply reveal the temporality of literary taste, and the contempt of a modern writer for the work of his immediate predecessors. Rachel's reading (especially its subject-matter) is robustly dismissed as passé – material which 'no one dreams of reading'. It is the social realism of these texts - presumably the Ibsen plays and *fin-de-siècle* novels which we have earlier seen Rachel reading - which Terence sees as outdated. His enthusiasm for poetry, a genre conventionally associated with greater formal rigor than fiction or drama, suggests his privileging of form over social realism. The writer's remarks suggest that, for him, true modernity lies in form rather than content. Although Terence's comments may be undercut by their patronizing tone, they nonetheless draw attention to the preeminence of form in modern writing – and in Modernist aesthetics.[28] His comments seem to suggest that Rachel's rapturous response to *fin-de-siècle* writing may have been an aesthetic false step, a step away from properly modern art. But they also, as we shall see, indicate why her integrity as a musician – and the integrity of music – are ultimately endorsed in the novel.

Woolf places unswerving emphasis on Rachel's attention to musical form. The accounts of Rachel's performances emphasize the fierce intellectual concentration that characterizes her playing. Rachel is absorbed by the formal structure of the pieces she plays; for her, aesthetic satisfaction lies in the uncovering of formal structure through performance. Even when she studies works with dramatic or representational qualities (such as when she reads the libretto of *Tristan*) rather than absolute music she is uninterested in the subject-matter; it is form which holds her attention. Her concentration on form is depicted in architectural imagery; Rachel's performances are imagined as processes during which the formal structures of the work become apparent to performer (and listener). They are compared to buildings or staircases, the temporal sequence of the performances imagined as processes of construction. In the early passage when Rachel plays a 'very difficult' Bach fugue:

> an invisible line seemed to string the notes together, from which rose a shape, a building. She was so far absorbed in this work, for it was really difficult to find how all these sounds should stand together, and drew upon the whole of her faculties, that she never heard a knock at the door (58-9).

In the second account of Rachel's playing we are told that the guests at the hotel ball:

> sat very still as if they saw a building with spaces and columns succeeding each other rising in the empty space. Then they began to see themselves and their lives, and the whole of human life advancing very nobly under the direction of the music. They felt themselves ennobled, and when Rachel stopped playing they desired nothing but sleep (187).

And later in the novel her playing is described for the third time:

> Up and up the steep spiral of a very late Beethoven sonata she climbed, like a person ascending a ruined staircase, energetically at first, then more laboriously advancing her feet with effort until she could go no higher and returned with a run to begin at the very bottom again (339-40).

From Rachel's first performance of the Bach fugue, she finds 'complete absorption and anxious satisfaction' in the formal structure of these works. Where the other characters turn to music for occasional emotional stimulation, or as a prop to the social occasion of the hotel ball, Rachel displays unswerving concentration on the musical texts themselves. And whereas other characters, such as Clarissa Dalloway, relish music's emotive effects, Rachel is identified as the 'true' musician and artist because of her concentration on form. Her concentration is characterized as demanding, both intellectually and technically, and whilst her performances are far from flawless, her integrity as an artist is unquestionably endorsed. Woolf's emphasis on musical form thus links music with modern art, and Rachel with modern artists.

Rachel's implicit sympathy with the formalism of modern art is suggested too by the development of her musical tastes. After her dalliance with late nineteenth-century literature, Woolf provides us with two substantial accounts of Rachel playing (the hotel ball and the Beethoven sonata), and Rachel is seen discussing and defending music to Terence. In other words, her identity as a serious musician (she describes herself as 'the best musician in South America, not to speak of Europe and Asia' [340]) is increasingly fore-grounded as the novel progresses.[29]Rather than appearing as an impressionable young woman who is an enthusiastic but somewhat unformed artist, in the later parts of the novel Rachel is characterized as a dedicated and accomplished musician. She shows less interest in literature, and indeed dismisses it in a heated exchange with Terence: '"Think of words compared with sounds!" […] she stirred the red and yellow volumes contemptuously' (340).[30] Her increasingly self-confident dedication to music goes hand in hand with her emerging modernism as an artist. As the novel unfolds, Rachel is increasingly associated with the music of Bach and Beethoven rather than that of the mid-nineteenth century. Whereas the explicit allusions to mid-nineteenth-century music occur in the early part of the novel in the references to Wagner's work, her concentrated interest in Bach is stressed as the narrative progresses.[31] Wagner's work – and, by extension, late Romantic music - is thus associated with the period of Rachel's immaturity and naivety, the stage in which '[h]er mind was in the state of an intelligent man's in the beginning of the reign of Queen Elizabeth' (31). By the twelfth chapter we are told, however, that Bach 'was at this time the subject of her intense enthusiasm' (187). The shift in Rachel's taste and in the novel's musical allusions indicate her emerging modernism, as she is aligned with an artist associated with formal perfection (Bach) rather than the emotive, high Romantic music and subjects of Wagner's dramatic works.[32] The shift represents too a move from dramatic or programme music to absolute music – symbolically, a move from subject matter to form. Although Rachel's musical tastes are increasingly for the music of a more remote historical period, the move towards a modern musical aesthetic is discreetly implied. Even though the shift in Rachel's taste as a performer and student does not explicitly enhance her knowledge of contemporary life (as her reading of Ibsen did), it indicates that her aesthetic tastes are becoming more contemporary. Her preference for Bach indicates a move towards a formalism that is tellingly 'modern'.

Although the accounts of Rachel's responses to *fin-de-siècle* literature in the earlier sections of the novel seem to suggest that fiction and drama will provide Rachel with the means of developing as a modern artist and individual, the novel describes her re-absorption in music after her emotional responses to the writing of Ibsen and his contemporaries. Woolf endorses Rachel's dedication to music, as I have just noted, through the increasing formalism of Rachel's musical tastes. But Woolf also suggests that her protagonist's development is a positive one because Rachel finds a social role as artist. Rather than, as in the early parts of the novel, using music as an escape from contemporary life and playing in isolation (she is even disconcerted when overheard by Clarissa), the scene at the hotel ball indicates that Rachel has found a valuable social role for her music. Playing for the assembled guests at the ball, she provides them with entertainment and pleasure, but also enables them to realize unspoken emotions:

> Susan rose […] "I do adore music," she said, as she thanked Rachel. "It just seems to say all the things one can't say oneself". She gave a nervous little laugh and looked from one to the other with great benignity, as though she would like to say something but could not find the words in which to express it (187).

The performance enables the shy and reserved guests to dance together joyously, and then to listen contentedly to Bach. In contrast to the solipsism previously associated with Rachel's playing, this performance brings her into closer contact with her peers and also serves a beneficial purpose for the community. Rachel's performance makes the audience feel 'ennobled', conscious of their mutual affection and conscious too of music's capacity to reveal and affirm these relationships. Although music certainly acts as a means for Rachel to 'defend […] her own solitude and autonomy' it also, in the later parts of the novel, provides her with a social – and a sociable – role.[33] This shift is indicated too by the fact that in this scene Rachel plays Bach, an artist associated with a genial family life, in contrast to Beethoven and Wagner, who were conventionally perceived as tortured, alienated geniuses.[34] What these developments suggest is that Rachel has found a way of being a modern artist that is sympathetic to her own art and to her own character.

Although this *Bildungsroman* is usually read as an account of Rachel's failure to mature or 'find a voice', there are some positive aspects to Rachel's development, aspects that suggest an innovative and valuable role for the modern female artist.[35] Whilst Rachel's development is certainly limited and problematic – most obviously because the novel concludes with her death - Woolf's portrait of the musician suggests some of the promise as well as the difficulties of Rachel's aesthetic principles and practice. Despite eschewing contemporary and recent music, and showing no interest in a public or professional career, Rachel is discreetly associated with modern art. In satirizing overtly 'modern' art (the problem plays, which quickly appear out-dated, or Mrs Flushing's eccentric paintings), and in associating music with the past, Woolf may be suggesting that the future for modern art lies not in ostentatiously innovative subject-matter or forms but in more subtle innovations – such as the formal innovations of her own work. Like the music that Rachel performs, *The Voyage Out* is not an overtly 'contemporary' text, but it may be more modern than it first appeared. Even though, as contemporary critics recognized, [36] it is not an ostentatiously experimental novel, it anticipates the significance of music in Woolf's later fiction, much of which drew its experimentalism from her study of musical form.

Works Cited

Forster, E.M.. *A Room With a View*. Ed. Oliver Stallybrass. London: Penguin, 1988.

Lee, Hermione. *Virginia Woolf.* London: Vintage, 1997.

Marcus, Jane. "Thinking Back Through Our Mothers" in *New Feminist Essays*. London: Macmilllan, 1981.

Pater, Walter. "The School of Giorgione" Ed. Adam Philips. *The Renaissance: Studies in Art and Poetry*. Oxford: Oxford University Press, 1986.

Raitt, Suzanne. "Finding a Voice: Virginia Woolf's Early Novels" in Ed. Sue Roe and Susan Sellers. *The Cambridge Companion to Virginia Woolf,* Cambridge: Cambridge University Press, 2000.

Sutton, Emma. *Aubrey Beardsley and British Wagnerism in the 1890's.* Oxford: Oxford University Press, 2002.

Woolf, Virginia. *Melymbrosia.* Ed. Louise DeSalvo. San Francisco: Cleis, 2002.

—. *The Complete Shorter Fiction of Virginia Woolf.* Ed. Susan Dick. London: Hogarth, 1985, 1989.

—. *The Essays of Virginia Woolf*, Vol. I, 1904-1912. Ed. Andrew McNeillie. London: Hogarth, 1976.

—. *The Flight of the Mind, The Letters of Virginia Woolf*, Vol. I, 1888-1912. Ed. Nigel Nicholson. London: Hogarth, 1975.

—. *The Question of Things Happening, The Letters of Virginia Woolf*, Vol. II, 1912-1922. Ed. Nigel Nicholson. London: Hogarth, 1976.

"DEAR EZZROAR," "DEAR ANTHILL": EZRA POUND, GEORGE ANTHEIL AND THE COMPLICATIONS OF PATRONAGE

ERIN E. TEMPLETON

American composer George Antheil recalls his first encounter with the infamous Ezra Pound in his autobiography, *Bad Boy of Music* (1945). As Antheil remembers the event, he and Pound first crossed paths in 1923 at the behest of Margaret Anderson, former editor of the *Little Review*. Recently expatriated herself, Anderson invited Antheil and Pound to a tea for actress Georgette LeBlanc, convinced that two such vivid personalities would certainly have interesting things to say to each other. In his memoir, Antheil recalls:

> There for the first time I met Erik Satie and a Mephistophelian red-bearded gent who turned out to be Ezra Pound. Margaret [Anderson] had given Ezra quite a spiel about me; according to her I was a "genius," and Ezra was vastly intrigued by all this, for, as everyone knows, Ezra was at that time the world's foremost expert in genius; in fact he frankly called himself an expert in genius.
>
> He was unusually kind and gracious to me; and as I left he asked for my address and said that he would someday come around to see me.
>
> Ezra turned up early the next morning, in a green coat with blue square buttons; and his red pointed goatee and kinky red hair flew off from his face in all directions . . . .
>
> Ezra asked me to get some of my music and go with him to the home of a friend who had a piano. I did so, went with him, played for hours, and Ezra seemed very pleased with it all. He accompanied me back home and asked if by any chance I had written anything about my musical aims, and I said "Yes, I have"; which accidentally happened to be the truth . . .
>
> Ezra was most delighted with all of this and asked if he could keep the "precious sheets" for a while, he would take scrupulous care of them. . . .
>
> After Ezra's visit, and as the weeks went by, it became more and more apparent that Ezra was working with the stuff I had written. Sylvia [Beach]—who like Eva Weinwurstel, always got to know everything first—told me that Ezra was planning to write a book about me, and that a friend of Ezra's, Bill Bird, would publish it in Paris.
>
> This scared me (117-118) [1]

From the tone of this passage, one might never guess that Antheil took Pound or his advice seriously. Casting him as the devil himself, the composer suggestively mocked Pound's self-proclaimed position as Modernism's talent scout. To do business with Ezra Pound, he implied, is to sell your soul. Indeed, the "deal" Antheil struck with Pound seems to be one he would rather forget entirely. Although the two artists knew one another and worked together throughout the 1920s, Antheil scarcely mentioned Pound in the remainder of his memoir, and when he did, he continued to portray Pound as manipulative and domineering.

Over the years, scholars who have attempted to study Pound's relationship with Antheil have drawn heavily upon Antheil's memoir. They either disregard the relationship completely, or like Antheil, they seek to demonize Pound. Modernist scholars like Hugh Kenner, by virtually ignoring the relationship, effectively write it out of history and, in doing so, suggest that the creative interchange between the two men was of little significance.[2] Musicologists Linda Whitesitt and Murray Schafer accept Antheil's version of the story, that Pound "merely wanted to use me as a whip with which to lash out at all those who disagreed with him" (119). Corroborating Antheil's account, they rely heavily not only upon the evidence offered in *Bad Boy of Music* but also upon a letter that Pound wrote to Antheil in October of 1927. This letter is cited as evidence of Pound's cruel and abrupt dismissal of Antheil and his work. I will argue, however, that this reading of the relationship is mistaken.

These accounts are flawed because both Pound's October letter and Antheil's memoir have been taken out of context. While *Bad Boy of Music* provides an entertaining description of the composer's life, the perils of equating Antheil's autobiography with "fact" should be readily apparent. By the early 1940s, the years when Antheil penned the document, Pound had fallen out of grace, both in the United States and in Europe, and Antheil himself had lost most of the fame he had once enjoyed. In retrospect, it seems likely that in the hopes of preserving what little artistic status he had left, Antheil fictionalized his doings, exaggerated his importance, and distanced himself purposefully from Pound in order to preserve his own reputation. He even admits, "It seems terribly unfair of me to criticize Ezra Pound now that the poet has fallen into disgrace. But, I emphasize, I would write these pages exactly this way if Ezra had become an international hero instead" (119). Antheil clearly tried to present himself as artistically independent in the hopes that future generations might remember his contribution to American music divorced from any association with the overtly fascist Ezra Pound. [3]

This relationship was not merely a case where Pound took advantage of a young and unknown talent to further his own ends as Antheil has suggested, nor is the relationship insignificant. It had real consequences for both men: it shaped the entire course of Antheil's career and helps to explain Pound's attraction to Mussolini and the Fascist State. Finally, in addition to furthering our understanding of two important Modernist figures, it reveals a great deal about the importance of patronage in the early Twentieth century. Antheil, like many artists in the early twentieth century, felt torn between pleasing his patron and remaining true to his artistic vision. Ultimately, he and Pound tried to have the best of both worlds: Antheil wrote the "mechanical" music he wanted to write, and he and Pound together schemed to manipulate Antheil's patron and manage the public reception of work. Ultimately, they succeeded not only in misleading his patron and American public, but an entire generation of scholars as well.

Pound's 1927 letter to Antheil also poses specific problems for scholars investigating Pound's relationship with Antheil. By all existing accounts, Pound and Antheil's friendship ended with Pound's letter of October 27, 1927. In this letter, Pound openly criticizes the bulk of Antheil's *oeuvre* as a composer. "I am not interested," he writes to his former charge, "in anything that you have done since *the Ballet Mechanique*."[4] Read as a single, isolated utterance, Pound's letter does seem to close the door on Antheil and his work. The context of this letter, however, has not been properly understood, primarily due to gaps that exist in the archival record of the event. While most of the letters that Pound wrote to Antheil are presumed lost, Antheil's replies to Pound still exist and are part of the Ezra Pound Collection at the Beinecke Library at Yale University. Unpublished, they serve to revise the current critical understanding of Pound's apparently dismissive letter and of his wider relationship to the American composer.[5] Ultimately, these letters add an entirely new dimension to readings of Pound's association with Antheil. Pound, in my view, did not simply use the young and unknown Antheil to suit his own artistic ends. Antheil's association with Pound not only helped him gain access to the previously closed Parisian salons—it also led to serious conflicts with his patron and the ultimate compromise of his artistic career. Pound's investment in Antheil's artistic success and despair at his failure helped to fuel Pound's attraction to Mussolini's Fascist State.

In 1920, disillusioned with postwar London, Ezra Pound and his wife moved to Paris. Not only a locus of literary experimentation and innovation, the "City of Lights" was also ripe for revolutions in music and the visual arts. In the early twenties, a group of avant-garde composers led by Eric Satie, known as "Les Six," made their mark on French music while Russian expatriates in Paris celebrated Diaghileff's Ballet Russe. American musicians, however, offered no apparent counterpart to these revolutionary musical movements. The conspicuous absence of American talent bothered Pound who had been writing music criticism for A. R. Orange's *New Age* since 1917. Consequently, Pound himself began to consider composing in an attempt to fill the void. He had been thinking about writing an opera based upon the poems of Francois Villon, one of his favorite medieval French troubadours but knew that he lacked the formal musical training to accomplish such a task.

In 1921, Pound attended a performance of Debussy's *Pelleas et Mellisande.* Describing the evening in a letter to Agnes Bedford, he wrote:

> Sat through *Pelleas* the other evening and am encouraged—encouraged to tear up the whole bloomin' era of harmony and do the thing if necessary on two tins and a washboard. Anything rather than that mush of hysteria ... Probably just as well I have to make this first swash without any instruments at hand. Very much encouraged by the *Pelleas,* ignorance having no further terrors, if that damn thing is the result of musical knowledge *(Collected Letters, 167).*

Apparently, his disgust with Debussy was enough to inspire Pound to try to compose the Villon opera in spite of his inexperience. Unfortunately, the "first swash without instruments" did not go very well, and Pound ended up trying to play his imagined melodies first on the piano and then on the bassoon. He became increasingly frustrated because, musically illiterate, he could not translate his ideas into notes and staves.

Meanwhile, across the Atlantic, wary of provincial American audiences, a 22 year-old George Antheil went to Europe in 1922 to launch his career as a concert pianist, a career he hoped would support his greater ambition of composing new and ultramodern music. He received money for his travels from his patron, Mary Louise Curtis Bok, a wealthy philanthropist and loyal patron of American music. Mrs. Bok, as Antheil addressed her, is best remembered for founding the Curtis Institute of Music in Philadelphia, PA. Antheil's former composition teacher, Constantin von Sternberg, had sent the young musician to her with hopes that she might support him. Thus, "[while] living the simplest possible life, he could devote himself entirely to his work without having to earn money for his bodily maintenance" (Shirley, 2). After much persuasion, Mrs. Bok reluctantly agreed to help the young musician get his start.

Antheil planned to win over the more conventional audiences of the United States by first establishing his reputation in Europe—a common ploy for American musicians at the time. Like many Americans of his day, Antheil imagined that European audiences would be much more receptive to artistic and musical innovation than their unsophisticated American counterparts. Once abroad, however, he soon learned that European audiences could also be hostile to an unestablished artist, especially a brash, young composer from the United States. Placing a loaded revolver on top of his piano before each concert, ostensibly to protect himself from abusive audiences, Antheil soon earned, or perhaps crafted, the reputation of *L'Enfant Terrible*. The gun not only, according to Eustace Mullins, served to "identify him unmistakably as an American artist, but it also served notice on the audience that he would not tolerate the riots that had characterized his public appearances before he had armed himself" (143-144).

The outrageous performances and "revolutionary" music of the self-proclaimed "Bad Boy" might have incited riots around the continent, but they also received enthusiastic reviews from critics. His successful streak seemed to continue when Antheil met his musical hero, Igor Stravinsky, in Berlin in 1922. The following year, he followed Stravinsky to Paris and moved into one of the apartments above Sylvia Beach's famed bookstore, Shakespeare and Co. Antheil, however, apparently had a falling out with Stravinsky soon after his arrival in Paris. He immediately became acquainted with several American expatriates and other members of the Parisian avant-garde but nevertheless had a difficult time breaking into Europe's artistic circles. He ultimately concluded that European audiences would accept new music only if it were written by an already well-known composer such as Stravinsky or Arnold Schoenberg.

Antheil and Pound crossed paths at an important point in both their lives. Just as Antheil was growing dissatisfied with the conservative tastes of European audiences, Pound was becoming increasingly frustrated with his own musical limitations. Antheil saw in Pound a way into the closed Parisian salons, as well as an established and respected voice to validate his "ultra-modern" music. Pound saw in Antheil an accomplished musician who echoed the Vorticist ideals in a new medium: music.[6] Soon discovering their mutual interest in music, Pound convinced Antheil t o help him notate and orchestrate the score of his opera. As they worked together on the opera, they also spent a great deal of time discussing their ideas about music and art. Antheil's musical concepts of rhythm and time-space fascinated Pound, who thought he had finally found the musical equivalent of the vorticism of Henri Gaudier-Brzeska and Wyndham Lewis. His article, "George Antheil," which appeared in a 1924 issue of *Criterion* proclaimed Antheil's work the musical counterpart to Lewis and Pablo Picasso and argued for recognition of Antheil's genius. According to Pound, Antheil, like Picasso, Lewis, and Gaudier-Brzeska, wanted to "revive and revivify the perceptions of musical form" (Schafer, 256). When contemporary composers were preoccupied with musical color, Antheil was more interested in rhythm and "time-space" in music. "Antheil," Pound proclaims, "has not only given his attention to rhythmic precision, and noted his rhythms with an exactitude, which we may call genius, but he had invented new mechanisms, mechanisms of this particular age" (259). Soon after, "George Antheil" appeared in print, Pound published a book titled *Antheil and the Treatise on Harmony*.

Despite Pound's obvious investment in *Treatise*, the book has received almost no critical attention. Most scholars simply view the work as another of Pound's propagandist efforts to boost the career of his latest protégé. Initially, one might assume that the book contains a summary of Antheil's theories of music, rhythm, and criticism, but in actuality, only the section titled "Antheil" actually deals with Antheil's ideas; the rest of the ideas in the volume belong to Pound himself.[7] The book is difficult even for musicians to understand, and some of Pound's ideas, such as absolute rhythm, are abstract and fanciful.[8] Its real importance lay in publicly identifying Antheil and Pound as collaborators working together to develop a new musical aesthetic. It also placed Antheil in the spotlight amongst the Parisian intellectuals. He became Pound's newest protégé, following in the footsteps of T. S. Eliot and James Joyce. Pound also introduced Antheil to another young American musician, violinist Olga Rudge, and commissioned him to write two violin sonatas for her. Antheil agreed. Pound's commission not only gave him additional compositional and performance opportunities, but it also suddenly provided him with access to previously closed Parisian venues such as Natalie Barney's salon and the Champs Elysses Theatre. According to *Bad Boy of Music*, Antheil played additional concerts in Paris, and he and Rudge toured Europe. "One could not announce a concert of mine between autumn 1924 and autumn 1926," he perhaps idealistically claimed, "without it being sold out far in advance' (137). In any case, the favorable reviews his concerts received from contemporary newspapers in 1925-1926 support his statement. One reviewer even described his concerts as "historical events."[9] Finally, with Pound's help, the European public began to recognize him as an important figure in the international music scene.

During the mid-twenties, Antheil focused on developing his "mechanical" aesthetic, a style that the Parisian avant-garde found interesting and attractive. Examples of this style include his "Airplane Sonata (1921)," "Sonata Sauvage," "Death of Machines," "Jazz Sonata," and "Mechanisms" (all 1923). Linda Whitesitt described his mechanical style as "constructed out of the addition and manipulation of rhythmically activated musical blocks delineated by different ostinato patterns. These musical blocks, the "time-space" components that Antheil superimposes upon his musical canvas, derive their energy from the rhythmic momentum of the repeated musical fragments" (88). Pound was even inspired to write a book about "Machine Art," which he did not complete but has been published posthumously. In a section titles, "The Acoustic of Machinery," Pound argues "One [has] to think of music as a definite entity in itself . . . a composition of sound, not merely the expression of something else."[10] He wrote that it was "not a question of taking an impression of machine noise and reproducing it in the concert hall or of making more noise, but composing, governing the noise that we've got" (76). The idea, he admitted, was inspired by Antheil's compositions.

Antheil's "mechanical" music culminated in the notorious *Ballet Mechanique*. The *Ballet* would surpass his previous "mechanical" pieces, such as the "Airplane Sonata," in both length and orchestration. First performed on multiple player pianos, its orchestration was soon expanded to include some rather unconventional "instruments." At the 1926 Paris premiere of *Ballet Mechanique,* the audience rioted under the attack of nine pianos and an odd battery of percussion that included whistles, electric bells, and a working, full-size airplane propeller. According to Noel Stock, Pound "played a heroic role in the attempt by Antheil's supporters to shout down the rioters and give the work a chance to be heard" (263). After Antheil performed *Ballet Mechanique* a second time in Paris that summer, he told Mrs. Bok that "My two concerts have established me as easily the leading young composer of Paris, now the leading music center of the world as far as new things go."[11] He may have exaggerated his success a bit for his patron, but Kay Boyle and Robert McAlmon have documented Antheil's position in the expatriate circle of the Parisian Left Bank in their memoir, *Being Geniuses Together.* McAlmon remembered "various musical affairs at which George Antheil's music was played" (219). Hosted by Natalie Barney and other prominent members of Parisian society, these events were "well attended by both French and Americans of the art and diplomatic worlds" (219). Even if Antheil had exaggerated his celebrity to Mrs. Bok, McAlmon's reports demonstrate that he was building a serious reputation for himself among the avant-garde artistic elite of Paris in 1926.

Later the same season, Pound's opera, *Le Testament de Villon,* premiered at the Salle Pleyel. Apparently, not only did Pound help Antheil break into the inner artistic circles of Paris, but Antheil returned the favor and helped Pound to secure a live performance of *Villon.* Most of Paris's "Modernist" circle turned out to hear the opera: Joyce, Hemingway, Djuna Barnes, Mina Loy, Sylvia Beach, Robert McAlmon, American composer Virgil Thomson, and even T. S. Eliot all attended the event. Although Antheil played piano in the performance and helped Pound notate and edit the piece, it is important to recognize that *Villon* was, musically speaking, very different from the mechanical pieces Antheil was composing at the time. While both composer emphasized rhythm and rhythmic innovation in their work, Pound's opera had little incidental (non-vocal) music, and what instrumental melodies there were, did little more than double the vocal music of the text. A comparison of the two styles illustrates that Pound and Antheil did not want to confine their work to a singular musical aesthetic. Instead, they hoped, each in his own way, to broaden the current conceptions of music and to challenge the notion that Americans had nothing worthwhile to contribute to the international music scene.

In 1927, Antheil decided America was ready for his music. He arranged for a performance of his famous *Ballet Mechanique* in Carnegie Hall that spring. Antheil's American concert promoter, Donald Friede, highlighted Antheil's controversial reputation in the pre-concert publicity. Apparently the promotional material and program notes exaggerated the riots at his European concerts, and such antics offended many critics and listeners before they heard a single note of Antheil's music. In addition to the sensational publicity, technical errors plagued the performance. The performers missed cues, and the airplane propeller, aimed directly at the audience (unintentionally), assaulted those unfortunate enough to be sitting in the first eleven rows. Finally, the fire siren sounded, not at the climax of the piece as it should have, but several minutes later as Antheil rose to take his bow. In other words, the concert was a complete disaster. Afterwards, reviewers lambasted the performance. The *St. Louis Dispatch* declared the piece to be a "Mountain of Noise Out of an Antheil." "Boos Greet Antheil Ballet of Machines," reported the *New York Herald Tribune*.[12] Finally, in *Bad Boy of Music,* Antheil recalled a headline he found especially offensive: "Forty million Frenchmen CAN be wrong!" (196). These reviews discounted the young composer's years of European success based on a single botched performance. Antheil returned to Europe rejected and scorned by the American audience he had long hoped to win over.

This concert shattered Antheil's reputation both in the United States and Europe, and the censure of his work wounded him deeply. Determined to become a successful composer, both financially and artistically, Antheil began to write music which sounded more conventional in an attempt to regain an audience. Like his former mentor, Igor Stravinsky, he abandoned his avant-garde ways and turned toward a more conservative, neoclassical style. According to most of the standard scholarly accounts, Pound, like the rest of the American public, turned his back on Antheil after his humiliation in New York. Pound, however, dropped Antheil not because of the disastrous performance, but because of the composer's shift in modus operandi. Like several other scholars, Linda Whitesitt concludes, "Pound, especially, could not forgive Antheil's abandonment of his earlier mechanical style" (41). As proof of her conclusion, she offers the often-invoked letter from Pound to Antheil, dated October 30, 1927:

> Dear George,
>
> I am not particularly interested in anything you have done since Ballet Mechanique. The third violin sonata an excellent piece of work, but am not sure it needed you to write it.
>
> I was not aware that I had ever had any influence on your work. I succeeded in getting or in helping to get some of it performed several years ago but do not consider that that constitutes an obligation on your part. Am not interested in la rue de l Odeon, or in neo'classics, neo-thomists, or even neo-Ulyssism.
>
> The yawps of the N.Y. press are certainly of no importance. Nothing is to be expected of that country, and least of all any sort of comprehension of anything.

> Get your stuff printed, and the three dozen people capable of understanding it will eventually discover that it exists.
>
> E. P.[13]

According to the standard accounts, while the two men met two or three more times during their lifetimes, they never worked together nor were close friends again. This letter allegedly ended both their personal and professional relationships. Pound evidently regarded Antheil's newest compositions as regressive excursions into “mere neoclassicism,” a style he deemed “the enemy” (Shirley, 13).

The Beinecke Rare Book and Manuscript Library at Yale University, however, has several lengthy letters from Antheil to Pound written after October 1927. The tone of the letters remains amicable and even intimate at times. Antheil writes of vacations to Africa and shares tales of his various antics and latest musical ideas as well as gossip about mutual acquaintances. He even invited Pound and Olga Rudge to visit him repeatedly. This archival evidence suggests that their friendship and even their working relationship surely did not end with Pound's dismissive letter, as critics have long believed. At the center of many of these affable letters are accounts of his lately vexed relationship with Mrs. Bok, his Philadelphia patron. Indeed, Antheil's relationship with Mrs. Bok was a theme central to much of Antheil and Pound's from the beginning. As a matter of fact, an examination of this archival evidence reveals the large extent to which Antheil tried (with Pound's help) to manipulate his patron and manage the public reception of his work.

From the earliest days of their acquaintance, Antheil and Pound both suffered financial difficulties. As friends, they shared the frustrations of their common commitment to art forms that the general public could not accept or appreciate. Both thought they could make more money if they conformed their work to meet the demands of popular venues, but they tried to resist the financial temptations of the mass market in order to preserve the integrity of their art. As Antheil wrote to Pound in 1925:

> If I print my translation from the German I would get more than Frank Harris for his book, while his book has all beat. I would make a fortune (printing a translation of pornography—the worst book in Vienna) on the other hand I know damned well that *you* will probably never make any more money in your lifetime upon the publication of your books than I will by the publication of my present pile of manuscripts. I'm just talking about composers and writers in general, and how the situation lays . . . You and I have been in the same financial boat for such a long while and so far you will do all the laying out . . .
>
> The reason you never saw more than 2000 bucks in your lifetime is because these animals we call people think that it ain't poetic for a poet to have enough to eat, and hate to profane the gorgeous ruin, etc.

Nuts, we are in the same boat and must work a way out.[14]

Because they were not willing to compromise their artistic standards to please the general public, neither Pound nor Antheil could count upon much steady income, at least during their lifetimes. Both yearned for the financial rewards of a mass audience but seem to have accepted the fact that such an audience would never understand their work. At the same time, neither was willing to compromise the integrity of their art to achieve financial success.

As a writer, Pound was able to support a meager existence, but Antheil, as a musician, faced a much greater financial burden. He not only had to pay for the printing, copying, and publishing costs of his work, but he also had to bear the additional financial burden of hiring musicians to perform his pieces and covering his own touring expenses. Such costs would be prohibitive to a struggling artist, for as Antheil stated in an interview with the *Paris Tribune*, "it costs several thousand dollars to give a single recital with a symphony orchestra."[15] As a result, Antheil relied heavily upon the financial support of Mrs. Bok. She not only provided him with a monthly stipend to cover his living expenses, but she also paid for the printing and publishing of many of his works, and bankrolled his travel and concert costs. It is safe to assume that without her support, Antheil would have faced severe financial hardship

In her account, Linda Whitesitt observes that Mrs. Bok had conservative musical tastes and frequently disapproved of Antheil's life and music (7). Because he was so dependent on her financial support, Antheil often felt pressure to appease her at the expense of writing music he wanted to write. As long as Antheil enjoyed some success and received favorable reviews, she did not object to his avant-garde tastes. The response to the American premiere of *Ballet Mechanique,* however, was more than she could bear. She thought the pre-concert publicity scandalous and despaired that it emphasized only the outrageous aspects of Antheil's career. Offended by such distasteful reports, she did not attend the Carnegie Hall premiere. Several of Mrs. Bok's friends and associates attended the performance in her place and conveyed their thoughts on the concert to her afterward, and she reported to Antheil "their opinion of the music offered is unanimously adverse" (Shirley, 16). As a composition, the *Ballet* was already dangerously close to offending her conservative tastes, and the negative reports and damning reviews of its performance further injured Antheil's precarious situation. Shortly after the Carnegie Hall debacle, Bok wrote to Antheil and informed him that she would give him no further funding beyond his monthly stipend. Antheil had already lost money on the Carnegie Hall concert, and the additional loss of Bok's support proved financially devastating.

In the wake of such a catastrophe, Antheil became determined to regain both Mrs. Bok's support and his former status as a prominent composer. He knew that she did not like the influence that the Parisian avant-garde had on his music, and she had a particular distaste for Pound. Earlier in his career, Antheil had sent Bok Pound's laudatory articles about his music and written to her about Pound's influence in the artistic circles of Paris. Pound even wrote to Bok himself in the early days of his acquaintance with Antheil to boast of the young composer's achievement, He stated: "It may interest you to know that George Antheil . . . scored no inconsiderable success here at the Salle du Conservatoire on Tuesday."[16] Mrs. Bok, apparently, was not impressed by these efforts, as she later informed Antheil, "I don't care for the group you quote, nor their work . . . Pound, Joyce and so forth."[17] Obviously, she altogether disapproved of Antheil's European acquaintances and must have feared their influence on the young composer.

After the Carnegie Hall fiasco, facing financial ruin, Antheil must have thought that if he could convince Mrs. Bok that Pound and the Parisian avant-garde had little influence on his work, she might change her mind and renew her financial aid. Without her subsidy, Antheil had little hope of regaining his former position as one of the leading American composers. To regain Bok's backing, he enlisted Pound's help. In mid-October 1927, Antheil wrote to Pound seeking his help in a complicated plot. Having faced financial hardships himself, Pound understood Antheil's plight and apparently agreed to help. Pound, Antheil decided, should write a letter to Mrs. Bok criticizing the musician's latest work and disavowing any friendship or artistic collaboration between himself and Antheil. The following letter to Pound, previously undiscovered, reveals Antheil's strategy:

> Here is Mrs. Bok's letter. She promises to take me up again when she is convinced that I have changed from the bad, evil Ballet Mechanique *which she has* heard.....remember that... its deadly evidence.
>
> Now I see no Goddamned use in waiting .... for I HAVE written a whole bunch of music to please her ....but she won't listen to it, she's so certain I'm especially under your influence (I've always quoted you the most, so it's you she really means in this letter).
>
> Do you see any harm in sending her some of the simplest examples of my LATE post-Mozartian music couched in simple piano keys for her oun fingers . . . together with a recent letter from you.....scolding me good and proper (don't use cuss words) for writing Mozartian music... reactionaire! Instead of the Beautiful Ballet Mechanique music. If I send this, I might immediately have a check for a great deal of money, for I know Mrs. Bok very well. You see that you, "Joyce crowd" and the Ballet Mechanique worry her.
>
> If you send this letter, send it in an envelop so I can send all.
>
> AFTER I get the money, I shall take pains, I PROMISE to have her see the right side of you, and your somewhat larger views upon music that [sic] the Ballet Mechanique, but just at present she has the argument upon her side. She doesn't understand you, that's all, and I shall take pains... the very greatest I am

> capable off [sic] that she shall... afterwards. She is a powerful ally, and we need these kind.
>
> Remember, at present, you are in a dreadful perplexity about me ... but later, after I get the money, you shall write me a letter, saying that you are convinced that the WAY I HAVE TAKEN TOWARDS my music was correct, and you are convinced. This will make her feel good and make her feel that she has done right. This does not mean that We cannot do exactly as we wish. Likewise don't worry about the Criterian [sic] article, I'm sure she's forgotten it, or has never read it .... besides you could have been thinking it over and over, and thinking more and more that this new classic music of mine is all wrong. Try to get me from wayward path if you care. But if you decline, in all cases send me your opinion of the situation. I sent her the letter you advised, and also the newspaper clipping made for her in the Herald the other morning, but no favorable answer yet.[18]

The newspaper clipping that Antheil cites in his letter ran in the Paris Edition of the *New York Herald* on October 24, 1927. Antheil mailed a clipping of the article to Mrs. Bok that same day. [19] In the article, titled "Father of Mechanical Symphonies Dislikes Being Called Jazz Artiste," Antheil claims that he is a serious composer who has "been exploited solely as a cymbal smashing exponent of mechanical Jazz." Aligning himself with the more reputable Classical tradition of symphonic music, Antheil takes pains to distance himself from jazz, a genre that would have been scorned by Mrs. Bok and her circle. He further comments on the *Ballet Mechanique* disaster stating:

> What hurt me about my experience in America was that it put me in a wholly false light in my own country. I was advertised, without my knowledge, as a circus performer, and the audience that packed Carnegie Hall was there to see a circus. They were so intent on seeing it that they didn't even hear the music. Now I suppose it will be years before I can be recognized as a serious artist in America.[20]

Depicting Antheil as a victim, the article tried to convince readers that instead of orchestrating the entire Carnegie Hall fiasco, he knew nothing about it. The article fits well with Antheil's plan to distance himself from Pound and the "bad evil Ballet Mechanique."

The new evidence offered in Antheil's letter forces us to reconsider Pound and Antheil's relationship. Both the *Herald* article and Antheil's letter to Pound predate Pound's October 1927 letter of "dismissal." Clearly, Pound had nothing to gain by helping Antheil in this situation, yet help he clearly did. Read in the context of Antheil's correspondence regarding his financial difficulties, Pound's letter and the *Herald* article seem obvious efforts to mange the public reception of his music and mislead his patron into renewing her support. These documents also help to explain the lack of quirky spellings and colorful language in Pound's October 30 letter—a signature mark of his usual correspondence. Instead, he followed Antheil's script faithfully and drafted the letter in a formal, impersonal tone because his audience was not "Jarge" or "Anthill" (nicknames which open his other letters to the young musician), but rather Mrs. Bok. Pound's letter follows Antheil's instructions almost exactly. In this fraudulent letter, Pound gives the impression that he and Antheil have not been working together since the completion of the *Ballet Mechanique* two years earlier. It suggests that the two men are not even friends, let alone collaborators (or co-conspirators).

In sum, Pound's letter was a sham. He wrote it to convince Mrs. Bok that Antheil was free from the clutches of the evil "Joyce crowd" who had "driven" him to compose the dreaded *Ballet Mechanique*. The letter along with the *Herald* article and further pleas from Antheil finally persuaded her to renew her support in the fall of 1928. Mrs. Bok, however, was not the only person taken in by Pound's letter. Both music and literary critics have accepted this constructed version of Pound's relationship with Antheil (See Goss, Shirley, and Whitesitt for examples). Antheil himself perpetuated this myth in his autobiography by minimizing their connection and distancing himself from Pound as much as possible. Nevertheless, Ezra Pound and George Antheil did not part ways in 1927 over this letter as most scholars have supposed. On the contrary, they remained friends and worked together for the next six years.

Pound and Antheil continued to try to build a space for American music in the United States and Europe even though America had rejected Antheil's music. *Ballet Mechanique's* Carnegie Hall failure persuaded Antheil to remain abroad until he was convinced that the American people were ready to recognize his talent and the merit of his music. By 1928, Antheil had not been able to redeem his fallen reputation, and he desperately wanted to prove to the world that he could still write serious music. So, in an attempt to reestablish his reputation as an avant-garde composer, he turned from instrumental music to opera, the form in which he had long ago tutored Pound. Rumor had it that the Weimar Republic had begun to invest large sums of money into the arts and that German audiences were eager for new and experimental operas. Apparently, "American" plots and jazz themes were the latest rage in Germany. Renowned European composers like Oscar Krenek and Kurt Weill had already achieved considerable success writing in this "American" medium. Hoping for similar recognition, Antheil began to work on composing a uniquely American opera infused with Jazz and popular American dance rhythms.

In the later years of their correspondence, he and Pound renewed their earlier discussion of operatic aesthetics, and almost from its inception, Antheil sought Pound's advice about his opera-in-progress, eventually titled *Transatlantic: The People's Choice*. Their discussion lasted until the premiere of the work in 1930. Some months before opening night, Antheil sent Pound a score of the opera and a copy of the libretto. Even as late as 1930, Antheil obviously still valued

Pound's artistic advice and, when the Frankfurt State Opera accepted *Transatlantic* for its 1930 season, he wrote to Pound as soon as he learned the news—even before the theater itself had made the announcement—to ask Pound to come to Frankfurt a week before *Transatlantic's* premiere and advise him on the work. Antheil's letter to Pound upon the acceptance of *Transatlantic* indicates that he still conceived of the promotion of his opera and American music generally, as a joint venture between he and Pound. In the following letter, he outlined their preliminary plan:

> I am in immediate need for the sheltered mountains, for the health necessary to strike, as I now must, for our common interests, and for my reinstatement, financially, in America.
>
> Likewise, in the meantime also think up something to tell the reporters *when they come to you.*
>
> This is positively the first time that an American Grand opera is to be given at State expense in Europe. If you say anything to the papers, it would be *well to emphasize* that ... but don't say that the opera is on a *political* subject whatever you do....
>
> *This acceptance assures me of the most prime position of importance at next seasons most important music festival.*
>
> Now sit back and figure how we can strike hard. This, of course, is visibly the greatest victory for the musical culture of the U.S.A. and everybody can't help seeing it, if at all fairly represented.
>
> Meanwhile, during these hard two years and a half—You stuck to me—and were the only one who did. Words do not suffice.[21]

Pound and Antheil had clearly remained friends and collaborators all along. Antheil's repeated use of "we" and his mention of "our common interests" indicate that Antheil saw the creation of an American grand opera as yet another of their collaborative projects. The letter also reveals a great deal about the continuing tenor of their friendship. The emotional nature of final lines lends a special poignancy to the letter—a sincerity that transcends issues of money and aesthetics. In other letters, Antheil frequently addressed Pound as his "artistic father"[22] or "the best friend I got in this world."[23] He even dedicated his second violin sonata (November 1923) to Pound with the inscription, "For E. P., best of friends" (Whitesitt, 219).[24] Such evidence contradicts all existing scholarly explanations of their friendship, including accounts by Antheil himself that all Pound wanted from their relationship was to use the composer to further his own ends. In my reading of the archival evidence, he and Pound not only maintained their professional relationship; they also remained friends.[25]

Antheil also remained indebted to Pound's counsel on the subject of public relations. He feared that the opera's reception would suffer of the premiere's location. He had heard the Frankfurt audience described as the "most notoriously cold public in Europe."[26] He asked Pound to round up a group of

Americans to come to the premiere and "clap hands" to ensure the opera's success. As he wrote to Pound, "Ezra, if I can put this over, I can do, in the future, practically any darned thing I want in the world of music. Now strikes the fatal hour."[27] Apparently, Pound again did as Antheil requested and began to ask "the Paris gang" to attend *Transatlantic's* premiere. Pound also purposefully tried to keep his association with *Transatlantic* quiet as not to alarm Mrs. Bok, but somehow word of his involvement got out. Once again, Pound was forced to disavow his efforts on Antheil's behalf. The following letter from Pound appeared in the Paris Edition of the *Chicago Tribune* on April 19, 1930:

> I think there must be some misunderstanding. So far as I know Mr. Antheil's opera is not dedicated to me. I have not seen Mr. Antheil for some time. I have never heard Mr. Antheil express the slightest intention of dedicating an opera to me.
>
> As long as the American musical world *y compris* the Metropolitan Opera House, the private Philadelphia back garden and its heavy chested musical foundations remain the pocket boroughs that they are now, I shd strongly advise Mr. Antheil or any other good composer to refrain from dedicating anything to me, or from being seen in my company. . . . (Qtd. Schafer, 319).

In the light of Pound's previous efforts save Antheil from poverty, this letter, like Pound's previous apparent dismissal, takes on a new meaning. Pound is, as Murray Schafer argues, killing a rumor that *Transatlantic* is dedicated to him, but he is not, as Schafer assumes, extinguishing this rumor because he is disgusted with Antheil's work. Instead, Pound was trying yet again to protect his friend. He knew that if Mrs. Bok suspected that he and Antheil still kept in touch, she might very well cut Antheil off again. He did not want Antheil to lose any more money.

Mrs. Bok apparently remained convinced of Antheil's loyalty because her support continued as Pound busily rounded up influential people to attend *Transatlantic's* premiere. Antheil was, in any case, pleased with Pound's efforts. In a letter to Pound, dated May 5, 1930, he wrote: "Hurray for Youse! Hurray for Youse! Nancy Cunard, Natalie Barney, Duchess de C. T. Polignacs should set them upon their heads in Frankfurt."[28] He proceeded to tell Pound of his plans should the opera succeed:

> Ezra, my solemn word has it that you are the best friend I ever did have. You and Olga watch my smoke, if I ever do break through. It won't be long, anyhow, until something or another very definite is decided. And if the ayes have it . . . the first thing that is going to happen is a tour for Olga, and a performance of "Le Testament" at Darmstadt (which is only 80 minutes from Frankfurt) next season, revision by G.A. (orchestral) and we will still live to burn the tails of some people.[29]

Confident of his upcoming success, Antheil's gratitude to his collaborator (and conspirator) is obvious in his letter. Unfortunately, after Pound had recruited a "Paris gang" of "hand clappers" for the audience, Antheil found out from his publisher, Hans Heinsheimer, that the plan might not be such a good idea after all: apparently, just weeks before, French composer Darius Milhaud had tried to guarantee himself a friendly audience in Berlin, and his plans had backfired. As Antheil explained the blunder to Pound: "Milhaud's French friends who came up from Paris got the Germans sore by applauding after the first act, and very conspicuously at that, so that the Germans all got cold, and remembered the war, and everything."[30] Panicked, Antheil wrote several frantic letters to Pound asking him to be very careful which Americans he invited to the premiere. He stated, "A few of these kind Americans, coming specially to Frankfurt could not only put this performance on the blink, but possibly put the largest possible kink in all my future career."[31]

Still feeling the sting of his Carnegie Hall debacle, Antheil remained quite defensive, almost paranoid, about *Transatlantic's* premiere. He did not want the critics to have any preconceived notions about the performance as they had had for *Ballet Mechanique*. He also feared that his fellow Americans would sabotage the opera by intentionally creating a stir in the audience thus offending the Germans. Still attempting to manage his own public reception, he sent Pound explicit instructions about the audience's behavior:

> NO AMERICAN SHOULD ATTRACT ATTENTION TO HIMSELF IN THE AUDIENCE.
>
> NO AMERICAN SHOULD BEGIN THE CLAPPING, IF ANY, BUT SHOULD TAKE THEIR CUE FROM THE GERMANS.
>
> DONT CLAP OR DEMONSTATE [sic] IN ANY WAY AFTER THE FIRST ACT.
>
> THEY SHOULDN'T SPEAK TOO MUCH DARNED ENGLISH IN THE FOYERS BETWEEN ACTS, BUT WITHDRAW TIFEMSELVES AS MUCH AS POSSIBLE UNTIL THE END. . . .
>
> Now any kind of riot means death to an operatic work, under heavy financing by the state, and it also means it will never be played again, and my contract with the U. E. imperiled....
>
> If any damned fool American takes it into his head to shout 'ata Boy, Antheil! After the first act....... you can take my future career out and shoot it for dinner tomorrow, and no fooling either.[32]

Antheil drastically wanted to regain prominence as an American composer. To Pound he admitted, "This premiere involves three years of struggle of a most desperate kind. I don't mind it being a flop on legitimate grounds, but if it is a flop just because of some wrong deadly diplomatic policy, especially involving my deadly enemies ... the Americans...... I shall be heart-broken."[33]

When it premiered, *Transatlantic* did, in fact, receive rave reviews: for example, in the *Chicago Daily News,* Irving Schwerke proclaimed: "*Transatlantic* [is] one of the most exciting spectacles on the operatic stage today."[34] Unfortunately, despite its critical success, the opera did not appear again after its initial run in Frankfurt and once again Antheil was denied financial success. Antheil's publisher attributed the work's failure to two factors: difficulty of adapting a Homeric plot into German and the loud and ostentatious manners of Antheil's friends who had traveled from Paris to see the opera. Their attitude, he believed, proved that the opera was very chic, but not serious or profound (Whitesitt, 129). A more likely reason for *Transatlantic's* demise was the opera's exorbitant production costs. Because Antheil took advantage of all the latest staging and cinematic techniques, presenting *Transatlantic* was extremely expensive, and it virtually barred the work's production in all but the most sophisticated opera houses (Cook, 507). Finally, the depiction of Americans and the United States in the opera insulted several Americans, including Mrs. Bok. She charged that it was "sordid" and "cheap ... [and] far from representative of real American life" (Qtd. in Shirley, 19, 20).

Antheil made several operatic innovations in *Transatlantic* and enjoyed a brief window of success, but ultimately he gained none of his desired recognition either in Europe or in the United States. He and Pound remained friends for another three or four years after *Transatlantic's* "failure" while he traveled between the U.S. and Europe before finally settling permanently in the United States in August 1933. The men kept in touch off and on through the 1930s, but by the mid-thirties, Antheil's days as America's "Bad Boy of Music" were over. In addition, Antheil tried to arrange an American concert tour for Olga Rudge, but nothing materialized. He also asked Pound to collaborate on another project: "if you would give me the idea for a stage work (not an opera, although there would be occasional solo) with your poetry I would set it, and produce it here in New York with the American Ballet."[35] Pound declined the offer, replying, "The honor of succeding [sic] Erskine as yr/ collaborator is NOT tempting."[36] At this point, the archival records indicate that their partnership had finally ended as Pound and Antheil parted ways. By 1934, Pound was no longer interested in developing a scene for American music abroad; instead, he and Olga Rudge had begun to revive Italian music by composers such as Antonio Vivaldi. Antheil, constantly fighting to stay financially secure, finally succumbed to the commercialism of Hollywood. He intended to compose movie music just to earn enough money to support his "serious" music, but during his first years in Hollywood, he devoted most of his time to writing film music and neglected his other compositions.

Antheil's final surrender to Hollywood in the 1930s marked the end of his relationship with Pound. This defection happened during a crucial moment in Pound's career. Since the end of the First World War, Pound had been intrigued by the ideas of Major Douglas's concept of social credit. In the early 1920s, while composing the "Malatesta Cantos," Pound developed *Bel Esprit*, a program designed to fund worthy artists. In "Credit and the Fine Arts" (1922), he stressed that his program "is NOT a charity. [It] is definitely and defiantly not a charity."[37] Pound intended for *bel esprit* to give artists enough money to live on, not live luxuriously, but enough to have the basic necessities so they could focus their time and energy on their art.

During the years of the Great Depression, Pound had become increasingly interested in economics. In 1933, he wrote *The ABC's of Economics* to define his theory of economics and Social Credit. In addition, in the early 1930s, Pound also became increasingly attracted to Fascism, an attraction that was in some ways linked to the struggles he and Antheil had faced as artists in the twenties. Throughout the 1920s, Pound witnessed artists like Antheil fail repeatedly in their quest to establish himself as an artist, not because they lacked talent or ambition, but ultimately because they lacked money. Pound had struggled himself to make ends meet for his entire life and relied often on his wife's money. Gaudier-Brzeska labored to scrounge up marble for his works. Wyndham Lewis often could not afford food and relied upon the Sitwells to provide for him. T. S. Eliot worked in a bank and was forced to moonlight as a poet, one of the causes of his nervous breakdown in the early 1920s. James Joyce could not afford to publish either *Portrait of the Artist as a Young Man* or *Ulysses,* so he too had to rely upon the money of others. Harriet Weaver funded the first novel; John Quinn and Sylvia Beach contributed to the second. Antheil, like the rest of these artists, relied upon the support of a patron, and without her money, he could not afford to be a musician. As Hugh Kenner has noted, "These are not the conditions of freedom" (303).

For Pound, Antheil's submission to Hollywood was further proof that truly gifted and original artists could not survive unless they had some sort of subsidized income. The logical answer to the plight of the artist, as he saw it, was state support. Pound felt that artists made contributions to society that were at least as valuable as the average laborer. The general public, however, could not be expected to understand, appreciate, or support real art so as a result, artists were forced beg, borrow, and prostitute themselves to patrons like Mrs. Bok in order to survive. Government subsidy might have proved to be a viable alternative, it the government could be persuaded not to interfere with artists and their work. Pound, it seems, had found such a system in Italian history with its patron states. There, at least in the idealized version Pound presents in canto VIII, artists could find support in beneficent patrons like Sigismundo Malatesta. To Pound, Malatesta would have been the perfect sponsor:

> But I want it to be quite clear, that until the chapels are ready
> I will arrange for him to paint something else
> So that both he and I shall

Get as much enjoyment as possible from it,
And in order that he may enter my service
And also because you write me that he needs cash,
I want to arrange with him to give him so much per year
And to assure him that he will get the sum agreed on.
You may say that I will deposit security
For him whenever he likes.
And let me have a clear answer,
For I mean to give him good treatment
So that he may come to live the rest
Of his life on my lands-
Unless you put him off it-
And for this I mean to make due provision,
So that he can work as he likes,
Or waste his time as he likes,
... never lacking provision. [38]

Malatesta is, as Lawrence Rainey argues, Pound's ideal patron; Pound wrote, "Ma<l>atesta got the goods. And he was enough of an artist himself to know that you can't always tell when an artist is loafing. Real work may be done on tennis court or in a trolley car, and sham work at a desk" (70). Moreover, Malatesta wanted to provide for artists and let them produce their own art. Unlike the Mrs. Boks of the artistic world, Malatesta, Pound asserts, did not attempt to pressure his painter to conform to his tastes. Instead, he wanted artists to follow their own creative visions.

Perhaps Pound equated Mussolini with Sigismundo Malatesta who took pride in his role as a patron of the arts.[39] Such an equation seems likely not only because they were both Italian, but also because, in Pound's eyes, both Malatesta and Mussolini truly understood great art and the conditions necessary for its creation. A system like Mussolini's Italy, led by a man who could realize and value the importance of fine art, might be the last chance for the true artistic genius to survive. Mussolini read Dante. Better yet, he played the violin, and he knew a great deal about music. He even invited Olga Rudge to play for him at his residence in 1933. In the end, perhaps Pound believed Mussolini would provide for the artist, unlike the governments of Britain, France, or the United States.

Ultimately, Antheil's surrender to Hollywood and commercialism reinforced Pound's belief in Mussolini and fascism. Pound could not have been immune to Antheil's constant setbacks and disappointment. When Antheil finally returned to America in the 1930s in defeat, it is likely that Pound became more determined than ever to secure some sort of economic reform that would break the cycle of the "starving artist" once and for all. Ultimately, however, his turn toward Fascism would have serious and tragic consequences. While most critics condemn Antheil for compromising his artistic standards in Hollywood, he did not forfeit serious music entirely. He composed several more "artistic" works and was able to achieve at least some degree of personal fulfillment. Unlike Pound, determined to fix all of the world's evils, Antheil was able to live the rest of his life with some degree of financial independence and security.

Acknowledgements

I am grateful to the following people: the estate of George Antheil and its executor Charles Amirkhanian for permission to include previously unpublished correspondence between Antheil and Ezra Pound; the librarians and staff at the Beinecke Rare Book and Manuscript Library for their assistance; Steve Nelson for his tireless work as research assistant; and Professor Robin Schulze of Pennsylvania State University for her guidance in this project and so much more.

Works Cited

Antheil, George. *Bad Boy of Music.* Garden City, N.Y.: Doubleday, Doran and Company, Inc., 1945.

—. Letters to Ezra Pound. 1925-1933. Ezra Pound Collection: Yale Collection of American Literature 43, Box 2, Folders 69-74. Beinecke Rare Book and Manuscript Library, Yale University.

Chotzinoff, Samuel. "Mountain of Noise Out of an Antheil." *St. Louis Dispatch*, April 11, 1927;

Cook, Susan C. "George Antheil's *Transatlantic*: An American in the Weimar Republic." *Journal of Musicology* 9.4 (Fall 1991): 498-520.

"Father of Mechanical Symphonies Dislikes Being Called Jazz Artiste." *New York Herald.* Oct. 24, 1927. Paris Edition.

Ford, Hugh, ed. *The Left Bank Revisited: Selections from the Paris Tribune 1917-1934.* University Park, PA: Pennsylvania State University Press, 1972.

Goss, Glenda Dawn. "George Antheil, Carol Robinson and the Moderns." *American Music* 10.4 (Winter 1992): 468-485.

Hoffa, William Walter. "Ezra Pound and George Antheil: Vorticist Music and the *Cantos*." *American Literature* 44 (March 1972): 52-73.

Kenner, Hugh. *The Pound Era.* Los Angeles: University of California Press, 1971.

"Paris to Hear Percussive Music Again, Pound and Antheil to unleash their 'Horizontal Minstrelsy' at Salle Pleyel," *Paris Times* June 29, 1924.

Pound, Ezra. *Antheil and the Treatise on Harmony,* 1924. New York: Da Capo Press, 1968.

—. *The Letters of Ezra Pound: 1907-1941*. Ed. D. D. Paige. New York: Harcourt, Brace, and World Inc., 1950.

—. *Ezra Pound's Poetry and Prose: Contributions to Periodicals.* Lea Baechler, A. Walton Litz, and James Longenbach, eds. 10 vols. New York: Garland Publishing Inc., 1991.

—. *Machine Art and Other Writings: The Lost Thought of the Italian Years.* Ed. Maria Luisa Ardizzone. Durham, NC: Duke University Press, 1996.

Rainey, Lawrence S. *Ezra Pound and the Monument of Culture: Text, History, and the Malatesta Cantos*. Chicago: University of Chicago Press, 1991.

Schafer, R. Murray, "The Developing Theories of Absolute Rhythm and Great Bass." *Paideuma* 2 (Spring 1975) 23-35.

—. ed. *Ezra Pound and Music: The Complete Criticism.* New York: New Directions, 1977.

Schwerke, Irving. "Antheil Given Ovation after Premiere of Opera *Transatlantic* in Frankfurt" *Chicago Tribune*, Paris Edition, May 26, 1930.

Shirley, Wayne D. "Another American in Paris: George Antheil's Correspondence with Mary Curtis Bok." *The Quarterly Journal of the Library of Congress* January 1977: 2-22.

Whitesitt, Linda. *The Life and Music of George Antheil: 1900-1959.* Ed George Buelow. Ann Arbor, Michigan: UMI Research Press, 1983.

"NOT JUST TANGLE AND DRIFT": MUSIC AS METAPHOR IN THE POETRY OF W.B. YEATS

JULI WHITE

> One thing [Stobrod] discovered with a great deal of astonishment was that music held more for him than just pleasure. There was meat to it. The groupings of sounds, their forms in the air as they rang out and faded, said something comforting to him about the rule of creation. What the music said was that there is a right way for things to be ordered so that life might not always be just tangle and drift but have a shape, an aim. It was a powerful argument against the notion that things just happen.
>
> Charles Frazier
> *Cold Mountain*

I. Introduction

The Yeats family were interested in the visual arts, not music. John Butler Yeats was a portrait painter, and the poet's brother Jack was an artist, too. His sisters Lily and Lolly were embroiderers and book publishers/printers. Music must have seemed foreign to Yeats; it was not the family business. He did not receive either informal or formal education or in music. Neither Ellmann, Brown, nor Foster mention Yeats's receiving any kind of musical training. Only Terence Brown mentions anything having to do with music when he claims that Yeats probably had "a tone-deaf ear" (26). The standard interpretation of Yeats's comments about music is that he completely disliked music. In a letter to a London newspaper in 1902, Yeats confessed "that he knew nothing of music, could not tell one note from another and even disliked music" (Brown 131). Victor Clinton-Baddeley, in 1941's *Words for Music*, claims that music for Yeats "was an aid to the performance of poetry and nothing more" (151), and that he "was not so much interested in the art of song as in the art of the public presentation of poetry" (155). However, I believe that this conclusion oversimplifies a complex issue.

First of all, Yeats deliberately set out to overcome this deficiency in his education, which would suggest not that he rejected music altogether, but that he had very strong ideas about its proper uses and its role in the total integration of the arts. Secondly, taking into consideration all of his comments about the nature and function of rhythm, about how music should accompany his poems, as well as all of his efforts to combine music and poetic recitation to invent a new art form, scholars should instead see the efforts of someone who may not have been naturally gifted in music, but who understood its potential and sought to incorporate it into poetic practice. In "The Symbolism of Poetry," Yeats says that the purpose of rhythm "is to prolong the moment of contemplation, which is the one moment of creation, by hushing us with an alluring monotony, while it holds us awake by variety, to keep us in the state of perhaps real trance, in which the mind is liberated from the pressure of the will, is unfolded in symbols" (*E & I* 159). These comments suggest that Yeats understood the impact of rhythm on the human body and soul; rhythm is one of the major points at which music and poetry intersect. These biographical details suggest that in spite of his lack of formal music training, Yeats instinctively knew and understood how music elevates mere speech or words and makes them more elegant and communicative.

Furthermore, his knowledge of folk songs came from a concerted, independent effort during his early adulthood. In an article in the June 1966 issue of the *Southern Folklore Quarterly*, Yeats's son Michael explains that "As a young man, [the poet] collected tales and folklore from the country people around Sligo who, though by now almost entirely English speaking, had not yet quite forgotten the Gaelic tradition which had been handed on to them" (155). In fact, Michael Yeats asserts that his father "was exaggerating when he claimed—as he did so often—that he was unable to distinguish between one tune and another" (163). However, in the same article, Michael acknowledges that "where the tunes [of folk songs] were concerned, he appears to have realised and accepted his ignorance of music" (165), and that his father's "attitude towards music seemed in many ways extremely inconsistent" (169). Because the poet's opinion was that music should accompany poetry and not the other way around, but also because of the reality that "he knew no music, and, indeed, was tone-deaf and incapable of of recognising a simple tune" (169), the reader can see that inconsistency quite clearly. The source of this ambivalence lies in Yeats's recognition that poetry set to music enhances the experience of poetry immeasureably. Michael Yeats explains that

> no man can ever have spoken so ill of the professional musician, yet have been so willing to give him advice. This seeming inconsistency, though, reflected not so much a real dislike of music as it did a firmly held belief in the separate, indeed opposite needs of words and music. Music as such he did not dislike, though he often chose to pretend that he did. (169)

Yeats objects to music because of his "constant fear that the meaning or the rhythm of the words would be lost, once set to music" (169). Fearing the loss of the meaning of his poetry is not the same thing as disliking music as a whole. The 1922, 1924, 1926, 1928, and 1931 editions of *Later Poems* all had this note as part of their prefaces: "A musician who would give me pleasure should not repeat a line, or put more than one note to one syllable. I am a poet not a musician, and dislike to have my words distorted or their animation destroyed, even though the musician claims to have expressed their meaning in a different medium" (*Variorum* 844). In other words, he was opposed to music's being given preference over poetry, not to music itself. This desire for capitalizing on music's potential for poetic performance would lead him to an abiding friendship with Florence Farr, his partner in his efforts to create a unique performance art. Yeats was quite taken with Farr's beauty and her melodious voice; additionally, he claimed that she had "an incomparable sense of rhythm, the seeming natural expression of the image" (*Autobiographies* 121). He began his experiments with the vocal performance of poetry set to the music of the "psaltery" (a stringed instrument somewhat like a lyre he and Farr used for their performances), relying on Farr's enthusiastic cooperation, in 1902.

Furthermore, Yeats recruited the help of musician Arnold Dolmetsch, who not only taught Yeats about music's forms and structures but also designed and created the psaltery. In doing so, he went out of his way to learn about music, to try to understand it. This was a period in his life when he was inspired by the "theatrical possibilities" (Brown 131) that music offered to poetry and drama. In addition, he was also excited by an opera performance he attended in March 1901; this opera performance was designed by Gordon Craig, whose philosophy of "total theatre," in which scenery, music, action and words all operate cohesively, strongly appealed to Yeats and his ambitions for his own theatrical enterprise. As Roy Foster observes in *The Apprentice Mage*, Yeats's dream of an Ireland unified by an integrated culture "led, unsurprisingly, to the illustration of music and poetry combined in his and Farr's performances with the psaltery" (308). So even though he may have professed (or affected) a dislike of music, a tin ear, and musical ignorance, he worked very hard to integrate music with poetry, especially in the poems themselves, which is actually a manifestation of his grand ambition of a culture whose elements had been completed integrated.

The traditions about music passed down from the ancient Greeks and Pater's widely read philosophy form the basis of the thinking about music that Yeats inherited from the Western canon and culture which permeates his attitude about music's role in human life and its power to both reflect and influence human emotions, character, and spiritual and intellectual life. Rather than a complete rejection of an entire art form, I believe that Yeats used music as a huge conceptual metaphor for speech and language, an elevated way of conceiving language, and an improvement on mere communication and expression. In looking closely at all of the lyric poems, I could see that there were many in which music was used for a specific purpose or in a specific way by Yeats. These fall into naturally-occurring groups of poetic references, revealing emergent themes. Ten different thematically-oriented groups naturally appeared, each containing more than one poem containing a reference to music, even though many poems only had one musical reference in it. My rationale for the forming of groups was based on the following: first, what the poem is *about*; second, how music is used in the poem, or how music is manifested in the poem; and finally, how music influences the interpretation of the poem's meaning. Above all, I wished to group the poems based on naturally-occurring texts and sub-texts; I tried to resist the urge to force poems together, so that the resulting groups would not be contrived, but "organic." These are the ten categories of poems that naturally occurred: 1) youth, vitality, sex and seduction; 2) magic and mystery; 3) verbal expression and communication; 4) war/call to arms/politics/ political causes; 5) responsibilities, cares and worries; 6) identity and identifying characteristics; 7) praise and worship; 8) life experience, wisdom, and learning; 9) lament and regret; then healing and comfort; and 10) peace and contentment. In the interest of brevity, I will discuss only one representative poem from each group in this paper.

The pattern formed by the groupings suggests the chronology of a human life, as well as the progression of chords in music. The standard musical figure in Western music begins with a chord (two or more notes played simultaneously) made up of notes in harmony at the quiet dynamic level, called *piano*. Discord is then introduced into the chord, usually by introducing notes that clash with the established notes of the chord; this discord then propels the movement of the line forward and upward on the scale, also increasing in dynamics, until the line climaxes at the top of the phrase, usually at the *forte* level of loudness. The line then begins to descend the scale, returning to the *piano* dynamic as the chords return to harmony and end finally in a satisfying resolution. I will show at the end of this chapter how this traditional pattern is a metaphor for the pattern of a human life: innocence and childhood give way to discord and disharmony, rising to a crescendo at mid-life, which then begins to decline into resolution and peace at the end of life. It is this progression which forms the basis of the pattern I found in the poems. I will follow the contour of this line in organizing my discussion of the poems themselves, followed by a more detailed explanation of the metaphor of music as I see it at the end of this chapter.

II. The "Music Poems"

Group One: Music's Role in Youth, Beauty, Infatuation, Vitality, and Energy

Appearing in *The Winding Stair and Other Poems* in 1933, "Lullaby" subverts the reader's expectation of a sweet, soothing song intended to lull a child to sleep. While this poem contains elements of soothing someone to sleep and watchful protection, the love here is not between a parent and a child, but between the Lover and his Beloved. The peace that the poem's persona wishes for his Beloved is the same peace a child would receive from feeding at his mother's breast, indeed the same peace she herself found at her own mother's breast: "Beloved, may your sleep be sound / That have found it where you fed" (ll. 1-2). The poem then takes a decidedly adult turn and makes a graphic reference to the peace found by lovers after enjoying each other's bodies. Yeats then invokes famous lovers (and familiar figures in Yeats's poetry) Helen and Paris, Tristram and Isolde, and Leda and the swan (Zeus), here the "holy bird" (ll. 15). Paris "found / Sleep upon a golden bed / That first dawn in Helen's arms" (ll. 4-6). Tristram slept "such a sleep" when the "potion's work" is "done" (ll. 7, 9). Even Zeus, after he raped Leda (in the form of a swan, a subject Yeats had already given his full poetic attention to in "Leda and the Swan," published in 1928's *The Tower*), sleeps the sleep of a satisfied lover. Yeats includes also the implication of loving protection for Zeus from his victim, Leda, since as he drifted off to sleep he may have "from the limbs of Leda sank / But not from her protecting care" (ll. 17-18). In this poem, Yeats significantly problematizes the concept of the lullaby. First of all, the poem itself is a lullaby for one adult to his lover, presumably after a night of physical passion, not from a parent to an innocent child. Elizabeth Cullingford, in her book *Gender and History in Yeats's Love Poetry*, also acknowedges these questionable aspects of this poem. She suggests that in this poem, Yeats "conflat[es] desire and hunger," a conflation which "eroticizes the lullaby" (218). Furthermore, Yeats's examples of peaceful sleep are troubling. Paris and Helen fled together, betraying Helen's husband, thus instigating a war that would eventually culminate in the downfall of one of the greatest civilizations the Western world has ever known. Tristram was supposed to have been delivering Isolde to his king, to be the king's bride; when he and Isolde drank the love potion, they betrayed their king and betrothed. Leda was the victim of a brutal rape, a rape which eventually results in the birth of the ill-fated Helen. While this poem is given the title "Lullaby," both the examples of "peaceful" sleep given by the Lover and the use of this music to soothe his Beloved to sleep (rather than an infant) are clearly intended for the complex adult relationship shared between the Lover and his Beloved. The sleep may be peaceful, but it has a disturbing and complicated undertone. Music is thereby made significantly more complex as a result, used here in such an unexpected context. This poem stands in stark contrast to the sweet, simple lullaby offered in a much earlier Yeats poem, "A Cradle Song." The difference between the younger Yeats and the older, perhaps more bitter Yeats is here made clear, and music, particularly the music of a lullaby, plays a very large role in the reader's understanding of this development.

The music in this poem reminds the reader that complicated relationships do, in fact, exist; not all lullabies are as pure and as untainted as those sung by mothers to their babies. While the musical references in this poem centers around the confusions, misdirections, and consequences of strong, sometimes irrational passions often associated with youthful emotions, Yeats also suggests that to live life without the intensity of these passions is to live a life only halfway. Passions give life sometimes hellish ups and downs, but, as is suggested here, life lived without such eruptive forces is not worth living.

Group Two: Music as a Signifier of Magic and Mystery

The next poem shows that in Yeats's early career, the magic of the faeries and the role of mystery often appear in the poems in the form of music. In this poem, "Cuchulain's Fight with the Sea," and others like it, music metaphorically represents those things which, literally, mystify people in their youth, but seem not so mysterious in later years. Music has long been associated with magic and ritual (Grout 3). Yeats, steeped in ancient Irish legends of his upbringing, often drew upon these legends for his inspiration and his subject matter in his early work, since he was determined to further the Irish Rennaisance as much as he could. Furthermore, Yeats, more than any other modern poet, believed passionately in the ritualistic aspect of life: that human life is often marked by cyclic rituals, such as those celebrating births, graduations or rites of passage, weddings, worship, and even death. Yeats's intense interest in the occult is also strongly tied to magic, ritual, and mystery. This interest in ritual and magic and the role of music in that ritual can easily be seen in "Cuchulain's Fight with the Sea," in 1893's *The Rose*. In this poem, the Druids "chaunt" "delusions magical" in Cuchulain's ear for three days, and in so doing, they "took [Cuchulain] to their mystery" (ll. 80-83). Yeats deliberately uses the older spelling of the word "chant," *chaunt* (which has evolved without the "u" in modern spellings), in order to emphasize the ancient, mysterious aspect of the Druids' magic. This word has significant connotations, associated strongly with the Gregorian chants of priests, monks (and others whose lives are devoted to worship, praise, service, and self-denial) and mystics of all kinds.

"Chaunting" is singing, usually on a single, repeated note, usually used for the purpose of focusing concentration, sending the singers into a trance-like state. It is intended to invoke the presence of other-worldly spirits or beings, either because the worshippers need protection, or because their presence is requested by the worshippers so that they may be given homage. In this poem, music is the delivery system by which Cuchulain is exposed to the mystery and magic of the Druids, the ancient prophets and holy men of Ireland's mythological past. The story of this poem would become the subject of one of Yeats's plays, *On Baile's Strand*, and the archetypal father-son conflict drives Cuchulain into madness and a futile fight with the sea and his own death. It is a story that is rife with symbolic and metaphorical importance to both the Irish Rennaisance and Western culture. Insanity also has a certain amount of mystery associated with it in Western culture, simply because by definition, it represents the unexplainable, especially unexplainable human behavior. In this poem, the Druids' "chaunting" of "delusions magical" into Cuchulain's ear, mesmerizes and hypnotizes him. This chaunting is the direct cause of his madness. Ordinarily, the role of holy men is not to instill insanity in people, but rather to guide them down the righteous paths of life, in accordance with the wishes of the gods they serve. In this poem, however, music plays the role not of soothing a man who is tortured by his own action—the killing of his son in a one-on-one battle—but of infecting him with the madness that would end his own life, in retribution for the murder he committed. Ritualized music, in the form of the "chaunting" by the Druid priests, has the awesome potential, as is suggested by this poem, to lead Cuchulain into madness, self-destruction, and seemingly self-imposed judgement.

Sometimes people do not even realize their own feelings for another until the other person is no longer in their lives. Sometimes the connections between people are more spiritual than physical, more suggested and misunderstood than acted upon. Magic, instigated by music, seems the only way to express these inexpressible and often dimly understood relationships, relationships that sometimes mark individual lives with tragedy and poignance. Music is only the harbinger of magic and mystery here, carrying with it no judgment or value. It is merely the vehicle which brings magic to experience. At this early point in Yeats's career, he seems satisfied with the acknowledgement that there are some things that mortals are not meant to understand, and very often, the movement of mysterious forces in human life is signaled by the presence of music.

Group Three: Music as Verbal Expression/Communication

Even poets have moments when words fail them; at such times, music has the extraordinary ability to step in and fulfill needs unmet by verbal expression. Yeats habitually invokes music when words fall short. His use of music in such circumstances seems more deliberate than incidental, which indicates another aspect of music: It is always available for use as a means of expression, even when words *are* available; and sometimes, music is just a better way to communicate than words, no matter how good the words are. For example, in "The Two Trees" (*The Rose* [1893]), he says, "The shaking of its leafy head / Has given the waves their melody, / And made my lips and music wed, / Murmuring a wizard song for thee" (ll. 9-12). The trees have power here to bestow the act of expression, "wedded" with music, upon the persona, giving his words and music the magic and power of wizardry (yet another example of music carrying magical properties to its hearers). The trees even have the power to endow the waves with music. Tree imagery has important significance for Yeats. He saw in it: Druidic/paganistic nature-oriented philosophy; allusions to Blakean and Coleridgian Romanticism; cabalistic and Christian theology; and the potential for a unifying pattern that could reconcile oppositions into synthesis. Blake used trees to symbolize the overall balance of life: trees absorb the carbon dioxide exhaled through human respiration; they "exhale" the oxygen that human beings need to breathe. The inherent balance of this system offers a model of harmony and order that intensely appealed to Yeats; additionally, in Blake's "antinomial, dialectic vision of reality" (Brown 151)—that without contraries there is no progression—Yeats found one of the principles that seem to underlie all organic life. Additionally, according to Frank Kermode, in the Blakean terms that Yeats incorporated into his aesthetic, art is the Tree of Life and science is the Tree of Death; the "first symbolized the creative and redemptive imagination and the second all barrenly discursive and prudential knowledge" (*Romantic Image* 97). The Tree of Life is "the good tree [that] is divine energy, [the Tree of Death is] the bad [that] is morality and nature, the fallen world, selfhood and abstraction" (97). Although Kermode points out that Yeats may not have "had the historical background of the tree image in mind when he used it" (96), it is clear that his work editing Blake's poetry made "a very large contribution to Yeats's aesthetic" (96).

Furthermore, the movement of the wind through the trees alludes to Coleridge's "Eolian Harp," an instrument from ancient Greece that is named for Aeolus, the god of the winds. This harp has strings stretched over a rectangular box; when placed in an open window, the strings respond to the altering winds by sounding sequences of musical chords. This instrument was said to be "the voice [of] nature's own music" (Abrams 287), and is therefore a popular image for the Romantic poets who celebrated All Things Natural. In Yeats's version of this image, the breeze through the trees' branches gives the gift of music to both the waves and the poem's persona. Trees therefore are naturally-occuring aeolian harps. Furthermore, the Cabala, a body of mystical teachings said to be of rabbinical origin based on an interpretation of obscure Hebrew scripture, had been introduced to Yeats through his friendship with MacGregor Mathers, the translator of *The Kabbala Unveiled* (Foster 103-104). In this esoteric philosophy, as well as in the Christian Bible, trees are symbolic of life's progressions, light, knowledge of both good and evil, and unity of structure. Blake's "profound consciousness of warring forces invigoratingly at work in the world and in his human nature" (Brown 151), Coleridge's use of an image for the intellectual mind "trembling into consciousness" (Abrams 287) by the touch of inspiration or perception, and the cabalistic and Biblical traditions of trees encompassing the whole of human experience are all brought together in this poem by Yeats into the coherent picture of the balance, synthesis, harmony and order for which he continually sought.

Finally, "murmuring" is also a word that has special significance to Yeats. He uses it often to signify a special language used by lovers, one that is not quite singing, not quite speaking, and not quite sighing. This method of communicating resides somewhere in the grey areas between those things. The "words" expressed this way are sometimes not at all articulate words, but are "words" that are comprehensible by a lover's heart, words that are understood on some deep, profound level that goes beyond words articulated by the mouth and tongue. This kind of communcation is intuitive and sub-literal. Music is sometimes the only way to articulate such feelings, and sometimes, music is the *best* way to do so.

Communication on this level is not always successful, and sometimes, the failure to communicate points out some shortcoming on the part of the one who fails to *hear* the music of the heart. This poem seems to suggest that a life without being open to hearing what is communicated through music is one that is ultimately cold and comfortless. A life without hearing music—and therefore without the possibility of growth toward understanding and peace—is dreary and sad. Music is the means by which people communicate most effectively, especially when what is being communicated is held so close to the heart. Both music-makers and listeners must participate in the activity in order for the communication to be considered "successful." But even when the attempts at communication fail, music remains the best possible means of making the attempt, especially since it is inherently more elegant and more memorable than ordinary speech, just like poetry, which Yeats would probably argue is no coincidence.

Group Four: Music that Calls to Arms/War/Revolution and Political Causes

Music is commonly used as a battle cry, to summon men to war, to call them to arms. Although he never served in the military or fought in a war, Yeats makes use of this common understanding of a certain kind of music in "To Some I have Talked with by the Fire," in *The Rose* (1893). He makes a direct association between music and the sounds of battle when he envisions "the embattled flaming multitude / Who rise, wing above wing, flame above flame, / And, like a storm, cry the Ineffable Name, / And with the clashing of the sword-blades make / A rapturous music, till the morning break" (ll. 10-14). The sounds made by the clashing of swords in battle is music, and not just any kind of music, either; it is *rapturous* music. Rapture is not a concept traditionally associated with the horrors of war; rather, rapture is defined as a state of ecstasy, supreme happiness and bliss. Yeats's diction here is indicative of the delayed gratification of an abstract, distilled victory, an internalized victory which is assumed by those who take up arms against their foes. The music implied is the music of revolution, rebellion, and freedom through sacrifice. According to the *Variorium* edition of the poems, an earlier version of this poem used the adjective "continual" to describe this music, which would connote a sense of urgency and insistence (137); Yeats changed it later to "rapturous," intimating that the music made by this sacrifice is one that leads to joy, freedom, and happiness for war's beneficiaries, its victors. This also alludes to the idea that the ultimate reward of that victory—freedom—will be just recompense for those who lost loved ones or who were injured or maimed in the war.

As in so many of Yeats's poems, however, there is more to this music of revolution than the relatively small efforts of one group to overthrow another. The revolution that Yeats has in mind in this poem is not just another war between embattled groups of human beings. This revolution is much larger and far more significant to the evolution of humankind than one more human war could accomplish. Rather than a revolution that would overthrow one powerful group of people and replace them with another powerful group of people, Yeats is looking more for a revolution that would return the old gods of ancient times to their seat of power, gods who could do a better job of leading human beings toward positive growth. In this poem, Yeats combines Irish folklore ("the wayward twilight companies" [ll. 6]), the cabalistic and biblical doctrine of God's "Ineffable Name" (ll. 12), and prophecy of both the political revolution discussed above *and* the larger spiritual and religious revolution that could potentially return the old gods to power and begin a new cycle, a new turn of the gyre of time: "And the white hush end all but the loud beat / Of their long wings, the flash of their white feet" (ll. 15-16). This implies that the ultimate reward is not just political victory, but spiritual and religious freedom that will allow, encourage and even induce the beginning of that new cycle that Yeats could envision and for which he longed. Music is an integral part of that evolutionary progression.

Group Five: Music That Provides Identity/Identifying Characteristics

Questions of identity are intricately bound up in questions of political loyaties and are therefore crucial for every Irishman, since the Irish identity has been seriously challenged by hundreds of years of English occupation. These poems celebrate and clearly define a national identity; furthermore, these poems are closely related to those in which music plays an integral role in the articulation of Ireland's political cause. In the following poem, music plays a critical role in establishing a uniquely Irish identity.

"To Ireland in the Coming Times," appearing in *The Rose* (1893), is one of Yeats's most famous poems. In this poem, he uses music as a means of defining himself as Irish: "Know, that I would accounted be / True brother of a company / That sang, to sweeten Ireland's wrong, / Ballad and story, rann, and song" (ll. 1-4). Those forms of storytelling, ballad and story, are mentioned in the same breath as poetry and music, conflating singing and storytelling, both activities strongly associated with Irishness. Yeats's parallel structure, since a ballad is merely a story that is sung, and a "rann" is a portion of a poem (i.e., stanza or refrain) or song, emphasizes this equation of poetry, music, and narrative. These songs are important, for they not only articulate Irishness in terms of its landscape and scenery, but also in terms of the eternal truths and timeless, mystical beauty associated with that landscape. In this way, Yeats is very consciously identifying his poetry as significantly different from the supposedly "more patriotic" poetry of the popular Irish poets "Davis, Mangan, and Ferguson" (ll. 18) (Ellmann 118-123). This poem is significantly more complex—but also more "Irish," perhaps—than traditional patriotic poetry or even patriotic songs, such as "The Little Black Rose" (which Michael Yeats identifies as "the most celebrated of all the Gaelic patriotic songs" [157]), or "Remember the Glories of Brien the Brave" (attributed to Thomas Moore by N. Clifford Page in his *Irish Songs: A Collection of Airs Old and New* (1907) [98]).

The "patriotism" in this poem stems not from a vaguely revolutionary rhetoric, but rather from the eternal truth, timeless beauty and ancient mysticism of Ireland, symbolized by the Rose—Yeats's symbol of perfect unity of form—which is what "made Ireland's heart begin to beat" (ll. 12). The rose appears in this poem as the "red-rose-bordered hem" (ll. 6, 30, and 48) of the garment Ireland metaphorically wears that signifies her cultural and national identity, since embodied in that embroidery is the whole Celtic tradition of ancient Ireland. The other identifying characteristic of Irishness, directly associated with singing, is love: these two things are what make them who they are: "And we, our singing and our love, / What measurer Time has lit above, / And all benighted things that go / About my table to and fro, / Are passing on to where may be, / In truth's consuming ecstasy, / No place for love and dream at all" (ll.

37-43). The hope is that someday, there will be no need to spell out an identity, since once everyone lives in the place of truth, national divisions will be irrelevant. Until that time, however, Yeats "cast[s his] heart into [his] rhymes," so that those who come after him will know who they are; and in so identifying what it means to be Irish for future generations, Yeats found himself as well, and one of his primary missions as a poet, the poet that is "of Ireland."

Group Six: Music of Responsibilities/Cares/Worries

Music is flexible enough in its forms to serve many purposes. In the following poem, Yeats moves from "singing" (writing poetry) about the overpowering sense of patriotic responsibility (and its possible failure) to the responsibilities one feels toward oneself and one's higher calling, since at least these responsibilities are within one's own purview. Yeats takes advantage of the idea that music can sometimes be a seduction away from responsibilities and obligations, which is a concept that has a long history, from Homer's Sirens in *The Odyssey* to Tennyson's "Lotus Eaters." "The Spirit Medium" (in *New Poems* [1938]) could be about Yeats's wife George, since she acted as the "medium" through which spirits communicated via the automatic writing she practiced during her marriage to Yeats. This poem acknowledges poetry and music as the two pursuits she—the "spirit medium" of the title, whose work it is to conduct seánces and contact the spirits of the dead—has loved the most, but they are also the two things that distract the medium from her work. She therefore "banishes" both poetry and music, so that she may carry on the business of being available to host the spirits of those "begotten or unbegotten" (ll. 1, 5) who need her as a vehicle for communication. Furthermore, the activity substituted for music and poetry is "bending" her body "to the spade" (ll. 7), which suggests digging. While the digging she is doing could be gardening, providing food for herself, it more likely is gravedigging, an enterprise of far more significance given her occupation of talking to the spirits of the dead. But why would she be digging graves, which are designed to hold the used-up shell of a person, but not his spirit? Moreover, gravedigging is traditionally work assigned to men, not women, for it demands much physical strength. However, there is no indication of gender in the poem; there is only an "I" speaking. For whatever reason, which Yeats is especially vague in offering his readers in this poem, the medium is compelled to the graves of the "new dead," those who are desperate to "escape / confusion of the bed" of death, and those who are "perning in a band" (ll. 3-4, 6), or suffering terribly. The needs of those in the graves where she digs are far more pressing and consuming of her attention, even though it is suggested in this poem that her work as a medium gives her no pleasure. She would much rather give her time and attention to music and poetry. The "stupidity / Of root, shoot, blossom or clay / Makes no demand" (ll. 20-22) on her; in other words, the natural things that grow in the ground are not the ones who make demands of her. Only those who at one time were alive, dead *people*, have sentience, even in the afterlife, and they make great demands on her, indeed. Poetry and music are not just equated here syntactically; they are also equal in their power to distract her from her work, and they are equal sacrifices made for the sake of one's calling, one's higher responsibilities.

Group Seven: Music of Praise and Worship

It would be difficult to envision any kind of worship service that did not include music at its core, especially for people so steeped in the ancient Western traditions that provide music its meaning and significance; however, Yeats subverts those expectations. He secularizes these forms by focusing worship on a mortal, flawed human being rather than a god or goddess. As in so many other poems by Yeats, music and poetry are nearly indistinguishable here; both are used for the explicit purpose of creating a portrait—both a musical portrait and one created through word-imagery—of the kind of human beings worthy of worship. He focuses that creative attentiveness on, of course, Maud Gonne. In this way, she becomes an apotheosized, larger-than-life example of great human potential. In this regard, she ceases to be the actual, flesh-and-blood Maud Gonne and becomes rather the poetic realization of the kind of woman who would have been written about by Homer, like Helen of Troy, who often represents Yeats's poetic ideal. Helen in her time and Maud Gonne in Yeats's are women of heroic proportions, women who can influence an entire culture for centuries beyond the scope of a single lifetime, Helen through her role in the Fall of Troy, and Gonne by virtue of her heroic efforts to affect Irish political independence.

All of these assumptions underlie "A Woman Homer Sung," one of a series of seven poems, all appearing in *The Green Helmet and Other Poems* (1910), that expand on Yeats's integration of poetry and music in worship. This poem is written from the point of view of a once-white-hot flame of passion that has cooled; the poem's persona is both remembering how he once felt and commenting on how his feelings have changed. He remembers that at one time, if any other man even "drew near" (ll. 1) to his Beloved, he viewed that man as a rival for her affections, "And shook with hate and fear" (ll. 4). However, it was "bitter wrong" (ll. 5), for any other man to have "pass[ed] her by / With an indifferent eye" (ll. 6-7) as well. His worship of his Beloved is so complete that he could not have tolerated either others' attention or others' indifference to the woman he deems worthy of such worship. Time has worked its magic and now, "being grey" (ll. 9), he can see the extremes of his own feelings. While a reader might expect the persona to realize his own foolishness, Yeats again turns that expectation around. Given the gift of objectivity by time, he can now see that the female object of his obsession "had fiery blood / When I was young" (ll. 15-16) and that she "trod so sweetly proud" (ll. 17). "Proud" is usually a perjorative term in the Yeatsian aesthetic when applied to women, but that pride is qualified with "sweetness," a far more traditionally feminine adjective. However, his more realistic appraisal of her passion and her pride has not diminished her worthiness. Rather, her worthiness seems to have increased, because at this point in the poem, he claims that she is the kind of woman that great, epic poems—those that define an age—are written about by poets who have been given the awesome task of recording such moments for posterity. She is, even now, "A woman Homer sung" (ll. 19). Singing here is equated with poetry of the highest order, and this poetry/music is that which carries with it profound implications for centuries of cultural influence. In this context, poetry that sings this woman's praises is more like the Psalms of the Old Testament: It is music intended to be sung in praise of the most holy and most cherished of all human beliefs.

Group Eight: Music of Intellect/Learning/Education/Life Experience/Wisdom

The second largest group of like-minded poems focuses on learning, wisdom, and the nature of human intelligence. This goes far beyond the old argument about the difference between youthful ignorance and mature wisdom, or the difference between formal and informal education. Even in some of Yeats's earliest poems, he exhibits a wisdom that far exceeds his years; in his later years, he stubbornly refuses to relinquish his passion for things that are supposedly the exclusive province of young men. Yeats is a poet who finds wisdom in youthful innocence and enthusiasm for remaining youthful for as long as possible.

At the end of *The Green Helmet and Other Poems* (1910) show Yeats writing with the insight gained from experience. Yeats shifts his focus from distractions from his work to the nature of love in the last poem of the *Green Helmet* collection, "Brown Penny." Twenty-one years earlier, Yeats wrote in "Down by the salley Gardens" that to fall totally in love without regard to the possible outcomes is one of the characteristics of youth, and it leads inevitably to heartache and loss. Yeats was forty-five years old at the publication of the *Green Helmet* collection, and his understanding of the nature of love has changed considerably. In "Brown Penny," the persona, already "looped in the loops" (ll. 8) of some beautiful young girl's hair, somehow realizes that he is both "too young" (ll. 1) and "old enough" (ll. 2); therefore, he hopes for advice by throwing a penny, presumably in a wishing well (ll. 3-4). These first few lines succeed in convincing the reader only of the persona's immaturity, since he thinks he is both too young and old enough, and he seeks guidance from a wishing well rather than from a more reliable source: his own heart. Of course the answer from the wishing well is a foregone conclusion, since the persona "hears" from it only what he wishes to hear: " 'Go and love, go and love, young man, / If the lady be young and fair' " (ll. 5-6), which of course she no doubt is.

But then, in the second stanza, the poet bestows wisdom on the personified penny, having it "sing" this "truth" to the young man: Falling in love is so completely out of the realm of human control, it makes no difference what those consequences may or may not be, since human beings are not able to control it anyway: "And the penny sang up in my face / 'There is nobody wise enough / To find out all that is in it' " (ll. 9-11). The penny, also a symbol of monetary worth, "sings" truth, which is an interesting conflation of poetry, music, and the commodities market, suggesting that the real source of "riches" may perhaps lie not in material things, but in experiencing love in all of its permutations. The truth coming from the mouth of the personified penny is that it makes no difference how wise one grows from living and loving and losing love. Love is so profound, so beyond human intellectual understanding, and so beyond human control, that no one is wise enough to fully grasp it. Real wisdom lies in acquiescing to its power and just accepting it when it comes, appreciating gratefully how it enriches human life. Because young men will *always* be "looped in the loops" of beautiful young girls' hair, attempts to prevent that from happening or to manage it or direct it in anyway are all foolish wastes of time and energy. This truth is delivered, to both the persona and the reader, in the form of music. Music is the voice of truth in this poem, a poem above love and about wisdom.

Group Nine: Music as Regret/Grief/Mourning followed by Healing and Comfort

Part of the aging process is coming to terms with the mistakes made in youth. Often, that "coming to terms" manifests itself in feelings of regret, in lamenting those mistakes for their consequences, often tragic ones. In order to fully reconcile oneself to the reality that those mistakes cannot possibly be un-made, psychologists say that before people can achieve true and lasting peace of mind, they must allow themselves to feel that regret, to mourn, literally, for lost or missed opportunities, for poor judgments that led their lives in unwanted or regrettable directions, or for failing to make changes that could have made a difference in one's own life as well as possibly in others'. The poems in this group express that regret, followed by resolution, and music, once again, figures prominently in the process.

The entire poem called "The Shepherd and Goatherd," also in *The Wild Swans at Coole* (1919), is one long, sad lament, or elegy, for the tragic, early loss of Major Robert Gregory in the First World War, the son of Yeats's friend, mentor and patron, Lady Gregory. Yeats's previous elegy for Gregory, "In Memory of Major Robert Gregory," is a poem marked by overwhelming sadness and poignance for the passing of not just Gergory but other loved ones as well. In that poem, Gregory becomes a symbol for good breeding, noble largesse, and the loss of an entire generation of young men of remarkable potential to the First World War. "The Shepherd and Goatherd," though, differs from "In Memory of Major Robert Gregory" in that it uses the classical Greek model of the rustic, pastoral personas to grieve for the passing of a paragon of aristocratic virtues. Yeats draws upon the tradition of the elegy established in poems such as Milton's "Lycidas" and Tennyson's "In Memoriam A.H.H.," which grieves poignantly for the loss of Tennyson's friend and fellow gentleman, Arthur Hallam. In much the same way, Yeats's "In Memory of Major Robert Gregory" uses the death of Gregory in the First World War to comment on the futility and waste of war. However, in "The Shepherd and Goatherd," Yeats expands on this established tradition to elevate the elegy beyond social commentary and into the more signficant area of the loss of human potential and how the loss of a single individual can impact an entire culture. In this poem, peasants sing the virtues of the nobleman; in this way, Yeats elevates the elegy beyond social class, since everyone, peasant and nobleman alike, can appreciate the loss of great human potential.

In this poem, music is the means of mourning, as both the shepherd and the goatherd use music to express their grief. Music is also strongly associated with the deceased, as the goatherd remembers that "He had often played his pipes among my hills, / And when he played it was their loneliness, / The exultation of their stone, that cried / Under his fingers" (ll. 24-27). The goatherd tells the shepherd to "Sing [his] song," for he also has "rhymed [his] reveries" (ll. 42-43), giving approval and validation to the act of singing as an appropriate memorial. The shepherd concurs: "And now that he is gone / There's nothing of him left but half a score / Of sorrowful, austere, sweet, lofty pipe tunes" (ll. 55-57). To honor his memory, they sing, and comment on each other's songs. The goatherd says of the shepherd's song: "You sing as always of the natural life, / And I that made like music in my youth / Hearing it now have sighed for that young man / And certain lost companions of my own" (ll. 75-78). The goatherd not only remembers the similar music he made in his own youth, he also remembers others who have died as well. The goatherd even sees the deceased "practis[ing] on the shepherd's flute" (ll. 102) in the afterlife. While the Shepherd focuses on the shortness of life and cannot find consolation for Gregory's loss, the Goatherd "feels sorrow not so much for the young man dead as for the mother who survives him" (Unterecker 138). He consoles himself with his beliefs concerning the process by which a soul is reincorporated into the eternal flux from which it had first sprung, part of the system Yeats designed in *A Vision* (Ellmann 234-235). In this system, the soul of a deceased person begins living his life backwards, as if his living years had wound upon a spool, and his afterlife unwinds it, from death toward birth. While the Goatherd is hopeful, there is no certainty in this system, only faith and hope. The Shepherd's lack of consolation represents the lamentation for the loss of one so gifted, and the Goatherd represents the continual hope for his miraculous return/reincarnation. However, both Sorrow and Hope, the Shepherd and the Goatherd, express themselves through and with music and memory. Music in this poem is mourning and grief, but it also comfort, healing, and validation.

Group Ten: Music as Peace, Contentment, Bliss

The final group of poems is centered around images of music that represent peace of mind, utter contentment, and moments of bliss. The placement of this group of poems at the end of this discussion is deliberate, and I will discuss this placement later; for now, suffice to say that this peace of mind is that which comes only after many years of struggle, heartbreak, disappointments, miscommunications, and regrets. This is the peace of mind that comes at the end of a life fully lived. This peace and contentment, however, is not limited to that time of a person's life that immediately precedes death. Yeats is not so predictable or clichéd to suggest that peace of mind can only come to the very elderly and the very wise, although it is true that much of this peace does, in fact, come only after having achieved maturity and much experience. Sometimes this peaceful contentment can come from living simply, living an uncluttered and uncomplicated life.

The music that is both Music and Time can be simply the source of the most profound and yet most simple of happinesses. Reminicent of Keats's "Ode on a Grecian Urn" and conflating music with the art of pottery/vase/sculpture, "Lapis Lazuli," from 1938's *New Poems*, shows the Chinese figures on the ancient vase carved out of the beautiful blue stone as made to permanently—at least as permanent as anything can be—have music within their reach. The one figure that the persona assumes is a "serving-man" follows behind the other two, carrying an unnamed "musical instrument" (ll. 41-42). The persona imagines that one of the men "asks for mournful melodies; / Accomplished fingers begin to play" (ll. 53-54). Even though the music being played is "mournful," the persona imagines that the Chinese men, caught in a contradictoty moment of profound emotion, are "gay." The happiness offered to them by the music supersedes the mournfulness of the tune being played. They are "ancient" and their eyes are surrounded by "many wrinkles," but they are unsurpassingly happy while they listen to beautiful, achingly sad music being played well by practiced, accomplished hands. Ironically, sad music often satisfies on a deeply profound level. Music makes sorrow more bearable this way, as both the experience of sorrow and the experience of the music are enhanced in an inexplicably reciprocal relationship. In this poem, even four of the most famously unhappy characters in the Shakespearean canon, Hamlet, Ophelia, Lear, and Cordelia, are also happy-sad. The persona claims that even in their misery, they are gay. In the same way that the lapis vase is made even more beautiful by the "discolouration of the stone, / [and] Every accidental crack or dent" (ll. 43-44), human life is made full and rich by not just the happiness experienced, but also the sadness, the pain, and the disappointment as well. This bittersweet quality of life marks human beings as fully human, fully cognizant of the wide variety of human experience, and fully awake to every experience. Suffering, and enduring beyond the suffering, makes the peace of mind one eventually achieves far more meaningful since it is so hard won. Being touched by mournful music encapsulates this truth of human experience without reducing it to mere truism or cliché. Moreover, this poem also maintains that in order to face death, either one's own or the death of an entire civilzation when the gyre turns, without fear and without irrational, hysterical behavior, one must embrace music, painting and poetry, for they provide the best defense against such fears and such destruction. In Yeats's view, in fact, it is the musicians, artists, and poets of the world who are the most brave in the face of certain defeat and destruction, since it is they who will ultimately be the architects of renewal.

III. The Metaphor

These are the ten groups of poems I have discussed at length in this chapter: 1) youth, vitality, sex and seduction; 2) magic and mystery; 3) verbal expression and communication; 4) war/call to arms; 5) responsibilities, cares and worries; 6) identity and identifying characteristics; 7) praise and worship; 8) life experience, wisdom, and learning; 9) lament and regret; then healing and comfort; and 10) peace and contentment. Stepping back and looking at the pattern created by my groupings of poems according to their thematic components reveals a pattern that closely resembles both the chronology of a person's life *and* the chronology and forward movement of a piece of music.

When human beings are young, their lives are marked by innocence and an overriding preoccupation with sex, being in love, and seducing the opposite sex, all of which are approached—usually—with a great deal of energy. There are many things that young people do not understand, which they often attribute to magical forces beyond human power and understanding. People's attempts to communicate with each other are often dismal failures, or at least halting or only partially successful. People are often swept up in and by causes, hearing and heeding the call to arms, barely comprehending all the possible ramifications that would come from such recklessness. All of these things—attempts at relationships and communicating, failure to understand cosmic forces, war and politics—are often chaotic, eruptive aspects of youth. They are like land mines that explode, propelling people forward headlong across the field seeking shelter and safety. Once the chaos of youth is left behind, human lives then take on heavy burdens and responsibilities that can cause existential doubt. People often seek answers during this middle time of life, even while accepting and dealing with those responsibilities. Mid-life crises are often marked by searching for individual identities. To some people, institutional religion offers solace.

But a certain amount of wisdom comes out of simply surviving. Life experience gives human beings the confidence to feel wise. Learning and knowledge are enhanced by witnessing life as it progresses. "Book" knowledge stands beside life experience and provides people with the bedrock they need to be able to claim wisdom. Part of that life experience, in addition, is the feeling of regret and lamentation for things lost along the way. True healing can only begin when wounds are acknowledged. The salve that covers those wounds is the understanding that comes from acceptance and reflection. Peace of mind is the end result, the resolution to all the discord that came before. The poems then, reflect the same progression of most lives, which looks and sounds like music. This is the larger metaphor reflected in, suggested by, and that seems to emerge organically from the poems themselves. In this chapter I have argued that for Yeats, music appears in his poems as a metaphor for this progression. Because Yeats was also influenced by the attitudes about music of the nineteenth-century philosopher Walter Pater, he, like Pater, saw that music expresses what is inexpressible by any other means.

In the broadest sense, music can be defined as the interplay between the disparate elements of sounds, rhythms, and dynamics that moves in a forward progression toward a resolution. Tension, discord, and disharmony are inherently a part of the chord progression, and this dissonance is actually the force that propels the line toward its resolution. The beginning of the line is often expected to be played or performed softly; as the dissonance increases, so does the volume. The top of the line is the loudest dynamic, which then begins to fall in volume as the notes move down the line, returning eventually to the same softness where the line began. The rests, or silences, in the measures create anticipation for the next chord; the dissonance makes the listener's ears hunger for the next chord in which that dissonance will be somehow resolved, while it often introduces a new dissonance, and the forward movement continues. The resolution is expected to come at the end of the composition, and it should be aesthetically and emotionally satisfying.

At this point I should point out that there is a distinct difference between *metaphor* and *metonymy,* and this difference is one of the markers of modernism. According to Katie Wales's *Dictionary of Stylistics*, with metonymy, "there is no transfer of field of reference as with metaphor" and that both metonymy and synedoche "work by substitution: of an expected word by the unexpected" (297). In metonymy, a part substitutes for a whole; for example, the White House is often used metonymically to refer to the U.S. Presidency. The White House, in meaning, is "close to" the Presidency, and is a part representing the whole of the Presidency, but it is not *similar to* the Presidency, in Roman Jakobson's terms. Linguist Roman Jakobson studied these differences in patients suffering from aphasia, a neurological disorder which manifests itself by the inability to distinguish or choose words correctly. In those patients whose disorder prevents them from understanding and using metaphors, they fail to see *similarities,* or they choose a word that is metaphorically *similar to* the word they actually intended. For example, an aphasic who is having this sort of manifestation will call "a gas-light a 'fire' " (Lodge 11). In patients who suffer a similar but different manifestation of aphasia, they cannot distinguish between what Jakobson calls "contiguities," or words that are *close to* the word they intended, and that closeness is marked by a closeness in time or space. For example, calling for a " 'knife' when they mean 'fork' " (Lodge 11) is a contiguity based on the spatial, physical closeness between the two objects. They are physically close, in their construction, in their uses, even in where they are kept in the kitchen, *and* in their meanings.

Metonymy, the rhetorical device of using a part to represent the whole, is marked by "a directly or logically contiguous relationship between the substituted word and its referent" (Wales 297). It is this continguous relationship that Jakobson noted as absent in certain apahasia patients. Metaphor, on the other hand, is marked by significant and profoundly meaningful similarities. As Jakobson maintains,

Similarity connects a metaphorical term with the term for which it is substituted. Consequently, when constructing a metalanguage to interpret tropes, the researcher possesses more homogenous means to handle metaphor, whereas metonymy, based on different principle, easily defies interpretation. (81)

While metonymy and metaphor are both non-literal, they are differentiated by the subtle differences between *similarity* and *contiguity.* According to David Lodge, "metaphor juggles with the selection and substitution [of words and concepts]; metonymy juggles with combination and context" (11).

This distinction between metaphor and metonymy, between similarity and contiguity, is actually a key marker of Modernist literature that distinguishes it from non-Modernist literature. For example, James Joyce's *Ulysses*, probably the quintessential Modernist text, is, according to Lodge, "essentially metaphorical, based on a similarity between things otherwise dissimilar and widely separated in space and time" because it is the metaphorical transference of Homer's *Odyssey* to modern-day Dublin; while other, non-Modernists texts have a tendency to "imitate, as faithfully as discourse can, the actual relations of things to each other in space-time. Characters, their actions and the background against which they perform these actions, are all knitted together by physical contiguity, temporal sequence and logical cause and effect" (Lodge 11-12). Modernist literature, for the most part, being so focused on taking the tradition handed to them by those who came before them to "make it new," is highly metaphorical in nature. Modernist writers were intently interested in finding new and startling relationships between things ordinarily disconnected in the minds and expectations of the reader. Metonymies, being based on closeness, would not work in the same way or have the same effect on the reader. While metonymy as a poetic device is still present, and quite regularly, in Yeats's poetry, as well as in the poetry of other Modernist writers, it cannot serve the purposes of the movement in the same way that metaphor does.

Finally, the distance between metaphor and metonymy and the regular fluctuation between these two poles by writers of different literary periods also helps to explain the "cyclical rhythm to literary history" (Lodge 12), an observation which fits perfectly into Yeats's broad understanding of the cyclical nature of human life and history. As Lodge points out, "if Jakobson is right, there is nowhere for discourse to go except between these two poles" (12). Therefore, literary trends tend to swing back and forth between preferences for one mode of thinking/writing or the other. The literature of the period previous to the Modernist era was heavily metonymical, based on the closeness of ideas and time and space and displaying a distinct preference for sequential cause and effect (the serialized novels of Dickens are a good example of this). Therefore, the Modernists' swing toward a preference for metaphorical representations of likeness between disparate things is only representative of the "natural" movement of history in its cycle. While "making it new," then, the Modernists were participating in long-established tradition. Their unique contribution lies in their choices of things to compare metaphorically, and in the depth and complexity of—and the insight gained from—those metaphors.

It is indeed the "right way for things to be ordered" that has been the subject of this chapter. The shape taken by Yeats's poems which use music and musical imagery becomes the shape of music, which in turn reflects the shape of human experience, which in turn is perceived by the faculty of imagination and understood through metaphor. What may *seem* like "tangle and drift" actually reveals itself to possess a form which bestows meaning upon that which it orders. The process of revelation and meaning-making is different for everyone, revealing another truth about music that it shares with human life, and that is this: Whether one's life follows a linear or circuitous path, one can still, hopefully, move forward in a grand chord progression of personal evolution in order to reach a level of understanding and peace that makes all the confusion experienced earlier worthwhile. No matter how many times a piece of music is played or how many codas are repeated, the music itself can offer new and insightful truths, affording the opportunity to glean wisdom, insight and peace, in recompense for pain, confusion, and turmoil.

Works Cited

Abrams, M.H., ed. *Norton Anthology of English Literature.* Vol. 2. New York: Norton, 1974.

Allt, Peter and Russell K. Alspach, eds. *The Variorum Edition of the Poems of W.B. Yeats.* New York: Macmillan, 1973.

Brown, Terence. *The Life of W.B. Yeats: A Critical Biography.* Oxford: Blackwell, 1999.

Clinton-Baddeley, Victor. *Words for Music.* Cambridge: Cambridge UP, 1941.

Cullingford, Elizabeth Butler. *Gender and History in Yeats's Love Poetry.* Syracuse: Syracuse UP, 1996.

Ellmann, Richard. *Yeats: The Man and the Masks.* New York: Norton, 1979.

Foster, Roy. F. *W.B. Yeats: A Life: I: The Apprentice Mage, 1865-1914.* Oxford: Oxford UP, 1997.

Frazier, Charles. *Cold Mountain.* Hampton Falls, NH: Beeler, 1997.

Grout, Donald. *A History of Western Music.* 3rd ed. New York: Norton, 1980.

Jakobson, Roman and Morris Halle. *Fundamentals of Language.* The Hague: Mouton & Co., 1956.

Jeffares, Norman. *A New Commentary on the Poems of W.B. Yeats.* London: Macmillan, 1984.

Kermode, Frank. *Romantic Image.* London: Routledge and Paul, 1957.

Lodge, David. *Working with Structuralism: Essays and Reviews on Nineteenth- and Twentieth-Century Literature.* Boston: Routledge, 1981.

Page, N. Clifford. *Irish Songs: A Collection of Airs Old and New.* Boston: Oliver Diston Co., 1907.

Parrish, Stephen M. and James A. Painter, eds.. *A Concordance to the Poems of W.B. Yeats.* Ithaca: Cornell UP, 1963.

Unterecker, John. *A Reader's Guide to William Butler Yeats.* Syracuse: Syracuse UP, 1959.

Wales, Katie. *A Dictionary of Stylistics.* London: Longman, 1991.

Yeats, Michael. "W. B. Yeats and Irish Folk Song" in *Southern Folklore Quarterly* 31.2 (June 1966): 153-178.

Yeats, William Butler. *Autobiographies.* William H. O'Donnell and Douglas N. Archibald, eds. New York: Scribner's, 1999.

—. *The Collected Poems of W.B. Yeats.* Ed. Richard J. Finneran. New York: Macmillan/ Collier, 1989.

—. *Essays and Introductions.* New York: Collier, 1961.

—. *Mythologies*. New York: Macmillan, 1959.

THE SOUND OF AN IDEA: MUSIC IN THE MODERNIST WRITINGS OF MINA LOY AND GERTRUDE STEIN

TANYA DALZIELL

Among the many confidants and antagonists of whom Gertrude Stein writes in *The Autobiography of Alice B. Toklas*, the poet, actor and artist, Mina Loy, is singled out for special consideration: "She has always been able to understand," Stein records with great affection.[1] Loy, in turn, "felt an affinity with this large, intelligent woman,"[2] and she memorably nominated her friend and intellectual compeer "Curie/of the laboratory/of vocabulary" in the 1924 poem-portrait, "Gertrude Stein."[3]

Now celebrated as distinguished *émigré* participants in experimental modernism and the internationalist avant-garde, even as both women are routinely conscripted to signify that amorphous category of 'American modernism,' Loy and Stein most obviously share a profound appreciation of language. Stein transforms prosaic words into sophisticated meditations on being and reality through periphrasis and syntactical innovation; Loy's logophilic inclusion of cryptic archaicisms in her notoriously esoteric poetry has disconcerted and fascinated readers from the time of its initial publication to the present day. Furthermore, and despite various champions and detractors (not to mention the authors themselves), who have insisted on the distinct disinterest in the outside word of these women's written texts,[4]Loy and Stein were exceptionally attuned to the debates and developments that were occurring in the arts adjacent to their own.

Most famously, perhaps, Stein's left bank salons in Paris brought together musicians, artists, actors and writers, and Stein herself, in her seemingly inexhaustible writings, signposted repeatedly her curiosity in the works (and personal intrigues) of visual artists such as Pablo Picasso, Paul Cézanne and Juan Gris. Loy too, by all accounts, was a cerebrally energetic and engaging figure in artistic circles in New York, Florence and Paris. Jane Augustine has suggested that: "By the nineteen-twenties, Loy was important in New York avant-garde, traveling frequently from Paris to bring information on the latest aesthetic ideas on the French 'scene.'"[5] Carolyn Burke, Loy's biographer, concurs: "It is not surprising that American modernists welcomed a poet with this impressive background in European avant-gardisms. They saw Loy as a sophisticated expatriate at home with the latest developments of modern art, as well as an ally in their battle with the genteel tradition."[6] Alongside these aesthetic and political commitments, and as a consequence of fiscal necessity (a pressure that Stein did not feel so keenly), Loy also involved herself in the 'murky business' of the commercial arts. Given such details, it is understandable that much scholarship on these writers in recent years has pursued the complex relations between their writings and concurrent 'discoveries' in the plastic arts. In particular, much erudite discussion has centred on Stein's imaginative engagements with cubism,[7]and Loy's aesthetic admiration for the polished abstract sculptures of Constantin Brancusi.[8]

This chapter proposes to extend such venturesome regard for the permeability of creative boundaries by focusing on the role of music in the works of Stein and Loy. However, and in consideration of the enormous amount of work that these women produced between them (with Stein unquestionably contributing the most significant share in quantitative terms), it should be noted that the aims of the chapter are comparatively modest. There is no presumption to address these writers' respective *oeuvres* comprehensively. Instead, the spirit is one of *bricolage* - to deploy a favourite trope of modernism - in the sense that works are selected on the basis that an engagement with them opens up possible readings of their relations with music. It must be acknowledged, furthermore, that no attempt is made here to employ the technical dexterity of musicology that Daniel Albright exercises admirably in his recent book on modernism in the arts.[9] Nor is the aim to offer an extensive survey of the historical debates over music that were taking place at the time that Stein and Loy were writing.[10] Rather, the emphasis of this chapter is on the tropic economies, the thematic preoccupations and the cultural conditions of production that allow for a discussion on the intersections of music and language in various texts by Loy and Stein.

The reason for this concentration is at least two-fold. Firstly, the contexts in which these authors worked, in France and in America in particular, were alive to the changes that music was undergoing and the challenges it was posing to accepted ideas of rhythm and tonality as well as 'civilisation' and 'history'. The apparently vital and fatiguing 'new' music of jazz was finding increasingly popular expression during and after the Great War in Chicago, New York, Berlin and Paris. Contemporaries too singled out the premier in Paris, May 1913, of Igor Stravinsky's *Le sacre du primtemps* (*The Rite of Spring)*, as a radical moment that represented, for better or worse, a seismic shift in the history of music, if not western society itself.[11]

Secondly, Loy and Stein make recurrent and explicit remarks in their works to various aspects of musical culture. Stein details in *The Autobiography of*

Alice B. Toklas, for instance, how the composer "George Anthiel brought Virgil Thomson to the house and Virgil Thomson and Gertrude Stein became friends and saw each other a great deal."[12] Thomson, himself a distinguished composer,[13] engaged Stein to write operatic librettos including *Four Saints in Three Acts,* which opened in 1934 in Connecticut and later on Broadway: the production was "met with a warm, if somewhat puzzled reception from audiences and critics."[14] If Stein's contemporaries were bewildered by her works, later composers, dancers, actors and artists, including John Cage and Willem de Kooning, would cite Stein's writings as major influences on their own enterprises.[15] By contrast, until recently Loy's poetry had been all but erased from cultural memory, even as it was highly regarded and admired by her avant-garde companions. Among its many qualities, Loy's poetry (which was written "with almost stoic slowness for half a century",[16] in contrast to Stein's ostensibly irrepressible logorrhoea), explicitly calls on musical figures with significant effects. Recent discussions on her work, for example, have pointed to the ways in which jazz operates in instances of Loy's poetry as a trope by which to grapple with an ethics of mourning.[17]

More than this, and as this chapter will examine, each of these authors turns approvingly at times to music as an approach to her own writings (and in the case of Loy, as a means by which to delineate the central conceits of Stein's work). However, not only do Stein and Loy recruit musical metaphors to describe their works: there is a sense that their written texts seek ways of becoming music. At first glance, this ambition seemingly rehearses Walter Pater's grand romantic dictum that "all art aspires to the condition of music."[18] Underpinning this contentious claim is the assumption, of course, that music, as a supposedly non-referential form, is the highest and most pure of the arts.[19] Yet, the suggestion that this chapter follows is that for Stein and Loy, music and language constitute a continuum, rather than a hierarchy as Pater would have it. Furthermore, to the degree that it can be argued that their written works aspire to music, it must also be recognised that Loy and Stein simultaneously seek to make the sound and rhythm of music visible on the page in words and spaces.

It is profitable to be reminded that a parallel project – the rendering of music in a medium reputedly distinct from its immediate form - was taking place in the avant-garde visual arts during the first decades of the twentieth century. With elemental structures such as line, colour and light at hand, cubist works including Georges Braque's *Clarinet and bottle of rum on a mantelpiece* (1911), Picasso's *Man with a Clarinet* (1911) and *Woman with Guitar* (1913), and Gris' *The Violin* (1916), to identify but four immediately familiar paintings, feature as pictorial content pre-fabricated musical motifs. Scores, staves, time signatures and instruments, implicative of geometrical patternings rather than any aspiration to representational accuracy, lend themselves to compositional planes that arguably seek to approximate to music, to rhythm, to beats.[20]

Musical designs were also a convenient and culturally available resource for the surrealists. Man Ray's photograph, *Le Violon d'Ingres* (1924), comes to mind as an excellent example. The image, featuring Kiki, or more precisely, Kiki's naked back, overlayed with orientalist tropes and F-holes, is exemplary of the surrealists' characteristic effort to eroticise feminine corporeality. However, it is by no mean unique. After all, it is a representation that rehearses uncritically, if 'unconsciously' (as the surrealists would have it), Picasso's preoccupations with the apparently revealing similarities between the curvatures of the female body and certain musical instruments, including the guitar and the fiddle, which found regular expression in his cubist works.

Notwithstanding the certainty that Loy, principally, produced some of the most impressively satirical and withering critiques of the gendered power relations which underscored many avant-garde movements,[21] (although Stein too gave discriminating consideration to "Patriarchal Poetry"),[22] it is clear that the visual arts and the written works of Stein and Loy had a similar intense interest: the rendering of music in forms that might not easily or immediately lend themselves to the task. With the sensitive calibration of a sonograph, and within a similar logic that turns around the relations between sound and graphic forms, the works of these two women are especially attentive to the mutual acoustics and rhythms of language and music as they self-reflexively negotiate the historical moments and movements in which (and to which) they write.

Indeed, it is not incidental that Loy turned to the most audacious and obstreperous of modernist genres to examine the relations between music and poetry – the manifesto. In the grip of the Futurists, with whom Loy had highly ambivalent allegiances during the development of her writing career,[23] the manifesto, with its typographical experimentations and didactic directives, sought to give the impression of aggressive sound as it 'shouted' bombastically from the page at the unsuspecting bourgeoisie.[24] As it turned out, the bourgeoisie did not founder, or even quiver, in the face of the promised ruin issued in the name of velocity. Instead, capitalism quickly co-opted these devices as it sought to create markets for its products through the relatively new and professionalised business of advertising. Loy too came to use the techniques of the manifesto against the intents of the Futurists, albeit with very differing ends to those envisaged by the capitalists. She endeavoured to exploit the idiosyncrasies of the manifesto in the development of her (presently much discussed) feminist politics.[25] Yet, when Loy came to write her only known treatise on poetry, "Modern Poetry," which was published in 1925, she declined to entertain by then such well-worn contrivances, choosing instead to take seriously as a topic the noise that the Futurists evoked graphically. More specifically, Loy was interested in charting what she posited as the intimate relations between modern poetry and jazz.

At the time that Loy's piece was published – the mid-1920s - jazz was routinely conceived of as a mainstream form of entertainment, with some commentators even proclaiming its imminent demise. During the Great War, and in the period immediately following it, jazz enjoyed considerable distinction and notoriety with audiences in America and cities in Europe. In part, this popularity came about as a consequence of the African-American military bands that transported with them the music across countries during wartime.

Yet, Loy grants little notice to such recent histories of jazz in "Modern Poetry". Instead, she posits an analogous relationship between this musical mode and the works of American modernist poets including Ezra Pound (whom she praises lavishly), Marianne Moore (whom she admits "has written at least one perfect poem"),[26]e.e. cummings, Laurence Vail and William Carlos Williams (whom she attests demonstrates most perfectly "the new rhythm" she is attempting to arrest in her account).[27] Whereas jazz enjoys universal acclaim because of its seductive appeal to the emotions, Loy argues, the appreciative audience of modern poetry is comparatively minor as a consequence not only of the intellectual demands of this art, but also its very form – "the cold barrier of print". Jazz appeals to the ear, and so too must we "listen to poetry," urges Loy. Further, what invites an extended correspondence between these arts, she contends, is the actuality that both forms share a commitment to rhythms, which rebel "against tradition." In other words, these arts are in close dialogue on evidence of their disapproving regard for 'regular' rhythm, rhyme and line phrasing. In addition, they are each thought to have "received fresh impetus from contemporary life," in particular from the streets of New York City.[28]

Stein, it is worth noting, was similarly attracted to this singular locale. Having spent the past thirty years in France, she returned to the United States in 1934 for a lecture tour as a celebrity: Stein was enjoying the spectacular success of *The Autobiography of Alice B. Toklas*. Yet, if her explication in *Everybody's Autobiography* of her experiences in New York is considered, then Stein travelled in New York not only as a literary luminary, but also predisposed to the peripatetic possibility of consumption: "In between everything I wandered around the streets of New York. The ten cent stores did disappoint me but the nut stores did not,"[29] she writes. A little later in the same narrative, Stein records that: "And we were always in New York and I was always walking and I liked best Seventh Avenue. I bought a stylograph there for a dollar, it is a good one. I bought an American clock that was not so good but the stylo is an excellent one."[30] In the context of this chapter's concerns, it is tempting, if somewhat fanciful, to speculate on Stein's stated preference for the fountain pen and its role in creative possibilities, over a positivist device depended upon for its presupposition to measure time with its steady beat. It is also appealing to note the way in which the passage formally registers in its rhythms the thematic focus on walking through the streets of New York that the passage details.

Nevertheless, the principal point to be made in the context of Loy's manifesto on modern poetry is that Stein's emphasis on consumption gives way to the peddlers of produce; specifically post-war European exiles, refugees and migrants typified by "an adolescent Slav who has speculated in a wholesale job-lot of mandarins and is trying to sell them in a retail market on First Avenue".[31] Why? Well, these migrants play an important role in the ongoing transmutation of the English language and its rhythms, "enriched and variegated with the grammatical structure and voice-inflection of many races."[32] For Loy, the inhabitants of the post-war New York streets have given rise to, or at least furnish a context for, jazz and free-verse poetry. Taken together, such claims result in an exemplification of *lingua franca*,"[33] wherein jazz is valued for its purported qualities of unprecedented freshness and sedition, which Loy imagines modern poetry written (only) in America to hold. In this way, jazz is also implicitly regarded as a culturally recognisable and serviceable discourse that enables the interpretation of modern poetry which otherwise has a reputation of being 'difficult,' if Loy's comments on its limited audience is taken seriously.[34]

In making these remarks, it is necessary to acknowledge that elsewhere in Loy's poetry, as with Stein's prose, jazz is called upon as something more than an evocative parallel to modernist poetry. Jazz becomes modern writing and modern writing becomes jazz, with dissonance underpinning this continuum. In *Lectures in America*, for example, Stein writes: "The jazz bands made of this thing, the thing that makes you nervous at the theatre, they made of this thing an end in itself. They made of this tempo a something that was nothing but a difference in tempo between anybody and everybody."[35] This ephemeral 'thing,' the idea of the improvised jazz swing with its syncopations and inconsistent sounds, is not so much described or represented here: the phrase is not something that strives for directness of signification. Instead, jazz is enacted in the composition, rhythm and 'tempo' of the sentences: it is made 'an end in itself' whereby language is called upon to perform operations other than that of naming, namely phonic However, this 'thing' also evokes a discordant experience - it 'makes you nervous at the theatre' – that registers wider cultural opinions about jazz as a symptom of and elixir for modern life.

As a consequence of its close associations with African Americans, who were habitually encoded in the early twentieth century through the twinned lenses of popular ethnography and evolutionary theory as primitive and unhindered by the trappings of modernity, jazz was seen by many non-African Americans as manifest of everything amiss in post-war society and a panacea for this condition.[36] For many writers and artists associated with the Harlem Renaissance, jazz struck an affirmative note which also carried with it a particular charge: it could signify on past interpretations of African American histories and identities to make meanings anew.[37] Yet, for others, jazz seemed to promise, bodily and emotional emancipation from the world of war and its neurasthenic aftermath, with its polyrhythms, syncopation and improvisation. Stimulation for war-weary nerves was sought in jazz, while for its critics, this music was the cause of such enervation. For those who favoured the former - 'you,' presumably, if Stein's assertions are adhered to - 'slumming' at cabaret jazz clubs and theatres became a popular past time,[38]as is suggested in Stein's aforementioned sentences and moments of Loy's poetry.

In Loy's poem, "Lady Laura in Bohemia", the apparently English figure of Laura, "Trained in a circus of swans" and "inseparable from the genealogical tree", descends into the "half-baked underworld" where an "abbess-prostitute/presides/Jazz-Mass".[39] Jazz is erotically and ecstatically thrilling, an encoding that finds similar expression in "The Widow's Jazz."[40] This poem details "black brute-angels" who "bellow through a monstrous growth of metal trunks/ and impish musics/ crumble the ecstatic loaf/ before a swooning flock of doves."[41] From the first lines of the poem - "The white flesh quakes to the negro soul/ Chicago! Chicago!/ An uninterpretable wail/ stirs in the tangle of pale snakes" - jazz is expressly linked to a 'black' essence or soul,[42]and it is also imagined to signal "the encroaching Eros/ in adolescence" which enraptures young (white) women:

Haunted by wind instruments
in groves of grace

the maiden saplings
slant to the oboes

and shampooed gigolos
prowl to the sobbing taboos. [43]

Furthermore, the music the 'black brute-angel' musician produces is clearly marked out in terms of white consumption. For the white patrons of this Chicago cabaret club, jazz is a fantasy of release founded on racial assumptions that are examined and exposed in other, later poems by Loy such as "Negro Dancer."

"Negro Dancer" (which might be read propitiously alongside Claude McKay's poem, "Negro Dancers" and Langston Hughes's piece, "Jazzonia),[44] formally enacts the sounds and cadences of jazz with its unexpected stresses, as these opening sections of the poem suggest:

Exile solarium
pulsate! percuss!

Puppet
of skeletal escapade
wired with tropical liana
shaking your lumbar
moulding of mahogany. [45]

At the same time that the poem aspires to jazz rhythms, it signals a thematic curiosity with primitivism that underpinned much contemporary discussion on jazz, which the African-American dancer, Josephine Baker, famously symbolised. For bedazzled white audiences in Berlin and Paris, Baker in her banana skirt was emblematic of a primitivist fantasy that saw African-Americans possess a spirituality and innocence (of a savage kind that could also be artlessly sexual), an idea apprehended in the lines of Loy's poem: "The ancestral smoulder/ of jungle ritual/ excites the satin limb". Yet, Baker mimicked and mocked such presumptions in her exaggerated performances of them,[46] and in "Negro Dancer," as in Baker's dance routines, the interest in jazz primitivism is informed by a critical self-awareness of the artifice of the primitive. Reference is made in the poem to the dancer as a "Puppet/ of skeletal escapade/ wired with tropical liana", and there is suggestion of both deliberate moulding and posturing - "to excel in/ posturing/ these aboriginal innocencies" - as well as performativity: "The cosmic spasm aquiver/ in the glare of the theatre," Loy writes.

The trope of the theatre, as it is respectively deployed in Loy's poem and Stein's prose piece (or at least that section from *Lectures in America* quoted), is that which differentiates the positions of each work on the possibilities of jazz. Stein's interest in jazz points to an aspiration of rhythmic resemblance and improvisation in words. At the same time, it registers a concern with the nervous effect of the theatrical spectacle on the likely white audience in a way that suggests an ambivalent regard for African-American popular musical culture, which subsequent critics have also noted. In her reading of Stein's prose piece, "Melanchtha," which was published in *Three Lives*,[47] Carla L. Peterson, for example, has argued that Stein was both "powerfully drawn" to such musical culture" and "repulsed" by the images it carried.[48] Loy's poem shares Stein's concern for mimesis however it also disassembles the staged, erotically-charged fantasies of primitivism with which jazz was intimately associated.

However, if Stein's prose registers some unease with respect to jazz and its cultural resonances, it is interesting to note Stein's approval of the contemporary comparisons made between her writing and the music of Bach. In *The Autobiography of Alice B. Toklas*, Stein twice refers to Marcel Brion, a

French cultural commentator, who remarked on Stein's sentences to this effect, as the author herself relates it:

> The sentences of which Marcel Brion, the french critic, has written, by exactitude, austerity, absence of variety in light and shade, by refusal of the use of the subconscious Gertrude Stein achieves a symmetry which has a close analogy to the symmetry of the musical fugue of Bach.[49]

Towards the end of the same text, as Stein details the "close understanding" between herself and Gris, on the basis of their commitment to the "conception of exactitude," she recalls again Brion's observations, writing that: "It is because of this [her desire for exactitude] that her work has often been compared [...] by a certain french critic to the work of Bach."[50] This triangulation – Stein, Gris, Bach – is one that deserves attention. The connections between Stein and Gris have already been established, with their shared interests in the rendering of music in other media, yet the question to be posed is this: why might Bach be called upon (contrapunctually) as an ally in this project? Further, how might this corresponding insistence on 'exactitude' be interpreted?

As Karin von Maur has persuasively outlined in her research on the cubist paintings of Gris, intellectual interest in Bach was notably rejuvenated in the early years of the twentieth century. In part, this revival was a reaction to the widespread devotion to Wagner. Further, the 'rediscovery' of polyphony in Bach's constructivist composition coincided with cubism that, if it did not intend always to settle on pictorial syncopations, certainly lent itself to comparison, as suggested earlier. In addition, and as von Maur has argued, while it cannot be claimed that Bach was "the presiding genius of Cubism," it can certainly be asserted that the repeated, affirmative resemblances that were identified between cubism and Bach in chronicles of the time attest to "the Cubists own desire for system and law"[51] - an order or symmetry typified by the musical fugue - in the same way that myth would provide an order for the imaginative, fragmenting worlds of T.S. Eliot and James Joyce.

It may be said, then, that Bach came to be seen as a figure that signalled not only the 'newness' for which modernism strived (against the backdrop of Wagner), but also an ordered aesthetic of spruce abstraction – a broader interest beyond Bach in 'exactitude' - that motivated much modernist work across the various arts, including Piet Mondrian's Neoplasticism and Brancusi's highly stylised golden birds as well as Stein's writing and Loy's poetry. Hence Stein's commendatory repetition of Brion's observations regarding her writings. Further, it is arguably not by chance that in Loy's 1922 poem "Brancusi's Golden Bird,"[52] which shapes in words the idea of the abstract to which the artwork aspires (rather than putting into language – describing, representing – the non-representational sculpture itself), she writes of "an incandescent curve/licked by chromatic flames".[53] 'Chromatic' here brings together at once the linguistic, colour and music (at a time when Arnold Schoenberg was introducing his ideas on the chromatic twelve-tone method which "sought relief from [atonal] anarchy"),[54] and gestures towards the exactitude of abstraction and the abstraction of exactitude.

Indeed, this raises the question as to what this 'exactitude' might actually entail. The paradox is that it is impossible to speak of exactitude exactly. To do so would mean to presume that the primary function of language is to name when the very idea of exactitude is to move language away from this dreary social function to seek out its essence, to "extract/a radium of the word", as Loy wrote of Stein's work in "Gertrude Stein," and as Pound wrote of Loy's own poetry when he declared enthusiastically that it was "akin to nothing but language."[55] If one thread of the modernist undertaking is to turn language to itself (keeping in mind that whether or not this intent can be agreed with, or achieved, is really not the point here), then the phenological qualities of language are necessarily foregrounded. Consider, for example, "sing/ing/in Ming/Syringa/Myringa/Singer/Song-winged/sing-wind/syringa" in one of Loy's later poems - "The Song of the Nightingale is Like the Scent of Syringa."[56] Words are sound - the analogy to music disappears – and what is 'extracted' in this process, at least for Loy in her reading of Stein, is the "core of a 'Being':"[57] the musicality of language grasps intuitively the otherwise inexplicable exactitude of being.

As Loy acknowledges, and like modernity itself, "Bergson was in the air" when she began to engage with Stein's writings, and the philosopher's ideas, Loy reflects, "seemed to have found a literary conclusion in the austere verity of Gertrude Stein's theme – 'Being' as the absolute occupation."[58] Bergson, the great defender of creative intuition against analytic intellect and theorist *par excellence* of *durée*, was a significant figure for many modernists. This was the case not least because his ideas about the primary role of artistic intuition in comprehending the essence of being held a definite appeal for those artists and writers who were newly faced (at least it seemed this way), with the ceaseless flow of an ever-changing reality, which Stein's disappointing 'American clock' could not ever quantify. Bergson, it should be recognised, was not averse to using musical tropes to elaborate the necessarily inexact concept of duration, writing that it might be conceived of as something akin to "the notes of a tune, melting, so to speak, into one another."[59] Perhaps, it is not unexpected that Loy would make similar analogies to music, as well as to sculpture, in her writings on Stein and their apparent realisation of Bergson's philosophies:

> For Gertrude Stein obtains the *belle matière* of her unsheathing of the fundamental with the most dexterous discretion in the placement and replacement of her phrases, of inversion of the same sequences that are so

closely matched in level, as the fractional tones in primitive music or the imperceptible modelling of early Egyptian sculpture.[60]

With its references to 'early Egyptian' sculpture and 'primitive music', the passage points to an interest in not only the possibilities of certain forms of writing, music and sculpture to grasp the essence of Being but also the importance of time for this aspiration. That Stein's work uncovers 'the fundamental' it is because of its close resemblance to art forms of 'the past', which as a result of their purported proximity to some 'origin', are likely to have more immediate access to this apparent essence. In addition, this intuition is possible because of another temporal patterning – rhythm. Rhythm is given a structural importance in Loy's assessment of Stein's writing. It is that which holds together Stein's work even as, or because, it promises to collapse the conventional sentence and its (now redundant) efforts to communicate meaning directly and in a developmental, linear fashion. Furthermore, with its rhythmic emphasis on inversions and repetitions, Stein's writing presents itself to Loy as an unparalleled manifestation of Bergson's theories: "For by the intervaried rhythm of this monotone mechanism she uses for inducing a continuity of awareness of her subject, I was connected up with the very pulse of duration."[61] The rhythms in Stein's work are neither ill-disciplined nor wildly confused, as some of her less generous critics have proposed. Rather, they represent a new effort in words to create a rhythmic sense of subjective time, of duration, and in so doing reach the exactitude of being.

Indeed, Stein's insistence on repetition, which has infuriated, perplexed and wearied many readers, even as it has enthused others, finds a historical and aesthetic parallel in the musical arts with which it has shared rhythmic interests. Most notably, the 'primitivist' works of Igor Stravinsky are renowned for the challenges they level at conventional meter, rhythm and musical time, with scholars of musicology such as Jonathan Cross recently suggesting that: "It is, in particular, his positive attitude toward repetition [...] that Stravinsky defines his particular modernist strand and clearly differentiates himself from others".[62] Stein too seeks to distinguish herself from others, including Stravinksy. She claims authoritatively in *The Autobiography of Alice B. Toklas* to have never heard Stravinksy's *Le sacre du primtemps*. She attended a performance of the ballet in Paris, she admits, but "no sooner had it commenced when the excitement began [...] We could hear nothing, as a matter of fact I never did hear any of the music of the Sacre du Printemps because it was the only time I ever saw it and one literally could not, throughout the whole performance, hear the sound of music,"[63] she insists.

To say that Stein heard nothing is inexact: what she heard was various sections of the crowd hissing and applauding as the audience members were confronted with one of the most defiant musical experiments of their generation. And without wishing to suggest a direct influence of Stravinksy's innovations on Stein's work, it is disingenuous to accept the writer's disclaimer that she heard nothing of the music. Even if the music was not immediately available at the time of her viewing of the ballet, it is nevertheless the case, as Stein herself admits that: "All Paris was excited about it." [64] It would seem unlikely that she would not have gleaned some knowledge of it from the discussions that were taking place among avant-garde artists and popular audiences alike. Whatever the situation, it is not an exaggeration to say that Stein and Stravinksy share a deep interest in the possibilities of repetition and rhythm to dominate the 'sense' of their works, to divine an 'exactitude,' with Loy commenting on both of these creative artists in this way in her poetry. Whereas Stein's extraction of this exactness is conceived of in "Gertrude Stein" to take place through processes of crushing and congealing, a crystallised reduction by repetition, Stravinsky's orientation, as Loy imagines it in "Stravinski's Flute," is expansive and transcendental. She writes of "A voice-evangel of loud ice/soars through a cloven dome" and "To this listening/the mouth and the ear/of music/ are one". Further, with the inclusion of signalled pauses in lines such as "Arise/shrill star-striker—" there is a sense that the musician's intake of breath – inspiration – is of as much importance as the music itself in achieving a sense of aesthetic truthfulness.[65]

From this, and despite the inferences of the title of Loy's poem, "Stravinski's Flute," it should now be evident that the piece is not at all 'about' Stravinsky's flute as a material object. Like the Stein of *Tender Buttons* who deliberately and satirically confuses and exposes the indexical conventions of language, particularly the noun, Loy is not seeking to describe the instrument in her poem. Nor is the design to replicate in words the music possibly made by the flute. Rather, her poetry resonates with "the sound of an idea" to return to the first lines from "Modern Poetry" which read: "Poetry is a prose bewitched, a music made of visual thoughts, the sound of an idea."[66] Loy's poem estimates in the rhythms of words the sound of an idea of music that is not transparently accessible. On this point, Stein's conception of "A Sound" in *Tender Buttons* is suggestive of a similar concern. She writes: "Elephant beaten with candy and little pops and chews all bolts and reckless reckless rats, this is this." This prose piece gestures towards both an idea of a sound and the sound of an idea; it does not easily solicit a search from some material referent as the parodical taxonomic title of 'Objects' under which this piece appears in the volume mischievously proposes. Rather, to paraphrase Loy, it intuits a sound made of visual thoughts in a way that refigures conventional modes of understanding, as both women understood.

For Stein and Loy, music was very much a part of their shared intellectual and cultural milieu and it is not astonishing, given the common curiosity of the avant-garde arts in cross-disciplinary stylistic and thematic preoccupations, that it should feature in their written works. Perhaps what is surprising, though, is that these writers' complex engagements with various aspects of musical cultures have been hitherto under-discussed in otherwise informed and inspiring scholarship. This chapter has aimed to outline but a few of the moments in which Stein and Loy sought to craft a new intelligence that directly engaged with contemporaneous debates and discoveries in music while denying any sense of comfortable immediacy in its approach to exactitude. Music, for these writers, is not something simply to emulate in words. Words, with their rhythms and sounds, are not an effortless means of representation and music too is seemingly non-referential, although it is undeniable that musical styles, like language, also carry social and historical import. Instead, ideas and sounds and visual thoughts are the substance of music and writing alike, they aver. As such, creative coalitions as well as dissonances may form productively between writing and music in ways that may not be readily anticipated, but which result in stimulating meditations on art and existence that continue to resonate today.

Works Cited

Adorno, Theodor. *Philosophy of Modern Music*, translated by Anne G. Mitchell and Wesley V. Blomster. London: Seabury Press, 1973.

Albright, Daniel. *Untwisting the Serpent: Modernism in Music, Literature and Other Arts*. Chicago and London: The University of Chicago Press, 2000.

—. *Modernism and Music:An Anthology of Sources*. Chicago and London: The University of Chicago Press, 2004.

Arnold, Elizabeth. "Mina Loy and the Futurists." *Sagetrieb: A Journal Devoted to Poets in the Imagist/Objectivist Tradition* 8.1-2 (1989): 83-117.

Augstine, Jane. "Mina Loy: A Feminist Modernist Americanizes the Language of Futurism." *Mid-Hudson Language Studies* 21.1 (1989): 89-101.

Bergson, Henry. *Time and Free Will: An Essay on the Immediate Date of Consciousness*, translated by F.L. Pogson. New York: Macmillan, 1910.

Blau du Plessis, Rachel. *Genders, Races and Religious Cultures in North American Poetry 1908-1934*. Cambridge: Cambridge University Press, 2001.

Bocher, Jay. "Architecture of the Cubist Poem." In *Architecture and Cubism*, edited by Eve Blau and Nancy J. Troy. Cambridge and London: The MIT Press, 1997.

Burke, Carolyn. "The New Poetry and the New Woman: Mina Loy." In *Coming to Light: American Women Poets in the Twentieth Century*, edited by Diane Wood Middlebrook and Marilyn Yalom. Ann Arbor: University of Michigan Press, 1985.

—. *Becoming Modern: The Life of Mina Loy*. New York: Farrar, Straus and Giroux, 1996.

Butler, Christopher. *Early Modernism: Literature, Music, and Painting in Europe, 1900-1916*. Oxford: Clarendon Press, 1994.

Cross, Jonathan. *The Stravinsky Legacy*. Cambridge: Cambridge University Press, 1998.

Cunningham, David. "A Time for Dissonance and Noise: On Adorno, Music and the Concept of Modernism." *Angelaki* 8.1 (2003): 61-74.

Dalton, Karen C.C and Henry Louis Gates Jr. "Josephine Baker and Paul Colin: American Dance seen through Parisian Eyes." *Critical Inquiry* 24 (1998): 903-934.

Dalziell, Tanya. "Mourning and Jazz in the Poetry of Mina Loy." In *Modernism and Mourning*, edited by Patricia Rae. PA: Bucknell University Press, 1995 (forthcoming).

DeKoven, Marianne. "Gertrude Stein and Modern Painting: Beyond Literary Criticism." *Contemporary Literature* 22 (1981): 81-95.

Gates Jr., Henry Louis. *The Signifying Monkey: A Theory of Afro-American Literary Criticism*. New York: Oxford University Press, 1988.

Kachur, Lewis. "Picasso, popular music and collage Cubism (1911-12)." *The Burlington Magazine* 135 (1993): 252-60.

Keck Stauder, Ellen. "Beyond the Synopsis of Vision: The Conception of Art in Ezra Pound and Mina Loy." *Paideuma: A Journal Devoted to Ezra Pound Scholarship* 24.2-3 (1995): 195-227.

—. "The Irreducible Surplus of Abstraction: Mina Loy on Brancusi and the Futurists." In *Mina Loy: Woman and Poet*, edited by Maeera Shreiber and Keith Tuma. Maine: The National Poetry Foundation, 1998.

Knapp, Benita. *Gertrude Stein*. New York: Continuum, 1990.

Kouidis, Virginia M. *Mina Loy: American Modernist Poet*. Baton Rouge and London: Louisiana State University Press, 1980.

Larsen, Nella. *Passing* (1929). New York: Penguin, 1997.

Lemke, Sieglinde. *Primitivist Modernism: Black Culutre and the Origins of Transatlantic Modernism*. Oxford: Oxford University Press, 1998.

Locke, Alain, ed. *The New Negro*. New York: Atheneum, 1992.

Loy, Mina. *Lunar Baedeker & Time-Tables*. Highlands: Jonathan Williams, 1958.

—. *The Last Lunar Baedeker*, edited by Roger L. Conover. Highlands: The Jargon Society, 1982.

—. *The Lost Lunar Baedeker: Poems of Mina Loy*, edited by Roger L. Conover. New York: Noonday Press, 1996.

Martin, Wendy. "Remembering the Jungle: Josephine Baker and Modernist Parody." In *Prehistories of the Future: The Primitivist Project and the*

Cultures of Modernism, edited by Elazar Barkan and Ronald Bush. California: Stanford University Press, 1995.

Monson, Ingrid. "Jazz improvisation." In *The Cambridge Companion to Jazz*, edited by Mervyn Cooke and David Horn. Cambridge: Cambridge University Press, 2002.

Nemo, Nancy. "Femininity, the Primitive, and Modern Urban Space: Josephine Baker in Berlin." In *Women in the Metropolis: Gender and Modernity in Weimar Culture*, edited by Katharina von Ankum. Berkeley: University of California Press, 1997.

Norris, Christopher, ed. *Music and the Politics of Culture*. London: Lawrence & Wishart, 1989.

Paddison, Max. *Adorno's Aesthetics of Music*. Cambridge: Cambridge University Press, 1993.

Palatini Bowers, Jane. *Gertrude Stein*. New York: St. Martin's Press, 1993.

Pater, Walter. *The Renaissance*, edited by Donald L. Hill. Berkeley: University of California Press, 1980.

Peppis, Paul. "Rewriting Sex: Mina Loy, Marie Stopes and Sexology." *Modernism/Modernity* 9.4 (2002): 561-579.

Perloff, Marjorie. *The Poetics of Indeterminacy: Rimbaud to Cage*. Princeton: Princeton University Press, 1981.

Peterson, Carla A. "The Remaking of Americans: Gertrude Stein's "Melanctha" and African-American Musical Traditions." In *Criticism and the Color Line: Desegregating American Literary Studies*, edited by Henry B. Wotham. New Jersey: Rutgers University Press, 1996.

Piolo, Richard J., ed. *Stung by Salt and War*. New York: Peter Lang, 1987.

Pound, Ezra. "Others" *Little Review* (1918): 56-58.

Sayre, Henry M. "The Artist's Model: American Art and the Question of Looking like Gertrude Stein." In *Gertrude Stein and the Making of Literature*, edited by Shirley Neuman and Ira B. Nadel. Boston: Northeastern University Press, 1998.

Stein, Gertrude. *The Autobiography of Alice B. Toklas* (1933). Harmondsworth: Penguin, 1966.

—. *Lectures in America*. New York: Random House, 1935.

—. *Everybody's Autobiography* (1937). Cambridge: Exact Change, 1993.

—. *Gertrude Stein: Writings 1903-1923*, edited by Catharine R. Stimpson and Harriet Chessman. New York: The Library of America, 1998.

Tommasini, Anthony. *Virgil Thomson: Composer on the Aisle*. New York and London: W.W. Norton and Company, 1997.

Vaught Brogen, Jacqueline. "The "Found Mother": Gertrude Stein and the Cubist Phenomenon." In *Challenging Boundaries: Gender and Periodization*, edited by Joyce W. Warren and Margaret Dickie. Athens and London: The University of Georgia Press, 2000.

Von Maur, Karin. "Music and Theatre in the Work of Juan Gris." In *Juan Gris*, Christopher Green with contributions by Christian Deouet and Karin von Maur. London: Whitechapel Art Gallery in association with Yale University Press, 1998.

Weiss. M. Lynn. *Gertrude Stein and Richard Wright: The Poetics and Politics of Modernism.* Mississippi: University of Mississippi Press, 1998.

Winters, Yvor. "Mina Loy." *The Dial* 80.6 (1926): 496-499.

MUSICAL AND IDEOLOGICAL SYNTHESIS IN JAMES WELDON JOHNSON'S *THE AUTOBIOGRAPHY OF AN EX-COLORED MAN*

MICHAEL KARDOS

Like the author himself, the protagonist in James Weldon Johnson's 1912 novel *The Autobiography of an Ex-Colored Man* was a talented musician who believed that racial uplift could be facilitated by individual artistic achievement. Because of this belief, *The Autobiography* can be seen as prognosticating the Harlem Renaissance. The unnamed narrator has a deep and life-long connection with music, and until he decides to pass as white at the novel's end, music is his passion, his career, and, above all, his means of bringing "glory and honor" to himself and his race.[1]

The narrator's conviction that an individual's art could foster "cultural synthesis"[2] conforms to W. E. B. Du Bois's view of racial uplift ideology, where the individual achievements of an educated and talented minority would lead to a reduction of prejudice toward all African Americans. Johnson's narrator subscribes to Du Bois's ideology of a "Talented Tenth" who will move the race forward, explaining that "the position of the advanced element of the colored race is often very trying. They are the ones among the blacks who carry the entire weight of the race question."[3] He views his personal attainments, such as being the best ragtime player in New York City, as not only gratifying in themselves, but more importantly as means to a greater humanitarian end. Therefore, his dream of collecting African-American folk music and turning it into high art is in his view an inherently valuable project not only because of the art it will produce, but also because whatever glory it brings the narrator will be glory brought to his race.

The Autobiography tells a Horatio Alger story of rags to riches, except that the material riches obtained by the novel's end are exposed by the narrator as a coward's compensation for betraying his race, or at least for failing to live up to his potential as one of Du Bois's Talented Tenth. While in the American South collecting musical material, the narrator witnesses the lynching of a black man, and "unbearable shame" overtakes him, causing him to abandon his project of combining Negro spirituals and ragtime with the aesthetics of European art music. He decides to return to New York, change his name, and "let the world take me for what it would."[4] He takes a job in business and eventually begins buying real estate. In New York he falls in love with a white woman to whom, after much internal struggle, he confesses his secret. She eventually decides to marry him, and though she dies at a young age she leaves the narrator with two children who are healthy and wealthy—but not wise, for they know nothing about their mixed heritage. It is assumed that they never will, and the novel ends with the narrator feeling "small and selfish" beside the "gallant band of colored men who are publicly fighting the cause of their race."[5]

Instead of putting his talents to use for the good of his race, the narrator has chosen to live his life as "an ordinary successful white man" and, alluding to the Biblical story of Abraham's grandson, Esau, in Genesis (25:29-34), claims that he has traded his "birthright for a mess of pottage."[6] The narrator hasn't, like his own father, abandoned his children. Nonetheless, he has followed metaphorically in his father's footsteps by abandoning music, which has been his primary connection to his African-American heritage. Nathan Huggins expresses a commonly held critical view that the tragedy at the end of the novel "was not merely the protagonist's abdication of his art…but, more, that the society had lost the cultural synthesis that might have been possible through the genius of this marginal man."[7]

Much criticism of *The Autobiography* has concentrated on the array of causes behind the narrator's decision to abandon his dream and pass as white. Absent, however, has been a critical examination of the narrator's conception of his musical project itself. And yet this project, particularly its ethnological agenda, sheds as much light on the narrator and his ideology of racial uplift as does the tragedy of his dream going unrealized. An examination of the role of music in *The Autobiography* uncovers the narrator's ambivalence about racial uplift ideology. It is an ambivalence that was shared by Johnson himself. However, while the narrator's failure at the end of the novel results from his need for synthesis—both musical and ideological—Johnson himself avoids the failures of his fictional narrator through a process of ideological accommodation.

In his biography of James Weldon Johnson, Eugene Levy writes that in *The Autobiography*, Johnson was able to "explore the essential quandary of his own life—that of the educated black in America's caste society."[8] Johnson's decision to publish his novel anonymously rested partly on his insecurity as a novelist, but mainly on his desire for the novel to be perceived as a "human document" that would spark curiosity about its author.[9] Despite his desire that the novel "pass" as autobiography—the book even included a faux attestation by the publisher as to the work's authenticity—reviewers tended to read the work as fiction.[10] Reviews were mainly positive, but they were scarce, and sales of the novel were slight. Partly the book's commercial failure is attributable to the publishing company's limited resources. (The publisher—Sherman, French, and Company—soon went out of business.) But also, Levy claims that in 1912 "the white reading public was not interested in a novel critical of national racial practices," and yet there wasn't a large enough black readership to produce significant sales on its own.[11]

Not until 1927, when Johnson was already a nationally well known and well respected African-American leader, was the novel reissued—this time by a major publishing house, Alfred A. Knopf—with Johnson's authorship identified, to more eager black and white audiences. The reissued book achieved wide recognition for its insights into the state of race relations in the United States and has since then remained in print. Charles Willis Thompson's 1927 review in *The New York Times* is representative of critical praise, claiming the book was "an all-embracing study of the race question from every angle."[12]

The novel chronicles the narrator's life from boyhood, when he first discovers that he is of mixed heritage, to his missed opportunity to attend Atlanta University, through a series of careers at a cigar factory, as a gambler and pianist in New York City, and later as the accompanist—both musically and personally—for a white millionaire on his trips to Europe. While in Europe, the narrator realizes how he can achieve his childhood dream of "bringing glory and honor to the Negro race":[13] when he returns to the United States, he will travel the American South collecting slave songs and ragtime music and, using his musical expertise, transform this music into "high art" according to the aesthetics of European classical music.

The narrator's belief that an individual's musical project could help bring glory to the race is consistent with Johnson's faith in art's ability to offset racial prejudice. In the preface to *The Book of American Negro Poetry*, published in 1922, Johnson wrote:

> A people may become great through many means, but there is only one measure by which its greatness is recognized and acknowledged. The final measure of the greatness of all peoples is the amount and standard of the literature and art they have produced. The world does not know what a people is until that people produces great literature and art. No people that has produced great literature and art has ever been looked upon by the world as distinctly inferior.[14]

This view not only echoes that of his fictional protagonist in *The Autobiography*, but also neatly summarizes the theoretical underpinning of the Harlem Renaissance, which emphasized the collective fruits of individual artistic achievement. *The Autobiography* portrays a character brimming with artistic potential. He is deeply affected by music, beginning as a child listening to his mother play old Southern songs on the piano. "I used to stand by her side and often interrupt and annoy her by chiming in with strange harmonies which I found on either the high keys of the treble or the low keys of the bass."[15] The narrator's music-making begins in the folk tradition, where songs, rather than being transcribed, were passed on aurally, and where improvisation played an important role in creative expression. The identification that the narrator feels with his mother's music is expressed with his symbolic remark, "I remember that I had a particular fondness for the black keys."[16]

The narrator's proclivity for self-expression, however, is rooted not only in inner passion but also in a desire to impress others. For instance, he explains that when providing accompaniment on the piano, "I constantly forced my *accelerandos* and *rubatos* upon the soloist, often throwing the duet entirely out of gear."[17] His expressiveness, rather than benefiting the performance, hinders it. Later in the novel, at a concert to raise money for his education in Atlanta, he admits that his choice to perform Beethoven's flashy Sonata Pathétique was "a bit of affectation."[18] The self-centered nature of the narrator's passion suggests a psychic distance from the world around him that helps to explain his retreat from art and his own heritage at the end of the novel.

When the narrator arrives in New York and first hears a pianist performing ragtime in a gambling club, he is captivated by the music's "barbaric harmonies" and "audacious resolutions" that demand a physical response.[19] In one of the essay-like expository passages in the novel, he articulates his belief that ragtime music is proof of black America's creativity and a tangible contribution to America's image abroad. As high praise, he notes that ragtime has been given the European stamp of approval: "In Paris, they call it American Music."[20]

The nature of such praise reveals the narrator's deep-rooted ambivalence toward black folk culture. While there is no reason to doubt the narrator's veracity when he claims, "there will come a day when this slave music will be the most treasured heritage of the American Negro,"[21] the text often professes a reverential view of European culture, which accounts for his desire to fuse slave songs and ragtime music with European art music. There is a paradox, however, in proclaiming the greatness of African-derived folk music—great, specifically, for its authenticity—while simultaneously viewing Europe as the gold standard for artistic achievement. The view that European classical music was more developed or of a higher class than African or African-American music stemmed from a racial uplift ideology that emphasized the morality of a bourgeois middle class. Kevin K. Gaines, in his book *Uplifting the Race*, explains that many Harlem elites stressed "temperance, thrift, chastity, social purity, patriarchal authority, and the accumulation of wealth."[22]Although the novel's narrator did not grow up wealthy, his household nonetheless had the accoutrements of a "proper" middle-class: horse-haired chairs in the parlor, a piano, books in a glass-doored case, a bible. When his father came to visit, he would hand the narrator a "bright coin," which his mother encouraged him to save in his "little tin bank." The narrator, summing up his childhood, boasts that he was "a perfect little aristocrat."[23] The novel depicts an uplift ideology rooted in the hierarchy of cultural values, favoring Victorian bourgeois sensibility. It was an ideology emphasizing class distinction, which later got challenged by a younger group of Harlem elites, such as Jean Toomer in his 1923 book *Cane* and Langston Hughes in his 1926 essay "The Negro Artist and the Racial Mountain."

In contrast, "The Old Guard," writes Steven Tracy, referring to W. E. B. Du Bois, James Weldon Johnson, and Alain Locke, "tended to be more ambivalent in their attitudes toward folk materials, attempting to balance their own racial pride with their middle-class values." For them, writers like Langston Hughes, Zora Neale Hurston, and Sterling Brown, whom Tracy refers to as the New Guard, "relied far too much on black underworld characters and 'lowlife' types in their depictions of African-American experience, rather than setting up examples of respectable Negroes for others of their race to follow; and they drew too much on and identified too fully with folk forms for their experimentation, particularly the 'vulgar' blues and jazz."[24] Consequently, the NAACP tended to publicize "'proper' music for the middle classes," such as a performance of operatic arias, rather than jazz or blues. Arnold Rampersad explained that the typical "notable musical event" as reported in the *Crisis* was "a black performer interpreting serious Western music, or a white composer or musician introducing African or Afro-American themes into his work"[25]

A drawback of the Old Guard's vision of racial uplift to which Johnson's narrator subscribes is that in drawing attention to class distinctions, "elite African Americans were replicating, even as they contested, the uniquely American racial fictions upon which liberal conceptions of social reality and 'equality' were founded."[26] Hence the narrator's pride about having resembled, as a child, a little aristocrat. When he arrives in Washington DC and for the first time comes across large numbers of lower-class African Americans, he feels repulsed by their "unkempt appearance," their "slouching gait" and "loud talk and laughter."[27] Later in the novel, when the narrator travels to Macon, Georgia to begin collecting folk music, he experiences a schism between his musical pursuit and the people who have given rise to that very music. He explains, "The houses in which I had to stay were generally uncomfortable, sometimes worse…the food was at times so distasteful and poorly cooked that I could not eat."[28] Descriptions of his project have a condescending tone, such as his stated process of "jotting down in my note-book themes and melodies, and trying to catch the spirit of the Negro in his relatively primitive state."[29] The narrator's apparent aversion to lower-class black Americans reveals his confusion of the effects of racism with its causes; he has internalized the belief that the lower class lacks the social customs and material achievements of the bourgeois because of some inherent—indeed, essential—flaw, rather than because of a racist society's years of cruelty and neglect. Thus he is disengaged from the creators of the very music that he is so intent on collecting.

It is likely this tension between the narrator's simultaneous regard for an authentic black folk culture and his internalized acceptance of bourgeois notions of "high" culture that causes him to be genuinely moved by the ragtime music he hears, and yet at the same time to downplay the art form. Several times he refers to ragtime music as "charming," and when he sits down next to the expert for the first time, he looks for "the trick."[30] Certainly he would not have described learning Beethoven's Sonata Pathétique in this way. Even when he becomes an accomplished ragtime pianist himself, he notes that everybody's favorite song is not one of the standard rags, but rather his own "novelty," a ragged rendition of Mendelssohn's Wedding March.[31]

Johnson's musical project is problematic because, despite his appreciation of folk culture, he nonetheless brings to the project a preconceived conception of "low" and "high" art as defined by the dominant group, a corresponding privileging of so-called high art, and, by extension, a privileging of the dominant group itself. And so the question becomes whether the narrator's motivation is to celebrate the music of his heritage, or to "appropriate, ennoble, and commodify" it.[32]

Ironically, ragtime music arguably is *already* a blend of the very musical traditions that the narrator intends to unite. While ragtime music's rhythmic basis, particularly the syncopation and stomping bass, derive from African-American folk tradition, its emphasis on formal, written structure and its particular harmonic features[33] have a European influence.[34]Typically, ragtime music is played on the piano, an instrument historically linked with European classical music. As well, its discrete tones do not acoustically permit a flexible rendering of "blue notes" (which lie between the major and minor modes), or the bending of notes as is possible with, for instance, the guitar or the human voice. "The best ragtime," writes Marshall Stearns in *The Story of Jazz*, "incorporates the horizontal rhythmic flow of all good American Negro music. It also retains its European form. The blend is a rare and sophisticated piano music that can be well played only by a very few, highly gifted virtuosos."[35] Looked at this way, ragtime is a successfully hybridized music that to some degree obviates the task of Johnson's narrator.

The narrator's cultural synthesis presumably was to result from the symbolic act of musical synthesis; the novel seems to suggest, however, that the narrator doesn't intend to "synthesize" the two musical styles, as much as to "fix" or "improve" the folk music through a process of musical alchemy. That the narrator fails to appreciate fully the intrinsic value of African-American folk music is an irony not necessarily intended.

Typically, it is unwise to attribute a character's beliefs to that of the author; however, in this instance there is sufficient documentation of Johnson's own views that closely mirror those of his narrator—specifically both men's emotional ardor for African-American folk culture, yet an intellectual appreciation of it that rests mainly on its *potential* to become high culture according to a European standard. Both Johnson and his fictional narrator express ambivalence about folk culture and its role in racial uplift. On the one hand, Johnson writes in his preface to *The Book of American Negro Poetry* that "the Negro" was the "creator of the only things artistic that have yet sprung from American soil and been universally acknowledged as distinctly American products."[36] Johnson placed tremendous value in the wide range of African-American folk music such as Negro spirituals, the blues, and ragtime. And yet, in the same preface, he writes:

> Now, these dances which I have referred to and ragtime music may be lower forms of art, but they are evidence of a power that will some day be applied to the higher forms.[37]

This latter excerpt matches almost exactly the words of Johnson's narrator in *The Autobiography*, in a discussion of the same artistic achievements:

> These are lower forms of art, but they give evidence of a power that will some day be applied to the higher forms.[38]

In fact, several of the didactic expository passages in the novel reappear in Johnson's essays and in his autobiography *Along This Way*. However, while Johnson and his narrator might share ideological ambivalences, they differ markedly in their approach to dealing with them. Through the symbolic act of synthesizing the music from his heritage with the music of the dominant group, the narrator hopes to synthesize the various parts of himself and achieve not only personal acclaim but also a resolution to his racial ambivalences. When synthesis proves impossible, he chooses to pass as white—a path with the least day-to-day resistance, but one that causes lifelong regret.

Unlike his fictional narrator, James Weldon Johnson led a career—artistic, diplomatic, political, and educational—marked not so much by attempts to *synthesize* as to *accommodate* competing ideologies. For instance, Dickson D. Bruce Jr. argues that Johnson stressed the importance of racial distinctiveness in some poems and racial assimilation in others. In "O Black and Unknown Bards," the slaves wielded spirituality, rather than the weapons of war:

> O black slave singers, gone, forgot, unfamed,
> You—you alone, of all the long, long line
> Of those who've sung untaught, unknown, unnamed,
> Have stretched out upward, seeking the divine.[39]

Bruce argues that "the slaves were closer to the ideals of faith than were the heroes of a militant life that, by implication, Johnson ascribes to the white world."[40] And yet Johnson's best-known poem, "Fifty Years," written in 1913 to celebrate the fiftieth anniversary of the Emancipation Proclamation, strikes assimilationist tones:

> Courage! Look out, beyond, and see
> The far horizon's beckoning span!
> Faith in your God-known destiny!
> We are a part of some great plan.[41]

By expressing black distinctiveness motifs in some poems and assimilationist in others, Bruce argues, "Johnson actually became, in a sense, two writers."[42]

Early in his career, Johnson was part of the successful songwriting team (including his brother Rosamond and musician Robert Cole) that composed "Labor is tiresome sho,'" "My Castle on the Nile," and many other songs that, while arguably humanizing its African-American subjects more than had been done in the past, nonetheless employed black stereotypes and perpetuated "coon song rhetoric" that "catered to the lowest levels of contemporary musical taste."[43] And yet he and Rosamond also co-wrote the stirring and optimistic "Lift Every Voice and Sing," a song that became known as the Negro National Anthem.

During his tenure working for the NAACP, Johnson had the complete personal and literary respect of W. E. B. Du Bois, and yet he also maintained a close and, it appears, sincere friendship with the controversial Carl Van Vechten. He even praised Van Vechten's novel *Nigger Heaven*, though most Harlem elites thought it exploitative in its presentation of the "debauched tenth."[44]

Perhaps the most obvious and telling example of Johnson's accommodation of multiple ideologies was his belief that race prejudice was most effectively attacked *indirectly* through works of art,[45] and his simultaneous belief in *direct* political activity, evidenced by his decade-long stewardship of the NAACP.

Johnson considered, but ultimately rejected, his brother Rosamond's suggestion of titling *The Autobiography* "The Chameleon." Nonetheless, it is a title that accurately describes the narrator. He is able to put on whatever skin, whatever mask, is most practical. When one considers how well Johnson got along with people, how deftly he understood his audiences, it is tempting to think of him, too, as a chameleon. After all, he befriended Booker T. Washington *and* W. E. B. Du Bois. And Johnson's poem "Fifty Years" was "assertive enough to please Du Bois and [Charles] Chestnutt," yet "also counseled patience and hope in the future, themes which fitted both the views of Tuskegee and the white racial bias of the *New York Times*."[46]

But Johnson was not a chameleon. Although his 1928 essay "The Dilemma of the Negro Author" underscores his intimate understanding of audience, Johnson wasn't tailoring his work simply so that particular groups of people would find it agreeable. Rather, he was expressing various parts of himself, ideas held simultaneously. Dickson Bruce explains that Johnson viewed both racial distinctiveness and assimilation "as valid, valuable goals; and for a variety of reasons, he could find no compelling reason to choose between them."[47] It is a quote that highlights Johnson's complexity and his strength: instead of forcing himself to choose a stable ideological position, Johnson allowed himself to be many things simultaneously, and his manifold talents gave expression to the various parts of himself, contradictions and all. He didn't necessarily synthesize the contradictions and paradoxes that confronted him; rather, he lived with them.

Works Cited

Berlin, Edward A. *King of Ragime: Scott Joplin and His Era*. New York: Oxford UP, 1994.

Bruce, Dickson D. Jr. *Black American Writing From the Nadir: The Evolution of a Literary Tradition, 1877-1915*. Baton Rouge: Louisiana State UP, 1989.

Cataliotti, Robert H. *The Music In African American Fiction*. New York: Garland Publishing, Inc., 1995.

Fleming, Robert E. *James Weldon Johnson*. Boston: G. K. Hall & Co., 1987.

Gains, Kevin K. *Uplifting the race: Black Leadership, Politics, and Culture in the Twentieth Century*. Chapel Hill: University of North Carolina Press, 1996.

Griffiths, Frederick T. "Copy Wright: What Is an (Invisible) Author?" *New Literary History* 33 (2002): 315-341.

Huggins, Nathan Irvin. *Harlem Renaissance*. New York: Oxford UP, 1971.

Levy, Eugene. *James Weldon Johnson: Black Leader, Black Voice*. Chicago: The U of Chicago Press, 1973.

Johnson, James Weldon. *The Autobiography of an Ex-Colored Man*. 1912. New York: Penguin Books, 1990.

—. *Along This Way*. New York: The Viking Press, 1933.

—. *The Book of American Negro Poetry*. New York: Harcourt, Brace, and Company, Inc., 1922.

—. "The Dilemma of the Negro Author." *Speech and Power: the African-American essay and its cultural content from polemics to pulpit*. Ed. Gerald Early. Hopewell, NJ: The Ecco Press, 1993.

Review of *Autobiography of an Ex-Colored Man*, by James Weldon Johnson. "An Ex-Colored Man." *The New York Times*. 26 May, 1912: BR319

Review of *Autobiography of an Ex-Colored Man*, by James Weldon Johnson. *Muncy's Magazine* 49 (1913): 794-98.

Review of *Autobiography of an Ex-Colored Man*, by James Weldon Johnson. *The Crisis* 5 (1912-13): 38.

Sundquist, Eric J. *The Hammers of Creation: Folk Culture in Modern African-American Fiction*. Athens, GA: The U. of Georgia P, 1992.

Thompson, Charles Willis. "The Negro Question." Rev. of *Autobiography of an Ex-Colored Man. The New York Times*. 16 Oct. 1927: BR14+.

Tracy, Steven C. *Langston Hughes & the Blues*. Chicago: U of Illinois P, 2001.

Vincent, Ted. *Keep Cool: The Black Activists who Built the Jazz Age*. East Haven, CT: Pluto Press, 1995.

OPERA, MATERNAL INFLUENCE, AND GENDER IN ERNEST HEMINGWAY'S *THE ASH HEEL'S TENDON*

LISA TYLER

"The Ash Heel's Tendon" is an exceptionally neglected Hemingway short story. It is not included in *The Complete Short Stories of Ernest Hemingway: The Finca Vigía Edition*, which includes several previously unpublished short stories. There is no article on it in Susan Beegel's massive, nearly 400-page collection *Hemingway's Neglected Short Fiction*, and it does not rate space in Paul Smith's otherwise admirably comprehensive 400+-page *A Reader's Guide to the Short Stories of Ernest Hemingway*. It does not even garner a mention in the index of the 600+-page biography of Hemingway written by the otherwise indefatigable Carlos Baker.[1]

Now, there are arguably valid reasons for its critical neglect: It is admittedly a pretty terrible short story, and, given its lack of quality and its 1920 date of composition, it more or less qualifies as juvenilia. (Hemingway would have been 20 or 21 when it was written.) James Mellow describes it as "the most improbable of the early stories."[2] Michael Reynolds suggests that the story's introduction, "which illustrates how much [Hemingway] had yet to learn," is derivative of Kipling's "slightly condescending but knowledgeable narrator" and judiciously concludes that while "Kipling can get away with it," unfortunately "Hemingway cannot."[3]

Although the story is admittedly a weak member of the Hemingway canon, it nevertheless richly repays critical exegesis. "The Ash Heel's Tendon" anticipates the hard-boiled prose style of some of the author's later works, such as the short story "The Killers" and the novel *To Have and Have Not*. Hemingway remained fascinated with its sordid underworld populated by bartenders, professional criminals, and prostitutes, drawing on it again in such later short stories as "The Killers" and "The Light of the World." The themes of "The Ash Heel's Tendon" also anticipate themes that would remain important to the writer in his maturity, including the value of stoicism, the corresponding disdain for emotional display, and the equation of masculinity with a tightly wrapped emotional self-control. Finally, it is the story in which

Hemingway most directly addresses the artistic power and the seductive dangers of music, and specifically the threat opera poses to masculinity.

The Role of Opera in "The Ash Heel's Tendon"

Given the neglect in which this story languishes, it is perhaps appropriate to review its plot before beginning to address its significance. The story opens with the conventional truism that under the influence of alcohol, a man sheds his reserve and shows his true self, and it is clear that what constitutes the true self is emotional expression: "laughing, sloppy crying and fighting jags."[4] But some men, Hemingway observes, do not experience this effect of alcohol. After a somewhat awkward transition, Hemingway then moves on to distinguish between a "gunman," which he describes as a Hollywood caricature, complete with chaps and chewing tobacco, and a "gun," which he bills as "a professional death producer" (175). While the gun is "colorless" and unemotional, Hemingway contends, "Also every gun has his weak point, what Jack Farrell . . . called his ash heel's tendon" (175). Thus Hemingway both invokes Greek mythology and, by emphasizing Irish police detective Farrell's mispronunciation of the Achilles heel allusion, mocks it.

Hemingway then properly introduces his principal character: Hand Evans, better known as the Hand of God for the facility with which he dispatches his victims. Rocky Heifitz, the bartender, speaks of him with appropriate awe, for he has seen Hand execute Scotty Duncan right outside Rocky's bar. Hemingway makes clear that Hand is unmoved by his professional accomplishments; the killer shoots Duncan and then chats blandly with the bartender about the merits of soft-nosed ammunition before having a whisky. The bartender, impressed, offers to shake hands with the killer, who refuses, saying he doesn't shake hands with anyone.

Predictably, Hand promptly leaves town, and there are reports of subsequent successful murders in various cities. Hemingway repeatedly emphasizes Hand's utter lack of vulnerabilities: "He gave allegiances to no one and he split with no one," for example, and "The members of the oldest profession could get no hold on him and his only possible weakness was drink" (176). But though he drinks to excess, he invariably shows no ill effects afterward.

When he returns to Rocky Heifitz's bar two years after dispatching Duncan, "The district wondered who was going to die" (175). Pinky Miller and Ike Lantz, two "stool pigeons" (178) convinced that they are his next targets, appeal to Jack Farrell to save them from Hand. But because no witness will testify against such a dangerous man, Farrell can only arrest him for vagrancy or hold him for investigation, and neither of those would stop him for long since Hand can prove he isn't a vagrant and he's already been investigated as thoroughly as possible, given the reluctance of witnesses to testify against him. "Somebody's due for a one way trip to the land out of which's bourne no travellers return," Farrell tells them, in what may be Hemingway's first use of the quotation from *Hamlet* that he found so compelling throughout his writing career. Farrell suggests that they drink with Hand in an effort to get him to incriminate himself, but Miller insists Hand has no weak points.

Once Miller and Lantz leave, Farrell calls Rocky and learns that Farrell himself is on Evans's list of targets. Farrell, unsurprised, asks Rocky to wait for his call at 11:30 p.m., then play a record Farrell's sending over for the bar's phonograph, and be prepared to duck afterwards. The record that Farrell sends over and Heifitz plays is the great Italian tenor Enrico Caruso singing the aria "Vesti la giubba" from Ruggero Leoncavallo's *I Pagliacci*, in which Canio, the tragic clown who plays Pagliacci in the play within the opera, dons his costume and makeup to prepare for his show despite his heartbreak at discovering his wife's infidelity (Kohrs 435-38).[5] The opera ends tragically, with Canio's murder of his wife onstage during their performance. It is probably not coincidental that Hemingway chose this particular lament from an Italian opera, first performed in Milan, about a woman's infidelity, as he himself had so recently been jilted by Agnes von Kurowsky, the woman he had perhaps naively expected to marry. She had sent her breakup letter from Italy in March of 1919.[6]

Upon hearing Caruso's recorded voice, Hand reacts emotionally for the first time in "The Ash Heels Tendon." His expression changes, and instead of closely monitoring the mirror behind the bar, he gazes at the floor, presumably under the powerful spell of the compelling music. "At the last note he raised both hands impulsively to applaud" (179), and Farrell arrives just in time to pull a gun on Hand and cuff him. Farrell gloats, not very attractively, that the killer's real name is Guardalabene: "And what brought his hand away from his pocket was the wop voice. Your ash heel's tendon, Mr. Guardalabene, was Music" (180).

Opera and the Hemingways

In order to understand fully the implications of this story about a hitman defeated by his own passionate love of opera, it is necessary to examine the significance opera held for the Hemingway family, especially for Hemingway's mother, Grace Hall Hemingway. In the fall of 1895, Grace Hall, then about 23 and not yet married, traveled to New York City to train as an opera singer with Madame Louisa Cappianni, a well-known opera coach.[7] The Metropolitan Opera Company offered her a contract, but she delayed responding until after a concert at Madison Square Garden, during which the footlights hurt her sensitive eyes. Grace chose to sacrifice her potential opera career and later claimed to her children that she might have "occupied the spot on the

Metropolitan's bill then taken by the great Austrian-American contralto Ernestine Schumann-Heink."[8]

While that claim may have been a bit suspect, Grace was no dilettante. She gave music lessons for five years after graduating from high school,[9] and in her marriage she remained dedicated to her music:

> When Grace Hall Hemingway designed their Kenilworth house, she included a music studio and recital hall thirty feet square with a vaulted ceiling and narrow balcony. Here she gave music and voice lessons, scheduled her student recitals, and composed and practiced her own music, which was marketed by different publishing houses.[10]

During much of her marriage, her income from her work as a professional musician exceeded her husband's even though he was a doctor.[11] There was, as Michael Reynolds observes elsewhere in his essay, "nothing shabby about the music that drenched Hemingway during his early years,"[12] and "The impact of his musical training, both formal and casual, was long lasting. He listened to classical music throughout his life. During his courtship of Hadley Richardson, piano concerts were part of their shared interests; after their marriage, Hadley replaced his mother at the piano they rented in Paris."[13]

In raising her children, Grace Hall Hemingway emphasized aesthetic appreciation: She said repeatedly that she wanted her children to enjoy life. To her this meant above all an awareness of the arts. She saw from the first that they all had music lessons. As soon as they were old enough, she bought them tickets for symphony concerts, operatic performances, and the better plays that came to Chicago, and they were encouraged quite early to acquaint themselves with the paintings and drawings at the Chicago Art Institute.[14]

Ernest had season tickets to the Columbia Opera Company in 1915 and began taking piano lessons when he was five.[15] His sister Marcelline recalls seeing *Romeo and Juliet*, *La Bohème*, *Faust*, *Aïda*, and *Norma* while she was still in her teens and specifically recalls taking the El to Chicago with Ernie to see *Madame Butterfly*.[16] Kenneth Lynn has persuasively suggested that Marcelline may have been named after not the saint but "Mozart's Marcellina, the aggressive spinster who is finally revealed to be the mother of the hero in *The Marriage of Figaro*."[17] Marcelline later studied music at the Oberlin Conservatory for a semester,[18] while her sister Sunny became a harpist with the Memphis Symphony Orchestra.[19]

Music was a central part of Hemingway's upbringing and education. Ernest sang in the church choir as a boy, sang in the glee club in high school[20] and played the cello for the school orchestra for two years.[21] He "spent long hours of orchestra rehearsal for the ambitious production of Balfe's three-act operetta, *The Bohemian Girl*."[22] One of his puppy loves as a teenager stemmed from opera: "His interest [in Frances Coates] dated from a performance of the three-act opera, *Martha*, in which Frances had appeared during April. Playing his cello in the orchestra pit, Ernest could hardly keep his eyes on the score."[23]

Hemingway remained vitally interested in opera as an adult. While he was recovering from his war wound in Italy, Hemingway wrote his mother that he had attended operas at La Scala, including *Moses*, *Aïda*, and *The Barber of Seville*, conducted by Toscanini, and complained that he'd rather see *Carmen* or *La Bohéme*.[24] He wrote his sister, "You know, Milano is some town, about 690,000, good opera and everything."[25] When he returned to Oak Park, an Italian-American society organized a party to celebrate his bravery, and the party included three members of the chorus of the Chicago Grand Opera Company, who gave a concert of opera arias in Grace's music room.[26] Marcelline later attended the opera with some members of the group who organized the part, and in 1920, Ernest went to see the Chicago Opera's performance of *Andrea Chenier* twice.[27] During his courtship with his first wife, Hadley, he wrote his mother that he had heard Bennie Moisewitsch perform and compared him knowledgeably to four other contemporary pianists.[28]

Hemingway's first wife, whom he met the year "The Ash Heel's Tendon" was composed, was arguably as deeply interested in music (and specifically musical performance) as his mother had been, although she seems to have lacked Grace's confidence in her own abilities. Hadley herself took piano lessons twice a week when she was a child. She studied piano for eight years and after dropping out of college practiced for several hours a day.[29] She dreamed of a career as a concert pianist but, discouraged by her mother's assurances that she was too sickly to succeed, she lacked the self-assurance to devote herself seriously to her goal. More than once she cancelled a planned concert at the last minute.[30] In Paris with Ernest, she rented an upright, moved the dining table into the bedroom to make room for it, and practiced three hours a day.[31] She continued to play, mostly for pleasure, throughout her life.

Hemingway's own artistic ability might easily have led in another direction, had he possessed more aptitude for music. Hemingway scholar and professional pianist Hilary K. Justice has traced the musical elements in Hemingway's style, attributing them to "his indebtedness to Grace Hemingway as his earliest artistic mentor."[32] Marcelline recalls Hemingway proposing that they and some friends make up an opera and describes at some length the development of their theme about Moses and the bulrushes.[33] Ernest retained his interest in opera for many years, telling Lillian Ross in 1949 that he loved all music, including opera, although he had no musical talent himself.[34]

Given what we know of Hemingway's upbringing and young adulthood, it seems reasonable to conclude that for him, music was coded as feminine, and opera specifically was coded as not just feminine but maternal.

Opera, Gender, and the Western Tradition

It is perhaps important to recall that in Greek mythology, Achilles' tendon is the only vulnerable part of him, and it is vulnerable because it is where his mother had touched him as she dipped him into the River Styx "to make him invulnerable" ("Achilles" 4).[35] Hilary K. Justice has called our attention to a "Hemingway who, like Achilles, knew that his greatest vitality and vulnerability was where his mother had touched him—in his art" ("Lion" 42).[36] For Hemingway, his mother had touched him through her love of opera, and this story suggests that he perceived his own love of opera as effeminate and dangerous.

There is cultural support for seeing opera as feminine and feminizing. In *The Queen's Throat: Opera, Homosexuality, and the Mystery of Desire*, Wayne Koestenbaum traces the connections between opera and gender. Citing the case of one boy who nearly faints at a performance of *Tristan* and another who gets goosebumps at the opera, Koestenbaum observes, "Opera in the theater as well as in the home can interrupt lessons in gender conduct, particularly lessons in how to be masculine."[37] As Koestenbaum acknowledges, there is an ancient tradition in Western culture of associating music and gender. He cites Plato's contention in the *Republic* that listening to music is "effeminizing" and notes that St. Augustine reached a similar conclusion.[38]

Guardalabene's emotional and aesthetic response to Caruso's voice betrays him and leads to his arrest for murder in an era when capital punishment was the sentence typically administered to convicted murderers. His love of opera leads inevitably to his death. Koestenbaum writes, of Puccini's *Madama Butterfly*, "Opera kills the thing it loves. . . . I long to remain outside the frame of opera, immune to its dangerous charms, but I also feel narrative's seduction: I want to enter the story and I want the plot to proceed."[39] Koestenbaum notes the self-destructive qualities inherent in the opera queen's obsession: "Opera queendom isn't suicidal. But it feels like throwing the self away, giving up autonomy and production, becoming pure receiver,"[40] adding a few pages later, "The dogma underlying the opera queen's body: love of opera entails a sacrificing of one's own flesh."[41] Guardalabene similarly becomes pure receiver and sacrifices his own flesh.

Opera demands that Guardalabene respond; he cannot resist. As Koestenbaum observes of Santuzza and Turiddu's duet in Pietro Mascagni's *Cavallier Rusticana* (1890), "Musically it is an ultimatum: *weep*. The codes of female and effeminate conduct demand that I react hypersensitively, that I identify with both soprano and tenor, and that I let their doubleness speak my divided solitude." [42] Koestenbaum further suggests that gays in particular respond emotionally to opera because it invokes their own experiences: "The singer and the homosexual each appear to be a closed-off cabinet of urges. But the body that sings and the body that calls itself homosexual are not as sealed as we think. Nor are they as free. They are looseleaf notebooks, filled with scrap-pages of inherited prohibitions: page after page of pain."[43]

It is possible to see Guardalabene's response as an inadvertent admission that he is not only Italian and a music lover, but that he is also effeminate and perhaps gay. It is important to remember the story's opening reference to alcohol as "the cup that *queers*" (174, emphasis added). Hemingway is blunt about Hand's lack of interest in prostitutes: "The members of the oldest profession could get no hold on him" (176). Farrell mocks him by saying, "You didn't care any more about a woman than a slot machine" (179). And it is specifically a man's voice, not a woman's, that moves Hand to applaud and make the fatal error of letting down his guard long enough to allow Farrell to arrest him. Even the reference to Achilles has undertones of cross-dressing and sexual ambiguity, since Achilles's mother, knowing that he was fated to die in Troy, dressed him as a maiden to protect him from the Trojan War ("Achilles" 4)[44]—a development that likely seemed particularly resonant to Hemingway since his mother had "twinned" Ernest with his older sister Marcelline by dressing him in girl's clothes until he was five years old (Lynn 38-42).[45]

Interestingly, given Hand's identity as a "gun," in the Greek myth Odysseus disguises himself as a peddler to gain entrance to the royal court, where Achilles inadvertently reveals his identity when he prefers the weapons Odysseus has for sale to the trinkets over which all the maidens exclaim.[46] True masculinity, the myth implies, means choosing violence over beauty.

Given Hemingway's repeated use of the word "shell" to describe Hand's impervious exterior, the obvious implication is that there is something else inside, something very different. What is most disturbing about this hidden part of the personality, however, is what Hemingway compares it to: first, "the shrunken, misshapen nudity of an unprotected hermit crab" and later the caskets within a pyramid (174). What is hidden is apparently either deformed, naked, and in desperate need of protection, or dead, entombed within an artificial shell of masculinity.

It's not a coincidence that Hand's true name, Guardalabene, translates roughly as "guard to the good"; by maintaining his shell, he is desperately trying to protect the deformed interior self. But the love of opera (which, for Hemingway, as we have seen, is always coded as feminine and maternal) opens a man up emotionally, which leads to vulnerability and ultimately, death. To borrow Gertrude Stein's curious syntax, to love opera is to be emotional is to be feminine is to be vulnerable is to be trapped, caught, and killed.

Works Cited

"Achilles." *Oxford Companion to Classical Literature.* 2nd ed. Ed. M.C. Howatson. New York: Oxford University Press, 1989. 4-5.

Baker, Carlos. *Ernest Hemingway: A Life Story.* New York: Scribner's, 1969.

Beegel, Susan F., ed. *Hemingway's Neglected Short Fiction: New Perspectives.* Ann Arbor, Michigan: UMI Research Press, 1989.

Diliberto, Gioia. *Hadley.* New York: Ticknor & Fields, 1992.

Hamilton, Edith. *Mythology.* New York: New American Library, 1969.

Hemingway, Ernest. "The Ash Heel's Tendon—A Story" in Peter Griffin, *Along with Youth: Hemingway, The Early Years.* New York: Oxford University Press, 1985. 174-80.

Hemingway, Ernest. *The Complete Short Stories of Ernest Hemingway: The Finca Vigia Edition.* New York: Scribner's, 1987.

Justice, Hilary K. "Alias Grace: Music and the Feminine Aesthetic in Hemingway's Early Style." In *Hemingway and Women: Female Critics and the Female Voice.* Ed. Lawrence Broer and Gloria Holland. Tuscaloosa: University of Alabama Press, 2002. 221-38.

—. "The Lion, the Leopard, and the Bear." *Hemingway Review* 19.1 (Fall 1999): 39-42.

Kohrs, Karl, ed. *The New Milton Cross' Complete Stories of the Great Operas.* Rev. and enlarged ed. Garden City, New York: Doubleday, 1955.

Koestenbaum, Wayne. *The Queen's Throat: Opera, Homosexuality, and the Mystery of Desire.* New York: Poseidon Press, 1993.

Lynn, Kenneth S. *Hemingway.* New York: Simon & Schuster, 1987.

Mellow, James R. *Hemingway: A Life without Consequences.* Reading, Massachusetts: Addison-Wesley, 1992.

Reynolds, Michael. "High Culture and Low: Oak Park before the Great War." In *Ernest Hemingway: The Oak Park Legacy.* Ed. James Nagel. Tuscaloosa: University of Alabama Press, 1996. 23-36.

—. *The Young Hemingway.* New York: Basil Blackwell, 1986.

Sanford, Marcelline Hemingway. *At the Hemingways: With Fifty Years of Correspondence between Ernest and Marcelline Hemingway.* Centennial edition. Moscow, Idaho: University of Idaho Press, 1999.

Smith, Paul. *A Reader's Guide to the Short Stories of Ernest Hemingway.* Boston: Hall, 1989.

Villard, Henry S. and James Nagel. *Hemingway in Love and War: The Lost Diary of Agnes von Kurowsky.* New York: Hyperion, 1989.

MUSIC: WALLACE STEVENS' SUPREME FICTION

KARL COULTHARD

Music: musical ideas and aesthetics, musical figures, musical performance, figure prominently in much of Wallace Stevens' poetry over the entire course of his literary career. However, thus far most scholarship on the subject of music in Stevens' work has focused on close formal analyses of musical structures in his poetry or involved traditional close readings of the significance of particular instruments, performance styles, and composers within a specific historical context. Kinereth Meyer and Sharon Baris, for example, attempt to read "Peter Quince at the Clavier" within the context of a historical discussion of Baroque music. Barbara Holmes, on the other hand, devotes an entire book to studying musical figures and forms in Stevens' compositional strategies, engaging in structural analysis akin to that of the music theorist. Both of these interpretive strategies are, to my mind, too empirical and fail to consider Stevens' focus on aesthetics. Stevens, however impenetrable his "gaudy surface" may appear at times, maintained a remarkably consistent focus throughout his career on the nature and processes of perception. For Stevens, the significance of music lies not within its formal structures: its harmonies, rhythms, and overtones, but in the impact that music has on the listener.

In his essay "The Noble Rider and the Sound of Words," Stevens celebrates the power of art to transform the world around us and describes the poet as one who "creates the world to which we turn incessantly and without knowing it and… gives to life the supreme fictions without which we are unable to conceive of it."[1] Stevens, like most artists and philosophers of his generation, was faced with a world in which the old order of Christianity had lost its force and relevance. In the absence of a divine power to order the world, Stevens sought to fill this void with "a notion of a 'supreme fiction' or an 'idea of order' governing all things and towards which the poet-philosopher must aspire without hope of ever encompassing it."[2] In "The Noble Rider," Stevens' describes this supreme fiction as "a force and not the manifestations of which it is composed."[3] Thus, like the *ding an sich*, the supreme fiction cannot be perceived directly, but can only be observed through the effect that it has, like a wave, on the substances through which it passes. Stevens' supreme fiction manifests itself in many ways in his poetry, such as through "beauty" or a "blessed rage for order"; indeed, Stevens clearly sees poetry itself as having the potential to manifest supreme fiction. However, in his lecture on "The Irrational Element in Poetry," Stevens articulates an obvious attraction to music when, while discussing the idea of "pure poetry," he longs for the day "that a poet may arise of such scope that he can set the abstraction on which so much depends to music."[4] Music, for Stevens, would seem to represent the purest sensory expression of his supreme fiction.

George Santayana's discussion of music in *The Life of Reason* is particularly useful in connecting the aesthetics of music to the ideal aesthetic that Stevens envisions creating through poetry. Where Stevens discusses the abstraction of pure poetry, Santayana describes music in remarkably similar terms: "Pure music is pure art. Its extreme abstraction is balanced by its entire spontaneity, and, while it has no external significance, it bears no internal curse."[5] The abstract nature of music, its lack of "external significance," would seem to be of considerable significance to Stevens. Music, at least in its wordless forms, does not signify the way language does. A word can have a definite meaning or a limited number of possible meanings within a specific context. A musical motif, on the other hand, remains elusive to definition, operating on an ineffable, sensory, emotive level with the listener. Stevens, on several occasions, expresses a preference for art that does not signify, that cannot be explained. In "The Noble Rider," he states that "nobility" must not be defined, must not be fixed: "As in the case of an external thing, nobility resolves itself into an enormous number of vibrations, movements, changes. To fix it is to put an end to it."[6] In "The Irrational Element in Poetry," Stevens similarly criticizes explanation in art: "When we find in poetry that which gives us a momentary existence on an exquisite plane, is it necessary to ask the meaning of the poem? If the poem had a meaning and if its explanation destroyed the illusion, should we have gained or lost?"[7] Clearly, Stevens is seeking through art to capture a sense of the divine, wholly independent from any earthly meanings or interpretations.

In seeking the divine, Stevens focuses most prominently on the experience elicited by art, rather than on the composition of art itself. In "The Noble Rider," he describes thoughts and feelings as "all the truth that we shall ever experience."[8] Once again, Stevens is favouring the role of perception, emphasizing the fact that we can never really interpret or comprehend art, but only experience it. However, he is also emphasizing the "irrational" nature of experience, that we do not appreciate art on the basis of intellectual evaluations of its form, structure, and meaning, but based on the purely subjective emotional impact that it has on us. Santayana praises music for its ability to elicit emotion, to touch the soul, based on its temporal nature:

> … what gives music its superior emotional power is its rhythmic advance. Time is a medium which appeals more than space to emotion… The visible world offers itself to our regard with a certain lazy indifference. "Peruse me," it seems to say, "if you will. I am here; and even if you pass me by now and later find it to your advantage to resurvey me, I may still be here." The world of sound speaks a more urgent language.[9]

Music as performance can only be experienced as a process, a sequence of events in time; this is true even for sound recordings, although the process can be repeated *ad nauseam*. In contrast, there is no process for experiencing physical art such as painting or sculpture; the whole experience is instantly presented to our senses. While for that instant such art may provoke feelings or visions of the sublime in the imagination, its continued presence allows us time to scrutinize and that initial pure experience is soon replaced in the memory by thoughts of analysis and interpretation, precisely the kind of "explanation" that to Stevens' mind destroys the divine illusion of art. As he explains when discussing our imaginative perception of art, "while its first effect may be extraordinary, that effect is the maximum effect that it will ever have."[10] For Stevens, the goal is to preserve that "first effect" in the memory such that we only remember the emotional experience of art, rather than our futile efforts to perceive art itself. In this context, music would seem to be an ideal model, for it is the most "real" artistic expression of experience, a force existing only for "a single moment, gone while we try to apprehend it."[11]

It is the combination of abstraction and temporality in music that seems to render it particularly appealing to Stevens as a subject and an aesthetic model for poetry. By virtue of its temporality, music is inherently difficult to scrutinize and seems to encourage a purely emotional reception to an extent far stronger than in most other art forms. As a non-signifying art form, music would also seem to express the "irrational" in the Stevensian sense of things that cannot be accounted for rationally,[12] of which emotion is a prime example. Santayana clearly echoes this point: "Hence the singular privilege of this art: to give form to what is naturally inarticulate, and express the depths of human nature which can speak no language current in the world."[13] Music is for Santayana, and I would argue for Stevens, a more primal, essential, and therefore authentic expression of the complexities of human experience than language.

Also of interest within this context is an article by Michael Faherty exploring the connections between Stevens' poetry and the musical theory of the abstract painter Wassily Kandinsky. In this article, Faherty describes how Kandinsky, like Walter Pater, believes that all artists should seek instruction from music, "since it this art form, above all others, that is free of the mimetic dictates of natural phenomena."[14] Like Santayana, Kandinsky regards human emotions, human nature, as abstract forces wholly foreign to the sensory phenomena that surround us. Therefore, since music also has little or no basis in natural phenomena, but does exist in the sensory world, Kandinisky employs it as a bridge through which he can translate emotion into visual images. As Faherty explains, "the note itself is merely the 'material' expression of a particular emotion."[15] This being the case, "Kandinsky argues that an individual form or color is, in a very similar sense, a 'symbol' of its own unique 'sound' capable of communicating a particular emotion."[16] I would argue that Stevens follows a very similar model in his poetry, creating tone or mood paintings through words instead of colours. Music, therefore, functions as an aesthetic rather than a formal model for Stevens, as he attempts to convey not its structure but its mood through his poetry.

This transition between emotion, music, and visual stimuli is very clearly illustrated in one of Stevens' early poems, "Peter Quince at the Clavier." This poem begins with a discursive proposition concerning the connection between music and emotion:

> Just as my fingers on these keys
> Make music, so the self-same sounds
> On my spirit make a music, too.
>
> Music is feeling, then, not sound;
> And thus it is that what I feel,
> Here is this room, desiring you,
>
> Thinking of your blue-shadowed silk,
> Is music.[17]

Stevens would seem to concur here with Kandinsky's proposition that music is the "material" expression of emotion, for Peter Quince claims that music is not merely remembered as feeling rather than sound, but that it is essentially feeling rather than sound.[18] Meyer and Baris make a particularly useful observation when they mention that in English "clavier" can sometimes refer to a toneless practice keyboard: "when practicing upon such a clavier the performer touches the silent keys while his mind 'knows' the sounds his fingers trace."[19] While there is no evidence in the poem to specifically support such a reading of "clavier," it would certainly fit with the proposition that Quince is making, for in this case both his feelings and the literal music are internalized, thus emphasizing the abstract nature of music and feeling in contrast to the story of Susanna that Quince uses as a metaphor to illustrate his feelings.

Stevens' use of the biblical story of Susanna in this context has puzzled and frustrated many readers and critics, prompting historical and feminist readings of the poem and numerous discussions of its moral implications. However, despite the content of the extra-textual biblical story, "Peter Quince" itself does not appear to express any strong moral tone, but rather attempts to manifest and explore the nature of aesthetic experience through a series of tone paintings, both auditory and visual. Quince's desire and that of the "red-eyed elders" is described in musical terms: "The basses of their beings throb/ In witching chords, and their thin blood/ Pulse pizzicati of Hosanna."[20] Thus, here the material expression of desire encompasses the sound of throbbing basses, witching chords, and pulsing Hosannas. This motif is contrasted by a tone painting of contentment. Susanna lies in "green water, clear and warm," feels "the touch of springs" and "the dew of old devotions," and sighs with pleasure at the melody of the whole setting.[21] In this case, the melody and the mood are created by a combination of sensory elements. It is a far more eclectic expression than the sharp sounds of the elders and may suggest a more "authentic aesthetic experience"[22] in contrast to their baser emotions. Other tone paintings include the more overt exhilaration of the elders upon seeing the fully nude figure of Susanna, manifested by crashing cymbals and roaring horns, and the sense of alarm from "her attendant Byzantines," expressed by "a noise like tambourines."

Stevens begins the last section of this poem with an unorthodox observation on the nature of beauty:

> Beauty is momentary in the mind—
> The fitful tracing of a portal;
> But in the flesh it is immortal.[23]

Here, I would regard beauty as a manifestation of Stevens' supreme fiction, immortal because it always exists in the flesh of youth, whether that of Susanna or the unnamed woman to whom Peter Quince addresses this poem. That "beauty is momentary in the mind" is amply demonstrated by the elders, who are exposed to Susanna's pure beauty but perceive only their own lustful impulses. They fail to appreciate "the substance and meaning of aesthetic experience"[24]; it traces only the portal of their senses, "the basses of their beings," and not that of their souls. This criticism also applies equally well to Peter Quince, who in *A Midsummer Night's Dream* constantly fails to appreciate the aesthetics of the theatre and interprets everything literally, and may explain Stevens' apparently otherwise idiosyncratic choice for placing this literary character in the poem. Ultimately, however, it is Susanna's music that escapes and, "in its immortality… makes a constant sacrament of praise." Stevens ends "Peter Quince at the Clavier" with music rather than the flesh serving as the material expression of beauty.

While the musical content of "Peter Quince at the Clavier" is obvious, in a number of Stevens' other poems in *Harmonium* he attempts to convey the mood of music without any specific reference to the medium itself. Two examples of this are "Thirteen Ways of Looking at a Blackbird" and "Six Significant Landscapes." In both of these poems Stevens employs a format similar to that of a concerto, connecting multiple independent movements by only a general and somewhat abstract theme. One of the unique characteristics of music is its ability to join seemingly incoherent juxtapositions together. This process would have been particularly appealing to Stevens, for the imagination and the thought processes of the mind also function in an irrational pattern, rather than following a logical or linear format. By utilizing disruptive rhetoric and juxtaposition, Stevens attempts to "escape simple representation and generate a relationship to reality comparable to the non-figurative expression of music."[25] In this sense, some of Stevens' work could be said to foreshadow the stream-of-consciousness style of many later twentieth-century poets.

Stevens describes "Thirteen Ways of Looking at a Blackbird" as a "group of poems… not meant to be a collection of epigrams or of ideas, but of sensations."[26] In this poem, the unifying theme is the figure of the blackbird, a symbol of the quotidian. While I feel that it would be a far too symbolic reading of this poem to equate the colour of the blackbird with darkness or evil, "Thirteen Ways" clearly expresses a somber tone. The quotidian is neither attractive, exciting, nor pleasant, but rather vaguely unsettling, since we do not "know" it as well as we often presume to. This sense of anxiety is most strongly articulated in the eleventh strophe, where a passenger in a glass coach mistakes "The shadow of his equipage/ For blackbirds."[27] The most obvious tone painting in the poem occurs in the sixth strophe:

> Icicles filled the long window
> With barbaric glass.
> The shadow of the blackbird
> Crossed it, to and fro.
> The mood
> Traced in the shadow
> An indecipherable cause.[28]

Here, a clear connection is made between a visual image and an ominous sense of foreboding. When Stevens speaks of "the mood traced in the shadow," he may be specifically referring to the way music evokes feeling, since the image of the shadow crossing the icicles is similar to the visual appearance of notes crossing a musical staff. The connection between mood and music is also emphasized in the eighth strophe, where Stevens concedes the influence of the quotidian, the blackbird, on our more powerful emotions, our "noble accents/ And lucid, inescapable rhythms,"[29] despite our preference for the more exotic "golden birds." Overall, in "Thirteen Ways" Stevens uses the "non-figurative expression of music" to present a juxtaposed collage of perceptual and cognitive constructions of the quotidian.

Unlike "Thirteen Ways," "Six Significant Landscapes" does not possess a single unifying theme, but rather presents a variety of cognitive perspectives on the world. Therefore, this poem is more abstract and "irrational" in its approach, focusing on the processes rather than the subjects of experience. However, like "Thirteen Ways" it explores how mood and sensation can be manifested through material expression. The first strophe is very much a visual tone painting designed to evoke a mood through visual description. In contrast, the second strophe presents a far more abstract image, a word painting designed to evoke a mood in much the same way that Kandinsky manifests mood through abstract forms and colours:

> The night is of the color
> Of a woman's arm:
> Night, the female,
> Obscure,
> Fragrant and supple,
> Conceals herself.
> A pool shines,
> Like a bracelet
> Shaken in a dance.[30]

While this passage does contain visual elements, they are irrational insofar as they have no basis in natural visual experience. "The color of a woman's arm" is a highly ambiguous image and certainly bears no literal relation to the colour, or lack thereof, of night. The image of the pool shining "like a bracelet… in a dance" represents a similar non sequitur. However, this passage clearly evokes an erotic mood by emphasizing and personifying the sensual connotations of night. Like Kandinsky, Stevens conveys the "sound" of a particular emotion, in this case through words rather than colours. This passage represents one of Stevens most successful attempts to capture the mood of music through words, for in this case his words are, like music, "free of the mimetic dictates of natural phenomena."[31]

Thus far, I have focused on the manifestation of musical emotion in Stevens' poetry. However, Stevens was also very interested in the impact that music can have upon the world we perceive, in "the notion of the imagination as a force that creates order through musical gestures."[32] The most famous example where Stevens explores this subject is "The Idea of Order at Key West"; however, many of the themes expressed in "Idea of Order" are foreshadowed in an earlier poem from *Harmonium* called "To the One of Fictive Music." This poem begins with an invocation praising the Muse as "sister and mother and diviner love," but the subject soon shifts in the second stanza to an intriguing discussion of how the imagination transforms the world around us:

> Now, of the music summoned by the birth
> That separates us from the wind and sea,

Yet leaves us in them, until the earth becomes,
By being so much of the things we are,
Gross effigy and simulacrum…[33]

The imagination may appear to be "the birth that separates us," removing us cognitively from natural phenomena while leaving us in it physically. However, given Stevens' general emphasis on the potential for abstraction and irrationality in the imagination, I would read this passage as illustrating a failure on the part of the Muse to truly remove us from the paradigms of natural phenomena. While this music may separate us from a literal awareness of "the wind and sea," the imaginative construction with which it replaces "the real world" is based on the same forms and structures, such that we are left with a "gross effigy and simulacrum."

This observation is further emphasized in the third stanza when Stevens describes how "That music is intensest which proclaims/ The near, the clear, and vaunts the clearest bloom/… That apprehends the most which sees and names."[34] Here, Stevens sees the imagination in a degenerated state, as a hollow shadow, a "gross effigy" of its former greatness. People find pleasure and hear music not in true aesthetic beauty, but in those things that are familiar and convenient; they also conceive the world only through explanation, by seeing and naming, in direct contrast to Stevens' preference for art that cannot be fixed or defined. Therefore, Stevens concludes the poem with a directive addressed to "the one of fictive music":

Yet not too like, yet not so like to be
Too near, too clear, saving a little to endow
Our feigning with the strange unlike, whence springs
The difference that heavenly pity brings.
For this, musician, in your girdle fixed
Bear other perfumes. On your pale head wear
A band entwining, set with fatal stones.
Unreal, give back to us what once you gave:
The imagination that we spurned and crave.[35]

Clearly, for Stevens art that is but a simulacrum of the sensory world we perceive is a waste of the imagination. In this passage, he exhorts the musician to convey "the strange unlike", the unreal, all those abstract and irrational elements of the human soul that both frighten and delight us, that we spurn and crave. For Stevens, the great power of the imagination is its ability to take us beyond the confines of the known, rational world, and here he declares the musician to be the artist best suited to this task.

In "The Idea of Order at Key West," Stevens finds the figure and the imaginative force that he seeks in "To the One of Fictive Music." While in the latter poem music creates only a "gross effigy," in "Idea of Order" the woman's singing is clearly distinguished from the natural phenomena surrounding her:

The sea was not a mask. No more was she.
The song and water were not medleyed sound
Even if what she sang was what she heard,
Since what she sang was uttered word by word.
It may be that in all the phrases stirred
The grinding water and the gasping wind;
But it was she and not the sea we heard.

For she was the maker of the song she sang.
The ever-hooded tragic-gestured sea
Was merely a place by which she walked to sing.[36]

This passage articulates a clear repudiation of the classic Romantic motif of natural inspiration. Like Wordsworth among the daffodils, Stevens' woman is wandering through a natural setting of obvious beauty, a bonanza for the senses. He concedes this, referring to "the dark voice of the sea" and "bronze shadows heaped/ On high horizons." "If it was only" this, the entire scene would be a very familiar one, almost a cliché. However, there is no apparent connection between the force of the sea and the force of the woman's singing. Here, once again, Stevens finds music to be free from the "dictates of natural phenomenon."

"But it was more than that"; the woman's singing is not merely independent of her surroundings; it actually "assimilates and transforms physical reality"[37]:

It was her voice that made
The sky acutest at its vanishing.
She measured to the hour its solitude.
She was the single artificer of the world
In which she sang. And when she sang, the sea,
Whatever self it had, became the self
That was her song, for she was the maker. Then we,
As we beheld her striding there alone,
Knew that there never was a world for her
Except the one she sang and, singing, made.[38]

This woman is the perfect embodiment of the potent poetic figure Stevens describes in "The Noble Rider" as one who "creates the world" and "gives to life the supreme fictions."[39] As "the single artificer of the world," she has full creative control, almost godly powers. Her order governs all things, mastering out the sky and portioning the hour. Furthermore, like the "pure music" that Santayana praises, it is wholly spontaneous and without "external significance."

The speaker in this poem can perceive no rational motivation for the woman's singing at this particular instant: the juxtaposition of her music against the physical setting is apparently pure coincidence. Hers is a kind of "ordered freedom, or free order,"[40] for she orders the world apparently without purpose, blissfully "striding" along the beach, unaware of the impact she is having on the world of the speaker's perception. Her art neither seeks nor requires any explanation; she seems content simply to enjoy the pure aesthetic experience of the world she has made and may, therefore, be expressing and experiencing a supreme fiction.

Stevens, assuming that he is the speaker/narrator of this poem, seems envious of this woman, for he provides no descriptive details about the content, the sound, of her singing, but rather dwells on her imaginative state. This woman seems wholly unaffected and uninfluenced by the rational world around her: her "fictive music, the voice of the imagination, because irrational, refuses to surrender to the pressure of reality."[41] This absolute freedom from reality, this utter indifference to comprehension and understanding, is precisely the kind of pure aesthetic experience that Stevens seeks in a supreme fiction. However, Stevens is also aware of the paradox that comprehending the nature of this experience leaves him incapable of experiencing it himself. As he explains in "The Noble Rider,"

> The case is, then, that we concede that the figure is all imagination. At the same time, we say that it has not the slightest meaning for us, except for its nobility. As to that, while we are moved by it, we are moved as observers. We recognize it perfectly. We do not realize it. We understand the feeling of it, the robust feeling, clearly and fluently communicated. Yet we understand rather than participate in it.[42]

As the observer, Stevens recognizes this woman's imaginative state but cannot realize it. The singer, by virtue of her blessed ignorance, her failure to recognize the "artifice" of imagination, is able to participate in an experience bordering on the divine. In contrast, Stevens' desire to participate in this same experience necessitates an awareness that renders this desire futile. Thus, he is left with his own Quixotic "blessed rage for order."

For Stevens, the act of experiencing art is more important than the nature of art itself. Art, like all the sensory material of the world around us, is something that we merely construct through our perception of it and therefore something that we can never truly know. Only the emotions, the aesthetic experiences generated by art, are real. Thus, art must be regarded as a process rather than a material product. Stevens, like Walter Pater, sees music as the ideal condition of art because it can only be experienced as process and therefore seeks to convey the emotional and aesthetic effects of musical process through poetry. Like the musician, he layers his poetry with disruptive rhetoric and discordant images, creating elaborate tone paintings designed to convey and evoke only pure emotion rather than impressions based on reference to external settings or experiences. At times, almost paradoxically, Stevens also attempts to comprehend, to "know" the aesthetic experience of music, despite his acknowledgment of the opposition between knowledge and experience. However, as the musician must practice constantly in order to be able to spontaneously and instinctually express beauty as the singer does in "The Idea of Order of Key West," so Stevens must practice his craft. Therefore, his efforts to understand the idea of order in music are undertaken with the goal of acquiring not the knowledge, but the skills of the musician, such that he may one day be able to spontaneously channel a supreme fiction through writing, embodying it in the process of reading.

Works Cited

Doreski, William. "Fictive Music: The Iridescent Notes of Wallace Stevens." *The Wallace Stevens Journal* 20, i (Spring 1996): 55-75.

Faherty, Michael. "Kandinsky at the Klavier: Stevens and the Musical Theory of Wassily Kandinsky." *WS Journal* 16, ii (Fall 1992): 151-60.

Holmes, Barbara. *The Decomposer's Art: Ideas of Music in the Poetry of Wallace Stevens*. New York: Peter Lang, 1990.

Meyer, Kinereth & Sharon Baris. "Reading the Score of 'Peter Quince at the Clavier': Stevens, Music, and the Visual Arts." *WS Journal* 12, i (Spring 1988): 56-67.

Needler, Howard. "On the Aesthetics of 'Peter Quince at the Clavier.'" *WS Journal* 18, i (Spring 1994): 50-62.

Pater, Walter. *The Renaissance: Studies in Art and Poetry*. Ed. Donald L. Hill. Berkley: U of California Press, 1980.

Santayana, George. "Music." *The Life of Reason*. New York: Prometheus Books, 1998. 315-24.

Sellin, Eric. *Valéry, Stevens, and the Cartesian Dilemma*. Brockport: Dept. of Foreign Languages, State University College of New York, 1975.

Stevens, Wallace. *Collected Poetry and Prose*. Eds. Frank Kermode & Joan Richardson. New York: Library of America, 1997.

—. *Letters of Wallace Stevens*. Ed. Holly Stevens. New York: Alfred A. Knopf, 1966.

III.

MUSICAL AESTHETICS AND THE MYSTICAL

UNSTABLE METAPHORS OF DIVINITY: PROUST'S THEOLOGY OF MUSICAL AESTHETICS

GREGORY ERICKSON

> Tones, which through rhythm and harmony are combined into melody and into the musical work of art, are not immediately natural sounds but are produced through mechanical art; not merely in order to subordinate them externally to the will of the striving spirit that rules them, but also to purify them of all special, finite meaning that, as alien content, would disturb and cloud the absolutely spiritual content with which they are to be imbued.[1]
>
> Christian Weisse

> And at the moment when, recovering my balance, I put my foot on a stone which was slightly lower than its neighbor, all my discouragement vanished and in its place was that same happiness which at various epochs of my life had been given to me . . . and of which the last works of Vinteuil had seemed to me to combine the quintessential character.[2]
>
> Marcel Proust

> Music is the catalytic element in the work of Proust. It asserts to his unbelief in the permanence of personality and the reality of art.[3]
>
> Samuel Beckett

Music/God

In his expansive novel À *la recherche du temps perdu*, Marcel Proust employs the ancient metaphor of God as artist that was resurrected in the late 19th and early 20th centuries. For Nietzsche, the creative artist "merges with the primal architect of the cosmos" (9); for Wallace Stevens, "God and the imagination are one" (178). Each author, as Mark C. Taylor puts it, "displaces divine creativity onto human creativity" (208), and this move is central in the work of Proust. Throughout À *la recherche*, God is rarely mentioned by name, but metaphorically the presence and absence of the Western God is felt in each carefully structured theme, character, and phrase. Proust's novel, however, is more about the *act* of creation than the presence of a divine. This focus is seen, for example, when Proust compares the creative powers of the painter Elstir to the divine creation of the world. The god-metaphor and the idea of art as religion are secondary to a never-ending process of creating and perceiving art. In Proust, neither pole of the metaphoric equation is as important as the cognitive efforts involved in reading the metaphor. Proust's implied "God," echoing thinkers from the medieval Kabbalah to Heidegger and Levinas, is a process, more verb than noun.

The very first paragraph of À la recherche establishes religion and art as interlaced themes. The famous opening, "for a long time I used to go to bed early," leads to the narrator describing his disorientation upon waking, after falling asleep reading. His semi-conscious thoughts juxtapose an item of religion with one of art: "it seemed to me that I myself was the immediate subject of my book: a church, a quartet" (I. 3). What further unites and complicates the two objects is that they each can be a work of art in themselves or a container for art. A church is a historical and political institution, an architectural structure, and a receptacle for art; a string quartet is a genre, a performing ensemble, and a piece of music. The triple movement of a container in its potential to surround, to take in, or to be an empty vacuum, is contained in the metaphorical play of both religious and artistic images.

If, for Proust, art is religion, then music is God. Music, as has often been pointed out, is the central artistic medium for the narrator of the novel. Music appears in the novel as the greatest of all the arts, and it provides the model on which the narrator seems to base his final epiphany. The music of Vinteuil and the famous "little phrase" resurface at important points throughout the work to both represent and initiate change in the narrator. Yet Proust's music, and in particular the "little phrase," creates a paradoxical god-idea that both suggests a unity and denies its possibility. Music's role in the novel strongly relates to and is created from the ideas surrounding both a determinate and the indeterminate God; one god that makes all meaning possible, and the other god who defies any possibility of knowledge. (The tension between a determinate and an indeterminate God is a theme of much postmodern theology, although it can also be located as far back as medieval Christian and Jewish mysticism.) [4]

We can first establish a superficial connection between the manner in which Proust portrays music and the traditional concept of a determinate Judeo-Christian god. As a metaphor, music represents, for the narrator, the artistic model by which he bases his path to a form of salvation. Although the moment of salvation—the moment in which he is touched by "grace"—happens through involuntary memory, it is clear that he feels music has prepared him for this moment. If we step back for a panoramic view of the world of the novel, music can be seen as the structuring device that holds the pieces together. The narrator clearly sees music as a model for organizing the pieces of his life—his loves, his friends, the places he has been—into a coherent whole. Like the determinate god-idea of totalization, the idea of music can create order out of chaos. How does this process happen? Is it convincing? Could there be a darker side, a negativity that reflects an indeterminate God? It is necessary to trace the path of music throughout the novel to begin to answer these questions.

*

An early scene, the narrator's first attempt at creating art to preserve or save a transcendent and religious moment, shows him struggling to achieve what he will later learn to do through music. As he is riding in a coach, Proust's young narrator is suddenly struck by the beauty and mystery of three distant church steeples. Beginning the connection between the life of art and its connection to the symbols and aesthetics of Christianity, the narrator first puts pen to paper to create a work of art. In an attempt to "penetrate to the core" of the church steeple's "impression," which "seem at once to contain and to conceal," he produces a "little fragment" of writing (I. 196). Getting carried away with his imagery, he describes the steeples moving and vanishing from his sight, comparing them to "three golden pivots," to flowers, and finally to "three maidens in a legend" (I.198). When finished, he feels that he has "entirely relieved [his] mind of its obsession with the steeples and the mystery which lay behind them" (I.198).

This short passage, about 200 pages into the work, richly suggests the theological and artistic themes that will permeate the rest of the novel. In Proust, art is experienced religiously and religions are experienced artistically. By putting the steeples in a frame where they switch positions, move, and shift, and by putting himself, the observer, in a moving position, the narrator participates in a characteristically modernist artistic experience.[5] But by sensing church steeples as pointers to a mysterious transcendence, the narrator is also taking part in a traditional Christian interpretation of steeples. The passage holds in it theologically related realizations that will hover over the whole work. Like all religious symbols and metaphors, the steeples both "contain and conceal." Like any art that attempts to capture religious or transcendent experiences, the narrator's piece is only a "fragment." As we shall see, these characteristics of Proust's whole project can perhaps subvert even his final realization and synthesis of art and religion. But more immediately, this scene of writing and religion is the first example in the novel of a pattern that will continue to be developed for the next 3000 pages.

When the narrator changes the steeples into three maidens we see the first example of a pattern that will continue throughout the novel: his insistence on eroticizing art into objects of desire. Each time he interacts with a work of art it will become inextricably intertwined in his memory with elements of his erotic desires, impeding his search for the essence of art. This is most significantly seen in his interaction with music and the composer Vinteuil.

As we follow these swirling but tightly organized themes of art and music through a complex systematic pattern of repetition and development, we can see how the narrator's changing perceptions of art mirror his developing view of the relationship between art and life, preparing him for his ultimate epiphany. His interactions with art repeatedly follow a similar process, a process that is in itself a microcosm of the narrator's life-long Search. When the narrator is exposed to a work of art, literature, or a piece of music, he will initially express confusion and a lack of comprehension. Following this confusion is a search for an explanation of the work, leading to partial or temporary truths. Finally, through memory, the essence of the work is seemingly penetrated.

This process is reenacted with every painting or piece of music in the novel, and it can be seen as a microcosm of the whole work. On the first page of the novel, the narrator is in bed half asleep, not understanding his surrounding world. The rest of the novel depicts the search for meaning, the partial truths, and the false paths that are recreated in his perception of art. Finally, at the end, the same process of memory leads him to what seems a complete understanding of both his life and art. As readers, our experiences mirror those of the narrator. As he experiences a deeper understanding due to the repetition of events, so we more clearly understand the repeated themes of the novel. As he experiences forgetting and partially remembering events, melodies and paintings, so do we barely remember a scent of these very things read a thousand pages before. It is this experience with each work of art and especially with music that mentally prepares both narrator and reader for the narrator's realizations in the last section of the novel.

While it is nothing new to point to these stages of perception,[6] what I want to focus on are the moments when the music is associated with desire, and then show through a musicological analogy, how the narrator's perception of music is a theological and religious quest that recreates the god-idea through its contradictory interpretive directions. From the musicological perspective, we will see in the narrator's aesthetic development, issues of perception that have been at the center of musicological and theological debate since before Proust's time to the present. By looking at the relationships between Vinteuil, his music, the narrator, and the novel, and by examining them in the light of theories of musical perception, we can more fully understand the relationship between the narrator's mental journey, the musical structure of the novel, and underlying religious and theological themes. Despite Proust's efforts to offer art and especially music as transcendent experiences that replace religion, the novel often resists this movement; it still exists within the paradoxical experience and epistemology of Western theology. From the religious and theological perspective, these aesthetic and musicological issues, like the church steeples will also both "contain and conceal."

These aesthetic and musicological issues are rooted in 19th century debate and discussion about the religion of art or "art religion," and about instrumental versus vocal music. The term "art religion" that was prevalent throughout the 19th century is thought to have been coined by Friedrich Schleiermacher.[7] In his *Lectures on Religion,* Schleiermacher urges a "religion of feelings" that can best be expressed by music.[8] This musical art/religion was a common way for writers to perceive music and the future of art and religion. For E.T.A. Hoffman, actual Christian art was on the decline while art religion, especially as practiced in music, was on the rise.[9] The future of both seemed clear. As Christianity faded as a practical source of spiritual enlightenment, secular art and especially music would take its place.

Listening to Proust's Music

Biographers of Proust have devoted much space to locating the real life "models" and events in Proust's life that he translated into Vinteuil, his music, and the famous "little phrase." Drawing from the novel's descriptions of the music, as well as Proust's life and letters, George Painter mentions Wagner, Fauré, Saint-Saëns, Franck, Debussy, and Beethoven as models for Vinteuil and his music. Painter connects Proust's description of the Vinteuil Septet ("continuous plane surfaces like those of the sea, amid a harsh silence, an infinite void" [III. 249]) as being "beyond doubt" the first movement of Debussy's *La Mer* (246).[10] The most direct source of Vinteuil and his septet, according to Painter, is César Franck. Painter cites as direct influences Franck's String Quartet in D, his Violin Sonata, and his Piano Quintet in F Minor. He also demonstrates some parallel passages in the Quintet and the Sonata that suggest the scene where the narrator is impressed by the further developments of themes from the Vinteuil Sonata in the later Septet.

What is more important than issues of direct influence is that these composers, especially Franck, Debussy, and Wagner, were composers writing *cyclical* works. These are pieces where themes and motifs repeat and echo across movements or, in Wagner's case, use a system of leitmotifs, where the essential musical structure of a work is composed of the appearance and reappearance of themes associated with a person or an idea. These innovative musical styles can be seen as models for Vinteuil's music and, in a larger context, as models for Proust's whole work. Although aspects of sonata form and the symphony can be located in Proust's structure, Wagner's leitmotif method seems the most apt model for the whole work.[11] The parallel is apparent in Proust's interweaving of many motifs that are prepared for, repeated, and transformed, but never completed; and in his use of this system to construct a work of epic proportion.

This structuring is not only musical but borrows from Biblical typology, where a theme from the Old Testament is perceived as being developed and ultimately completed in the New Testament. Each of the narrator's experiences with a place will be repeated both literally and in his memory. Each of the narrator's experiences with a woman, for example, follows and expands on the themes of the previous relationship; Odette becomes Gilberte who becomes Albertine. This is especially relevant when the path of music and its perception seems to lead teleologically to an ultimate completion that can only be understood from the point of view of this ending. This kind of cycle, by which the new completes the old, but where the new is never whole without the old, is characteristically Christian in its development, and cannot be fully appreciated outside of this context.

*

While Elstir and Vinteuil produce the most important works of art that the narrator encounters in his life, the significant difference is that while we really only "see" the work of Elstir once, the music of Vinteuil appears often. Presented with repeated opportunities to listen to the music of Vinteuil, the narrator must change how he "hears" before learning to hear the "truth" in the music. Only then is he able to seemingly understand the complex relationship between music and life, and to open his mind to his final redemptive vision.

The music of Vinteuil makes nine extended appearances during the whole of the work. Each of these scenes shows the same stages of development, shows the narrator (or in some cases his alter ego Charles Swann) struggling with the perception of the music, glimpsing some sort of possible truth or transcendence that the music can offer, and ultimately creating a feminized and erotic association that replaces the experience of the music and leaves him disappointed. Although music will ultimately claim a God-like power to reveal the absolute and to rule over the whole of the narrator's Search, it appears in most scenes to offer only a flash or glimpse of a possibility of a transcendent religious experience. So while music will come to appear as a form of God, it is best understood theologically as glimpses of the possibility of Proustian *grace*, to use Georges Poulet's label.

The music is first heard by Swann, who, like the narrator, has trouble initially comprehending a work of art: "At first he had appreciated only the material quality of the sounds which [the] instruments secreted" (I. 227). Following exactly the perception and associative pattern of the narrator's first writing experience, Swann first compares a phrase to "the fragrance of certain roses," and finally to a "woman he has seen for a moment passing by." This early scene starts to develop the idea of the necessity of memory to aesthetic perception. Swann is moved by the music, but as he has no memory of it, its effect is fleeting:

> But the notes themselves have vanished before these sensations have developed sufficiently to escape subversion under those which the succeeding or even simultaneous notes have already begun to awaken in us. And this impression would continue to envelop in its liquidity its ceaseless overlapping, the motifs which from time to time emerge, to plunge again and disappear. (I. 228)

What listening to the piece and especially the "little phrase" does for Swann, at least temporarily, is to give him the impression of a new hope for life: "It seemed, for a time, to open up before Swann the possibility of a sort of rejuvenation" (I. 229). Swann, trying to understand, "wished to acquire its secret" (I. 230), but he will never move past this temporary feeling of transcendence. What keeps him from understanding the music, the novel seems to suggest, is his obsessive association of the music, and especially the little phrase, with his desire, love, and jealousy for Odette. By giving the music human form, by making artistic desire erotic, he loses the access to pure experience.

Although the music appears several more times during Swann's narrative, the most important development occurs after the music has been passed along to the narrator. The music and the little phrase are introduced to the narrator in a scene at Swann's home where Odette is playing the piano. The narrator, like Swann, can hear nothing at first: "But often one hears nothing when one listens for the first time to a piece of music that is at all complicated" (I. 570). He moves beyond Swann's perceptions when he begins to understand that "probably what is wanting, the first time, is not comprehension but memory" (I. 570). This leads to a musing on the joys of difficult art, the examples of which are the late Beethoven string quartets. Difficulty, the narrator implies, and the longer it takes a listener or the public to come to understand a piece, is directly related to the work's greatness and the composer's genius.

But the narrator—again turning church steeples into maidens—is, like Swann, distracted by desire. "If I did not understand the sonata, I was enchanted to hear Mme. Swann play. Her touch appeared to me . . . like her wrapper, like the scent of her staircase, like her coats, like her chrysanthemums" (I. 573). One is reminded here of the narrator's description of his book as not "like a cathedral, but quite simply like a dress." *True* structure, this metaphor ironically suggests, is a container without the core. In each case we have a garment without a woman representing the essence of art itself. If we take, like Jacques Derrida, Mark Taylor, and Kenneth Burke, the "book" to be a theological unit, this reflects by analogy, a religious structure without the God; Christianity represented by only an empty tomb.

The process of artistic recognition and erotic diversion will continue throughout the novel. The Sonata and its little phrase become associated as emblems of desire as much for the narrator as they were for Swann. The narrator's association will pass in time from Odette to Swann's daughter, Gilberte, to his next love, Albertine, but it will continue to be his primary connection to the music.

The next significant appearance of the music of Vinteuil is much later, when the narrator plays the Sonata in solitude. This is the only time in the novel that he plays the Sonata himself. Feeling, for the moment, at peace about his relationship with Albertine, he is briefly able to separate the music from the feelings of jealousy and desire that it usually conjures up in him: "approaching the sonata from another point of view, regarding it in itself as the work of a great artist" (III. 155). Yet, he only hears the music "in itself" for a short time before he lets the music take him back to his childhood and his dreams of becoming an artist: "Could life console me for the loss of art? Was there in art a more profound reality, in which our true personality finds an expression that is not afforded it by the activities of life?" (III.155). As he plays the passage, the narrator's thoughts turn to Wagner. He murmurs "Tristan," and as he looks at the Wagner score he is

> struck by how much reality there is in the work of Wagner as I contemplated once more those insistent, fleeting themes which visit an act, recede only to return again and again, and, sometimes distant, drowsy, almost detached, are at other moments, while remaining vague, so pressing and so close, so internal, so organic, so visceral, that they seem like the reprise not so much of a musical motif as of an attack of neuralgia. (III. 156)

We can read this passage as Proust describing his method of composition, relating it to the Wagnerian leitmotifs; we can read it as an account of our experience of reading Proust; we can read it as an existential Kierkegaardian expression of the quest for a true Christianity. But we can also see here the narrator making an advance by beginning to break with the Wagnerian method of association as well as with the way he has perceived music up to this point in the work. For the first time music is described formalistically, unattached to specific emotions or memories. Although it is not clear from the text *how*, the narrator receives a temporary revelation as the music helps him to "descend into [himself], to discover new things" (III. 156).

The longest and most significant scene of music listening occurs late in the novel as the narrator hears a performance at the same salon where Swann first heard the Vinteuil Sonata. Vinteuil's final work is being performed: his Septet. In an extended passage, the narrator comes to the realization that art is more than a prolongation of life; it is "more real than life itself" (III.256). This realization seems to be triggered by his perception that the Septet contains many of the same themes as the Sonata, but that they have been transformed into a richer work. The "lily-white sonata" has become a "glowing" Septet, as it takes up "the same phrase again and again," exploring "profound" similarities and differences. This scene takes place after a long gap in time, and as the narrator listens he is surrounded and distracted by all the people and memories that have inhabited his world—the whole material of the novel so far: the narrator's "Sonata world," so to speak. Like Vinteuil, the narrator will ultimately have to rework his early material into a richer work of art. In the final scene he will again be surrounded by these same people; however, they will no longer be a distraction from art, but—reworked into a richer form—the very material of it—an artistic development the narrator learns from music, and that Proust learns from Christian art. Religious art, to produce a true response, cannot just represent the past, but must suggest and include the present.

The final appearance of Vinteuil's music occurs, appropriately, with the psychologically sinking narrator lying in bed while Albertine plays for him on the piano. As she plays, he realizes that music expresses something that is impossible to express any other way; that art is "something even more than the merely nerve-tingling joy of a fine day," and that if art did not "correspond to some definite spiritual reality . . . life would be meaningless" (III.381). It is in this scene that the narrator begins to understand that music can be "truer" to life than literature, not despite its abstract nature, but *because* of it:

> Music seemed to me truer than all known books. At moments I thought that this was due to the fact that, what we feel about life not being felt in the form of ideas, its literary, that is to say intellectual expression describes it, explains it, analyzes it, but does not *recompose it as does music*, in which the sounds seem to follow the very movement of our being. (III. 381, emphasis mine)

Music again is truer *becaus*e it is separate from life. However, desire and jealousy again pull him away from this realization:

> Vinteuil's phrases made me think of the "little phrase" and I told Albertine that it had been as it were the national anthem of the love of Swann and Odette, "the parents of Gilberte, whom I believe you know. You told me she was a bad girl. Didn't she try to have relations with you? She spoke to me about you." (III. 383)

Following the pattern we have been tracing, the narrator—again turning steeples into maidens—loses his trail to salvation just when he is on the edge of discovering it.

Although experiences with music have led the narrator to question his relationship to art and to life, it is literature, a reading of the "Goncourt

Journals," (Proust's fictional rendering of the well-known brothers's journals) that causes him to finally resign himself to a life without art, and to give up his life-long desire to write. He feels that he does not "know how to look or listen" (III. 737).

Reading the Journals, the narrator senses, but does not at first see, that the "realism" of the journals lacks "truth" because, while full of minute details, they ignore perception: the experience of the impression. This is a lesson he first learned not from music, but from painting. In Elstir's studio he realizes while looking at his impressionist seascapes that there is more "truth" in Elstir's paintings because he had "reproduce[d] things not as he knew them to be but according to the optical illusion of which our first sight of them is composed" (I. 897). Following the familiar pattern, however, this Ruskinian lesson is lost for the narrator when this visit provides his first view of Albertine ("Do you know that girl, Monsieur?"), with whom the works of Elstir will now be associated. What he will not realize until the end of the novel is that, like a religious mystic (or Dorothy in The Wizard of Oz), he has possessed the means to redemption within himself all along, given to him by art, and especially by the music of Vinteuil.

The Music of the Absolute

On the eve of his epiphany at the Guermantes party, the narrator tries to conjure up some feelings of happiness by recalling Venice. He feels nothing but boredom and disappointment at this mere mental and verbal "snapshot," which lacks the "reality" he craves. It is at this very moment that his stumbling over a paving stone reminds him of the *essence* of Venice and the "sensation" of being at St. Marks. Although it is not music that triggers his realization, through music and the ideas of music he can finally understand the relationship between art, life, and memory.

> And at the moment when, recovering my balance, I put my foot on a stone which was slightly lower than its neighbor, all my discouragement vanished and in its place was that same happiness which at various epochs of my life had been given to me . . . *and of which the last works of Vinteuil had seemed to me to combine the quintessential character.* (III. 898-899, emphasis mine)

This experience of involuntary memory enables him to discover his "true life," to discover "reality as we have felt it to be, which differs so greatly from what we think it is that when a chance happening brings us an authentic memory of it we are filled with an immense happiness" (III. 915). So how does music do this? With intensely experienced moments of art, beauty, and emotion in the narrator's life, what is it about the musical experience that makes it the primary art in the true "reality"? How is it that his experiences of listening to music, which have been intense since his youth, can suddenly combine with events of his life to offer an answer to his Search?

Some insight can be found in Proust's traversing of a fundamental debate among composers, musicologists and aesthetic philosophers that arose in the nineteenth and early twentieth centuries. This split is between what are often referred to as the absolutists and the referentialists. To absolutists the "meaning" of music lies exclusively in the musical process alone; the "language" of music can refer only to itself, not to anything outside of music. The leading proponent of this position in the nineteenth century was Eduard Hanslick: "Music can whisper, storm, roar— tenderness and anger are carried only in our own hearts."[12] On the other side of this debate are the referentialists, for whom the meaning of music is associated with its communication of images, experiences, and specific emotional states. Oratorios, masses, program music, and Arnold Schering's "hidden programs" in Beethoven's symphonies would be examples. In the middle we find someone like Schopenhauer, who, although he proclaimed the power of a textless "absolute" music, also saw it as the most powerful and precise language for art because it could directly represent human emotions. [13]

This debate began around 1800. Until then the prevailing idea of music—going back to Plato—was that it needed *logos*: language as an expression of human reason. Either music had to contain words or it needed to be supplied with a program. Around 1800, a whole new way of thinking about music developed. According to advocates of "absolute" music, words were "outside" of music, and purely instrumental music was no longer considered "beneath" language, but above it and, in fact, as containing the essence of musical experience. Gradually the idea of absolute music became the "aesthetic paradigm of 19th century musical culture," and this continued through the 20th.[14]

Both sides of this debate were caught up in a web of theological assumptions, both conscious and intentional and subconscious and unintentional. While earlier musical forms had derived from religious practices and settings of sacred and religious texts, absolute music found justification in that it could be listened to and appreciated with "devotion" despite its lack of specific reference.[15] Absolutists insisted that this "wordless" music would be "elevated" above speech.[16] This "pure" music then is justified on the ground that it is a *more* religious experience, *because* it is not connected to a sacred text. The issue centers around what kind of music leads one to the divine or the transcendent experience, leading to the ontological questions of defining just what it was they were aiming towards. Was the proper target of devotion the traditional Judeo-Christian personal figure that could be addressed or a more abstract "Absolute" that was an experience beyond words?

For many 19th century thinkers, "absolute" music was where the religious Absolute could truly manifest itself—a religious and spiritual idea that could only be realized through art. "What Hegel said of the ancient statue of a god—that the religious idea is not merely 'symbolized' but is immediately present in it—was transferred . . . to modern instrumental music."[17] On the other hand, for Kierkegaard, the "indeterminate" nature of instrumental music is an "imperfection."[18] But ironically, Kierkegaard's interpretation of a God that is unknowable proposes an essential nature of the Divine that is indeterminate. So although Kierkegaard shows his disapproval of instrumental and absolute music, he has linked it with a religious spirit in much the same way other more Hegelian thinkers have. Carl Dahlhaus contrasts Kierkegaard's with Adorno's view:

> As opposed to language that means something, music is language of a completely different type. In that type lies its theological aspect. What it says is an appearance simultaneously determined and hidden. Its idea is the form of the name of God. It is . . .the human attempt, though futile as always, to speak the name itself, not to impart meanings.[19]

The Idea in music, the statement without words, becomes the name of God, yet it still remains outside of human contact.

Writing about Proust, Beckett said "music is the Idea itself, unaware of the world of phenomena, existing ideally outside the universe."[20] Early 20th century composers, like Schoenberg, agreed that musical structure was non-referential but insisted that it still had ideas that needed to correspond to the "laws of human logic,"[21] which echoes Proust's narrator's realization that music seems to "follow the very movement of our being" (III. 381). As Proust wrote in his preface to *Sesame and Lilies*, "music, unlike language, bears no trace of material things . . . never speaks to us of men, but imitates the movements of the soul."

Early in the novel we can see these very issues played out and debated in the mind of Swann as, affected by the "little phrase" of Vinteuil, he perceives musical motifs as "actual ideas, of another world, of another order, ideas veiled in shadow, unknown, impenetrable to the human mind, but none the less perfectly distinct from one another, unequal among themselves in value and significance" (I. 379-380). These thoughts are close to those of an absolutist and sound like something Schoenberg could have said, but on further analysis of his impressions of the phrase Swann realizes that he is basing this "conclusion not upon the phrase itself, but merely upon certain equivalents, substituted (for his mind's convenience) for the mysterious entity of which he had become aware" (I. 380).

Swann here sets in dialogue the two sides of the issue, both trying to hear music as itself *and* as symbolic or representative of something else. This debate is very significant in our effort to understand the narrator and his search to make sense of life and art. As we have seen, he consistently associates music with his own emotions. Specific events and feelings of love, jealousy, desire, optimism, and hopelessness are all associated for him with the music of Vinteuil. Yet, as I have also tried to show, these same feelings seem to keep him from truly experiencing the music and from fully experiencing the transcendence that the music suggests to him. Because he attaches the music to specific emotion, and because specific emotions like love and jealousy—at least in Proust—will always fade, so will the music's "meaning." The theological side of this resides in the mystic argument—from Pseudo-Dionysius to Meister Eckhart—that to give any specific attribute to God is to lose some of what God essentially "is."

There is always a question of just how absolute music can be, and it is clear that it must have *some* meaning for the narrator. For absolutists from Hanslick to Schoenberg, the problem has been to articulate what music can *mean* if it has no referential meaning. For Wagner, who first coined the term absolute music (*absoluten musik*), and who was greatly influenced by Schopenhauer, "music can only be understood in forms drawn from a relationship to life. . . forms that, originally foreign to music, only receive their deepest meaning through music."[22] For Nietzsche, drama (i.e. Wagner) could only reproduce the appearance of things, while music could capture their true nature.[23] Hanslick pushed the idea of absolute music even further towards the abstract.

In the 1950's, in his influential *Emotion and Meaning in Music*, Leonard Meyer offered musicologists a new vocabulary for analyzing the effects and meaning of music. Recognizing the persuasive argument of the absolutists, Meyer also realized the problems inherent in their position: "[I]f the term 'meaning' is to have any significance at all as applied to music, then it must have the same signification as when applied to other kinds of experience." The challenge for Meyer, and for Proust's narrator, is to locate this meaning without falling victim to the "propensity to regard all meanings arising in human communication as designative, as involving symbolism of some sort.[24]

Meyer locates meaning in the listener, and more specifically in the way the music creates—and then fulfills, denies, or delays—expectations. A "musical event . . . has meaning because it points to and makes us expect another musical event. This is what music means from the viewpoint of the absolutist."[25] For the narrator, as well, the meaning is found in the perceiver: "It is only a clumsy and erroneous form of perception which places everything in the object, when really everything is in the mind" (III. 950). For Schopenhauer, music perception must be a "selfless aesthetic contemplation," concentrating on the music, not distracted by the "coincidental stirrings of one's own spirit."[26] Listened to correctly then, music will "seem to reveal the innermost sense of the things and appear as its most correct and clearest commentary."[27]

Only when Proust's narrator realizes that reality lies not in the feelings and emotions that music conjures up, but in the functioning of the pure music itself, is he able to understand the transcendent force of music. In the abstraction of music, not distracted by words or referential images, he feels a separate world created—a world that embodies a "purely mental character of reality" (III. 953).

In music, a phrase of music can never be the same from one listening to another, even within a single listening of a piece. For example, a formal analysis of Bach's *Goldberg Variations* would describe it as a theme followed by variations over the same harmonic progression followed by an exact repetition of the original theme. To a listener, however, when the theme returns it is enriched and changed by the experience of having listened to the variations. One hears different moods, rhythms and harmonies internally because of what has just been listened to. There can never be an exact repetition in art or life, and when the narrator begins to see this in music he can also relate it to his social experiences: "How often had all these people re-appeared before me in the course of their lives, the diverse circumstances of which seemed to present the same individuals always, but in forms and for purposes that were shifted and varied!" (III. 1019). The listening experiences the narrator has responded to have included the anticipation, remembering, and forgetting which Meyer associates with the "meaning" of music. Proust's narrator will also find that this applies to his impressions of events and people: "this forgetfulness which modifies for us our image of a human being" (III.1011). This forgetfulness, as much as memory, also applies to the reader's experience in the novel. Even the reading of the Proustian sentence is an experience in memory. Like a long melody by Mahler, part of the perception process involves trying to remember where the line began. It is music, then, that is most important to the narrator's realization that nothing is stable. Like the supposedly unchanging melody that is constantly being heard differently "all that seemed to be forever fixed is constantly being re-fashioned" (III. 1072).

The "reality" of music lies in its nature of creating (with the perceiver) a past, a present, and a future, *of its own*, through memory and expectations. Music teaches the narrator to see himself and others, not as a "snapshot," but as a succession of events and a succession of perceptions. Specific associations or referential memories can prohibit this experience from occurring. Ironically, only when music becomes separate from the outside material world does it acquire a reality more true than nature. Only when the narrator allows music to become absolute (and to become the Absolute), does it help him to see how he must live his life—and how he can merge his life *and* his art. Time is regained, not through static but fading memories and associations, but through the shifting, subjective reality for which the model is music.

Listening Again: The Absence of the Absolute

Having followed one specific path, at this point we seem to have come to a sort of closure. Our logical argument has led us to an understanding of the role of music in Proust's work and its relationship to his secular/religious aesthetic. But a path is never direct and never leads in only one direction. The tropes, themes, and metaphors around which we locate elements of the theological can always be seen to create fields of instability rather than stability. Relationships to the god-idea and its metaphors are always both determinate and indeterminate. Can this path lead us in another direction?

Barthes says that Proust's "good fortune" is that "from one reading to the next we never skip the same passages."[28] If we read and experience Proust's scenes of music yet again, using his method of circles, cycles, and folding back in upon himself, we can re-evaluate our conclusions and the idea of music as the determinate God of Proust's art religion.

Contemporary musicologists no longer engage in evaluative debates about absolute and referential or program music. Postmodern thought has questioned the assigning of inside and outside and the concept of "extra-musical" upon which theories of absolute music depend. The idea of absolute music is now seen as an impossible and idealized category. The latter part of the 20th century has seen a renewed interest in musical hermeneutics and in discussion of musical meaning, and all music and texts are interpreted within some type of context. This view is reflected in the title of Berthold Hoeckner's book *Programming the Absolute*, where he writes "today . . . the idea (and ideology) of absolute music has finally lost its privileged position in Western art music and it is no longer a dominating paradigm in the scholarly study thereof. Absolute music has become relative."[29] There is no more Absolute.

Musicologist Susan McClary points to an association of absolute music with traditionally gendered plot lines, something constantly questioned in Proust. Proust's eroticized musical experiences are both penetrating and embracing, both masculine and feminine, and if Proust's feminization and eroticizing of music is one way to point to a certain binary relationship, perhaps it is also a way to problematize it, to rip it away from history and binary relationships.[30] As Gilles Deleuze says, we are always reading Proust from two distinct viewpoints: from the viewpoint of an "apprenticeship in progress," and from the viewpoint of a "final revelation."[31] These terms apply as much to us as to the narrator, and my first conclusion puts too much emphasis on the final revelation; it is limited and Christian-rooted and implies a teleological movement towards the narrator's salvation. But that is only one type of movement. The movement of both plot and musical perception are much more complicated.

If "only art gives us what we vainly seek in our beloved,"[32] then once art has given us that do we still find desire? Julia Kristeva considers the "risk of desiring another person" to be the most interesting element of eroticism; theologian Charles Winquist sees "desire" as being the central theme of all theology. For both the reader of Proust and for his narrator, having escaped or transcended the erotic through art—in a pseudo-religious process that necessarily includes desire and the erotic—do we then double back to include it? Has it always already been there? Should we think of the narrator's perception of music as not *referentially* erotic but *absolutely* so? In other words, the narrator's musical experiences must contain the erotic and desire; they don't exist outside of this context.

In his reading of Proust, Deleuze focuses on the separation of the sign of art from the sensual sign. Each, he says, offers a different type of "time regained."[33] But as the text draws the reader back in, time reverses, and the eroticization of art seems a necessary step: a step that is *absolutely* part of the musical experience, and therefore of the music. It is impossible to separate Proust's ideas of the sacredness of music and erotic desire. (The narrator even compares not understanding art to being a virgin.) And in the "time regained" of art, the erotic moments are *saved* along with the rest of the narrator's life, so that they are not now distractions from the essence of art, but erotic moments in that art itself.

By concentrating on teleology we fall into the trap of viewing art through a traditional and Christian goal-oriented time frame. We ignore process: of reading, listening, desiring, and of metaphor. As Kristeva points out, Vinteuil's music exists entirely in metaphorical terms, and as she says, it is a "reversible" metaphor: both woman is music and music is woman. In the same way both religion is art and art is religion. And as musicologist Leo Treitler suggests, the "expressive effect of metaphor is musical."[34] The power of metaphor is not in what it says or even in what it describes, but in the creative process involved in its perception—an "erotics" of perception that exists in listening to music or in reading Proust. The process of reading Proust seems to suggest that if art does have a relationship to life, it is ultimately in the complexity of the response: the "unstable opposition, the original complication."[35] Music not only "contains and conceals," it also creates and erases the Absolute. So while the theological and dialectical tension of absolute and referential music provides a starting point, while Hanslick and Schopenhauer provide some context, perhaps the best way to listen to the language of music in Proust is through the metaphor of sleep and the sensuous dream—the scene of confusion where the novel begins.

Works Cited

Barthes, Roland. *The Pleasure of the Text.* Trans. Richard Miller. New York: Hill and Wang, 1975.

Beckett, Samuel. Proust. New York: Grove Press, 1931.

Dahlhaus, Carl. *The Idea of Absolute Music*. Trans. by Roger Lustig. Chicago: University of Chicago Press, 1989.

Derrida, Jacques. *The Gift of Death*. Trans. By David Wills. Chicago: University of Chicago Press, 1996.

—. "Living On," in *Deconstruction and Criticism*, ed. Harold Bloom. New York: Seabury Press, 1979, pp 75-82.

Derrida, Jacques and Gianni Vattimo, eds. *Religion*. Stanford: Stanford University Press, 1996.

Deleuze, Giles. *Proust and Signs*. New York: George Braziller, 1972.

Hanslick. Eduard. *The Beautiful in Music*. 1854. New York: Bobbs-Merrill Co., 1957

Hoeckner, Berthold. *Programming the Absolute: Nineteenth-Century German Music and the Hermeneutics of the Moment*. Princeton: Princeton University Press, 2001.

Hughes, Robert. *The Shock of the New*. New York: Alfred A Knopf, 1991.

Kierkegaard, Søren. *Either/Or. Trans. George L. Stengren. New York: Harper and Row,* 1986.

Kristeva, Julia. *Time and Sense: Proust and the Experience of Literature*. New York: Columbia University Press, 1996.

McClary, Susan. "The Impromptu that Trod on a Loaf: Or How Music Tells Stories." *Narrative* (Jan. 1997) 20-35.

Meyer, Leonard. *Emotion and Meaning in Music*. Chicago: University of Chicago Press, 1967.

Nattiez, Jacques. *Proust as Musician*. Trans. Derrick Puffer. Cambridge: Cambridge University Press, 1989.

Nietzsche, Frederich. *The Birth of Tragedy*. 1872. Trans. by Shawn Whiteside. London: Penguin Books, 1993.

Painter, George. *Marcel Proust: A Biography*. New York: Random House, 1989.

Prieto, Eric. *Listening in: Music, Mind, and the Modernist Narrative.* Lincoln: University of Nebraska Press, 2003.

Proust, Marcel. *Remembrance of Things Past* Vol. I-III. Trans. by C.K. Scott Moncrieff and Terence Kilmartin. New York: Vintage Books, 1981.

—. *On Reading Ruskin*. New Haven: Yale University Press, 1987.

Robinson, Jenefer, ed. *Music and Meaning*. Ithaca: Cornell University Press, 1997.

Schoenberg, Arnold. *Style and Idea: Selected Writings*. Trans. by Leo Black. Berkeley: University of California Press, 1975.

Stevens, Wallace. *Opus Posthumous.* Milton Bates, ed. New York: Vintage Books, 1990.

Taylor, Mark. *About Religion: Economies of Faith in Virtual Culture*. Chicago: University of Chicago Press, 1999.

Treitler, Leo. "Language and the Interpretation of Music." Robinson 23-56.
—. "Postmodern Signs in Musical Studies." *Journal of Musicology*, 13/1 (1995).
Winquist, Charles. *Desiring Theology*. Chicago: University of Chicago Press, 1994.

SILENT MUSIC IN JAMES JOYCE'S SIRENS

ENRICO TERRINONI

'Sirens', the eleventh episode of *Ulysses*, is a key passage to the understanding of many interwoven symbols, hidden behind the organization of the book and its structure. Its importance lies in the unveiling of particular truths concealed either by means of very subtle allusions, or by certain secret equations between distant levels of meaning, all pointing to a very subliminal underlying logic. An investigation about the actual nature of particular occult connections of the episode may help us to trace back narrative patterns leading to the revelation of both aspects. In 'Sirens', a peculiar complexity of narration unfolds itself in the subtle game of concealing and revealing some obscure implications of music.

On a textual and superficial level, the first obvious correspondence of the chapter is the one between the overture-like beginning and the developing of the themes alluded in the first pages, before the orchestral exhortation 'Begin'[1] takes place. The relationship is the first musical metaphor we encounter, and introduces us to the general atmosphere of 'Sirens', accordingly the most "musical" of all the episodes of the book.

The reasons of this assumption have become commonplaces in Joyce criticism; in fact, beside the mere musical effects of the episode on a textual level, in the *Ulysses* schemas we find explicit links to the musical dimension. 'Music' is the 'art', 'fuga per canonem' is the 'technique', 'sounds' and embellishments' are the 'symbols'. The musical aspects of 'Sirens' have been in fact explored by many critics so far, and the amount of pages written about them is so large to discourage anyone from the task of writing anything original on the subject. Yet I feel that some ground is still open to speculation, for certain narrative patterns of the episode happen to exhale distantly a faint odour of secrecy. Jules Law believes that the possibility of displacing the meaning of the episode appears to be 'framed by a political context (signalled most immediately by the passing of the viceregal cavalcade) which it is Bloom's project to repress and avoid'.[2] Despite the nature of the critic's conclusions, indeed opposite to mine, a general statement in the beginning of the analysis – the title of the first paragraph being 'The "outside" of music' – seems to suggest a useful approach to the present perspective:

> I begin not so much out of an active impatience with music in "Sirens" as with a conviction that some of the most intriguing developments in the chapter occur "outside" its psycho-philosophical meditation on music, and indeed, outside the Ormond bar, saloon, and restaurant altogether. [3]

In my view, the "outside" of music happens to be utterly distant from any political interpretation. As a matter of fact it is rather an "inside", it dealing with some occult implications of the chapter, and with the value they retain in connection with the development of certain themes in other particular places of the book seen as a whole. This way of appraising 'Sirens', and generally speaking *Ulysses* itself, will show also that some of the strange references we find in the schemas could be seen in a new light, and the link between them and the text can acquire a certain logical coherence. This is the case, for example, of 'the sweet cheat' as the 'sense/meaning' and 'promises' as one of the 'symbols'. One of the explanations, as we will see in due time, lies in what I call the Swedenborgian correspondence for the 'organ': 'ear'.

As always, with regards to *Ulysses*, we must distinguish several levels of understanding: those sharing a sort of superficial meaning and those which belong to the field of allusions. In this analysis I have decided to deal with a special kind of allusions which is far from general, and also distinct from any idea of metaphor we are commonly accustomed. I chose in fact to take into account what I call 'the secret level' of the text, and speculate whether or not it may correspond to any of the superficial levels. Obviously, when I say 'superficial' I don't mean either simple or futile. My intention is broader and rather refers to a kind of general sense of the episode, similar to the first effect upon the reader after a very linear reading.

Having stated this, in order to complete this brief *overture* of mine, I must add that, together with the Swedendorgian explanation, the second connection which can link superficial levels of understanding and secret ones, is the relationship with the tradition, the techniques and some general ideas of the Kabbalah. I will proceed now to analyze singularly the main features of the episode, distinguishing whether they belong to the first or to the second level of understanding, and try to explain what the connection between them might be.

The sad magic of music

Of all the various themes a chapter like 'Sirens' may suggest, I chose those I believe to be the most important in this context, their implications being the broadest and peculiarly fascinating. Any of them is double-faced, and the two aspects of each, the superficial and the secret, are correspondent. It goes without saying that despite their double nature, they are also interrelated and dependent on each other.

The first superficial theme, rather easily spotted by the reader, is a kind of pervasive air of sadness, incompleteness and failure which perspires through the chapter's pages. The eleventh episode of *Ulysses* is possibly the one in which we feel most Bloom's frustrated nature, and the psychological effects the condition of his existence inexorably produces. Beside Bloom's own failure, we are also faced with other personal sad stories, particularly the one recalled by the depiction of Simon Dedalus as a still-good-enough singer, even though not as good as in the old days.

It is interesting to note that, in my perspective, this general atmosphere led by a feeling of sadness and loneliness is the starting point of any reflection upon the episode, but also possibly the end of any speculation, it being a kind of "human sense" of the whole chapter. The first reference to such a feeling occurs in the *overture*, and precipitates some developments of the same idea in other parts of the episode: 'I feels so sad. P.S. So lonely blooming'.[4] Those words represent the fulcrum of Bloom's broodings. His very nature is a frustrated one, his blooming being castrated by the ways of life; yet some irony is recognisable in the passage. The 'P.S.' reference explains his intention to write a letter to Martha Clifford, and the following sentence, the poetic 'So lonely blooming', may very well be a trick to try and obtain from her a kind of maternal attention towards him. The whole line may be interpreted then also as an effort to establish a complex out-of-marriage relationship with a woman who has already shown her sadist intention to punish him.[5]

Of course, 'So lonely blooming' refers to a verse from 'The last rose of summer' by Thomas Moore, but also provides the link with another line in the same *overture*, where the title of the poem occurs, woven with *Rose of Castille* by Balfe. The result is an effect of both absolute and light sadness ('Last rose Castille of summer left bloom I feel so sad alone'[6] also anticipating oneirically the last line of *Finnegans Wake*: 'A way a lone a last a loved a long the'[7]

Another passage in the first pages of the episode suggests the same feeling, even though apparently it is not directly addressed to Bloom:

> Miss Kennedy sauntered sadly from bright light, twining a loose hair behind an ear. Sauntering sadly, gold no more, she twisted twined a hair. Sadly she in sauntering gold hair behind a curving ear.[8]

The passage is very interesting in many respects. First, it points to the fact that Bloom is not the only sad character of the episode, and somehow also suggests that, during that story of a day, we will encounter other lonely people absorbed in the same atmosphere of incompleteness.

Secondly, another detail suggests that there is something common between the ways of Miss Kennedy and those of Bloom. In the passage she is described as 'sauntering'. Twice the same verb has been previously used by Joyce: with reference to Bloom in 'Lotus-Eaters'[9], and to describe a girl in 'Calypso'[10].

Apart from discussing the arguable feminine nature of the act of sauntering, I believe that the use of the same verb to describe both Bloom and a girl may be a hint helpful in trying to understand the utter reason of the feeling of lonesomeness evident throughout the whole episode.

Men and women are correspondent in the book, as their attitudes and ways clearly show, but something which belongs to their terrestrial nature still divides them, and the feeling of sadness and frustration could be the effect of this ultimate truth. As a matter of fact, Bloom will "become" a woman only in the visionary *exploit* of 'Circe', but the allusions to androgyny are so frequent in the book, that they invite us to treat them rather as real than imaginary.

The circularity of the episode is given, as I said, by the feeling of loneliness being the starting point of any reflection, but also the arrival point of them, and the naturally unfulfilled tension towards androgyny and unity, being the ultimate reason behind that very feeling, may very well be the secret esoteric truth we need to unveil. But it is too early to touch on such conclusions, which eventually could somehow undermine the authority of another occult truth unmistakably connected, a critics have shown, with the technique of *Ulysses*: the *coincidentia oppositorum* of Bruno and Nicholas of Cusa. Could it be that the unfulfilled Neoplatonic belief in unity as reconciliation of the contraries is here only a pretext to suggest the sad destiny of men's terrestrial existence? The following quotation from the final part of the episode seems to point to this very truth: 'Hate. Love. Those are names'[11] It also contrasts the other statement occurring in 'Cyclops', where love is meant to be 'the opposite of hatred'. The ambiguity is final, and it would be rather difficult to discern whether Joyce is playing a parody of both the occult beliefs or not, accepting them as both possible. Being as being opposite to something could in fact be just a matter of disguises, therefore the possibility of returning to any primordial unity may be the cause of both frustration and irony at the same time.

The hermetic belief – first suggested by Plato's *Convivium* – that men and women shared once the same nature, but are divided by a distance which is merely corporeal and bodily, deserves attention. It is not a casualty that at the end of the episode Bloom spots a 'frowsy whore with black straw hat askew'[12]; she may be possibly corresponding to Blazes Boylan, who also uses to wear a straw hat. The same is to be said of Simon Daedalus who happens to reach his 'pouch and pipe' 'forth from the skirt of his coat'[13] This superficial truth is parallel to a secret reasoning, a subliminal esoteric logic, underlying the whole episode. We need to spot such an occult pattern and try to explain its implications. However, before attempting so delicate a task, let's allow the discussion to touch on the second superficial theme, the magical power of music, a theme purposely announced by the reference to the singer Simon Dedalus. It is very strictly linked with the first one, perhaps even depending on it.

It retains also a certain inter-textual relevance in Joyce's works for some passages, and the general atmosphere of the chapter, are clearly reminiscent of many echoes from the short-story 'The Dead'. This inter-dependence has been comprehensively analyzed by many critics. Among them, Jackson I. Cope has an illuminating chapter which suggests this relation in the famous collection of essays on *Ulysses* edited by Hart and Haymann. Cope doesn't only spot the many common features between 'Sirens' and 'The Dead'. He takes them as a starting point for a broader analysis of *Ulysses* as a kind of ciphered text, and brings the same discussion further in an essay called '*Ulysses*' Kabbalah', first published in *James Joyce Quarterly* in 1969, and then included in his valuable book *Joyce's Cities* in 1981. In the following pages, I will try to take Cope's useful suggestions and, in light of certain occult technique, shall see what results my analysis may achieve.

Between 'Sirens' and 'The Dead', some places suggest more evident resemblances than others. The performances of the singers, Aunt Julia and the tenor Bartell D'Arcy in the short-story, Simon Dedalus and Ben Dollard in the eleventh episode of *Ulysses*, are just the first and more superficial correspondences. They are characterised also by the fact that, while the songs lasted, silence had been made around the singers, and the audience had been attentively listening to them. With reference to the performances in 'Sirens', Bettina Klein states that:

> Dedalus', Dollard's and Cowley's music (voice and piano = string instrument) attracts more attention than the barmaids' seductive display. It is in particular Simon Dedalus's voice that enchants all the listeners, Bloom and the barmaids included. Male singing outdoes anything else brought forward in this episode. This is a clear reference to Apollonius' Orpheus who beats the Sirens with his songs.[14]

In 'The Dead' this is clear in both Aunt Julia's and Bartell D'Arcy's performances, but it is during Darcy's that we encounter an atmosphere which somehow anticipates that in which all the singing in 'Sirens' is set. Consider for instance the following passage, where the tenor is giving his version of 'The Lass of Aughrim', and Gretta Conroy, standing on the stairs, is absorbed in a most mysterious stillness:

> She was leaning on the banisters, listening to something. Gabriel was surprised at her stillness and strained his ear to listen also. [...]
>
> He stood still in the gloom of the hall, trying to catch the air that the voice was singing and gazing up at his wife. There was grace and mystery in her attitude as if she were a symbol of something. He asked himself what is a woman standing on the stairs in the shadow, listening to distant music, a symbol of.[15]

Gabriel is wondering what has stolen his wife's mind and thoughts; his thoughts are parallel to Bloom's ironical meditations on the same matter towards the end of the eleventh episode: 'What do they think when they hear music? Way to catch rattlesnakes'[16] Despite the shift towards materialism in Bloom's answer to his own question, it is quite evident that both he and Gabriel are somehow attempting to give response to the same dilemma, although in different attitudes.

Also the reference to 'distant music' has its counterpart in 'Sirens'. Here, instead of any sort of existentialist interpretation of a tune hardly heard from a certain distance, and in an imaginative completely silent atmosphere, it's the nature of the silence itself, considered both as a sound and as a vehicle for the act of listening, which catches Bloom's investigative character: 'That voice was a lamentation. Calmer now. It's in silence you feel you hear. Vibrations. Now silent air'[17]. The reference to vibration is fundamental to this analysis, for it also provides a link between the superficial side of the theme of music, and its secret explanation. We need to stress the value of silence intended as a state of the mind for, as Bloom believes, it gives one the opportunity to understand the real nature of music, and the attitude of listening as its *sine qua non*.

In the episode, music has a kind of magical/alchemical power: it can change the moods of people, as Bloom himself secretly acknowledges in his thinking about the above mentioned 'P.S.' in the letter to Martha Clifford: 'Too poetical that about the sad. Music did that. Music hath charms Shakespeare said'[18]. Critic Hallan Hepburn, discussing Bloom's thought that 'minor-key melancholy in music is performative, a pretence of feeling'[19], also agrees in admitting the magical implications of music:

> 'As Plato argues in his discussion of musical modes in *The Republic*, music affects emotions and inspires action for good or for bad. For Plato as for Bloom, this affectivity bypasses reason'[20]

This particular power of music influences people's moods also in 'The Dead', where both Gretta and Gabriel have to surrender to its secret force at last. Gretta is won by the recollection of the sad memories her Galway reminds her of, while Gabriel is finally defeated by the silent sound of the faintly falling snow, and dies an imaginary death in communion with it, and the destiny of all the living and the dead. Music can change moods then, and turn joy and desire into hopeless sadness. This happens in 'The Dead' as well as in 'Sirens', where the sound of desolation, though demystified, is the utter *leit-motif* of all of Bloom's reflections.

However, music has also a more superficial effect which may be possibly explained just as a Dublin, or rather Irish, peculiarity of the time: when it was performed in a bar, it usually obtained complete attention and willingness to listen from people gathered there. This happens also in the Ormond Bar, where we encounter the protagonists of 'Sirens' lending attention to the singers whenever they start to perform. Throughout the episode, many are the exhortations to hush and listen, and they are generally accomplished. It is the case of the gentle and charming *captatio benevolentiae* by which Simon Dedalus asks for attention, before starting his own song: 'I have no money but if you will lend me your attention I shall endeavour to sing to you of a heart bowed down'.[21]

A strong summons to listen, which resounds with the subtle murmur of a powerful sexual metaphor, comes also from Miss Douce, when she offers George Lidwell a 'winding seahorn' in order to make him hear the voice of the sea:

> - Listen! she bade him. [...]
> Ah, now he heard, she holding it to his hears. Hear! He Heard. Wonderful. She held it to her own and through the sifted light pale gold in contrast glided. [...]
> The sea they think they hear. Singing. A roar. The blood it is. Souse in the air sometimes. Well, it's the sea. Corpuscle islands.
> Wonderful really. So distinct. Again. George Lidwell held its murmur, hearing: they laid it by, gently. [22]

In the *Odyssey*, Ulysses providentially saves his companions from hearing the dangerous call of the Sirens by plugging their ears with wax. In Joyce's episode, despite the difficulty to state with a sufficient amount of certainty who the Sirens really are – whether the singers or the seductive barmaids – the Homeric connection is certainly parodied. Here everyone can hear, even deaf people, as if the power of music had something of the supernatural, of the miraculous:

> Listen. Bloom listened. Richie Goulding listened. And by the door deaf Pat, bald Pat, tipped Pat, listened.
> The chord harped slower.
> The voice of penance and of grief came slow, embellished, tremulous. [23]

In discussing briefly the hidden meaning of some references in the schemas, a similar parody-like effect occurs also if we take into account the first of the occult connections which may unveil the essence of a secret theme. I'm referring to certain visionary teachings to be found in a book Joyce had in his Trieste library – as Ellmann records[24]- by an author to whom he refers many times in his writings (*A Portrait, Giacomo Joyce*, *Finnegans Wake*, *Critical Writings*, *Letters*). I'm referring to Emmanuel Swedenborg who, in his *Heaven and Hell*, had imagined heaven as having a bodily form, and described the particular function of each of the organs of the other world. As a matter of fact, his idea of a somatic scheme of interpretation of the bible according to a body/organ correspondence, is very similar to Joyce's own intention of providing almost all of the episodes of *Ulysses* with a particular correspondence with an organ of the body.

Music inverted

In the schemas, 'ear' is the organ of 'Sirens'. In paragraph 96 of *Heaven and Hell* we understand that in the Scriptures, according to the mystic's system of correspondences, the ear is a symbol of 'hearkening and obedience'[25]. It seems to me that both the ideas happen to be subtly mocked in the episode, as well as in the schemas, where we read 'promises' as one of the symbols, and 'the sweet cheat' as the 'sense/meaning'. While those references may very likely be only half-serious reminiscences of the Homeric correspondence with the singing of the sirens, it is hard not to spot a link also to the two conceits Swedenborg spoke of, a link eventually structured according to the technique of the semantic overturn. In fact, although in 'Sirens' the protagonists are imaginatively plugging both their ears with their fingers, everyone actually happens to obey to the 'sweet cheat' of the magical power of music, and to hearken to its false promises.

Despite this, together with all the general exhortations to lend attention to music occurring in many places of the episode, the secret sense concealed behind the two ideas may dwell in a different ground than a strictly musical one, as the following quotation seems to suggest: 'Might be what you like till you hear the words'[26]. In *Ulysses* often apparently casual sentences like this may open a vast range of possibilities in terms of interpretation. They may point in fact to a once united and coherent knowledge, which in the text appears to be scattered into pieces to be reorganized. The suggestion to wait until the words make their appearance is subtler than it might seem at first. It alludes to the cheating spells which belong to the nature of music, bur also to an equation words=music which is fundamental in the episode as well as in the book, and in relation to Joyce's own aesthetics.

As a matter of fact, the relationship between words and music is one of the major genetic factors in other works by the Irish writer. The musical effects of the narrative play a central role, for example, in 'The Dead', especially in the perfect symphony-like architecture of its final paragraphs, in *Chamber Music*, in certain places of *A Portrait* such as the second part of the fourth chapter, and finally are one of the main structural figures in *Ulysses* and *Finnegans Wake*.

With regards to *Ulysses*, 'Sirens' is obviously, among all the episodes, the one where music alone plays the main part. One is reminded of what Joyce wrote to Harriet Weaver in the summer of 1919: 'Since I wrote the *Sirens* I find it impossible to listen to music of any kind'[27]. This quotation shows how fundamental music is for the understanding of the episode in the author's intentions, but also suggests a very strict relationship between music and language. The musicality of the chapter is in fact a product of the organization of the words which secretly give it its inner life. Richard Ellmann explains the whole argument as follows:

> During the later nineteenth century the claims of music were put forward with *brio*. Wagner understandably said so, and Pater apophthegmatized the going sentiment by writing 'All the arts aspire to the condition of music'. But Mallarmé argued that music had to work with relationships which words had already established, and Joyce, though a singer, put himself on the same side. For him all the music aspires to the condition of language, and being brought to that condition in the *Sirens* episode, reveals itself as less than supreme. [28]

Joyce's radical ideas about the relationship between words and music, so precisely explained by Ellmann, are certainly very helpful in achieving a comprehensive perspective when reading 'Sirens'. Yet I don't feel we can generalize so neatly and state openly that for Joyce 'all the music aspires to the condition of language'; at least we cannot do so if we consider only the eleventh episode of *Ulysses.* It would be easier to show how that statement works with regards to *Finnegans Wake,* where we may say that music, or rather harmony, being not only the starting point but also the final aim of Joyce's art, is somehow achieved at last through the attempt to reproduce polyphonic (polysemantic) effects. Instead I believe that, with regards to 'Sirens', one should be very careful before indulging in the temptation of drawing an exact parallel between 'the condition of music' and 'the condition of language'. In an early study, following Curtius' scepticism about the real achievements of the compromise between music and literature, A. Walton Litz states that:

> In trying to atone musical and literary forms, Joyce weakened the rational structure of his prose, exalting secondary qualities ('suggestion' and 'sound-imitation') at the expense of communication. The *Sirens* episode demonstrate the weaknesses of a compromise between the two arts. [29]

This judgement may seem overstated, especially in the light of the future developments of Joyce's intention to "create his own music" in the *Wake.* On the other hand, this relative failure in achieving what cannot be achieved, given the 'insuperable barrier to the simulation of musical form,'[30] is also parallel to Joyce's early frustration due to his wish to become a musician/performer, a frustration which led him to pursue a literary career as his second best choice[31]. Hepburn, in order to give a solution to the whole argument, and particularly to the relationship between literature and music, suggests to resort to opera, a genre indeed very dear to Joyce, as the place where the two arts are blended in a successful wedding:

> The degree to which music exceeds language and the degree to which music retains ambiguity suggests that opera, with its combination of narrative, voice, orchestration, and recognisable forms [...] often communicates symbolic structures and fantasies in *Ulysses*. [32]

Leaving aside the unsolved question of whether or not literature may aspire to, or achieve, the condition of music, and viceversa, the textual ambiguity of 'Sirens' may also encourage us to consider again carefully the secret system of references and the suggestions hidden by the writer between the lines, not as a surrogate for the failure of a compromise between the two arts, but rather as one of the main hidden features of the episode. In this context, a quotation such as the following sounds as a key-phrase to approach the occult message concealed behind the episode: 'Words? Music? No: it's what's behind'[33].

> 'What's behind', contrasting the "outside" of Jules Law, cannot but refer to some unconscious truth, neither invented nor understood by the protagonist, yet fully intended by the author. It is a truth which reminds us again of Hepburn's comment that 'music stands as the Freudian *Unberwusste*, or "unknown" component of identity that colours individual subjectivity and human interaction'[34].

What is the secret essence of music, and what links it with the ultimate secrets of words and language? The hint to the unveiling of this dilemma is eventually dropped at a certain point of 'Sirens' where, after Simon Dedalus has completed his performance and everyone is admiring, Richie Goulding eventually joins the praising crew by addressing Bloom in the following way: 'Grandest number in the whole opera, Goulding said'[35]. Despite the apparent plainness of the sentence, quoted also in 'Proteus'[36], Bloom's mind doesn't intend the sense Richie Goulding had meant by the expression. Oppositely, he is fascinated by another idea suggested by the word 'number'. For him the term stands no more for musical piece; instead he takes it literally. It starts a very peculiar train of thoughts, already implied in the earlier reference to vibrations:

> - It is, Bloom said.
>
> Numbers it is. All music when you come to think. Two multiplied by two divided by half is twice one. Vibrations; chords those are. One plus six is seven. Do anything you like with figures juggling [...] Musemathematics. And you think you are listening to the ethereal. But suppose you said it like: Martha, seven times nine minus x is thirtyfive thousands. Fall quite flat. It's on account of the sounds it is. [37]

The shift from the previous relation words/music to a more comprehensive perspective including numerical allusions is clear, and becomes always a structural factor if we consider that, as John Senior explains, the essence of music, according to the hermetic belief of the Pythagoreans, is numerical:

> Through numbers, the alchemists also identified themselves with the Pythagoreans. And since Pythagoras taught the relation between number and music, the alchemists said that the seven metals were the seven strings of the lyre and the seven notes of the musical scale.[38]

The idea of Joyce being fully aware of the connection between the numerological doctrines of the Pythagoreans, and those of the kabbalaists, seems to me to be shared by Sheldon Brivic, who ho explains that:

> He was aware of Giordano Bruno's statement that the wisdom of the Kabbalah "derives from the Egyptians, among whom Moses was brought up". And *Isis Unveiled* sees a connection between the Kabbalah and "the cosmological theory of numerals which Pythagoras learned from the Egyptian hierophants".[39]

Music unveiled

Acoustic science suggests that it's the number of vibrations in a unit of time which gives the sound its height and allows us to distinguish a sound from another. Moreover, its frequency gives a sound its timbre, and finally numbers are also at the basis of any idea of rhythm. This last idea seems to be just the hint dropped by another sentence occurring a few lines below: 'Time makes the tune'.[40] The assumption that the whole essence of music is numerical had been already established by the expression 'Musemathematics' quoted above, which in its first part also contains a reference to the inspirational process, but also to the ancient Greek world of the Pytagoreans.

As it happens, Bloom's reflections are the product of a seemingly half-scientific mind, and this somehow anticipate an attitude which will be more evident in a later episode such as 'Itacha'. However, they express an idea which is well established in the acoustic sciences: musical relationships are parallel to mathematic ones, insofar as they are dependent on the same kind of numerical rapports. The previous equation words=music, which has then been replaced by the one music=numbers, gives way now, by means of a simple logic syllogism, to a third and ultimate equation: words=numbers. In order to solve the whole words/numbers question we may take account of the ideas and techniques of that Jewish *corpus* of knowledge known as Kabbalah. As Gershom Scholem, possibly the main authority on the subject, puts it, 'the Kabbalah, literally "tradition", that is, the tradition of things divine, is the sum of Jewish mysticism'.[41]

Jackson I. Cope informs us that Joyce undoubtedly had access to important texts of the Kabbalistic tradition 'in the course of his weaving of *Ulysses*[42], and many other authoritative critics agree with such a statement. Despite this, Brivic, in an article on the Kabbalah in the *Wake*, argues that:

> Cope effectively expands our recognition of Joyce's knowledge of the Kabbalah, though some of his observations are more suggestive than conclusive. Actually, the work containing an account of te Kabbalah for which Joyce's use has been most solidly demonstrated is Helena Petrovna Blavatsky's *Isis Unveiled.*[43]

Let's start by saying that Joyce's awareness of some aspects of the Kabbalah seems undisputable, although, as Brivic argues, 'Joyce's version of the Kabbalah is thoroughly personal'.[44] With regards to *Finnegans Wake*, Atherton is right in including he Kabbalah in the list of those occultist sources (Spiritualism, occultism, alchemy) 'in which we are given to understand that Joyce was deeply read.'[45] Yet the scholar's remarks voluntarily point to an apparent inconsistency between his use of Kabbalistic doctrines and the actual provenience of his knowledge of them. An instance of this is the numerological relationship between Levy-Bhrul's books present in Joyce personal library at Buffalo, and the *Wake*. Atherthon, while stating that 'everything he uses in *Finnegans Wake* about the Kabbalah seemed to be contained in the article on that subject in the eleventh edition of the *Encyclopedia Britannica*'[46], had previously explained the above connection as follows:

> According to Levy-Bruhl, 'there is no number among the first ten that does not possess supreme mystical importance for some social group or other'. Furthermore, 'certain multiples of numbers of mystic value participate in the peculiar properties of those numbers'. This is the state of affairs in *Finnegans Wake*. So far as arithmetic is concerned there is simply unity and diversity. But each of the main characters has a number as well as a symbol, and certain numbers – of which 1123 is the most prominent – have a mystical value which has still not been satisfactorily explained. The particular character assigned to each number may have been obtained by Joyce from some works on occultism and the Kabbalah.[47]

In this perspective, the fact that Joyce's Kabbalistic sources may be contained just in one article of the *Enclypodiea Britannica* may sound odd. In fact, Kabbalah-derived ideas about the magical and mystical value of numbers literally permeate the whole eclectic corpus of occult works during the centuries, with which Joyce was acquainted. They are a major aspect of Rosicrucianism, as well as of modern theosophy, and no doubt inform substantially also the works of Levy-Bruhl which we may well regard as one of Joyce's direct sources. Therefore, if Kabbalah-related theories are present in detail in the *Wake*, there's no sufficient reason to dismiss the possibility that they are also present behind certain apparently odd allusions in *Ulysses*.

I will here review only a few implications of a kabbalistic technique, which concern my analysis. This is known as *Gematria*, and seems to provide the link with the reasoning explained above and with the final equation numbers=words. Scholem describes it as the 'interpretation through the numerical value of the Hebrew letters.'[48] In the Kabbalah, the *Gematria* is an occult and very precise technique: its fundamental issue, the correspondence of letters of the alphabet to numbers, together with the *Notarikon* which is the science of composing words mixing up letters, is undoubtedly what Bloom's monologue quoted above is all about. This is confirmed by a passage in 'Ithaca', where Joyce tells us directly about Bloom's knowledge of such a technique:

> and Bloom in turn wrote the Hebrew characters ghimel, aleph, daleth and (in the absence of mem) a substituted goph, explaining their arithmetical values as ordinal and cardinal numbers, videlicet 3, 1, 4 and 100.[49]

As Cope suggests in his essay on 'Sirens'[50], this technique has been alluded to previously in *Ulysses*. I'm referring for example to Stephen's mocking telephone call to Edenville in the third episode: 'Hello. Kinch here. Put me on to Edenville. Aleph. Alpha: nought, nought, [51] A further link to the episode is the above-mentioned mutual reference to 'the greatest number'. As with regards to most of Blooms allusions, it would be quite useless to look for more precise and schematic relations, firstly because a parodying and mocking will seems to me to be as always the main feature of the game, and secondly because Joyce was not a Kabbalist neither in the strict sense nor, like Jorge Luis Borges according to George Steiner, in a modernist one. What is interesting is the secret system of allusions made by Bloom – we shall consider also his bland and multifaceted Jewish background – and the secret general meaning of the episode from which this analysis has started.

The theory of these references to a Kabbalistic technique is in fact neither the main aim of Joyce's intentions in writing the episode, nor the ultimate cause behind its organization. It is nothing but a mean by which other more general statements and truths are affirmed. Those statements, providing, as I have said before, a kind of human sense or meaning of the chapter, are likely to be applied also to the book as a whole. Through this final step we may eventually find out that they are introduced to our attention both as superficial and as secret themes, the latter having being suggested by the strange numerical techniques belonging to the tradition of the Kabbalah.

In order to show this circularity and ambivalence of ideas, let's now take into account the general Kabbalistic assumptions and conceits which the numerical references seem to me to point to, and see how they can bring our discussion back to where it started from: the sense of incompleteness, failure and frustration symbolized by music, of which Bloom is a victim in the episode.

As it is implied in Scholem's definition of the Kabbalah as 'the tradition of things divine', this kind of mystic philosophy not only includes a practical side – the techniques of interpretation through numbers, letters and words – but also a theoretical side which is somehow distant from the traditional orthodox rabbinical doctrine. This theoretical side, which is utterly multifaceted, includes a series of what I would dare to call, from the Christian New Testament point of view, half-heretic about the nature and the essence of god and his law.

Here, I will focus only on what seems to me to be a clear connection between a revolutionary statement made by the Kabbalists and the very cause behind the sense of frustration and sadness as the prevailing figure of the episode. Scholem explains that:

> Most if not all Kabbalistic speculation and doctrine is concerned with the realm of the divine emanations or *sephiroth*, in which God's creative power unfolds. [...] Insofar as God reveals himself he does so through the creative power of the *sephiroth* [52]

Suffice our discussion to explain that the *sephiroth*, or manifestations of the power of god, are ten, and among them the first three are the more general ones, while each of the remaining seven, named the lower *sephiroth*, correspond to a part of the human body of the primordial man, Adam Kadmon. It is interesting to note that in the third episode of *Ulysses* we find also an allusion to Adam Kadmon. He is the man in his purest form, whom certain Kabbalistic traditions identify with the god of the *sepiroth*, or god as he reveals himself to men through the manifestation of his power.

Beside the general correspondence of the *sephiroth* with parts of the body, which very likely may have influenced some of Joyce's intentions in describing his book as having a bodily form, I am here referring to this very complex mystic idea just to introduce the theme of androgyny – a link back to the theorization of the perfect artist as an 'androgynous angel, being wife unto himself'[53] in 'Scylla' – which is in fact the revolutionary theory secretly elaborated by the Kabbalists, in manifest contrast with the orthodox Jewish traditional doctrine. Again I rely upon the valuable study of Professor Scholem in order to illuminate this discussion:

> Of the seven potencies that emanate from it [from the third *sephiroth*,[54]], the first six are symbolized as parts of the Primordial men's body and epitomized in the phallic 'foundation' [...]
>
> The tenth *sephirah*, however, no longer represents a particular part of man, but, as complement to the universally human and masculine principle, the feminine, seen at once as mother, wife, and as daughter, though manifested in different

> ways in these different aspects. This discovery of the feminine element of God, which the Kabbalists tried to justify by Gnostic exegesis, is of course one of the most significant steps they took.[55]

Relying on my previous demonstration that at some stage of his career James Joyce must have come in touch with the main texts of the Kabbalah, there's no doubt that a writer like him could very likely have been fascinated by such a complex and utterly obscure doctrine belonging to the tradition of Jewish mystical knowledge. Particularly, the kabbalistic doctrine of the *sephiroth*[56] was mentioned in the article on Kabbalah in the eleventh edition of the *Encyclopedia Britannica* which, as I said, Atherton believes is one of Joyce's major sources on the subject. Besides, given the fact that Joyce refers in his book to both Adam Kadmon and the androgynous being as the perfect artist, we still have to acknowledge what is the light – a serious commitment or rather a mocking parody – in which the conceit is presented to the reader.

I have suggested earlier that the straw-hatted whore of the end of the episode is reminiscent of Blazes Boylan, and that generally in 'Sirens' men seem to correspond to women; and finally, I have somehow assumed that the theory of the 'coincidence of the opposite', so dear to Joyce as everyone seems to agree in Joyce studies, might be affected by a congenital error. Now, my purpose is to try and clarify the idea of incompleteness of humanity as a debt, in part, to the Kabbalah, by providing further examples in order to establish a direct relationship between it and the atmosphere of sadness and failure of the chapter.

I doubt that when Joyce chose 'Sirens' as the title of the episode, he had been thinking solely of the two barmaids, Miss Douce and Miss Kennedy. I am inclined to believe, in fact, that he must have admitted to himself that the Homeric Sirens – as matter of fact, an almost sexless kind of beings – were actually participating of the androgynous nature. In the *Odyssey* they are not remarkable for the sexual potency of their appeal, but only in the light of the cheating powers of their chant. This is why in Joyce's 'Sirens', only men happen to sing, and why they are the only ones who may catch the attention and make the persons, gathered in the bar, listen to them.

The two sexy barmaids get only a little attention compared to that which is easily accorded to the male singers, Simon Dedalus and Ben Dollard. This may eventually lead us to think, by ways of another overturn, that if the singers are the sirens, the barmaids may possibly be the *Ulysses*' crowd. This seems to be confirmed by many passages such as the following one, where one of the girls actually pretends to prevent herself from listening by plugging her own ears:

> Sweet tea Miss Kennedy having poured with milk plugged both two ears with little fingers
>
> - No, don't, she cried.

- I won't listen, she cried. [57]

As a further evidence of this exchange of genders, we may quote a passage where Lydia Douce anticipates Bloom's most peculiarly masculine act in the whole book, his masturbation on Sandymount Strand:

> On the smooth jutting beerpull laid Lydia hand lightly, plumply, leave it to my hands. All lost in pity for croppy. Fro, to: to, fro: over the polished knob (she knows his eyes, my eyes, her eyes) her thumb and finger passed in pity: passed, repassed and, gently touching, then slid so smoothly, slowly down, a cool firm white enamel baton protruding through their sliding ring.
>
> With a cock with a carra.
>
> Tap. Tap. Tap.[58]

Having stated that a natural, although fictional, exchange of genders between the protagonists may very well be the fundamental issue of the chapter – a truth that is also authoritatively enforced by means of both occult allusions and more superficial references, all suggested by the secret numerological implications of music – the effort to return to the starting point of my reflections, with the help of a new and more comprehensive perspective, shall not come in so stressful a way.

I believe in fact that we can easily recognise the general air of incompleteness surrounding the whole episode as the result of the failed attempt of almost all the protagonists to achieve the perfect state of androgyny, a state which is suggested by the allusions to the occult *sapientia* of the Kabbalists. Unfortunately, men and women are prevented from achieving that kind of perfection due to an unavoidable terrestrial barrier: human nature. This secret wish, shared by many of the relevant characters of 'Sirens', and more generally of *Ulysses*, is destined to remain unfulfilled, and this truth proceeding from necessity, is the ultimate reason informing Bloom's and the other protagonists' feelings of sad failure and, more superficially, music's pervasive melancholy. As it happens, only the imaginary and oneiric evolutions of 'Circe', in which Bloom will become a woman, and Bella Cohen will become Bello, will partly satisfy such an aim; yet the 'Sirens' chapter stands firmly for an anticipatory key-passage in the acknowledgment of Bloom's latent androgynous nature. It is a two-fold status: while textually speaking it appears to be easily detectable, given the protagonist often unmistakably womanly behaviour, from an occult point of view Bloom's androgyny may also be linked with his "Jewishness", and his awareness, although incomplete, of some of the secret doctrines of Hebrew's mysticism. In fact, as Carolyn Heilbrun states: 'The woman as hero, like the man as hero, exists in one character in *Ulysses*, Leopold Bloom. […] his Jewishness in Dublin makes necessary a certain passivity and has developed in him a great kindness'[58]. Such a kindness, which is at once a misrepresentation of his failure and also the most important aspect of his great humanity, is parallel in the episode to the sad music which can magically change people's mood, and be, at the same time, a powerful symbol of the secrecy of narration in Joyce's text. Hence, Joyce's failure to achieve the condition of music in 'Sirens' is just another way to speak out silently the innate impossibility of terrestrial reconciliation – suggested by a series of occult references and allusions – which, being a fundamental issue in the hidden organization of his stories, often haunts his characters and intentions.

Works Cited

Atherton, James S.. *The Books at the Wake*. New York: Paul P. Appel, 1974.

Brivic, Sheldon. "The Mind Factor: Kabbalah in Finnegan's Wake," *James Joyce Quarterly* 21, 1: 1983.

Cope, J.I.. *Joyce's Cities*. Baltimore: Johns Hopkins University Press.

—. "Sirens" in *James Joyce's Ulysses*. Ed. Hart and Hayman. 236-37.

Ellmann, Richard. The Consciousness of Joyce. London: Faber and Faber, 1971.

Heilbrun, Carolyn G. *Towards a Recognition of Androgyny: Aspects of Male and Female in Literature*. New York: Norton, 1982.

Hepburn, Allan. "Ulysses, Opera, Loss" in *James Joyce Quarterly* (Vol.38, Is. 1- 2): 67.

Joyce, James. *Finnegan's Wake*. ed. Seamus Deane. London: Penguin, 1976.

—. *Letters I*. ed. Stuart Gilbert. London: Faber and Faber, 1957.

—. *Ulysses*. Ed. Declan Kiberd. London: Penguin, 1992.

Kiberd, Declan. "Theatre as Opera: The Gigli Concert" in ed. Eamonn Jordan, *Theatre Stuff*. Dublin: Carlsfort Press, 2000.

Klein, Bettina. "Traces of Homer: Between Sources and Models in Joyce's "Aeolus" and "Sirens" in ed. Frances Ruggeri, *Classic Joyce: Joyce Studies in Italy*. Vol. 6. Roma: Bulozi, 1999.

Law, Jules. "Political Sirens" in ed. K.J. Devlin and M. Reizbaun, *Ulysses- An Engendered Perspective: Eighteen New Critical Essays on the Episodes*. Columbia: South Carolina Press, 1999. 150-66.

Litz, A. Walton. *The Art of Joyce*. London: Oxford University Press, 1961.

Scholem, Gershom. *On the Kabbalah and its Symbolism*. New York: Schocken Books, 1965.

Swedenborg, Emanuel. *Heaven and Hell*. New York: Swedenborg Foundation, 2001.

IV.

MODERNISM AND POPULAR CULTURE

T.S. ELIOT AND UBIQUITOUS MUSIC, 1909-1922

T. AUSTIN GRAHAM

Recent criticism at the crossroads of literary, historical, and musical scholarship has begun to tackle the relationship between T.S. Eliot and the popular songs of his day, with most of it attempting to establish whether the poet tended to tap his foot or turn up his nose when someone put on a record. The goal, generally speaking, has been to determine just how he felt about his day's hit music, to get at his personal tastes and preferences by analyzing his poetic treatment of song. And as is usually the case in Eliot studies, conclusions vary widely.[1]

In one corner we have Alfred Appel, Jr., whose *Jazz Modernism* asserts that an open-minded, intertextual, ever-sampling ethos of musical "rag-picking" was central to the work of such artistic giants as Joyce and Picasso, but absolutely not to Eliot's. Indeed, Appel frets that the mere appearance of the word "modernism" in his title is a mistake, as it implies that Eliot could be included in the so-called "jazznocracy" despite the fact that he "cultivated and collected far fewer rags" than his contemporaries and "used vernacular lingo to connote vulgarity."[2] Appel's argument is a familiar one, resting on Eliot's well-worn reputation for cultural elitism and snobbery. The poet's tendency to quote from popular song is therefore dismissed as condescension, and his work judged to lack such vital musical characteristics as "accessibility; humor; a capacity for joy" (84). Responding in kind, however, is David Chinitz, who attempts to show in *T.S. Eliot and the Cultural Divide* that Eliot's sensibility was in tune with and even defined by the pop of his day. Thus we have biographical anecdotes of Eliot singing "Frankie and Johnny" in his bathroom, tripping the Foxtrot and Grizzly Bear with his wife at London's Hammersmith Palais de Danse, and generally embracing the vivacious spirit of the Jazz Age. In his literary analysis, meanwhile, Chinitz finds evidence of music appreciation in the poet's earliest notebooks and his subsequent major works, ultimately concluding *contra* Appel that Eliot had "an ear open" to popular song for most of his life.[3]

Attempting to enter this polarized critical debate from the outside is a dicey proposition, as it seems difficult if not impossible to definitively establish Eliot's stance on pop. Turning to his poetry does little to clear up the issue, as

Eliot never depicts music consistently there. For him, song is sometimes a free-floating, scene-setting effect, other times an invasive force that changes the very way people think, now a symbol of independence and authenticity, now an indication of squalor or of mechanized sameness. Eliot's treatment of it is as ambiguous as his rendering of modernity itself, and as such we cannot make cut and dried conclusions about his tastes. The best we can do is agree that pop for Eliot is ultimately tied up in his larger conception of the new, and agree that his opinions on both subjects are far too broad to define precisely.

The most glaring oversight in this taste-based mode of inquiry, however, is that it almost completely elides the question of how Eliot understands music to operate on listeners and interact with their senses — a question that has profound implications for how we read his poetry. Instead of pushing on the irresolvable issue of popular songs as "high" or "low" art, then, this paper will concern itself with Eliot's depiction of the human auditory process, a process that appears to be undergoing a kind of mutation in an increasingly music-suffused sonic environment. Again, Eliot's treatment of this subject varies. His listeners are sometimes beset by music, with songs stuck deep inside their heads and scrambling their thoughts in spooky or absurd ways (depending on one's reading). At other moments, they seem like nothing so much as song junkies, hooked on musical sensations and in need of the occasional auditory fix. Sharpening our critical focus in such a way, however, makes it considerably easier to find musical patterns in Eliot's work. Simply put, he seems to view his era's popular music as a powerful, almost hallucinogenic presence so entrenched in daily life that listeners cannot escape it, even if they want to.

Between Eliot's *Inventions of the March Hare* journals and *The Waste Land*, two important musical developments occur in his poetry. The first is an evolving conception of what I will refer to as ubiquitous music. Once a fleeting experience confined to specific places or occasions, music in Eliot becomes an omnipresent force that can erupt in one's ears at any time and without warning. Eliot's characters seem surrounded, almost oppressed by music; and even when they are not, sonic conditions have the potential to change at any moment. His interest in this topic, meanwhile, cannot be separated from his concern with recording technology and mechanized means of producing music, which during his early life were changing the aural landscape in obvious but nevertheless revolutionary ways. Music began to reach ever deeper into private experience, and Eliot's view of the world indicates that silence is growing increasingly hard to find.

As Eliot hears music moving towards a state of ubiquity, he perceives a second, parallel phenomenon: a change in the human capacity for processing auditory stimuli. Music has a generally obtrusive effect on listeners in Eliot's earliest *March Hare* sketches, with songs surrounding, haunting, and even torturing his characters from the outside. To borrow a phrase from Coleridge, it seems as though they cannot choose but hear the music around them, immersed in a steady stream of sound.[4] In Eliot's published works, however, music becomes considerably more invasive and people begin listening differently, with the distinction between externally and internally produced sensations starting to collapse. By the time Eliot produces *The Waste Land*, his listeners are absorbing popular songs directly into their minds and bodies, with music occupying the same interior space as their memories, observations, and desires. In other words, Eliot seems to believe that people are becoming something like record players themselves in an ever-shifting aural environment, altered by both the unprecedented amount of music in daily life and the technology responsible for disseminating it. It is a complicated concept, and to nail it down we must do more than simply consider Eliot's aesthetic judgment of pop. His poetry raises the question of just how it is that we listen to music in the first place.

The verse from Eliot's early years often has a soundtrack to it, and this is almost certainly due to the fact that he grew up in what was then one of America's most music-crazed cities. His childhood home as described by Lyndall Gordon was in "an unfashionable part of St. Louis, not far from the saloons and brothels of Chestnut and Market Streets, at a time when pianists in back rooms were joining 'rags' together as jolting tunes."[5] Jaunty, syncopated, piano-driven ragtime hits from the likes of Scott Joplin and Tom Turpin routinely rang in the air, making involuntary listeners and inadvertent pop connoisseurs out of everyday passers-by. Of course, this sensation of being constantly surrounded by music is unremarkable today, familiar to anyone who has ever set foot in a mall; but exposure on the scale of what the young Eliot would have experienced was still rather new at the beginning of the twentieth century. Intentionally or not, some histories of the early St. Louis ragtime scene create the impression that there was something strange, addictive, and even pathological in the songs, a peculiarly captivating quality that allowed them to circulate almost of their own volition. David A. Jansen and Gene Jones, for example, write that ragtime grew there "like Kansas grew wheat" and describe its spread as nothing short of a "virus," with their verbiage emphasizing just how relentless and catchy the new music was.[6] Eliot, it would appear, grew up in a unique, perhaps even unprecedented musical time and place, caught up in a fad that would serve as the foundation for virtually every subsequent form of American pop. The question of how much the budding poet enjoyed such sensations is rather beside the point — he and the rest of St. Louis had no choice but to live with them.

It becomes easier to imagine what Eliot's formative years sounded like if we turn to his *March Hare* poems, in which music seems as important and pervasive a part of the environment as buildings, nature, and people. Most significant are the pieces featuring the tinny sound of a "street piano," which Eliot uses to heighten the unpleasantness of his urban scenes. The instrument is actively sinister in his "First Debate between the Body and Soul," in which a protagonist "yet devoted to the pure idea" sits in a city square, "Forced to endure" the sound of "a street piano through the dusty trees/ Insisting: 'Make the best of your position.'"[7] As in some of his earlier verse, the sound of the piano in this poem is one in a series of sordid sensations, equated with houses of ill repute and a blind man who "coughs and spits sputters" in the alleyways. This time, however, Eliot includes what is presumably a song lyric — "Make the best of your position" — to accompany the piano's tune, creating an ironic disconnect between its sunny platitudes and the grimy scene. It is all apparently too much for the protagonist to bear, as his optimism "dies of inanition" after the music appears. He makes a final attempt to resurrect his devotion to the "Absolute!" and "pure idea", but the domineering sound remains the same: "Street pianos through the trees/ Whine and wheeze" (65). The idealist's defeat has come in the form of an unshakable piece of ambient music.

Eliot is making gestures towards the sensation of involuntary listening in this and others of his early poems, beginning to grasp an auditory phenomenon that he would develop further in coming years. The relationship between music and listener is relatively straightforward, with the two fighting for control over the listener's interior space (and music coming out on top). Simplicity aside, however, the 22-year-old Eliot has come upon an important truth: music has a uniquely invasive, forceful effect on listeners that distinguishes it from all other sounds, largely because the human brain is wired to pay particular attention to it. As Robert Jourdain has explained, we are drawn to musical tones because they represent perfect aural balance, something difficult to find in our everyday surroundings. By definition, a musical tone is sound vibrating "in simple ways," resonating with all its frequencies or "overtones" arranged in an unnaturally precise and orderly pattern.[8] Only objects vibrating in complete isolation, such as strings, reeds, or columns of air, can produce musical tones; and isolated vibrating objects almost never occur accidentally. As Jourdain puts it, "Wind may occasionally whistle and brooks may sometimes babble melodiously, but nature usually makes noise" (31). Tones are so unusual that the brain's response to them borders on being involuntary — and this is to say nothing of the attention demanded by even a few bars of music. Bearing this in mind, the Eliot protagonist's absorption in street-piano music makes perfect sense. Most city noise is a mishmash of sounds at jumbled, disordered frequencies, and the human brain can instinctively filter such noise out. But the more balanced vibrations of a rag are considerably harder to ignore.

The *March Hare* poems occasionally contain identifiable pop songs, with Eliot quoting their lyrics or referring to them by name. We find the title of the 1909 ditty "By the Light of the Silvery Moon" buried in "Suite Clownesque," a line from the 1907 song "You Found" quoted in the fragment "The smoke that gathers blue and sinks," and two Broadway shows (*The Chocolate Soldier* and

The Merry Widow) referred to in "Goldfish (Essence of Summer Magazines)." Chinitz has already pointed out that the songs' syncopated rhythms and unexpected rhymes appear to have influenced Eliot's prosody, imbuing his verse with a fractured, off-balance feel and jazzy vitality. It is important to note, however, that their presence also indicates just how music-suffused America had become during Eliot's youth. Snatches of song drop into the poems as if plucked out of thin air, creating the impression that they circulate freely as part of a broader cultural experience. To live in Eliot's world is to encounter popular music at frequent, even random intervals, and his poetry reflects this musical ubiquity. This early form of song sampling also functions as a salute to young, self-consciously modern readers, appealing to a communal musical sensibility that was becoming increasingly widespread in Eliot's day. There is a rebellious, defiant attitude here, with the poet cheekily deploying popular music so as to set "vulgar life against a romantic, genteel world of blue-delft china."[9] Indeed, when Eliot sets out to illustrate the superiority of his youthful perspective and break ranks with traditional literary convention, music is one of his favorite conceits — few characters in the *March Hare* poems, after all, come off as badly as their stuffy, pretentious opera fans.

Eliot's early musical ideas begin coalescing in "Portrait of a Lady," a poetic face-off between a high society woman and a young male protagonist that juxtaposes high and low art, maturity and youth, and extravagant and realistic outlooks. The lady, as A.D. Moody has noted, is something of a straw figure for Eliot as he seeks a "cure for romanticism," a showy *grande dame* who hosts teas in her drawing room and makes long, florid observations that appear to interest no one but herself.[10] The defiantly lowbrow narrator, meanwhile, is a youth who spends his mornings in the park "Reading the comics and the sporting page" and who chafes at the lady's attention.[11] The two are hopelessly divided, and the woman's invitations of friendship are doomed to fail for several reasons. Music, however, seems to be one of the most powerful wedges between them, and the poem contains all the musical phenomena that Eliot hints at in his earlier works: a pervasive aural presence, a capacity to invade and disrupt consciousness, and an uncannily effective ability to shed light on and even construct people's characters.

Eliot associates the lady and the youth with two very different styles of music. Readers meet the duo after a trip to hear "the latest Pole/ Transmit the Preludes, through his hair and finger-tips", with the lady speaking a few lines on Frederic Chopin and the exquisite intimacy of his piano compositions. The atmosphere in her salon has a similarly classical and delicate feel to it, with the stiff conversation among her guests ("velleities and carefully caught regrets") blending with "attenuated tones of violins/ Mingled with remote cornets". But as the lady's rhetorical meanderings become more irritating to the young protagonist, so too does the music. The violin grows aimless, "winding" though his thoughts, while the short arias now seem to come from unpleasant "cracked cornets" instead of pure-toned ones. And in what may be the cleverest musical description in the entire poem, the lady's voice at one point becomes the "insistent out-of-tune/ Of a broken violin on an August afternoon".[11] This is no mere out-of-tune *song* or out-of-tune *phrase*: the woman's voice and the classical tradition associated with it have merged to become tone-deafness itself, and it is hard if not impossible to say where one ends and the other begins.

The music associated with the young man, on the other hand, is more public, less sophisticated, and heavy on percussion — all key attributes of popular music. In one of the poem's most famous lines, the narrator hears a "dull tom-tom" playing inside his head as the lady speaks, "Absurdly hammering a prelude of its own" in a "Capricious monotone/ That is at least one definite 'false note'". This moment, widely commented on in Eliot scholarship, is generally understood as a semi-primitive and resolutely unsophisticated attempt on the young man's part to resist the lady's romanticized temptations. While I will address the drum line in more detail later, it suffices for now to point out that the tom-tom — an instrument at the foundations of almost all pop since Eliot's day — represents a decisive break with the lady's more refined art-music sensibility. Later, the youth reiterates his allegiance to this sort of "low" music by describing one of the few sensations able to distract him from his morning reveries in the park: Eliot's ever-present street-piano, "mechanical and tired" as it "Reiterates some worn-out common song" (12). If it were not already abundantly clear that the youth and lady have irreconcilable differences, the narrator's alignment with such a cheap and jangly instrument makes the point unmistakably.

Eliot's characters are not just expressing musical preferences in this poem. Music is actually part of who they are, an integral component of both personalities. As the protagonist lapses into doubt at the poem's end, unable to decide whether his modern consciousness is superior to the lady's romanticism, it is her violins and cornets — not her words — that seem to hold the ultimate "advantage" over him (13). "This music is successful with a 'dying fall'", he sighs in the final stanza, incapable of separating his foe from the classical tradition she admires. She *is* Chopin, he *is* a jazz drummer, at least up to a point; and as such, the twain can never meet. This concept of musical self-definition is of course eminently familiar today: Simon Frith has made the most convincing argument that listeners do not look for music that reflects them so much as change themselves to reflect music, and that in some ways we actually become the songs and performers we love. "In 'possessing' music, we make it part of our own identity and build it into our sense of ourselves," Frith writes, highlighting music's capacity to be absorbed in a variety of ways.[12] To find music seeping into and even constructing personalities in Eliot, however, is rather unexpected. Like so much else in his poetry, his idea of musical embodiment (pop and otherwise) is strikingly ahead of its time.

It is important, however, not to go too far and assign aural agency to Eliot's characters here, asserting as most critics do that the two styles of music serve the lady and the youth like weapons in a duel. Rather, music seems to be a force almost wholly unto itself in "Portrait of a Lady," appearing in relation to the characters with little regard for whether it has been called on or not. The youth, for example, does not seek out the street-piano that so moves him in the garden. The music appears to seize him and practice a kind of mind control over him instead, as he reflects that he had been able to "remain self-possessed" until the song came to him (12). The tom-tom in his head, so often described as an instrument of resistance to romantic ideology, is even further from his control. There is no decision on his part to enlist music in the conflict, no indication that he summons or remembers the beat in order to clear the lady's words out of his head. Instead, the "Capricious" drum simply "begins" as though it were in his mind already and needed no push to begin playing. Even the classical cornet and violin that so unsettle him seem to be associations that exist only within his thoughts, accompaniments that appear when the appropriate situation arises: the instrumental combination, after all, implies a comparatively large, unwieldy ensemble such as a symphony orchestra, unlikely background music at a tea. And even if there is any music playing in the salon, could the hostess reasonably be said to have evoked it? It is doubtful. Even the pianist who gives the Chopin recital does not appear to be in charge of the music he plays, as his fingertips passively "Transmit the Preludes" like radio antennae rather than summon, interpret, or even simply play them.

The conclusion at this point must be that, while music serves to construct conceptions of identity and the self in Eliot, it nevertheless remains an independent force that operates on listeners whether they will or no. The young protagonist is at the mercy of several outside influences: the smell of a hyacinth captures and transports his imagination, while his mental responses to his foil's statements often (and unwittingly?) rhyme with hers, forced into a more traditional prosody. Nothing in "Portrait of a Lady," however, takes command of him as often as music does, nor to such a radical extent; and while Eliot hints at music's invasive capacity in his earlier unpublished works, this poem seems to articulate something larger and considerably more complicated. It is his first depiction of music as a ubiquitous force, such a powerfully significant part of modern life that it can take control of people's minds without warning and command their very thoughts — even, in the case of the tom-tom, when there isn't any music playing at all.

It is vital to note that the first major phase of Eliot's career (spanning from his late childhood to *The Waste Land*) coincided almost exactly with the rise of the modern record industry and an associated explosion of what we might today call ambient music. In 1889, when Eliot was a year old, the first coin-activated jukebox received its patent and began appearing in public spaces all over America. In 1901, a so-called "golden era" of acoustic recording was underway, with record sales increasing steadily for two decades and radio broadcasting holding sway long after that.[13] By 1909, one year before Eliot began "Portrait of a Lady," more than 27 million records were being produced every year, featuring everything from classical ensembles to whistling virtuosos to performers of racial "coon songs." And this is to say nothing of the burgeoning sales of pianos and sheet music, Tin Pan Alley's most profitable product. Simply put, the amount of music in everyday life was increasing at an extraordinary rate, and it was all the more extraordinary because it was so subtle — as William Kenny has noted, the phonograph itself seemed to disappear into the background as manufacturers designed models that resembled furniture, pianos, overnight bags, and suitcases.[14] It did not take long before the sonic environment had changed utterly, and with it the world as depicted by modernist authors. Eliot's contemporary John Dos Passos nicely captures this new reality in his sonically rich novel *Manhattan Transfer*, depicting a man trying to read a newspaper at home: "Apartments round about emitted a querulous Sunday grinding of phonographs playing *It's a Bear*. The Sextette from *Lucia*, selections from *The Quaker Girl*."[15] By the first World War, the now-familiar sense of daily musical immersion was already well underway.

Theoretically speaking, the existence of recording technology has several implications for Eliot's poetry. As Walter Benjamin has so famously written, music's capacity to be mechanically reproduced and disseminated in the early twentieth century did away with much of its unique and evanescent character. No longer did listeners have to go to any great lengths to hear music, nor did they have to rely on their memories once it was over. Instead, mechanical reproduction enables music "to meet the [listener] halfway" at any time and in any place, just as it does in Dos Passos's sound-bombarded apartment.[16] Music on a record exists free of any context: "the choral production, performed in an auditorium or in the open air, resounds in the drawing room," representing a "tremendous shattering of tradition" (221). Meanwhile, listeners presented with mechanically reproduced, infinitely repeatable music come to regard it as a commodity as well as an art, unlike previous generations. Benjamin thus concludes his essay by predicting the rise of "distracted" consumers who absorb music into themselves rather than find themselves absorbed in music — a reversal of the traditional relationship (239). It is somewhat difficult to know from Benjamin's description just what a distracted, music-absorbing listener might actually be like, but Eliot provides us with vivid examples in "Portrait of a Lady." We cannot be certain, after all, whether his lady and narrator are listening to external music or the music in their heads and imaginations; the only certain thing is that music has actually become part of their fundamental selves.

Like so much else in Eliot's work, however, the presence of popular song reaches an apex of complexity and significance in *The Waste Land.* The poem was published in 1922, two years after radio broadcasting began, and it remains Eliot's best depiction of music as a ubiquitous agent in society. He is considerably more explicit here than in his previous poems, describing the ways in which music can hijack a listener's consciousness in blow-by-blow detail as well as mapping the world's larger sonic landscape more thoroughly. Music exists as both an external and internal force, but it is unavoidable in all states, appearing in unexpected places and almost always without warning. Working in concert with the prophets, bartenders, and long-dead writers who provide the poem's many interwoven fragments, music ensures that a reader of *The Waste Land* is never alone, ever walking, as John T. Mayer writes, "with voices singing in his ears."[17] Whether these voices can be filtered in such a way as to hear a coherent message is the poem's central question.

In the poem's originally published version, contemporary music makes its first and most surprising entrance in the "Game of Chess" section. After a 33-line, heavily allusive description of a gaudily decorated room, Eliot presents a squabbling couple. It is a strange argument, at least in the aural sense, because only one side — a woman's rapid-fire admonitions — seems to actually be audible. "Speak to me. Why do you never speak? Speak./ What are you thinking of? What thinking? What?" she demands of her silent partner.[18] The man's unspoken responses are more interesting, but they have a similarly fractured, off-balance feel to them. On the question of what he's thinking, he gives an ominous and inscrutable mental response: "I think we are in rats' alley/ Where the dead men lost their bones." Asked whether he can remember anything, his thoughts swerve to a line of Shakespeare's: "I remember/ Those are pearls that were his eyes." Having spent the last 15 lines literally inside the man's brooding consciousness, readers are at this point beginning to get the hang of the effect and are prepared for the next series of questions, "Are you alive, or not? Is there nothing in your head?" But this time, the man's response is jarring and nothing short of bizarre:

> "Are you alive, or not? Is there nothing in your head?"
> But
> O O O O that Shakespeherian Rag —
> It's so elegant
> So intelligent

The rag in question comes from the 1912 Ziegfeld Follies, and in Chinitz's judgment it isn't a particularly good one, a "rather forced" collection of puns and rhymes about characters from Shakespeare's dramatic works (47). The lyric and its placement in *The Waste Land* has inspired years of debate over just what Eliot meant by including it, and the discussion is usually framed in the familiar terms of cultural value. While the rag has often been dismissed as a symbol of vulgarity or mass taste, Chinitz suggests that Eliot in all probability enjoyed it "for its blend of brash irreverence and outlandish vacuity"; but as I have previously noted, the question of likes and dislikes seems rather beside the point here. While it would certainly be interesting to know what Eliot thought of the tune, it seems more important to explore the inventive way in which he has described something of a modern epidemic: the sensation of having a song stuck in one's head, one that pops up at the strangest moments.

Once readers get over the song's initial apparent randomness, they will likely notice the odd "O" sounds and fanciful spelling of "Shakespeherian." The devices, as Frank Kermode has noted, were Eliot's inventions, and they serve to both locate the music within the man's mind and create a uniquely musical effect (*The Waste Land and Other Poems* 101). The O's might be his mental rendition of a piano line, an attempt at some sort of scat singing, or the all-too-familiar practice of covering up forgotten lyrics in the middle of a line. The misspelling, in a similar vein, forces a pretentious, vaguely British accent, a syncopated rhythm, and a satiric edge on the lyric — perfect for a song claiming that Shakespeare's canonized plays are nothing more than an "old classical drag." (*The Waste Land* 52). Unlike so many of the allusions to outside sources in *The Waste Land*, "That Shakespearian Rag" is not quoted faithfully and left intact. The man has riffed on it as any singer might, interpreting the piece in the private space of his mind.

Further attention to the passage will show that, while the song's appearance is odd, it is anything but random — no more random, certainly, than the two preceding mental digressions. The simplest explanation is that the man, having already quoted from *The Tempest*, simply has Shakespeare on the brain and is making a mental association with one of The Bard's pop culture incarnations. More specifically, his "pearls that were his eyes" digression also comes a song, one sung by Ariel, and as such it is just the thing for Eliot's sardonic, associative narrator to riff on. In a more obscure vein, all this could be the man's way of adding onto the woman's question: if punctuation and the long space separating the lines are ignored, the phrase reads as a complete sentence. It thus becomes, "Is there nothing in your head but 'That Shakespearian Rag?" and casts the man as something of an improvising jazz musician, adding his own variations to a theme. But regardless of whether the song is inspired by the woman's needling questions or represents a continuation of the man's private thoughts, it is an improper response in a conversation of such gravity, and the song remains inaudible. The effect gets echoed to an extent in the poem's next scene, in which a speaker chats in a tavern and a bartender's shouted refrain of "HURRY UP PLEASE ITS TIME" punctuates the verse (10). The loud proclamation never actually disrupts conversation, for the speaker ignores it as background noise and continues talking. The henpecked husband would appear to be doing the same thing with his silly rag, noticing but not acknowledging yet another distracting sound inside the noisy, crowded barroom that his mind has become. To reiterate Benjamin's concept of the distracted listener, he has absorbed a piece of art into himself and must deal with the consequences as best he can.

The sudden appearance of "That Shakespearian Rag" is similar to the tom-tom effect of "Portrait of a Lady," but it differs in one key aspect: by making his point with an identifiable piece of popular music, Eliot makes the man's experience more universal and draws his audience closer into the scene. It is difficult to say with any certainty, of course, how widely known "That Shakespearian Rag" was among either the contemporary public or Eliot's cadre of readers. But for those who were already familiar with the song before encountering it in *The Waste Land*, the poem would presumably have caused the rag to begin playing within their own minds as well, replicating the experience of Eliot's aurally beset man. It is very much like the effect that Robert Crawford finds in Eliot's descriptions of the disembodied, whispering voices that haunt London's familiar landmarks, simultaneously appealing to and scrambling his audience's "normal notions of reality" (52). Eliot would later complain that critics misinterpreted him when asserting that *The Waste Land* captured the anxieties and sensations of an entire generation, but it is likely that many of his first readers understood all too well what it felt like to have "That Shakespearian Rag" stuck in one's head. And as is the case in so much of this poem, Eliot invests a familiar experience with a sense of creeping unease.

The passage of time and shifts in musical taste have made this rather antique song something of a dead link for modern audiences, and Eliot's reader-response sensation has thus lessened over time. One does not need to be familiar with "That Shakespearian Rag," however, to understand that its appearance points to a jumbled consciousness and confused, crowded sensorioum. This sort of musical eruption should be familiar to anyone who has ever found an unshakable pop tune stuck in his or her head, and Friedrich Kittler has posited that this kind of disoriented auditory sense is inevitable in a post-gramophone sonic environment. For Kittler, listeners have trouble differentiating between their own internal voices and ones heard from records, as the latter exist free of any obvious organic source. Listening to recorded music, then, has an almost hallucinogenic effect: an external, disembodied voice enters the skull and produces powerful, involuntary mental responses. As Kittler puts it, riffing on a Pink Floyd song, "To make no sound, to pick your feet up off the ground, and to listen to the sound of a voice when night is falling — we all do it when we put on a record that commands such magic."[19] The result, practically speaking, is that listeners actually become part of the overall recording process, with the impressions left upon their exposed brains resembling something like the grooves on a disc or cylinder. At least in musical terms, Eliot is writing during a historical schism, a moment marked by the transition "from active music-making to passive music consumption" and grappling with the issue of just what "performance" means in an era of mechanically produced and ubiquitous song (Garofalo 24). In *The Waste Land*, he seems to be showing that one does not even need to be near a phonograph and, as Benjamin puts it, meet music halfway to encounter a well-worn tune. His protagonist's immersion in an increasingly musical and mechanical culture has made him a walking collection of pop, something of a record himself.

Eliot makes the same point in a slightly different way in the poem's "Fire Sermon" section, when contemporary music and the process of making it take front-and-center roles. A young woman cleans her cluttered flat, which is covered with spread-out, drying clothes, tins of food, and the remains of her breakfast from earlier in the day. Her self-absorbed lover, a "young man carbuncular," drops in for a visit, which culminates in an unpleasant but mercifully brief sex scene: "he assaults at once;/ Exploring hands encounter no defence;/ His vanity requires no response,/ And makes a welcome of indifference" (13). He leaves her alone in her home after giving her "one final patronising kiss," and she gazes into a mirror.

> Her brain allows one half-formed thought to pass:
> "Well now that's done: and I'm glad it's over."
> When lovely woman stoops to folly and
> Paces about her room again, alone,
> She smoothes her hair with automatic hand
> And puts a record on the gramophone. (13-4)

Readers cannot know what the typist's musical selection is, as the scene shifts immediately afterwards. There are any number of possibilities: it might be a sad song that heightens the feeling of disillusionment lingering over the scene, or a peppy one that would provide the ironic, "Make the best of your position" contrast that Eliot exploits in a previous poem. It is crucial to notice, however, that the typist is attempting to force a song *into* her head, hoping that music will spring into her consciousness as it has (unexpectedly) for others of Eliot's characters. The line "her brain allows one half-formed thought to pass" casts the typist as a policewoman of her own mind, creating a sense — as if it were not clear already — that there are aspects of her life that she would prefer not to think about. And in such a situation, the following lines imply, it is well known to all that music can provide the necessary distraction. The next sentence has a feel of ritual to it, set up as an if/then condition reducible to something like, "When lovely woman stoops to folly, she puts a record on the gramophone." Benjamin asserts that music "becomes a creation with entirely new functions" in an age of mechanical reproduction, while Kittler writes that electronic devices like the gramophone stole the "powers of hallucination" that had once belonged exclusively to writers (225, 10). For the typist, it would appear that music has become her default drug of choice, a perception-altering force that she instinctively reaches for when she needs to block something out of her thoughts.

Indeed, there is much about this scene that is mechanical, an appropriate touch given that the music of Eliot's day was becoming increasingly intertwined with the technology that produced it. Most obviously, there is the description of the typist's "automatic hand," which carries connotations of both her machine-oriented typing job and the tone arm on her record player (which brings needle to disc). Then there is the regular pattern of rhyme and meter, which at 30 lines is one of the poem's longest sustained passages of traditional prosody, an uncharacteristically rigid versification that, in the words of Martin Scofield, "contributes a great deal to the effect of fastidious observation and holding at a distance."[20] Even the word "record" is indistinguishable from a technological process, coming as it does from the exact duplicate created when "stamper" master discs are pressed against ebonite rubber biscuits to produce copies (Garofalo 21). In one scene, then, we have a mechanical approach to sex, poetry, and music-making, all in the confines of the typist's home. This is what it must look like when life imitates art in an age of mechanical reproduction.

The mind-controlling music that the typist chooses may brighten her mood, heighten the scene's sadness, or simply provide a distraction; but in any event, Eliot does not allow readers to expend too much thought on her, leaving her in what Calvin Bedient calls "a limbo of mild mechanical throbs and habitual circlings as automatic and soothing as those of the gramophone."[21] Instead of dwelling with her, Eliot moves quickly to a scene in which music functions as it so often does in the literature before him — as a stumbled-upon, unexpected instrument of pure pleasure. The poetic consciousness moves down the same London streets that Eliot enjoyed walking during his lunch breaks, as music "crept by" — another phrase of Shakespeare's — and the "pleasant whining of a mandoline" becomes audible (14). It is a welcome contrast to the episode of the typist, a one-of-a-kind interlude produced by visible, identifiable human beings that, once over, will exist only vaguely in the protagonist's memory and never be heard in the same way again. It captivates but does not enter him, pleases him but does not command him, and ultimately represents an older way of listening that had become a "near anachronism in the jazz age" (Bedient 140). Music in Eliot's poetry is generally an overwhelming presence that forces listeners to take part in a process that is equal parts aural, mental, social, and mechanical. The moment of the mandoline, however, hints (as does the entire poem) that means of escape still do exist, even if they have become nearly impossible to find.

A previous draft of *The Waste Land* has a much higher musical volume, with "The Burial of the Dead" containing references to additional pop songs. Lyrics from a variety of tunes are penciled in at the margins as Eliot describes an all-night bender, in which the protagonist tries to "put my foot in the drum" at a club and hassles a police officer.[22] But the entire scene was later cut, and as such "That Shakespearian Rag" is the only extant pop song in the work, with the rest lurking in the background, exerting a shadowy and unheard influence on the poem as published. As a result, Michael North has noted, it would not be until the later *Sweeney Agonistes* that most of Eliot's readers fully understood how important popular music had been in shaping the changing, urban, mobile feel of his work.[23] But one of the few who did make the connection, Desmond Hawkins, wrote in 1948 that he had found Eliot's work every bit as catchy as the pop of his era, commanding his attention "because the poetry got into your head like a song-hit" (qtd Chinitz 6). Such a statement finally closes the loop interweaving music, words, thought, readers, and the poet himself. If the ubiquitous music of the day was forcing its way into the public mind whether it was welcome or not, it stands to reason that an astute cultural observer like Eliot might replicate the effect with new lyrics of his own.

As I have previously mentioned, Eliot's interest in the changing human auditory sense has gone generally unnoticed in critical studies, no doubt because modern readers are accustomed to the kinds of involuntary listening and song internalization that strike him as so new and strange. Music floats around us from the moment our clock radios go off in the morning to when we turn off the television at night, and we seldom give its ubiquity much thought. Even the pop hits and jingles that perennially bounce about in our heads give us little pause, and the number of people who have lived in any other kind of sonic environment grows smaller by the year. And yet, we still seem to have a sense that sound should be able to impinge only so far upon our interior spaces. In a recent *Esquire* overview of up-and-coming inventions, the magazine's editors profess unease over the so-called HyperSonic Sound laser, a device capable projecting music, advertisements, and other auditory sensations into an individual listener's skull as though through headphones, all from a distance of 150 yards. An illustration features a businessman standing in line at an ATM with concentric beams of sound targeting his brain, and the short article ticks off the various circumstances under which bystanders might be forced to hear the laser's operators, some "odious," others less so.[24] If the consciousness-busting idea of a sound laser can still unnerve us, then it becomes all the more important to understand Eliot's interest in music's peculiar, haunting character. His song-absorbing listeners remain early prototypes from a dawning age of mechanical sound, but when all is said and done they nevertheless anticipate our own concerns.

Works Cited

Appel, Afred Jr. *Jazz Modernism: From Ellington and Armstrong to Matisse and Joyce*. New York: Alfred A. Knopf, 2002.

Bedient, Calvin. *He Do the Police In Different Voices: The Waste Land and Its Protagonist*. Chicago: University of Chicago Press, 1986.

Benjamin, Walter. "The Work of Art in the Age of Mechanical Reproduction."

—. *Illuminations*. Ed. Hannah Arendt. Trans. Harry Zohn. New York: Schocken Books, 1968.

Chinitz, David. *T. S. Eliot and the Cultural Divide*. Chicago: University of Chicago Press, 2003.

Coleridge, Samuel Taylor. "The Rime of the Ancient Mariner." *The Complete Poetical Works of Samuel Taylor Coleridge*. Ed. Ernest Hartley Coleridge. Oxford: Clarendon Press, 1912.

Crawford, Robert. *The Savage and the City in the Work of T. S. Eliot*. Oxford: Clarendon Press, 1987.

Dos Passos, John. *Manhattan Transfer*. New York: Mariner Books, 2000.

Eliot, T. S. *Inventions of the March Hare: Poems 1909-1917*. Ed. Christopher Ricks. New York: Harcourt Brace & Company, 1996.

—. *The Waste Land*. Ed. Michael North. New York: W.W. Norton & Company, 2001.

—. *The Waste Land: A Facsimile and Transcript of the Original Drafts Including the Annotations of Ezra Pound*. Ed. Valerie Eliot. New York: Harcourt Brace Jovanovich, Inc.: 1971.

—. *The Waste Land and Other Poems*. Ed. Frank Kermode. New York: Penguin Books, 1998.

Frith, Simon. "Towards an Aesthetic of Popular Music." *Music and Society: The Politics of Composition, Performance and Reception*. Ed. Richard Leppert and Susan McClary. Cambridge: Cambridge University Press, 1987.

Garofalo, Reebee. *Rockin' Out: Popular Music in the USA*. Boston: Allyn and Bacon, 1997.

Gordon, Lyndall. *T. S. Eliot: An Imperfect Life*. New York: W.W. Norton & Company, 1998.

Jansen, David A. and Jones, Gene. *That American Rag: The Story of Ragtime from Coast to Coast*. New York: Schirmer Books, 2000.

Jourdain, Robert. *Music, the Brain, and Ecstasy: How Music Captures Our Imaginations*. New York: William Morrow and Company, 1997.

Kenny, William Howland. *Recorded Music in American Life: The Phonograph and Popular Memory, 1890-1945*. Oxford: Oxford University Press, 1999.

Kittler, Friedrich A. *Gramophone, Film, Typewriter.* Trans. Geoffrey Winthrop-Young and Michael Wutz. Stanford: Stanford University Press, 1999.

Mayer, John T. "*The Waste Land* and Eliot's Poetry Notebook." *T. S. Eliot: The Modernist in History.* Ed. Ronald Bush. Cambridge: Cambridge University Press, 1991.

Moody, A.D. *Thomas Stearns Eliot: Poet.* Cambridge: Cambridge University Press, 1979.

North, Michael. *The Dialect of Modernism: Race, Language, and Twentieth Century Literature.* Oxford: Oxford University Press, 1994.

Scofield, Martin. *T. S. Eliot: The Poems.* Cambridge: Cambridge University Press, 1988.

"The Sound Laser." *Esquire.* December 2003: 165.

THE BEATLES AS MODERNISTS

KENNETH WOMACK

The Beatles have been the stuff of serious scholarly attention since the release of their second album, *With the Beatles* (1963), when William Mann of the London *Times* famously saluted John Lennon's "Not a Second Time" for its deployment of an Aeolian cadence, a feature that Mann likened to the chord progression that ends Gustav Mahler's *The Song of the Earth* (1907-1909).[1] In one of the final interviews before his senseless murder, a baffled Lennon remarked that "to this day I don't have *any* idea what [Aeolian cadences] are. They sound like exotic birds." Yet way back in 1963, he could barely contain his excitement by Mann's sophisticated response to the band's work: "That was the first time anyone had written anything like that about us," he later admitted (qtd. in Dowlding 57). In 1968, the esteemed BBC critic Deryck Cooke branded Lennon and Paul McCartney as "serious" composers of a "new music" (199). In so doing, Cooke legitimized them for the ages. From the likes of Wilfrid Mellers and Ian MacDonald through Tim Riley and Walter Everett, a critical evolution emerged in which the Beatles's phenomenal accomplishments were treated from nearly every possible lyrical and musicological perspective. In recent years, the Beatles have enjoyed considerable interest from cultural theorists attempting to gauge the group's signal role in the sociohistorical construction of 60s culture, as well as the larger impact of the band's *oeuvre* as a sustained commentary about the nature of the human condition.

Not surprisingly, cultural and literary theorists inevitably aspire to situate the Beatles in terms of their overarching narrative and ideological intentions. This constitutes a vital function of literary studies and not mere fodder for self-propagating critical theorists. As *de facto* authors of a significant body of work, the Beatles surely merit the same sort of exacting analysis that our seminal writers undergo as we attempt to ascertain the breadth and scope of their achievements. This is important and ongoing work that continues to merge literary studies, musicology, and cultural theory in a variety of intriguing ways. Rather, my issue is with the increasing certainty with which the Beatles are framed as innovative postmodern visionaries. In such works as Henry W. Sullivan's *The Beatles with Lacan: Rock 'n' Roll as Requiem for the Modern Age* (1995), David Quantick's *Revolution: The Making of the Beatles' White*

Album (2002), Devin McKinney's *Magic Circles: The Beatles in Dream and History* (2003), Ed Whitley's "The Postmodern *White Album*," and Jeffrey Roessner's "We All Want to Change the World: Postmodern Politics and the Beatles' *White Album*," the Beatles are essentially—indeed, *unflinchingly*—categorized in terms of an increasingly popular reading of the *White Album* (*The Beatles*; 1968) as a series of arch parodies conducted in a den of sociopolitical chaos. That's right: we have collectively outed the Beatles as postmodernists—not that there's anything wrong with being a postmodernist *per se*.

This rather transparent critical desire to classify the Beatles as postmodernists most likely finds its origins in an effort to "update" the band by making them seem more trendy by virtue of postmodernism's relative contemporaneousness. This critical gesture might also be the explicit result of the myriad ways in which the band continues to "speak" to generation upon generation of listeners. One need only witness the unparalleled success of their recent greatest-hits compilation—an album that accumulated sales of some 35 million copies across the globe in a mere 18 months—in order to appreciate this latter impulse. The Beatles' apotheosis as a postmodern spectacle might also be understood as the express product of literary theory's rage for establishing coherent period terms. Postmodernism is generally recognized, of course, as a postwar phenomenon, and the Beatles are one of the most—if not *the* most—visible postwar phenomena of them all. Surely, postmodernism and Beatles are one and the same?

The glaring lack of scholarly debate about the Beatles' ostensible postmodernist credentials is particular troubling. For the most part, critics have already consigned them to postmodernism's increasingly eclectic scrapheap. Scholars generally ascribe the Beatles' alleged postmodernity to the brash experimentation of *Revolver* (1966) and *Sgt. Pepper's Lonely Hearts Club Band* (1967), as well as to the complex artistry and deliberate fragmentation inherent in the *White Album*.[2] In addition to discounting the significance of such formative Beatles albums as *Help!* (1965) and *Rubber Soul* (1965), this perspective mitigates the roles of *Abbey Road* (1969) and *Let It Be* (1970), respectively, in the twilight of the band's creative fusion.[3] Sullivan, for example, contends that the Beatles shared in the construction of postmodern culture by helping to bring modernism to a close. Yet other critics refuse to consider any linkage between the Beatles and modernism, preferring, instead, to read the Beatles as scions of postmodern art. Whitley perceptively addresses the manner in which the Beatles "shift the center of meaning from the text itself and onto [their] readers, who are then given a share of the responsibility for creating meaning." At the same time, Whitley argues that the Beatles resist modernist tendencies toward unity by engaging in "disparate musical styles" and "fragmentation of structure" (108). Whitley's position, as with so much contemporary Beatles criticism, neglects to account for the band's decidedly modernist rage for creating unity at nearly every turn—among individual songs, among albums, across their entire career. Do the Beatles create a sense of intentional fragmentation on *Sgt. Pepper* and the *White Album*? Absolutely. But they clearly do so as artists bent on establishing a form of controlled chaos in which every note, every utterance has its place. And, indeed, while the *White Album* seems to evince postmodern tendencies in a number of interesting ways, the Beatles' ideological stance might be more accurately described as modernist, given that many of their songs concern themselves with love, peace, and the genuine possibility of communal transcendence.

Simply put, the Beatles unashamedly believe in a form of moral center that exists in sharp contrast with postmodernism's subjective elevation of personal and cultural malaise. Yes, the Beatles are modernists alright, and—whether we care to admit it or not—their modernist stance is one of the factors behind their lasting popularity and influence. While we may look outwardly at an endlessly complex and nihilistic postmodern world, the Beatles afford us with a comforting firmament from which we can awake from our golden slumbers, bask in the glory of the morning sun, and simply let it all be. Time and time again, we can revisit their unifying vision of love, hope, and community. From their earliest work through the waning days of *Abbey Road*, the Beatles imagined themselves to be creating a coherent body of work. For Western culture, the Beatles clearly function as a master-text, as a sociohistorical touchstone, as a grand narrative. And make no mistake about it: the Beatles believed in the existence of a grand narrative, albeit not an exclusionary macronarrative for understanding the world. The Beatles' modernism involves the invocation of a universal, unifying ethical center and a persistent optimism about an unknowable future in contrast with a lingering nostalgia for the past. In *Sinking Island: The Modern English Writers* (1988), Hugh Kenner identifies nostalgia as a distinctive feature of modernism that involves a turning-away from contemporary life and a subsequent retreat into the soothing interstices of memory. The Beatles accomplish this end through an explicitly nostalgic reverence for the past that evinces itself in nearly every nook and cranny of their remarkable musical canon.

While Jean-François Lyotard famously challenges the notion of a single, subsuming grand narrative in *The Postmodern Condition: A Report on Knowledge* (1979), mass culture has always longed for the comforting unity of an all-encompassing human story. If the spirited religious furvor over Mel Gibson's controversial *The Passion of the Christ* (2004) reveals nothing else, the film demonstrates mass culture's unquenchable desire for a singular narrative within which to instill their most sacred beliefs. Although we may theorize about the nuances of its construction and the nature of its existence, mass culture constitutes a vast constituency that yearns (often unconsciously) for transcendence amidst the malaise and fragmentation of postmodern life.

While he acknowledges nostalgia's "semideluded state" and its function "as an act more of forgetting than remembrance," R. J. Warren Zanes argues that nostalgia finds its contemporary roots in our larger cultural urge to return to an unblemished past where we can revivify our notions of community and eschew the superficiality of commercialism's ceaseless engine. In contrast with our nostalgic desires for reasserting stability, the real myth, Zanes suggests, originates from "our ill-founded dreams" of a proverbial elsewhere in which our yen for consumerism replaces the emotional satisfaction that we derive from home, hearth, and humanity. As Zanes reminds us, the world of music—and rock culture in particular—"holds out the promise that such a longing might be satisfied" (62).[4] And why not? Hasn't popular music always dared us to embrace the restorative powers of love, friendship, and a universalizing belief in a redeemable past—a past to which, if our aim is really true, we can get back to where we once belonged?

Kimberly K. Smith argues that our contemporary notions of nostalgia first came into being through various nineteenth- and twentieth-century conflicts over the political significance of the past. According to Smith, nostalgia finds its origins in the historical transition from the relative stability of an agrarian society to the mounting anxiety of a largely industrial world. In this sense, nostalgia emerges as a means for recontextualizing the past in terms of the present, as a form of social constructivism in which the past accrues greater meaning because of its significance and desirability in contrast with an uncertain and highly volatile contemporary moment. "To experience a memory nostalgically is not just to have certain feelings along with that memory," Smith suggests, "but to adopt a particular attitude towards it: to understand the memory and its associated feelings as the product of a psychological propensity to romanticize the past, and to value it as a vehicle for a Proustian sort of heightened sensibility or self-awareness" (509). In this way, nostalgia exists as an acculturated behavior through which we develop a perspective towards the past as a place where we might fulfill our collective longing for an "archetypal paradise" (514). As the editors of the canon-making *Norton Anthology of English Literature, Volume Two* (7th ed.; 2000) remind us, modernism is frequently "characterized by nostalgia for the vanished past," and "modernists looked to the past as a time when subjectivity was unfragmented, communities were organic and nurturing, daily experience was meaningful, and social values were unquestioned. Postmodernists, by contrast, are unlikely to indulge in nostalgia for such a past, which seems increasingly distant, most probably fabricated, and—if it ever existed—more than a little sinister." Indeed, postmodern variations on nostalgia frequently involve stylistically motivated or retro-oriented desires for reconnecting with the past.

The Beatles' modernism finds its roots in their evolving need to perform nostalgia as a narratological device. The group's nostalgic imperative in their music fulfills a larger ethical desire—both for them *and* for us—to replicate sameness and to establish means of reconnecting with the past even as we make explicit attempts to break with that same past and create new inroads into an uncertain future. The Beatles inaugurate this process in their earliest recordings and begin, rather self-consciously, to refine their forays into nostalgia as their career reaches its zenith. While songs such as "There's a Place" and "I'll Be Back" reveal Lennon and McCartney on a utopian search for comfort and sameness, later numbers such as "I'll Follow the Sun" and "In My Life" find them looking backward—across increasing expanses of time—in a thinly veiled desire to memorialize the past and their relationship with its mysterious hold upon the present. These same impulses evolve along with the Beatles' lyrics and music. Intriguingly, recordings such as "For No One" and "Tomorrow Never Knows" find the Beatles engaging with the past even as they attempt to confront an overwhelming sense of presentness that threatens to undo their nostalgic feelings in nearly the same instant in which they first experience them. This narratological double-bind intensifies as the decade moves forward in such tracks as "A Day in the Life" and "Your Mother Should Know," songs in which the band waxes nostalgically about the past, while an enigmatic future unfolds before them. This trend assumes even darker textures on the *White Album* as the band comes to recognize their impending dissolution. Recordings like the self-referential "Glass Onion" and "Sexy Sadie" create makeshift memorials to a disintegrating creative fusion, while numbers like the schmaltzy "Honey Pie" and George Harrison's somber "Long Long Long" conjure up the past with utter abandon. By the advent of *Let It Be* and *Abbey Road*, they can only dream of transcendence in the face of an increasingly unknowable and irremediable past. Yet from beginning to end, the Beatles continue to embrace nostalgia—hoping against hope, as they always do, for the emergence of a more tolerant and loving world.

Without question, the Beatles exist as the historical product of the socially constructed nostalgia of the postwar world. In 1957—the year in which Lennon famously met McCartney in a Liverpool churchyard—Britons had ample reason to look back wistfully at an eminently more auspicious past in comparison to their mediocre present. As Philip Norman reminds us:

> The year was one of unparalleled national humiliation. It was the year that the British engaged with France in a ludicrous plan to invade Egypt and were foiled by, of all people, the Egyptians. After Suez, the world would never again function at the behest of British gunboats. England had become overnight a second-class power, barely noticed in the new, harsh glare of America's and Russia's nuclear cohabitation. (30)

For budding songwriters such as Lennon and McCartney, the act of reflecting upon the past—and upon its supposed glories—had become nothing short of a national pastime. As they grow as lyricists and musicians, their recordings begin to emerge as concentrated and humanistically driven searches for self-knowledge. While their songs reveal increasingly more elaborate uses of language and innovative musical textures, the Beatles' recurring performance of nostalgia reflects their highly literary effort to narrativize the past. At times, their narrative project seeks to memorialize an idealized past as a form of reassuring façade, although in other instances their music undermines that same notion of an idealized past by presenting a concerted meditation on the nature of loss. As their career comes to a close with *Abbey Road*, we witness the Beatles in a rather sobering search for interpersonal transcendence as they grapple with an irreparable, impermeable, and ultimately inconsolable sense of pastness. These three stages of development seem to find the Beatles devoting considerable creative energy to their narrative project in an attempt to reconcile their audience and themselves—modernists that they are—with the complex nature of memory and its refraction through nostalgia's lens.

The lion's share of the Beatles' musical explorations of nostalgia occur, rather pointedly, *after* 1966, when the band and their management had permanently relocated to London, leaving the comforting environs of Liverpool behind forever. In addition to the suffocating power of Beatlemania itself, this geographical shift from working-class Liverpool to the eminently more sophisticated London accounts for the band's understandable sense of emotional dislocation. Rather than functioning as their ultimate destination, London emerges for the Beatles as "a point of departure," according to Annette Hames and Ian Inglis, "from which to elaborate on other, non-localized themes—of nostalgia, consciousness, and history" (182). While their fascination with nostalgia assumes greater nuance with such albums as *Rubber Soul* (1965) and *Revolver* (1966), the Beatles offer intriguing portraits of nostalgia as early as *Please Please Me* (1963), their whirlwind first album. In Lennon's "There's a Place," the speaker imagines an otherworldly space where "there's no sorrow" and "no sad tomorrow." More likely a state of being as opposed to an actual physical locale, this personally inscribed place allows Lennon's speaker to be alone, and, rather significantly, to be liberated from the socially dislocating forces of the workaday world. In "Misery," the speaker, suffering from the understandable woes of a failed romance, maligns his gloomy present in contrast with the ostensibly joyful times of a rapidly fading past: "I'll remember all the little things we've done," he tells us, suggesting that his blissful memories of happier days might function as curatives for his broken heart. The song's implicit irony, of course, is that the speaker's nostalgic longings for his beloved serve to establish a vicious circle of sorts in which his miserable state will continue to plague him indefinitely.

Recordings such as *The Music Man*'s "Till There Was You"—written by Meredith Wilson and covered on *With the Beatles*—demonstrate the band's affinity for waxing nostalgic about romance in the very moment in which the love affair reaches its emotional pinnacle, rather than after its consignment to Cupid's scrapheap. Can those "bells on the hill" and "fragrant meadows of dawn" be anything other than nostalgia's unremitting hyperbole? *A Hard Day's Night* (1964) finds the Beatles in full acceleration with quasi-nostalgic tracks such as "If I Fell" and "I'll Be Back." In the former song, the speaker seems to be making tentative steps toward a new romantic relationship, although his attitude towards his former lover belies his alleged emotional growth: "I must be sure from the very start, / That you would love me more than her," he cautions his prospective girlfriend, conspicuously reminding her that his erstwhile love "will cry when she learns we are two." Nostalgia takes a similarly bitter form in "I'll Be Back"—a darker manifestation of the less-threatening "This Boy" (the B-side of "I Want to Hold Your Hand"—wherein the song's speaker, supported by a clutch of bristling acoustic guitars, offers what appears to be a fairly routine dirge about the emotional traumas of lost love. Yet, rather interestingly, the speaker learns an excruciating lesson about the fleeting nature of romance; claiming that "I'll be back" because "I'm the one who wants you," he discovers the agonizing truth about his lover's immutable discontent. Believing all the while that she would reciprocate his love, he "got a big surprise" instead. Will the speaker usurp the past and finally prove to his beloved that he has changed emotionally, or will he proffer an engagement ring, or is he referring to something sinister—her desire for a vengeful breakup perhaps?

As with the bitter nostalgia inherent in songs like "If I Fell" and "I'll Be Back," *Beatles for Sale*'s "I'll Follow the Sun" (1964) similarly concerns itself with the nature of sorrow and loss. The song brims with a sense of deeply felt nostalgia, as if the speaker were intensely self-conscious about his fleeting place within the temporal moment: "One day you'll look to see I've gone," McCartney sings. "For tomorrow may rain, so I'll follow the sun." The early Beatles' nostalgic dance reaches its apex with *Help!*'s "Yesterday" (1965), McCartney's masterpiece of sorrow and simplicity. The concept of "yesterday" itself denotes a sense of looking backward into an increasingly distant past, as well as a self-consciousness about a certain "shadow hanging over me" in the irreducible present. Performed in the darkish hues of a minor key—so dark, in fact, that listeners might understandably wonder if the speaker's former love had died, rather tragically, in youth, instead of merely dumping him summarily—"Yes It Is" (the B-side of "Ticket to Ride") cautions his beloved's successor that wearing a red dress will conjure up powerful memories of the past—a painful nostalgia for which he has no antidote. "I could be happy with you by my side," he admits, while claiming that his indefatigable pride in the face of a public breakup apparently prevents him from moving forward.[5]

In many ways, "All You Need Is Love"—the Beatles' 1967 utopian anthem recorded for the international *Our World* television broadcast—creates a musical amalgam of sorts regarding the early Beatles' fairly unsophisticated tangles with nostalgia. At the creative behest of George Martin, the Beatles' magisterial producer, the song's introduction famously references "La Marseillaise" in an obvious attempt to conjure up stereotypical notions of the French as the world's greatest lovers.[6] In addition to the French national anthem, Martin concludes the song with an instrumental montage that features "Greensleeves"—a rather appropriate choice, given the sixteenth-century tune's despairing phrases about a heart that remains forever in captivity—as well as a fragment from Glenn Miller's "In the Mood." Perhaps even more interestingly for our purposes here, "All You Need Is Love" witnesses the Beatles bidding farewell, in a manner of speaking, to their early forays into nostalgia's appealing web. As the song fades out, Lennon delivers a non-sequitur reference to "Yesterday," followed closely on the heels by McCartney, who provides a brief refrain from "She Loves You." As Alan W. Pollack astutely remarks, "To my ears, their quote from 'She Loves You' goes beyond the merely clever literary association of the lyrics to become the more profound musical equivalent of the wax models [of the Beatlemania-era band mates] on the cover of *Sgt. Pepper*." In so doing, the group offers a telling salute to the past as "All You Need Is Love" fades into oblivion.

The Beatles' narrative project clearly begins in earnest in the latter months of 1965, culminating in the release of *Rubber Soul*, a groundbreaking musical and lyrical event in the larger scope of their career. As Gary Burns notes, the Beatles' nostalgic forays during this era "softened and humanized" their recordings, thus "increasing their mass appeal." Rather than being politically motivated, he adds, "this was a benign use of nostalgia" (186). In short, the Beatles often employed nostalgia for nostalgia's sake as a comforting mechanism. Lennon and McCartney begin self-consciously fashioning a nostalgic façade with "In My Life," which fuses Lennon's nostalgic phrases with McCartney's hopeful, meandering music.[7] The resulting composition provides a spectacular opening gambit in a nostalgic trip that will take the band through "Penny Lane," "Strawberry Fields Forever," "A Day in the Life," "The Long and Winding Road," and the *Abbey Road* medley. With "In My Life," Lennon deftly examines the power and inevitable failure of memory. While some places and people remain vivid, others recede and disappear altogether. "Memories lose their meaning," Lennon sings, although he knows that "he'll often stop and think about them," referring, yet again, to the past's fecundating layers of character and setting. Fittingly, "In My Life" features Martin's wistful Elizabethan piano solo. With its baroque intonations, the piano interlude participates in establishing the track's nostalgic undercurrents. The song's closing refrain—"In my life, I love you more"—suggests obvious romantic overtones, as well as a lyrical posture in which the speaker commemorates the all-encompassing power of romantic love. Yet it also underscores our vexing relationship with the past, which exerts a powerful hold upon the present, in one sense, while slowly fading from memory and metamorphosing into other, perhaps more pleasing or less painful memories with each passing year. As Maurice Halbwachs reminds us, "The past is not preserved but is reconstructed on the basis of the present" (qtd. in Smith 517-18).

For the Beatles, of course, the past never really ceases to exist in the first place; it merely becomes transmogrified by the present. No two Beatles songs demonstrate this point more than "Penny Lane" and "Strawberry Fields Forever," the classic pair of tunes that the band produced after abandoning life on the road forever in favor of a schedule more sympathetically oriented to their work as recording artists.[8] Named after a Liverpool bus roundabout, "Penny Lane" offers a shrewd reading of the manner in which we frequently reconceive the past in our memories in order to imbue it with idyllic hues. "Memory," Nancy Martha West observes, "depends on a personalized narrative; nostalgia transforms that narrative (including the possible stresses and uncertainties of events in progress) into fullness, innocence, simplicity" (175). With its overarching "blue suburban skies" and perpetually convivial environs, "Penny Lane" effects a utopian neighborhood where life borders on perfection and even the banker eschews a raincoat despite the "pouring rain." In "Penny Lane," McCartney's dreamlike refrain—"very strange"—suggests the ways in which the stuff of memory might be all too easily manipulated in order to conform with our most palpable desires about the past's irrevocable course. Lennon investigates similar terrain in "Strawberry Fields Forever," a song that takes its name from a Liverpool Salvation Army home. A place where "nothing is real" and where there is "nothing to get hung about," Strawberry Fields emerges as a peaceful space where "living is easy with eyes closed," a sea of tranquility in dramatic contrast with the invariably more complicated reality of the present. The *White Album*'s "Mother Nature's Son" pursues a slightly different line of inquiry. With "Mother Nature's Son," McCartney imagines a pastoral environment in which his speaker lives in an interminably idyllic present: "Born a poor young country boy, Mother Nature's son / All day long I'm sitting singing songs for everyone." Rather than blithely memorializing the past in the vein of *Magical Mystery Tour*'s "Your Mother Should Know" (1967), "Mother Nature's Son" establishes an artificial present in which the speaker's yearnings for transcendence have seemingly already been satisfied. Yet as surely as the sun goes down, McCartney's "swaying daisies [that] sing a lazy song beneath the sun" will die. The song rather pointedly avoids discussion of life's cyclical maneuvers between birth and death, even though the recording's very fleeting subject matter necessarily prefigures a nostalgic experience in some distant (or perhaps not so distant) future.[9] As with "In My Life," "Penny Lane," and "Strawberry Fields Forever," "Mother Nature's Son" depicts life as a generally benevolent experience with scant regard for its corporeal limits.

In contrast with the Beatles' more dreamy forays into nostalgia, songs such as "Michelle," "For No One," and "Rocky Raccoon" evince a melancholic sadness in which the past, present, and (occasionally) future collide, resulting in a predictable, but no less significant mediation on the nature of loss. Meanwhile, recordings like "She Said She Said" and "A Day in the Life" ponder the sheer impossibility of escaping the interpersonal tensions of the present. With nostalgic feelings, Fred Davis remarks, "the emotional posture is that of a yearning for return, albeit accompanied by an ambivalent recognition that such is not possible" (21). In one of the band's most peculiar meditations on loss, *Rubber Soul*'s "Michelle" reveals an implicit nostalgia in which the song's speaker confesses his love for Michelle even as he already espies the death of love in their future. While McCartney's lyrics concentrate on providing the speaker's would-be French girlfriend with romantic "words that go together well," the Beatles' music—particularly the song's contemplative bass lines—establish a sorrowful subtext with desolate portents for the couple's future. As with so many other McCartney tunes for which nostalgia performs a central function, "For No One" concerns the aftermath of lost love. Complemented by Alan Civil's hauntingly beautiful horn solo, the song's lyrics rather intriguingly consider the interpersonal transformation that such loss engenders in the former lovers: "And in her eyes you see nothing / No sign of love behind the tears / Cried for no one / A love that should have lasted years." Originally entitled "Why Did It Die?" the lyrics of "For No One" examine the ways in which the erstwhile lovers' change in status defines their feelings toward each other—the warmth of their romantic connection has been replaced with the coldness of post-romantic distance; the meaning of their relationship has become transfixed by the present and dispersed among an impenetrable sense of pastness.

In one of his more complicated examinations of nostalgia, McCartney blends disquieting images from the past, present, and future in the *White Album*'s countrified "Rocky Raccoon," a song that shifts, rather astonishingly, from the improbable universe of cowboys, gunplay, and saloons into a gentle paean about nostalgia and loss. Having ventured into the "black mountain hills of Dakota," Rocky is dead, quite literally, before the song even starts. Future commutates into present when Rocky, with only Gideon's Bible to nurture his aching heart, pledges to avenge the loss of his beloved—in a masterstroke of ambiguous identity, "Her name was Magil, and she called herself Lil / But everyone knew her as Nancy"—who has left him, it seems, for another man. The expected showdown is intentionally anticlimactic, resulting, as it does, in Rocky's fatal shooting. As he teeters toward death on the drunken physician's table, Rocky optimistically plots his revival: "Doc, it's only a scratch / And I'll be better, I'll be better, Doc, as soon as I am able." With precious little time remaining, Rocky returns to his hotel room, where Gideon has already "checked out," leaving the gunslinger to die alone. In contrast with the Biblical Gideon's theophanic mission to inspire the Israelites, Rocky's spiritual savior sees scant value in rescuing yet another relic from the Old West. With no place in the future and a desolate present spread out before him, Rocky fades away into a quickly receding past. As with the lover's waning romantic aspirations in "For No One," Rocky can only contemplate the inevitable measure of his loss in an alien world in which nostalgia engenders nothing but sadness and death, spiritual or otherwise.

Amazing as it may seem at this juncture, the narratives of *Revolver*'s "She Said She Said" and "A Day in the Life"—the dramatic climax of *Sgt. Pepper's Lonely Hearts Club Band* (1967)—provide some of the Beatles' most disparaging portraits of contemporary life. In "She Said She Said," Lennon's speaker reacts to a woman who claims to "know what it's like to be dead" by rejecting her observations, which make him "feel like I've never been born." In short, her breadth of experience counters his inferior knowledge, which, in a moment of Blakean contrast, equates the innocence of birth—or, in the speaker's case, *pre*-birth. "When I was a boy," the speaker tells us, "everything was right." The woman's experiences with death ultimately bestow the speaker with a sense of overarching sadness, realizing, as he does, that he is engaged in the act of living a life whose resolution has already been foretold, whose experiences will be less than extraordinary, probably even trite. Filled with variegated sonic hues and other assorted sound effects, "A Day in the Life" trumps the inherent despair of "She Said She Said" by contrasting Lennon's impassive stories of disappointment and remorse with McCartney's deceptively buoyant interlude about the numbing effects of the workaday world. The song's luminous, open-ended refrain—"I'd love to turn you on"—insinuates a sense of interpersonal salvation on a universal scale. Yet Lennon and McCartney's detached lyrics seem to suggest, via their nuances of resignation and unacknowledged guilt, that such a form of emotional release will always remain an unrealized dream. As the music of the Beatles and a studio orchestra spirals out of control and into oblivion, a massive piano chord punctuates the song's melancholic ambiance. "In the end," Martin recalls, "the microphones were so live that you could hear the air-conditioning. It took forty-five seconds to do, and we did it three or four times, building up a massive sound of piano after piano after piano, all doing the same thing" (212). The chord's metaphorical open-endedness suggests—in dramatic contrast with the self-contained love songs of the Beatles' musical youth—the proffering of a larger philosophical question for which there is no immediate answer. "A song not of disillusionment with life itself but of disenchantment with the limits of mundane perception," MacDonald observes, "'A Day in the Life' depicts the 'real' world as an unenlightened construct that reduces, depresses, and ultimately destroys" (181).

During their final year together as recording artists, the Beatles' nostalgic musings involve a self-consciously futile search for the emotional and spiritual consolation that had eluded them in such songs as "She Said She Said" and "A Day in the Life." If nothing else, a number of their songs on the *White Album*, *Let It Be*, and *Abbey Road* find them in a state of resignation about nostalgia's counterfeit manna, yet still questing, nevertheless, for a narrative means for experiencing transcendence despite the unflinching reality of an irreparable past that so many of us long to surmount. The *White Album*'s brilliant psychosocial palette reveals a number of instances in which the band presents intentionally contradictory canvases for our inspection. In "Revolution I," for instance, Lennon sings about the tempting qualities of revolution and revenge: "when you talk about destruction / Don't you know that you can count me out—in."[10] As with the *White Album*'s "Happiness Is a Warm Gun," Lennon delivers his polemic against the dislocating backdrop of a 1950s-era doo-wop chorus. The Beatles conclude the album with what amounts to their most purposefully disconcerting trio of recordings: the unlisted "Can You Take Me Back?"; the fiercely chaotic "Revolution 9," a jarring montage of indiscriminate noise, tape loops, and sound effects; and "Good Night," the lushly over-sentimentalized lullaby that brings the *White Album* to a close. As the coda for Lennon's "Cry Baby Cry," McCartney's haunting fragment literally pleads for a transcendent return to a simpler past: "Can you take me back where I came from? / Can you take me back?"—a question that will be revisited with dramatically different results in *Abbey Road*'s "Golden Slumbers." The speaker's answer arrives in the menacing form, of course, of "Revolution 9," some eight minutes of nightmarish surreality. Pollack rightly describes the recording as a "random anti-narrative effect," which indeed it is. Yet by accruing disruptive layer upon layer throughout that same anti-narrative's stultifying vision, the track succeeds in establishing one of popular music's most disturbing listening experiences. The answer to McCartney's desperate appeal for a return to innocence is nothing short of a resounding negative. As the haunting landscape of "Revolution 9" recedes from view, a distant harp ushers in the seeming comfort and solace of "Good Night," complete with Ringo Starr's warm farewell to the band's understandably disoriented listeners: "Good night, everybody / Everybody everywhere." In this way, the *White Album* pointedly concludes with the intentionally syrupy mawkishness of "Good Night," the band's explicit attempt to console their audience, to provide palpable reassurance in the cataclysmic wake of "Revolution 9."

While the Beatles offer a host of nostalgic soundings on *Let It Be*, their bleak reflections about nostalgia's fallacious tendencies soften into a series of timely meditations on the agonizing power of regret. Lennon's "Across the Universe" picks up McCartney's nostalgic baton from "Two of Us" and produces one of the songwriter's most prophetic accomplishments. With "Across the Universe,"

Riley notes, "the free-floating imagery determines the musical flexibility—the words evoke the creative process as much as a creative state of mind" (296). The song's chorus of "nothing's going to change my world" complements McCartney's regretful tones throughout the album about the manner in which the past continues to elude us despite our best efforts to memorialize it and render it into permanence through the auspices of language. "Let It Be" and "The Long and Winding Road" provide similarly minded excursions into nostalgia's death-defying limbo, a place in which disillusionment and anguish commingle *ad infinitum*. While "Let It Be" counsels us to meditate upon "words of wisdom" during our hours of darkness and to embrace the gentle consolation of peace, "The Long and Winding Road," in many ways, knows better. For the speaker, nostalgia's circuitous road "will never disappear." And while it always leads us back to the memories of lost friends and loved ones, the long and winding road never quite gets us there. For the song's speaker, the panacea inherent in "Let It Be" merely produces "a pool of tears" in the harsher reality lost amidst the restless and unconvincing hopefulness of "The Long and Winding Road."

There is little question that, even during its production, the Beatles regarded *Abbey Road* as their final studio album.[11] Their growing interpersonal and financial tensions were exacting a seemingly immutable toll on their artistic relationship. As the workmanlike Beatles went about the business of recording their musical finale, McCartney and Martin began assembling the medley that would conclude the album. "I wanted to do something bigger, a kind of operatic moment," McCartney remembered (qtd. in Lewisohn 14). In contrast with the pop-operas of that era by the Who and the Small Faces, the Beatles' medley essentially consists of an assortment of unfinished songs.[12] Yet McCartney and Martin's inspired post-production efforts ensured that the medley enjoys a cohesiveness from which we can draw larger musical and lyrical motifs. After "I Want You (She's So Heavy)" brings *Abbey Road*'s more playful first half to a close, the second half's medley of unfinished songs—literally their farewell performance—grapples with nostalgia and its equally complex relationship with regret. While the medley highlights the Beatles' penchant for balladry via such literary characters as Mean Mr. Mustard, Polythene Pam, and the eccentric female protagonist who meanders in and out of the narrative of "She Came in through the Bathroom Window," the sequence reaches its most profound instances during such poignant numbers as "You Never Give Me Your Money," "Golden Slumbers," and "Carry that Weight." In "You Never Give Me Your Money," McCartney's plaintive piano strains give way to Lennon and Harrison's dueling rhythm guitars. As Harrison later observed, the song "does two verses of one tune, and then the bridge is almost like a different song altogether, so it's quite melodic" (qtd. in Dowlding 287). The lyrics bespeak the tragedies of misspent youth and runaway fame: "Out of college, money spent /

See no future, pay no rent / All the money's gone, nowhere to go." As "You Never Give Me Your Money" comes to a close, the song's bluesy guitar riffs segue into the chorus of a child's nursery rhyme: "One, two, three, four, five, six, seven / All good children will go to heaven." As Mellers shrewdly points out, the subsequent "electronic gibbering and beeping belies the nursery-rhyme paradise of the words," ultimately producing an emotional response that is "more scary than ecstatic" (119).

Later, in "Golden Slumbers," McCartney resumes the medley's earlier themes with a deft reworking of Thomas Dekker's 400-year-old poem of the same name. As the medley progresses toward its symphonic conclusion, the song's bitter nostalgia—"Once there was a way to get back homeward / Once there was a way to get back home"—yields itself to a larger realization, in "Carry that Weight," that we inevitably shoulder the past's frequently irredeemable burden for the balance of our lives. In "Carry that Weight," McCartney acknowledges his own culpability in the Beatles' dissolution, yet his rather humbling, self-conscious lyrics extend an olive branch to his increasingly distant chums: "I never give you my pillow / I only send you my invitations / And in the middle of the celebrations / I break down." In its highly polished, final form, the *Abbey Road* medley encounters the Beatles at the height of their literary faculties. In many ways, the medley functions as McCartney's clever reconfiguration of Shakespeare's "seven ages of man" in *As You Like It*. From "You Never Give Me Your Money" through "The End," his lyrics impinge upon the inherent difficulties that come with growing up and growing older. Only the power of memory, it seems, can placate our inevitable feelings of nostalgia and regret—not only for our youthful days, but for how we lived them. Appropriately, McCartney concludes the medley with a quasi-Shakespearean couplet—"a cosmic, philosophical line," in Lennon's words (qtd. in Dowlding 292): "And in the end the love you take / Is equal to the love you make." Everett perceptively reads the medley as "a very personal final gift from Paul McCartney to his mates, as well as from the Beatles to the world" (271). "Her Majesty," the album's belated coda, serves as an ironic footnote to the medley, subverting, as it does, our accepted notions of Queen Elizabeth II's regal decorum—"Her Majesty's a pretty nice girl / But she doesn't have a lot to say"; by normalizing her persona, the speaker's playfully nostalgic memories of the Queen's youth transport us back to a more innocent time, as with the group's more carefree, pre-Beatlemania days, before the onset of adulthood's inevitable burdens.

In this way, the *Abbey Road* medley functions as a fitting conclusion for the Beatles' textual musings about nostalgia's salve-like, albeit highly illusory possibilities. The medley also encounters the Beatles' enduring humanism, which, in itself, exists as yet another aspect of modernism—and particularly among such "high modernists" as James Joyce, William Butler Yeats, and D. H.

Lawrence, among others.[13] As Sanford Pinsker observes, "High modernism was fashioned from richer, more humane stuff, as anyone who takes the time to compare Joyce's Leopold Bloom with Pynchon's Benny Profane will readily attest. And that is really the essential point about the humanism that high modernism reflected," he continues. "High modernism taught us to see the work of art as sacrosanct, and its difficulties as worthy of our best efforts." Are the Beatles—fascinated, as they were, with the literary nuances of irony, memory, and the inevitable pull of the past—really so different from Joyce, Yeats, Lawrence, and their ilk? James O. Brecher astutely interprets cultural phenomena like the Beatles and the Beat poets as "the link between the 'high' art of the modernists and the popular 'art' of the masses" (122). By acting as a bridge to the past—as a virtual conduit for their vast audience of listeners in search of a reprieve from the ills of postmodern life—the Beatles espoused a sense of hope and the promise of sameness in the face of an increasingly inexplicable present. Consider, once more, the calming refrain of "Across the Universe" in which Lennon invokes the Sanskrit phrase, "Jai guru deva om," which we might loosely translate as follows:

Jai	Guru	Deva	Om
Live	Teacher	Heavenly	The Vibration of the
Forever	R	One	Universe[14]

In contrast with postmodernism's penchant for elevating malaise and fragmentation over optimism and community, the Beatles' ineluctable modernism shines ever brightly. "Nothing's going to change my world," Lennon sings. Is there any grander narrative than that?

Works Cited

Abrams, M. H., ed. *The Norton Anthology of English Literature, Volume Two*. 7th ed. NewYork: Norton, 2000. See: www.wwnorton.com/nrl/english/nael72/Period3Twentieth/Course-Sessions3/PostModernRushdie.html.

The Beatles. *Abbey Road*. 1969. Parlophone, 1987.

—. *The Beatles* [*The White Album*]. 1968. Parlophone, 1987.

—. *The Beatles Anthology*. San Francisco: Chronicle, 2000.

—. *Beatles for Sale*. 1964. Parlophone, 1987.

—. *A Hard Day's Night*. 1964. Parlophone, 1987.

—. *Help!* 1965. Parlophone, 1987.

—. *Let It Be*. 1970. Parlophone, 1987.

—. *Magical Mystery Tour*. 1967. Parlophone, 1987.

—. *Please Please Me*. 1963. Parlophone, 1987.
—. *Revolver*. 1966. Parlophone, 1987.
—. *Rubber Soul*. 1965. Parlophone, 1987.
—. *Sgt. Pepper's Lonely Hearts Club Band*. 1967. Parlophone, 1987.
—. *With the Beatles*. 1963. Parlophone, 1987.
Brecher, James O. "Connections: Modernism to the Beats and Beatles and on to a Future American Literature." Diss. U of South Florida, 2002.
Burns, Gary. "Refab Four: Beatles for Sale in the Age of Music Video." Inglis 176-88.
Cooke, Deryck. "The Lennon-McCartney Songs." *Vindications: Essays on Romantic Music*, by Cooke. Cambridge: Cambridge UP, 1982. 196-200.
Danger Mouse. *The Grey Album*. 2004.
Davis, Fred. *Yearning for Yesterday: A Sociology of Nostalgia*. New York: Free, 1979.
Dowlding, William J. *Beatlesongs*. New York: Simon and Schuster, 1989.
Everett, Walter. *The Beatles as Musicians: Revolver through the Anthology*. Oxford: Oxford UP, 1999.
Hames, Annette, and Ian Inglis. "'And I will lose my mind': Images of Mental Illness in the Songs of the Beatles." *International Review of the Aesthetics and Sociology of Music* 30 (1999): 173-88.
Inglis, Ian, ed. *The Beatles, Popular Music, and Society*. New York: St. Martin's, 2000. 105-25.
Jameson, Fredric. *Postmodernism or, The Cultural Logic of Late Capitalism*. Durham: Duke UP, 1991.
Jay-Z. *The Black Album*. Def Jam, 2003.
Kenner, Hugh. *Sinking Island: The Modern English Writers*. New York: Knopf, 1988.
Lapidakis, Michalis. "Variations on Gustav Mahler." *Musicology* 12-13 (2000). <www.musicol-ogy.gr/issue012013/lapidakis1en.html.>
Lennon, John, and Yoko Ono. *All We Are Saying: The Last Major Interview with John Lennon and Yoko Ono*. Interview by David Sheff. New York: Griffin, 2000.
Lewisohn, Mark. *The Beatles: Recording Sessions*. New York: Harmony, 1988.
Lyotard, Jean-François. *The Postmodern Condition: A Report on Knowledge*. 1979. Trans. Geoffrey Bennington and Brian Massumi. Minneapolis: U of Minnesota P, 1984.
MacDonald, Ian. *Revolution in the Head: The Beatles' Records and the Sixties*. New York: Henry Holt, 1994.
Martin, George, with Jeremy Hornsby. *All You Need Is Ears*. New York: St. Martin's, 1979.

McKinney, Devin. *Magic Circles: The Beatles in Dream and History*. Cambridge: Harvard UP, 2003.

Mellers, Wilfred. *Twilight of the Gods: The Music of the Beatles*. New York: Schirmer, 1973.

Miles, Barry. *Paul McCartney: Many Years from Now*. New York: Holt, 1997.

Norman, Philip. *Shout!: The Beatles in Their Generation*. New York: Simon and Schuster, 1981.

Pinsker, Sanford. "Was High Modernism a Humanism?" *The Midwest Quarterly* 36 (1995): www.english.swt.edu/cohen_p/Postmodern/Pinsker.html

Pollack, Alan W. "Alan W. Pollack's 'Notes On' Series." 2000: www.recmusicbeatles.com/-public/files/awp/awp.html

Quantick, David. *Revolution: The Making of the Beatles' White Album*. Chicago: Chicago Review, 2002.

Riley, Tim. *Tell Me Why: A Beatles Commentary*. New York: Knopf, 1988.

Roessner, Jeffrey. "We All Want to Change the World: Postmodern Politics and the Beatles' *White Album*." *Reading the Beatles: Cultural Studies, Literary Criticism, and the Fab Four*. Ed. Kenneth Womack and Todd F. Davis. Forthcoming.

Smith, Kimberly K. "Mere Nostalgia: Notes on a Progressive Paratheory." *Rhetoric & Public Affairs* 3.4 (2000): 505-27.

Stephens, Julia. "Cultural Outlaws, Political Organizers." *Australian Humanities Review* May1998: www.lib.latrobe.edu.au/AHR/archive/Issue-May-1998/stephens.html

Sullivan, Henry W. *The Beatles with Lacan: Rock 'n' Roll as Requiem for the Modern Age*. New York: Lang, 1995.

West, Nancy Martha. *Kodak and the Lens of Nostalgia*. Charlottesville: UP of Virginia, 2000.

Whitley, Ed. "The Postmodern *White Album*." Inglis 105-25.

Zanes, R. J. Warren. "Too Much Mead?: Under the Influence (of Participant-Observation)." *Reading Rock and Roll: Authenticity, Appropriation, Aesthetics*. Ed. Kevin J. H. Dettmar and William Richey. New York: Columbia UP, 1999. 37-71.

FOR FURTHER READING

The study of the interactions between music and literature has a long history. In the twentieth century, the field may be said to find its keynote in the works of Calvin S. Brown, a longtime professor at the University of Georgia, who wrote many articles and two principal volumes. In *Music and Literature* (1948), Brown showed the relations of these arts. He continued this work in *Tones into Words: Musical Compositions as Subjects of Poetry* (1953).

Shortly after Brown's first book was published there were some responses. Through an historical approach, in his article "The parallelism between Literature and the Arts" (1949), Rene Wellek discussed attempts by critics to demonstrate analogies between music and literature. Northrop Frye, who had previously offered his thoughts in "Music and Poetry" (1941-42), edited papers from an international conference in Paris that resulted in *Sound and Poetry: English Institute Essays*, 1956 (New York, 1957). More of Frye's thoughts on music and poetry would later appear in his fourth essay in *Anatomy of Criticism.* (Of continuing interest is Edward T. Cone's essay in the *Sound and Poetry* volume, "Words Into Music: The Composer's Approach to the Text.") In the years following Calvin Brown's pioneering work, Marshall Brown looked at the musical structures in Thomas Hardy, Charles Dickens, Anton Chekhov, and James Joyce. Charmenz Lenhart produced *Musical Influence on American Poetry* (Athens, GA. 1956) in which he looked at Poe, Whitman, Lanier and others. Gretchen L. Finney's *Musical Backgrounds for English Literature* (Rutgers UP, New Brunswick, N.J. 1962) appeared in the early 1960's. Likewise, *The Untuning of the Sky* (Princeton UP, 1962), John Hollander's important study of music and the English poetry of 1500-1700 appeared in 1961. Wilfred Mellers published *Harmonious Meaning: A Study of the Relationship Between English Music, Poetry, and Theatre 1600-1900.* (London 1965) Alex Aronson provided a reflection on music and fiction which included the discussion of many other authors, like Marcel Proust, Thomas Mann, Virginia Woolf, Aldous Huxley, Hermann Hesse, and others. (*Music and the Novel: A Study in Twentieth Century Fiction.* Totowa: Rowman and Littlefield, 1980) James Winn's book *Unsuspected Eloquence: A History of the Relations Between Poetry and Music,* (New Haven: Yale UP 1981) has also offered a very useful addition to reflection on music and literary relationships. Kevin Barry's *Language, Music, and the Sign: A Study of Aesthetics, Poetics, and Poetic Practice from Collins to Coleridge* (Cambridge: Cambridge University Press,

1987) deals primarily with the mid- to- late 18th century, or early British Romanticism.

Much of the most effective work in the field of intermediality has come from German scholars, or those concerned with the German romantic tradition. These include Walter Bernhart and Werner Wolf. Steven Paul Scher, as well, has often examined the field and particularly rewarding are his specific studies of German writers such as Tieck, Wackenroder, Hoffmann, Heine, and Mann in his valuable study *Verbal Music in German Literature*. Scher has since written many articles, chapters for the volume *Interrelations of Literature,* and has edited the German publication *Literatur und Musik* (1984). See "Comparing Music and Poetry: Beethoven's Goethe Lieder" in *Sensus Communis: Contemporary Trends in Comparative Literature* (Tubingen: Gunter Narr, 1986). Musicologist John Daverio has written *Nineteenth-Century Music and the German Romantic Ideology* (New York: Scribner's, 1993) and other useful studies.

Among the leading voices in this field, Lawrence Kramer, a musicologist and a professor of literature Fordham University, has offered sharp analysis and commentary in numerous books. Kramer's musicological perspective has been likened at times with influential scholars of his generation such as Susan McClary, Rose Subotnik, and Richard Leppert. (See Susan McClary, *Feminine Endings- Music, Gender and Sexuality*, Minneapolis: University of Minnesota Press, 1991. Rose Rosengard Subotnik, *Deconstructive Variations: Music and Reason in Western Society*. Minneapolis: University of Minnesota Press, 1996. Richard Leppert, *The Sight of Sound: Music, Representation, and the History of the Body* (Berkeley: University of California Press, 1993). In the development of the new musicology, in books like *Classical Music and Postmodern Knowledge* (Berkeley: University of California Press, 1995), Kramer has brought together the study of music with social and cultural issues. His literary scholarship has been equally vigorous and insightful. In *Music and Poetry- The Nineteenth Century and After* (University of California Press, 1984) for example, Kramer engages the reader in studies of Mozart, Wordsworth, Chopin, Shelley, and in thoughtful parallel discussions of Wallace Stevens and Charles Ives, Elliott Carter and John Ashbery. Among his recent books, *Musical Meaning- Toward a Critical History* (University of California 2002) offers chapters on mixed media and musical meaning and reflections on jazz, and on composers ranging from Bartok, Weill and Ravel to Shostakovich.

In journeying into the new musicology, one might also turn to the essays of Scott Burnham (such as "How Music Matters: Poetic Content Revisited," in *Rethinking Music*, edited by Nicholas Cook and Mark Evarist (Oxford UP, 1999). Nicholas Cook examines music and multi-media in *Analyzing Musical Multimedia* (Oxford: Clarendon Press, 1998). Also rewarding are studies by musicologists Leo Trietler (*Music and the Historical Imagination*, Cambridge:

Harvard UP, 1990), Charles Rosen (*The Classical Style: Haydn, Mozart, Beethoven*. New York: Norton, 1972), Ruth Solie, *Musicology and Difference: Gender and Sexuality in Music Scholarship* (Berkeley: University of California Press, 1993) and Patrick McCreles, *Contemporary Music Theory and the New Musicology: An Introduction.*

This is, of course, only a sampling. There are many others at work in the field of word-music studies today. The contributors to this volume have included bibliographical references for their essays. The end notes which follow will also assist you in locating books and articles. Readers with musicological interests will find several valuable studies produced by Cambridge Scholars Press. Likewise, invaluable for study in this field are the volumes of the International Association for Word-Music Studies founded in 1997, available from Rodopi Publishing in Atlanta and in the Netherlands. The reader might also consult *Literature and Music*, edited by Michael J. Meyer (Amsterdam: Rodopi, 2002) and Werner Wolf's *The Musicalization of Fiction: A Study in the Theory and History of Intermediality* (Amsterdam: Rodopi, 1999).

CONTRIBUTORS

Karl Coulthard is engaged in interdisciplinary studies at the University of Guelph, Canada where he is a doctoral candidate. He plays the trumpet and sings, although not at the same time.

Tanya Dalziell is a Senior lecturer in English, Communications, and Cultural Studies at the University of Western Australia. She is the author of *Settler Romances and the Australian Girl* (2004) and has published in the areas of modernism, postcolonial theory, gender studies and film.

Marc Derveaux is the author of *La poetique semiophone. Etude sur la sonorite du language dans la modernite et musicale* (Paris: L'Harmatton. 2004). A citizen of France, he teaches in Brighton, U.K..

Gregory Erickson teaches world literature and writing at Mannes College and New York University. His book *The Absence of God in Modernist Literature* is forthcoming from Palgrave Macmillan. He was the Director of Classical Music at the Brooklyn Conservatory of Music (2001-2005). He is an accomplished trombonist and the author of numerous articles.

T. Austin Graham is completing his doctorate in literature at the University of California- Los Angeles.

Zbigniew Granat is a classical pianist and musicologist. He studied musicology at Jagiellonian University in Krakow, Poland and Boston University, where he completed his doctoral dissertation on "Open Form and Work Concept: Notations on the Musical Work After Serialism." He has published articles on jazz and classical music and has delivered papers at conferences in England, Belgium, and the United States. He currently teaches at Boston University and Massachusetts College of Liberal Arts.

Michael P. Kardos studied music composition at Princeton University, holds an MFA in Creative Writing, and is a doctoral candidate in literature at the University of Missouri.

Robert P. McParland is a composer and performer of music. His writings include several articles on music and modernism, *Music-The Speech of Angels* (2004), and two book-length studies of the novels and readership of Charles Dickens: *Dickens and Melodrama* (2009) and the forthcoming *Charles Dickens's American Audience* (2010). He currently is Assistant Professor of English at Felician College in New Jersey.

Emma Sutton is a Lecturer in English at the University of St. Andrews, Fife, Scotland, U.K.. She is the author of *Aubrey Beardsley and British Wagnerism in the 1890's* (Oxford: Oxford Univesity Press, 2002).

Erin E. Templeton is completing her doctorate in literature at the University of California-Los Angeles. She has published articles on works by T.S. Eliot, James Joyce, William Faulkner, and Ernest Hemingway.

Enrico Terrinoni of Rome, Italy is a Government of Ireland Scholar in the Humanities and Social Sciences at the University College of Dublin. He has translated into Italian works by Brendan Behan, Muriel Spark, and Gerard Mannix Flynn. He has published several works on James Joyce in *Joyce Studies in Italy, James Joyce Broadsheet, To the Other Shore, PaGes.*

Lisa Tyler is Professor of English at Sinclair Community College in Dayton, Ohio. She is the author of the *Student Companion to Ernest Hemingway* and of several essays on Hemingway and on Virginia Woolf.

Juli White is an Assistant Professor of English at Arizona State University, where she teaches English composition, Introduction to Literature, and business and technical writing.

Kenneth Womack is Associate Professor of English and Head of the Division of Arts and Humanities at Penn State Altoona. He has published widely on twentieth-century literature and popular culture. He serves as Editor of *Interdisciplinary Literary Studies: A Journal of Criticism and Theory* and as Co-Editor of Oxford University Press's esteemed *Year's Work in English Studies*. His book-length publications include *Key Concepts in Literary Theory* (2001), *Postwar Academic Fiction: Satire, Ethics, Community* (2001), *Mapping the Ethical Turn: A Reader in Ethics, Culture, and Literary Theory* (2001), *Formalist Criticism and Reader-Response Theory* (2002), and *Reading the Family Dance: Family Systems Therapy and Literary Study* (2003).

Kiene Brillenburg Wurth is Assistant Professor of Comparative Literature at Utrecht University in the Netherlands. She has published on Immanuel Kant, Ludwig van Beethoven, Franz Liszt, Hector Berlioz, and American experimental music and poetry in relation to the idea of the postmodern sublime and has written several essays on Theodor Adorno and modernism.

NOTES

The Sonority of Language in Literary and Musical Modernity

1. *La poétique sémiophone*. Paris : L'Harmattan, 2003. The adjective "semiophonic" and the corresponding noun "semiophony" were forged for the purpose of this research. These terms refer to the acoustical dimension of language when it makes sense as such and yet has no verbal meaning.
2. About the theory of distanciation as "tradition of break within tradition", see Jurij Striedter, 1971.
3. …as it has been first defined by the Russian Formalists, among others by Viktor Sklovskij. See Jurij Striedter, 1971.Schallplatten, 1988.

"Sounds Like Now": Music, Avant-Gardism and the Post-Modern Sublime

1. Renée van de Vall, *Een subliem gevoel van plaats [A Sublime Sense of Place]*, Groningen: De Historische Uitgeverij, 1994, 337, my translation.
2. Mikko Lehtonen, 'On No Man's Land. Theses on intermediality', transl. Aijaleena Ahonen and Kris Clarke, at:
www.nordicum.gu.se/reviewcontents/ncomreview/ncomreview101/Lehtonen.pdf, 1999], online 2004. Basing himself on Guther Kress and Theo van Leeuwen, Lehtonen defines multimodality as the process whereby the production of a text is always already informed by different, multifarious modes of communication. Thus, a written text involves more than language, as it is written on a different medium, while a spoken text is not just visual but also verbal since it combines with non-verbal modes of communication such as facial expression, intonation, etc. See for this Guther Kress and Theo van Leeuwen, *Reading Images. The Grammar of Visual Design*, London: Routledge, 1996, 36.
3. In the practice of cultural studies, popular culture is not equated with mass culture, but rather typified as undermining mass culture from within by means of the very products and infrastructures (i.e. mass media) that mass culture provides. Thus, making do with what is available, popular culture is awarded a subversive and critical function that mass culture lacks.
4. Lehtonen, 'On No Man's Land', 75.
5. For one thing, as a mixture of drawing, design, typography, and poetry, visual poetry has been a common practice in Western high culture since the days of George Herbert and before, while the transgression of media borderlines can be traced all the way to the practices of epic theatre (Aeschylus) in Antiquity. Poetry and music have a long-lasting relationship in traditional artistic culture as regards the recycling or remediation of poems in songs, of narratives in symphonies and program music, or of songs in poetry. Painting and music likewise share an interactive past, culminating perhaps in that special

branch of symbolist painting that was inaugurated by Théodor de Wyzéwa in 1886 as Wagnerian painting. All this suggests that high culture actively embraces rather than shuns working at the limits, or in-between the borders, of different media.

6. [6]Wallace Stevens, 'The Man with the Blue Guitar', quoted in Thomas McEvilly, *Art and Discontent. Theory at the Millenium*, New York: McPherson & Company, 1991, 26.

7. See for this Kevin Barry, *Language, Music, and the Sign. A Study in Aesthetics, Poetics, and Poetic Practice from Collins to Coleridge*. Cambridge: Cambridge University Press.

8. Clement Greenberg, 'Towards a Newer Laocoön' in *Art in Theory 1900-1990. An Anthology of Changing Ideas*, Charles Harrison and Paul Wood, ed., Oxford: Blackwell, 1999 [1940], 554-560.

9. I have derived this definition of intermediality from Dick Higgins. See for this his *Horizons. The Poetics and Theory of the Intermedia*, Carbondale and Edwardsville: Southern Illinois University Press, 1984.

10. Greenberg, 'Laocoön', 557.

11. See for this Walter Pater, 'The School of Giorgione' in *Art in Theory 1815-1900. An Anthology of Changing Ideas*, ed. Charles Harrison and Paul Wood with Jason Gaiger, Oxford: Blackwell, 1998 [1877] 830-833.

12. Greenberg, 'Laocoön', 557. Greenberg maintains that this tendency towards the musical was motivated by a paradigm shift away from literature as a dominant art form in the hierarchy of the fine arts. Literature here being conveniently reduced to literary realism (or what Greenberg takes literary realism to be), Greenberg argues that the 'ideological struggles of society' had illegitimately infected the arts through the governing principle of 'subject matter'–and literature was 'subject matter at its most oppressive'. Differently put: because literature (again: this refers to Greenberg's conception of literature as literary realism) represented the scenes and struggles of a world 'out there', and because literature presumably exerted its dominance over the other arts, the other arts were representational only in so far as they were functioning under the oppressive paradigm of literature. Apparently, music–as an art that would be its own subject matter–pointed the way out of this problem: its presumed self-sufficiency inspired the other arts to claim 'respect for their own sakes, and not merely as vessels of communication'. Formerly figurative and representational art forms like painting now could 'expand the expressive resources of the medium, not in order to express ideas and notions, but to express with greater immediacy sensations, the irreducible elements of experience'. Evidently, this tale of liberation is based on, firstly, Greenberg's formalist desire to preserve art as a pure *sanctum* within the confusing flux of cultural and societal change, and, secondly, the formalist conception of music as revolving around the evoking and eliciting of immediate sensations, not about mediated thinking (a myth which has now been debunked successfully in the New Musicology). Greenberg, 'Laocoön', 556.

13. Eduard Hanslick, *On the Musically Beautiful*, transl. Geoffrey Payzant, Indianapolis, Indiana: Hackett Publishing Company, 1984 [1854], 73, 80.

14. Greenberg, 'Laocoön', 557.

15. Ibidem

16. Ibidem, 448

17. Jacques Derrida, 'Mallarmé' in *Jacques Derrida. Acts of Literature*, ed. Derek Altridge, New York: Routledge, 1992, 110-126, 114.
18. Jacques Derrida, 'Mallarmé', 121.
19. Martin Jay, *Downcast Eyes. The Denigration of Vision in Twentieth-Century French Thought*, Berkeley: University of California Press, 1994, 504.
20. See for this Jay David Bolter and Richard Grusin, *Remediation. Understanding New Media*, Cambridge, Mass.; London: MIT Press, 2000, 44-50, 51-62.
21. Bolter and Grusin, *Remediation*, 38.
22. *Ibidem*, 38.
23. Immanuel Kant, *Kritik der Urteilskraft*, Hamburg: Felix Meiner Verlag, 1990 [1790]. For a full account of the complexities and problematics of the Kantian sublime, see my *The Musically Sublime*, chapter 1 ('Sublimation'), at http://www.ub.rug.nl/eldoc/dis/arts/c.a.w.brillenburg.wurth/
24. Andrew Bowie, *Aesthetics and Subjectivity: from Kant to Nietzsche*, Manchester: Manchester University Press, 1993, 37.
25. Striving for absolute totality (that is, a totality without condition, relation, or limitation), reason is for Kant a faculty of transcendental ideas that have no object in experience, or by means of which no objects can be determined and cognized. No congruent object of sense can ever be given for these ideas, as no object of sense can ever meet their absolute requirements.
26. Andrew Bowie, *Aesthetics and Subjectivity*, 37.
27. Jean-François Lyotard, 'Response to the Question: What is Postmodernism?' in *Art in Theory 1900-1990*, 1008-1015, 1015.
28. Lyotard, 'Response', 1014. Interestingly, this tendency of avant-garde art to elude existing artistic categories also fits in with Dick Higgins' definition of intermediality as falling in-between such categories.
29. Lyotard, 'Response', 1010.
30. Jean-Francois Lyotard, 'Representation, Presentation, Unpresentable' in *The Inhuman. Reflections on Time.* Transl. Geoffrey Bennington and Rachel Bowlby. Cambridge: Polity Press, 1998, 119-129, 127.
31. Lyotard, 'Response', 1014-1015.
32. Lyotard, 'Representation', 126.
33. Matter has a privileged (or, as one would now say, re-centered) status in poststructuralist theory. In *The Truth in Painting*, for instance, Derrida criticizes Kant for focusing entirely on 'pure form' in his analytic of the beautiful, and relegating the material aspects of the arts (such as color in painting, or sound in music and poetry) to a marginal, secondary status. Thus, materiality in Kantian aesthetics must always be contained and absorbed by the play of form that would occasion a free interplay between the mental faculties. In imitation of Martin Heidegger, Derrida considers this privileging of form over matter symptomatic of traditional aesthetics. As an alternative, he points to philosophers like Emmanuel Levinas and Maurice Blanchot who have focused on experimental art works (nonfigurative painting, serial music, acoustic poetry) that would offer matter not yet forged into a recognizable form: matter not yet processed and refined in the meaningful totality of an imaginative synthesis. Significantly, however, Levinas nevertheless preserves the (Kantian) notion of autonomy in this revaluation of medial

materiality. As Nico van der Sijde has already pointed out, Levinas uses the term 'musicality' to circumscribe the effect of modern art works that offer an unformed materiality–music, such as the music of Iannis Xenakis, 'approaching unformed sound, [abstract-expressionist] painting consisting of almost unformed blots of paint, poetry [such as acoustic poetry] approaching unformed language'. In this context, the term musicality is attractive for Levinas for the same reasons as it was attractive for Greenberg: 'for Levinas, music and rhythm imply a relative autonomy with respect to the logical-discursive world'–the world, to put it very simply, of ideas, meaning, and rationality. Modern art, avant-garde art, approaches this state of musicality when it offers a substance that resists meaning-making, when it stops making sense, when it no longer refers to a recognizable reality–when, in short, it withdraws into the surface of its own medium and (to recall Greenberg) makes this surface, its sensuous matter, into its subject matter. This formalism without form, if you will, clearly echoes in Lyotard's analysis of the postmodern sublime. For Levinas, see Nico van der Sijde, *Het literaire experiment. Jacques Derrida over literatuur [The Literary Experiment. Jacques Derrida on Literature]*, Amsterdam: Boom, 1998, 87.

34. Theodor Adorno, *Filosofie van de nieuwe muziek [Philosophy of New Music],* transl. Liesbeth van Harmelen, Nijmegen: Sun, 53.

35. Jean-François Lyotard, 'Newman : The Instant' in *The Inhuman*, 78-88, 85.

36. Jean-Francois Lyotard, 'After the Sublime, the State of Aesthetics' in *The Inhuman*, 135-143, 141.

37. Van de Vall, *Een subliem gevoel van plaats*, 221, my emphases.

38. Lyotard, 'Newman: The Instant', 79

39. *Ibidem*, 83.

40. *Ibidem.*

41. In John Cage's music this 'sound come into its own' typically manifests itself as a chance-like, material occurrence in what Cage has called an indeterminate or experimental action: in a suspension of pre-set rules and intentions that allows the unexpected to present itself. Typically, for Cage an experimental action is one 'the outcome of which is not foreseen', so that sounds are not predetermined to appear in (the service of) a certain structural or narrative order with an established beginning, middle, and ending. They are rather allowed to just 'be' without one knowing or planning in advance if, how, or when they will be, how they will develop, or where they are going to. This music thus centrally revolves around the occurrence of a sound which can neither be foreseen, controlled, nor repeated. It 'simply', uniquely happens. As such, it requires a different, almost precarious sort of listening. It is not the structural listening of the musicologist, or the narrative listening associated with sonata form, granting the listener full oversight or orientation. Neither is it the emotive listening associated with much Classical and Romantic music, allowing the listener to project his or her own subjectivity into the sounds heard and be blissfully lost or borne away. It is, rather, an impersonal and suspended listening, a listening to silence (cf. Cage's *4'33''*) or a listening to 'undeveloped' sounds without an identifiable beginning or ending. See for this: John Cage, 'Lecture on Something' in: *Silence*, *Lectures and Writings by John Cage*. London: Marion Boyars, [1959] 1999, 128-140, 69.

42. Quoted in Michael Nyman, *Experimental Music Experimental Music. Cage and Beyond,* Cambridge: Cambridge University Press, 1991, 1.
43. Lyotard, 'Newman: The Instant', 84.
44. *Ibidem*, 85.
45 Lyotard writes that as a painter Newman is less concerned with the manipulation of space than the sensation of time. And not historical or narrative time but now-time, this moment now, the time of an instant, the occurrence of the momentary: that time, the instantaneousness of the instant, 'is the picture itself'. As Lyotard comments on Newman's fourteen *Stations of the Cross* (1958-1966): 'The time of what is recounted (the flash of the knife raised against Isaac) and the time taken to recount that time (the corresponding verses of Genesis) cease to be dissociated. They are condensed into the plastic (linear, chromatic, rhythmic) instant that is the painting'. The painting performs instead of recounts, it becomes the instant recounted in the verses of Genesis. The instant is performed, it happens, rather than being pictured as having happened: the place (makom) where Abraham stood before G-d (Hamakom) becomes a taking place, and this taking place is the painting itself. Lyotard, 'Newman: The Instant', 78, 83.
46. Wendy Steiner, *The Colors of Rhetoric. Problems in the Relation Between Modern Literature and Painting*, Chicago and London: The University of Chicago Press, 1985, 208.
47. Jean-Francois Lyotard, 'God and the Puppet' in *The Inhuman*, 153-165, 156.
48. Jean-Francois Lyotard, 'After the Sublime, the State of Aesthetics', 140.
49. *Ibidem*, 140.
50. Jean-Francois Lyotard, *Heidegger and 'the jews'*, transl. Andreas Michel and Mark S. Robert, Minneapolis; London: University of Minnesota Press, 1997, 32.
51. Lyotard, 'After the Sublime', 142, 141.
52. Philosophically, the problem of this rereading of the sublime is, of course, that matter conceived of as an 'in itself' cannot quite be disconnected from Kant's transcendental scheme of things: the notion of an 'in itself', thinking matter as an in itself, is already an idea of reason that cannot be made to fit the forms of sensibility (since the thing in itself always eludes the forms of time and space to which sensibility is bound). If 'raw' matter replaces ideas of reason in Lyotard's writings, there is always already an overlap between the two in so far as neither fits the 'forms and concepts…constitutive of objects'. Lyotard, 'After the Sublime', 140.
53. Clement Greenberg, 'Avant-Garde and Kitsch' in *Art in Theory 1900-1990*, 529-541, 531-532.
54. Lyotard, 'After the Sublime, the State of Aesthetics', 139.
55. Peter Conrad, *Modern Times, Modern Places. How Life and Art were Transformed in a Century of Revolution, Innovation, and Radical Change*, New York: Alfred Knopf, 1998.
56. Peter Conrad, *Modern Times, Modern Places*, 111,112.
57. Hans Richter, *Dada: Art and Anti-Art.* London: Thames and Hudson, 1997, 30.

Boulez, Joyce, Mallarme: Music as Modernist Literature

1. Pierre Boulez, "Current Investigations," in *Stocktakings from an Apprenticeship*, trans.

Stephen Walsh (Oxford: Clarendon Press, 1991; orig. publ. *Relevés d'apprenti*, Paris 1966), pp. 15-19.
2. Ibid., pp. 18-19.
3. Pierre Boulez, "Sonate, que me veux-tu?", in *Orientations*, trans. Martin Cooper (Cambridge, Mass.: Harvard University Press, 1986; orig. publ. *Points de repère*, Paris 1985), pp. 143-54. The title of Boulez's article, which alludes to a remark made in reference to instrumental music by the French author Fontenelle in the early eighteenth century, is clearly designed to call attention to the polemical nature of the Third Sonata. On Fontenelle, see William S. Newman, *The Sonata in the Baroque Era* (Chapel Hill: The University of North Carolina Press, 1966), p. 353.
4. The other three formants of the sonata in their incomplete versions are currently housed at the Paul Sacher Foundation in Basle. See Allen Edwards, "Unpublished Bouleziana at the Paul Sacher Foundation, *Tempo*, No. 169 (June 1989), pp. 4-6. Some of the writers that have discussed the formal layout of the sonata include: Dominique Jameux, *Pierre Boulez*, trans. Susan Bradshaw (Cambridge, Mass.: Harvard University Press, 1991; orig. publ. *Pierre Boulez*, Paris 1984); Manfred Stahnke, *Struktur und Ästhetik bei Boulez: Untersuchungen zum Formanten "Trope" der Dritten Klaviersonate* (Hamburg: Verlag der Musikalienhandlung Wagner, 1979); Iwanka Stoianowa, "La *Troisième Sonate* de Boulez et le projet mallarméen du Livre," *Musique en jeu* 16 (November 1974), pp. 9-28; Anne Trenkamp, "The Concept of 'Alea' in Boulez's 'Constellation-Miroir'," *Music and Letters* 57 (1976 no.1), pp. 1-10; Anne Piret, "Pierre Boulez: Troisième Sonate pour piano," *Analyse Musicale* 29 (November 1992), pp. 61-74; William G. Harbinson, "Performer Indeterminacy and Boulez's Third Sonata," *Tempo* 169 (June 1989), pp. 16-20.
5. Pierre Boulez, "Sonate, que me veux-tu?", p. 143.
6. *Ibid.*, p. 144.
7. Pierre Boulez, "Poetry – Centre and Absence - Music," in *Orientations*, p. 195.
8. György Ligeti, "Some Remarks on Boulez' 3rd Piano Sonata," *Die Reihe* 5, p. 58.
9. Pierre Boulez, "Sonate, que me veux-tu?", p. 147.
10. Pierre Boulez, *Conversations with Célestin Deliège*, p. 82.
11. Pierre Boulez, "Sonate, que me veux-tu?", p. 145.
12. Pierre Boulez, "Sound, Word, Synthesis," in Orientations, p. 179.
13. The concept of phrasing is described in "Alea," pp. 33-34; the reference to the "accelerando on a rest" comes from Boulez's essay on serial compositional methods entitled "…Near and Far," in Stocktakings from an Apprenticeship, p. 154.
14. See note 1 above.
15. Pierre Boulez, "Sonate, que me veux-tu?", p. 150.
16. Ibid.
17. For Boulez's detailed explanation see Boulez on Music Today, p. 78-9.
18. Boulez, "Sonate, que me veux-tu?", p. 150.
19. Quoted in "Sonate, que me veux-tu?", p. 148.
20. Umberto Eco, *The Open Work*, p. 10. Moreover, the very principle of circular permutation can be viewed as a reflection not only of the structure of Joyce's novel but also of Joyce's own model: Vico's cyclic view of history, in which each cycle, consisting

of four ages, ends with a transitional ricorso that heralds renewal. See, for instance, Eco, *The Aesthetics of Chaosmos: The Middle Ages of James Joyce*, trans. Ellen Esrock (Cambridge, Mass; Harvard University Press, 1989; orig. publ. Le poetiche di Joyce, Milan, 1962), pp. 63-4.
21. Umberto Eco, *The Aesthetics of Chaosmos* p. 86.
22. Ibid., p. 37.
23. Pierre Boulez, "Sonate, que me veux-tu?", p. 143-4.
24. See Jacques Scherer, *Le "Livre" de Mallarmé* (Paris: Gallimard, 1977), p. 59; also, Stoianowa, "La *Troisième Sonate* de Boulez et le projet mallarméen du Livre," pp. 11-4.
25. The quotes here are from Boulez, "Sonate, que me veux-tu?", p. 147.
26. Umberto Eco, *The Aesthetics of Chaosmos*, p. 48.
27. See Lucien Dällenbach, *The Mirror in the Text*, trans. Jeremy Whiteley with Emma Hughes (Chicago: The University of Chicago Press, 1989; orig. publ. *Le récit spéculaire: essai sur la mise en abyme*, Paris 1977), esp. p. 35.
28. Stoianowa, "La *Troisième Sonate* de Boulez," p. 26.
29. Charles Rosen, "The Piano Music," in *Pierre Boulez: A Symposium*, ed. William Glock (London: Eulenburg Books, 1986), p. 96.
30. Pierre Boulez, *Conversations with Célestin Deliège*, p. 83.
31. Pierre Boulez, "Sound, Word, Synthesis," p. 179.
32. Pierre Boulez, "Where Are We Now?", in *Orientations*, p. 462.
33. Boulez, *Conversations with Célestin Deliège*, p. 85.
34. *Ibid.*, p. 82.
35. Umberto Eco, *The Aesthetics of Chaosmos...*, p. 67.
36. Pierre Boulez, "Alea," p. 31.
37. See note 30.
38. Pierre Boulez, "Where Are We Now?", p. 461-2.
39. Anne Piret, "Pierre Boulez: Troisième Sonate pour piano," p. 62.
40. See chapter VI, "Towards the Dissolution of Classical Forms: The Second Piano Sonata" of Boulez, *Conversations with Célestin Deliège*, p. 40-42.
41. Jean-Paul Sartre, Preface to Nathalie Sarraute, *Portrait of a Man Unknown*, trans. Maria Jolas (New York: George Braziller, 1958; orig. publ. *Portrait d'un Inconnu*, Paris, 1956), pp. vii-viii.
42. Pierre Boulez, "Alea," p. 29.
43. Jean-Jacques Nattiez, ed., *The Boulez-Cage Correspondence*, trans. Robert Samuels (Cambridge: Cambridge University Press, 1994; orig. publ. *Pierre Boulez/John Cage: Correspondance et documents*, Winterthur 1990), p. 117.

Within A Space of Tears: Music, Writing and the Modern in Virginia Woolf's The Voyage Out

1. Some critics have identified as many as nine drafts or fragments of the novel; Woolf was repeatedly ill during this period. See Woolf, *Melymbrosia*, ed. Louise DeSalvo (San Francisco, CA.: Cleis, 2002),xxv and Woolf, *The Voyage Out*, ed. Lorna Sage (Oxford: Oxford University Press, 1992,2001) 239. Virginia Stephen was married in 1912; I use her more familiar married name throughout.

2. There are a number of thoughtful, though relatively brief, considerations of this relationship in the work of Woolf scholars. Examples include: Jane Marcus, 'The Years as Greek Drama, Domestic Novel and Gotterdammerung', *Bulletin of the New York Public Library* (Winter 1977), 276-301; Jane Marcus "Thinking Back Through Our Mothers' (1-30) and Nora Eisenberg, 'Virginia Woolf's Last Words on Words: Between the Acts and "Anon" (253-66) in Jane Marcus, ed., *New Feminist Essays on Virginia Woolf* (London: MacMillan, 1981); Mark Hussey, *The Singing of the Real World: The Philosophy of Virgina Woolf's Fiction* (Columbus: Ohio Sate University Press, 1986), 63-8; Jane Marcus, "Enchanted Organ, Magic Bells": Night and Day as a Comic Opera' in *Virginia Woolf and the Languages of Patriarchy* (Bloomington: University of Indiana Press, 1987); Peter Jacobs, "The Second Violin Tuning in the Ante-room": Virginia Woolf and Music,' in Diane F. Gillespie, ed. *The Multiple Muses of Virginia Woolf* (Columbia: University of Missouri, 1993) 227-60; and Suzanne Raitt, 'Finding a Voice: Virginia Woolf's Early Novels', in Sue Roe and Susan Sellers, eds., *The Cambridge Companion to Virginia Woolf* (Cambridge: Cambridge University Press, 2000), 29-49. A collection of essays on Woolf and music, edited by Adriana Varga, is currently in preparation.
3. She may have conceived of the novel as early as 1904, however. See Suzanne Raitt, "Finding a Voice" Virginia Woolf's Early Novels, in Sue Roe and Susan Sellers, eds. *The Cambridge Companion to Virginia Woolf* (Cambridge: Cambridge University Press, 2000) 29-49 (34).
4. 'The School of Giorgione', in Walter Pater, *The Renaissance: Studies in Art and Poetry*, ed. Adam Phillips (Oxford: Oxford University Press, 1986), 86.
5. See the 'Epilogue' of my Aubrey Beardsley and British Wagnerism in the 1890's (Oxford: Oxford University Press, 2002).
6. *The Voyage Out*, ed. Lorna Sage (Oxford: Oxford University Press, 1992, 2001), 46-7. Further references to this edition are cited parenthetically in the text.
7. See Hermione Lee, Virginia Woolf (London: Vintage, 1997), 143; Woolf's brother Adrian was an admirer of Wagner's work, as was Saxon Sydney-Turner, a Cambridge friend of her brother Thoby, whom Woolf knew from about 1905 [see Nigel Nicholson, ed. *The Flight of the Mind: The Letters of Virginia Woolf, Volume 1: 1888-1912* (London: Hogarth 1975) 308.]
8. *Letters* I: 263-4. Woolf's phrase is surely an echo of Pater's 'hard, gem-like flame' in the 'Conclusion' to *The Renaissance*. For an illuminating account of Woolf's relationship to Pater, see Perry Meisel, *The Absent Father: Virginia Woolf and Walter Pater* (New Haven and London: Yale University Press, 1980).
9. 'The Opera', *The Essays of Virginia Woolf, Volumel, 1904-1912,* ed. Andrew McNeillie (London: Hogarth, 1976) 26.
10. *Letters* I: 331 and 333.
11. Nigel Nicholson, ed. *The Question of Things Happening: The Letters of Virginia Woolf, Volume II: 1912-1922* (London: Hogarth, 1976) 26.
12. A couple of later short stories return to musical subjects: 'The String Quartet' (1921) and 'A Simple Melody', possibly written in 1925. (See Susan Dick, ed., *The Complete Shorter Fiction of Virginia Woolf*, London: Hogarth, 1985; 1989) 305.

13. Jane Marcus has stated, more broadly, that Woolf 'worked all her life to give her fiction musical form and operatic structure.' "Thinking Back Through Our Mothers", 22.
14. 'A Sketch of the Past', in *Virginia Woolf, Moments of Being: Unpublished Autobiographical Writings*, ed. Jeanne Schulkind (Sussex: Sussex University Press, 1976) 61-137 (68). Woolf made a number of references to Stephen's hostility to music: see, for example, her account of his reaction to the purchase of a gramaphone (*Letters* I:55).
15. It is suggestive, give Stephen's declared indifference to music, that in 'Street Music' Woolf criticizes the increasing number of individuals willing to declare their ignorance of music; the allusion may be a rebuke to Stephen's philistinism.
16. *Essays* I: 27-32 (30-32).
17. *Letters* I: 180,
18. *The Voyage Out*, xxi.
19. If we accept 1907 as the starting date, Woolf would have been twenty-five when she first started work on the novel; Rachel, we are told, is twenty-four (8).
20. There are surely traces of Stephen's character in Mr. Ambrose, the self-absorbed scholar of *The Voyage Out*, and in his relation with Rachel. Of all the literary critics and scholars in the novel, he is the most aloof from contemporary life: the comic account of Rachel's visit in chapter 13 depicts him as literally barricaded in by his books, 'some thousand miles distant from the nearest human being' (191).
21. Lorna Sage makes the same observation in her introduction to the Oxford edition of the novel, citing an example from a letter of 1901 (xviii).
22. 'A Sketch of the Past', 86-7.
23. Marcus, 'Thinking Back Through Our Mothers', 19.
24. Additionally, the music she plays is almost exclusively Germanic and by male composers. For a discussion of the extensive but often discreet Wagnerian allusions in *The Voyage Out*, see my article in the forthcoming collection edited by Adriana Varga.
25. Letters, I:410.
26. Woolf's half-sister Stella had herself been taught by Dolmetsch. See 'A Sketch of the Past', 97.
27. Rachel is frequently bored by the reading that her male companion recommends to her, finding it irrelevant to her life and experiences.
28. They also endorse, by their emphasis on the inevitabilityof change, the modernity of Woolf's novel and suggest the imperative of moving on from Victorian models of prose.
29. Her burgeoning confidence as a musician is shown by her comment to St. John Hirst at the ball: "I also play the piano very well[…] better, I expect, than anyone in this room" (171).
30. I hesitate to go as far as Nora Eisenberg, though, who sees Rachel's 'return' to music as an absolute break with language: 'Though, in the course of the novel, the inarticulate heroine voyages into a world of words, she returns in the end to her beloved sounds and silences. But forsaking language entirely, Rachel also forsakes her self and finally her life.' 'Virginia Woolf's Last Word on Words', in Marcus, *New Feminist Essays*, 253-66 (254).

31. The shift is not an absolute one; we are told early in the narrative that Rachel has cpies of lots of 'old music', but her interest in earlier (ie. pre-Wagnerian) music is increasinly stressed.
32. G.B. Shaw was unusual among his contemporaries in recognizing the formal discipline of Wagner's music; it was more commonly seen as having abandoned traditional musical structures. See, for example, *The Perfect Wagnerite: A Commentary on the Nibelung's Ring* (New York: Dover, 1967) 54-6 [1898].
33. Raitt, 35.
34. The perception of Beethoven as an isolated figure is evident, for example, in *A Room with a View* (1908) which Woolf reviewed whilst working on The Voyage Out (Raitt 48). His music alientates those who play it, such as Lucy Honeychurch, whose sense of isolation and subsequent defiance is attributed to 'too much Beethoven'. There are a number of suggestive similarities between the protagonists of these novels: both are inarticulate young pianists with little self-understanding, and both are described as playing Beethoven's Opus 111. The effects of music are very different in Forster's work, however; in contrast to Rachel, Lucy 'never knew her desires so clearly as after music'. E.M.Forster, *A Room with a View*, ed. Oliver Stallybrass (London: Penguin, 1988) 59, 60.
35. Raitt.
36. Its relationship to Victorian fiction was too close for some reviewers, who described the novel as old-fashioned. See Lee, 374.

'Dear Ezz-Roar', 'Dear Anthill'- Ezra Pound, George Antheil and the Complications of Patronage

1. In his memoir, Antheil belittles his own writings about music. Claiming they were merely "adolescent effervescence . . . how can one explain the writing of one's youth?" (118). For more information, see *Bad Boy of Music* (Garden City, NY: Doubleday, Dorian and Co, 1945).
2. In *The Pound Era* Antheil is mentioned only on pages 389-90. Here Kenner writes, "The rumor went about that Pound had abandoned words. He worked at music . . . and welcomed George Antheil as a Vorticist composer come late." Kenner proceeds to describe Pound's interest in Antheil, but he provides no real consideration of their professional relationship or recognition of the friendship Pound and Antheil shared.
3. Antheil's explanation of his "lost" paintings can serve as an example of his autobiographical tendency to "bend the truth." According to *Bad Boy*, Antheil had shipped the paintings back to the United States for storage when he moved to Paris, and then he had forgotten to whom he had sent them. For the next several chapters, finding these missing paintings is a sub-plot to the autobiography. This search serves to connect events and provide humor. In reality, Antheil never forgot where he sent the "lost" paintings. He had shipped the back to the offices of the *Little Review*. A letter to his patron, Mrs. Mary Louise Curtis Bok, reveals the true fate of the artworks; Mrs. Bok paid the shipping charges after Jane Heap forwarded the expense to an impoverished Antheil (Shirley, 8).

4. Pound to Antheil, October 27, 1927. This letter is quoted in Linda Whitesitt's book, *The Life and Music of George Antheil 1900-1959* (Ann Arbor, Michigan: UMI Research Press, 1983), 41.
5. Antheil's correspondence with Pound is part of the Beinecke Rare Book and Manuscript Library, Yale Collection of American Literature, Ezra Pound Collection (43). Hereafter, letters from this collection will be cited as YCAL.
6. Vorticism is an artistic movement that originated in London in 1913 with work of Wyndham Lewis. Ezra Pound, one of Lewis's close friends, gave the group its name from "vortex" or whirlpool. Vorticism sought to harness the force and energy of the vortex to draw the audience into the dynamics of the work. For more information about Vorticism, including the "Long Live the Vortex" and "Vorticist Manifesto," see volume one of *BLAST: Review of the Great English Vortex.*
7. Both William Walter Hoffa and Murray Schafer have argued that *Treatise* actually has more to do with Pound's poetic style in the *Cantos* than Antheil's actual musical composition theories. Antheil's accusation that Pound "merely wanted to use [him] . . ." (*Bad Boy*, 119) also supports the notion that the book was more about Pound than Antheil.
8. Pound's "Absolute Rhythm" was a mathematical formula which suggested that music was "pure" rhythm because even the variation in pitch could be reduced to a variation in rhythm of individual notes (their acoustical vibrations and harmonic overtones). R. Murray Schafer has noted that in his introduction to his Calvalcanti translation, Pound goes as far as stating that "the tempo of every masterpiece is exact and set by some further law of rhythmic accord" (25), For a more detailed discussion of these concepts, see Schafer, "Developing Theories of Absolute Rhythm and Great Bass," *Paideuma* 2, no 1 (1973) 23-35.
9. "Notes Struck in the World of Music: Antheil's Symphony Gets Ovation From Paris Audience," *Paris Times*, October 20, 1926.
10. Ezra Pound, *Machine Art and Other Writings: The Lost Thought of the Italian Years*, ed. Maria Luisa Ardizzone (Durham, NC: Duke University Press, 1996), 72.
11 Letter, Antheil to Bok, July 1926, Music Division, Library of Congress, George Antheil Correspondence. Also quoted in Whitesitt, 26.
12. Samuel Chotzinoff, *St. Louis Dispatch*, April 11, 1927; *New York Herald Tribune*, April 11. 1927.
13. Pound to Antheil, October 27, 1927, YCAL.
14. Antheil to Pound, 1925, YCAL.
15. Roger Fuller, "'Ballet Mechanique' to Wipe Out Big Orchestras, and Audiences Too," *Paris Tribune*, January 21, 1925, reprinted in *The Left Bank Revisited: Selections from the Paris Tribune 1917-1934* (University Park, PA: Pennsylvania State University Press, 1972) 213.
16. Pound to Mary Louise Curtis Bok, December 15, 1923. Quoted in Whitesitt, 20.
17. Mary Louise Curtis Bok, Letter to George Antheil, August 1, 1929, quoted in Glenda Dawn Goss, "George Antheil, Carol Robinson and the Moderns," *American Music* v10, n4 (Winter 1992) 473.
18. Antheil to Pound, 1927, YCAL.

19. Confirmation that Antheil sent this clipping to Mrs. Bok can be found in Linda Whitesitt's bibliography: ""Father of Mechanical Music dislikes being called Jazz Artiste," *New York Herald* Paris Edition [. . .] enclosed in Letter, Antheil to Bok, October 24, 1927 (p. 318). Unfortunately, Whitesitt makes no other mention of this article in her book.
20. "Father of Mechanical Symphonies Dislikes Being Called Jazz Artiste" in *New York Herald*, Paris Ed. October 24, 1927.
21. Antheil to Pound, undated but probably July 1929, YCAL. According to Antheil's autobiography, he received the letter from Universal Editions at the Hotel Moderne (where he wrote the letter to Pound) on his birthday, July 8, 1929.
22. Antheil to Pound, Winter 1927, YCAL.
23. Antheil to Pound, August 13, 1926, YCAL.
24. Antheil wrote this sonata for violin, piano and drums. In *Ezra Pound and Music*, Murray Schafer points out that Pound played the drums in several of the performances with Antheil (312). Antheil likely included drums in this piece so that Pound could accompany Olga Rudge and himself in their recitals.
25. Unfortunately, Antheil did not reciprocate his friend's loyalty and stand by the poet when he himself fell upon hard times later on.
26. Antheil to Pound, Spring 1930, YCAL.
27. Ibid.
28. Antheil to Pound, May 5, 1930, YCAL.
29. Ibid.
30. Antheil to Pound, May 9, 1930 YCAL.
31. Antheil to Pound, 1930 YCAL.
32. Antheil to Pound, 1930 YCAL.
33. Antheil to Pound, 1930 YCAL.
34. Irving Schwerke, "Antheil Given Ovation after Premiere of Opera *Transatlantic* in Frankfurt" *Chicago Tribune*, Paris Edition, May 26, 1930.
35. The plot of *Transatlantic* features Helen of Troy, Ajax, Hector, Jason, and several other characters drawn from Greek antiquity. The characters are placed in modern roles in New York City in the early 1900s. For example, Ajax is a politician, Hector is a Presidential candidate, and Helen, previously married to Jason and becomes Ajax's mistress.
36. Antheil to Pound, June 26, 1934, YCAL.
37. Antheil to Pound, July 7, 1934, YCAL. John Erskine collaborated with Antheil on the libretto for *Helen Retires*, which Antheil composed 1930-32
38. Ezra Pound, "Credit and the Fine Arts," *Ezra Pound's Poetry and Prose: Contributions to Periodicals,* ed. Lea Baechler, A. Walton Litz, and James Longenbach, v4 (New York: Garland Publishing, Inc., 1991) 223.
39. Excerpt taken from Canto VIII (11. 34-54).
40. In *Ezra Pound and the Monument of Culture* (Chicago: University of Chicago Press, 1991), Lawrence Rainey compares Malatesta with Mussolini. He writes, "In 1922 an analogy between Sigismundo Malatesta and Benito Mussolini had been only one possibility, and at that a remote one, among many; by 1932, however, it would strike

Pound as the central axis for the shape of his magnum opus and his understanding of its place in the modern world (74). See also pp. 46-47, 72, 75.

The Sound of an Idea; Music in the Modernist Writings of Mina Loy and Gertrude Stein

1. Gertrude Stein, *The Autobiography of Alice B. Toklas* (1933) (Harmondsworth: Penguin, 1966), 145.
2. Carolyn Burke, *Becoming Modern: The Life of Mina Loy* (New York; Farrar, Straus and Giroux, 1996), 129.
3. Mina Loy, "Gertrude Stein" [poem] (1924) *The Lost Lunar Baedeker: Poems of Mina Loy*, ed. Roger L. Conover (New York: The Noonday Press, 1997), 94. As Conover details on p.203 of the same volume: the pome was first published "as an untitled epigraph to a two-part letter in which ML [Mina Loy] discusses the influences on and maieutic effects of GS's [Gertrude Stein's] compositonal technique."
4. Ezra Pound, most notably, insisted on coining a term to describe the works of Marianne Moore, T.S. Eliot and Mina Loy, among others- logopoeia. For Pound, "logopoeia" refers to "poetry that is akin to nothing but language, which is a dance of the intelligence among words and ideas and modification of ideas and characters." Further, he seeks to define logopoeia by distinguishing this type of poetry from "melopoeia"- a poetry that has close ties to music- and "imagism"- that poetry that aspires to the image. As will be made clear, this essay does not propose to fix Loy's poetry into the secondary (and a priori) category of 'melopoeia'. Rather, it attempts to rehabilitate the relations to music that this work entertains, which have been largely overlooked in part as a consequence of the influence of Pound's frameworks. Ezra Pound, "Others", *Little Review* 4 (1918): 57.
5. Jane Augustin, "Mina Loy: A Feminist Modernist Americanizes the Language of Futurism," *Mid-Hudson Language Studies* 12.1 (1989): 57.
6. Carolyn Burke, "The New Poetry and the New Woman," in *Coming to Light: American Women Poets in the Twentieth Century*, eds. Diane Wood Middlebrook and Marilyn Yalom (Ann Arbor: The University of Michigan Press, 1985) 48-49.
7. For example, see Henry M. Satre, "The Artist's Model: American Art and the Question of Looking Like Gertrude Stein." in Gertrude Stein and the Making of Literature, ed. Shirley Neuman and Ira B. Nadel (Boston: Northeastern University Press, 1998), 21-41; Bettina L. Knapp, Gertrude Stein (New York: Continuum, 1990), 111-135; Jay Bochner, "Architecture of the Cubist Poem," in Architecture and Cubism, eds. Eve Blau and Nancy J. Troy (Cambridge and London: The MIT Press, 1997), 89-115; Jacqueline Vaught Brogan, "The Found Mother": Gertrude Stein and the Cubist Phenomenon." in Challenging Boundaries: Gender and Periodization, eds. Joyce W. Warren and Margaret Dickie (Athens and London: The University of Georgia Press, 2000), 248-266. By contrast, Marianne DeKoven argues that cubism is not an iporatnat influence on Stein's work. See Marianne DeKoven, "Gertrude Stein and Modern Painting: Beyond Literary Criticism," *Contemporary Literature* 22 (1981): 81-95.
8. For example, see Ellen Keck Stauder, "Beyond the Synopsis of Vision: The Conception of Art in Ezra Pound and Mina Loy," *Paideuma: A Journal Devoted to Ezra*

Pound Scholarship 24: 2-3 (1995): 195-227; Ellen Keck Stauder, "The Irreducible Surplus of Abstraction: Mina Loy on Brancusi and the Futurists," in *Mina Loy: Woman and Poet,* eds. Maeera Schreiber and Keith Tuma (Maine: The National Poetry Foundation, 1998): 357-77.

9. Daniel Albright, *Untwisting the Serpent: Modernism in Music, Literature and Other Arts* (Chicago and London: The University of Chicago Press, 2000).

10. A very useful volume that brings together many of these controversies is Daniel Albright's edited collection *Modernism and Music: An Anthology of Sources* (Chicago and London: The University of Chicago Press, 2004).

11. Theodor Adorno, of course, was one critic who lamented Stravinsky's work, to say the least. Theodor Adorno, *Philosophy of Modern Music*, trans. Anne G. Mitchell and Wesley V. Blomster (London: Seabury Press, 1973). For perceptive accounts of Adorno's work, see Max Paddison, *Adorno's Aesthetics of Music* (Cambridge: Cambridge University Press, 1993); David Cunningham, "A Time for Dissonance and Noise: On Adorno, Music and the Concept of Modernism," *Angelaki* 8.1 (2003): 61-74.

12. Stein, *The Autobiography of Alice B. Toklas*, 246.

13. For a recent biographical account of Virgil Thomson, see Anthony Tommasini, *Virgil Thomson: Compose on the Aisle* (New York and London: W.W. Norton and Company, 1997).

14. Jane Palatini Bowers, *Gertrude Stein* (New York: St. Martin's Press, 1993), 108.

15. Roger L. Conover, "Introduction" in *The Last Lunar Baedeker*, by Mina Loy, ed. Roger L. Conover (Highlands: The Jargon Society, 1982), xxxiii.

16. See my forthcoming chapter, "Mourning and Jazz in the Poetry of Mina Loy," in *Modernism and Mourni*ng, ed. Patricia Rae (Bucknell University Press, 2005).

17. Walter Pater, *The Renaissance*, ed. Donald L. Hill (Berkeley: University of California Press, 1980), 106.

18. For positions that contest this reading of music, see Christopher Norris (ed) *Music and the Politics of Culture* (London: Lawrence and Wishart, 1989).

19. For an overview of the influence of music on cubist works, see Lewis Kachur, "Picasso, Popular Music, and Collage Cubism (1911-12)" *The Burlington Magazine* 135 (1993): 252-60; Christopher Butler, *Early Modernism: Literature, Music, and Painting in Europe, 1900-1916* (Oxford: Clarendon Press, 1994); karin von maur, "Music and Theatre in the Work of Juan Gris," in *Juan Gris*, Christopher Green with contributions by Christian Derouet and karin von Maur (London: Whitechapel Art Gallery in association with Tale University Press, 1992), 267-282; Jonathan Cross, *The Stravinsky Legacy* (Cambridge: Cambridge University Press, 1988) 17-28.

20. Elizabeth Arnold, "Mina Loy and the Futurists," *Sagetrieb: A Journal Devoted to Poets in the Imagist/Objectivist Tradition* 8:1-2 (1989): 83-117.

21. "Patriarchal Poetry" was not published in Stein's lifetime. Gertrude Stein, "patriarchal Poetry," (1927) in *Gertrude Stein: Writings 1903-1923*, eds. Catharine R. Stimpson and Harriet Chessman (New York: The Library of America, 1998), 567-607.

22. Loy's "Aphorisms on Futurism," first published in 1914, registers an intense commitment to many of the central concepts of this avent-garde movement, including creative orginality, individual will, an appeal to the possibilities of speed and velocity. Loy writes with enthusiasm that: "The Futurist must leap from affirmative to affirmative,

ignoring intemittent negations- must spring from stepping stone to stone of creative explorations; without slippingback into the turbid stream of accepted facts." Yet, despite support for such Futurist precepts, the difficult relations between Fututis and feminism, as well the declared devotion of Futurism to the destructive potential of war, troubled Loy. Mina Loy, "Aphorisms on Futurism," (1914) in *The Lost Lunar Baedeker*, 150.

23. See, for example, Filippo Marinetti, "Futurist Manifesto" (1909) in *Stung by Salt and Water*, ed. Richard Pioli (New York: Peter Lang, 1987), 22.

24. See Loy's "Feminist Manifesto," which was written in 1914, but never published in Loy's lifetime. Most interestingly, this manifesto employs Futurist typography and proclamations to question the gender politics of both Futurism and then current feminist positions. Mina Loy "Feminist Manifesto," in *The Lost Lunar Baedeker*, 153-156. Most of the recent commentary on Loy's work has centered on her feminist interests. See, for example, Paul Peppis, "Rewriting Sex: Mina Loy, Marie Stopes and Sexology," *Modernism/Modernity* 9.4 (2002): 561-579.

25. Mina Loy, Modern Poetry in *The Lost Lunar Baedeker*, 160.

26. Ibid, 161.

27. Ibid, 157.

28. Gertrude Stein, *Everybody's Autobiography* (1937) (Cambridge: Exact Change, 1993), 193.

29. Ibid, 204.

30. Loy, Modern Poetry, in *The Lost Lunar Baedeker*, 159.

31. Loy, "Modern Poetry," in *The Lost Lunar Baedeker*, 158. It is a cnspicuous claim in the context of her own itinerant existence and the figure of the wandering Jew whom she mythically associated with her father in the long poem, "Anglo-Mongrels and the Rose." Rachel Blau du Plessis, *Genders, Races and Religious Cultures in North American Poetry 1908-1934* (Cambridge: Cambridge University Press), 159.

32. Jazz itself was often acorded the appellation of *lingua franca* at the time. For some, African Amerian cultures constituted the foundations of jazz. For others, the hybrid qualities of jazz and its indebtedness to a number of musical forms as diverse as the blues and "the Spanish cinquillo rhythm. See Ingrid Monson, "Jazz Improvisation" in *The Cambridge Companion to Jazz*, eds. Mervyn Cooke and David Horn (Cambridge: Cambridge University Press, 2002), 117.

33. This is a charge critics routinely levelled at Loy's own work. Writing in The Dial, Yvor Winters commented with exasperation and admiration: "She [Loy] moves like one walking through granitre instead of air, and when she achieves a moment of beauty it strikes one cold." Yvor Winters, "Mina Loy" *The Dial* 80.6 (1926): 496.

34. Gertrude Stein, *Lectures in America* (New York: Random House, 1935), 95.

35. For an overview of these debates, see Sieglinde Lemke, *Primitivist Modernism: Black Culture and the Origins of Transatalantic Modernism* (Oxford: Oxford University Press, 1998).

36. Henry Louis Gates, Jr. discusses the politics of signifying in his text *The Signifying Monkey: A Theory of Afro-American Literary Criticism* (New York: Oxford University Press, 1988).

37. Among the many white artists who pursued this form of entertainemnt was Carl Van Vechten, the model for Hugh Wentworth, the white writer who attends the Nefro Wefare

League dance in Nella Larsen's *Passing*, and the mutual friend of Stein and Loy. Nella Larsen, *Passing* (1929)) (New York: Penguin, 1997).
38. Mina Loy, "Lady Laura in Bohemia" (1931) in *The Lost Lunar Baedeker*, 98.
39. As I have argued elsewhere, this poem can be read as formally enacting the conversational mode of jazz. See Dalziell in *Modernism and Mourning.*
40. "The Widow's Jazz" is an involved poem marked by unresoved grief reflecting on theloss of Arthur Cravan, Loy's proto-Dada and pugilist husband. Mina Loy, "The Widow's Jazz," (1927) in *The Lost Lunar Baedeker*, 95-97.
42. Loy, "The Widow's Jazz", 95.
43. Ibid, 95.
44. Claude McKay, "Negro Dancers" and Langston Hughes "Jazzonia" in *The New Negro*, ed. Alain Locke (New York: Atheneum, 1992) 214-15, 226.
45. Mina Loy, "Negro Dancer" in *The Lost Lunar Baedeker*, 216. This poem was first published in 1961.
46. See, for example, Wendy Martin, "Remembering the Jungle" Josephine Baker and Modernist Parody" in *Prehistories of the Future: The Primitivist Project and the Culture of Modernism*, eds. Elazar Barkan and Ronald Bush (California: Standorf University Press, 1995)310-335; Nancy Nenno, "Femininity, the Primitive and Modern Urban Space: Josphine Baker in Berlin" in *Women in the Metropolis: Gender and Modernity in Weimer Culture*, ed. Katharina von Ankum (Berkeley: University of California Press, 1997) 145-161; Karen C.C.Dalton and Henry Louis Gates, Jr. "Josephine Baker and Paul Colin: American Dace seen through Parisian Eyes," *Critical Inquiry* 24 (1998): 903-934.
47. Gertrude Stein, "Melanctha" in *Three Lives* (1909) in *Gertrude Stein: Writings 1903-1932*, eds. Catherine R. Stimpson and Harriet Chessman (New York: Library of America, 1998), 124-239.
48. Carla L. Peterson, "The Remaking of Americans: Gertrude Stein's "Melanctha" and African-American Musical Traditions," in *Criticism and the Color Line: Desegregating American Literary Studies,* ed. Henry B. Wonham (Rutgers University Press, 1996), 155. It should be recognized, though, that Stein's work is often cited as a positive influence on African-American writers such as Richard Wright. See M. Lynn Weiss, *Gertrude Stein and Richard Wright: The Poetics and Politics of Modernism* (University of Mississippi Press, 1998).
49. Stein, *The Autobiography of Alice B. Toklas*, 57.
50. Ibid, 228.
51. von Maur, 270.
52. Virginia M. Kouidis mentions in passing that this poem "verge[s] upon pure sound." Virginia M. Kouidis, *Mina Loy: American Modernist Poet* (Baton Rouge and London: Louisiana State University Press, 1980), 122.
53. Mina Loy, "Brancusi's Golden Bird," (1922) in *The Lost Lunar Baedeker*, 79.
54. Albright, *Modernism and Music*, 194. For an introductory overview of Scoenberg's method, see Albright, *Modernism and Music* 193-223.
55. Pound, 57.
56. Mina Loy, "The Song of the Nightingale is Like the Scent of Syringa," *The Lost Lunar Baedeker*, 218. This poem was first published in the volume *Lunar Baedeker & Time-Tables* (Highlands: Jonathan Williams, 1958).

57. Mina Loy, "Gertrude Stein," [essay] in *The Lost Lunar Baedeker*, 289.
58. Loy, "Gertrude Stein," [essay] in *The Lost Lunar Baedeker*, 289.
59. Henri Bergson, *Time and Free Will: An Essay on the Immediate Data of Consciousness*, trans. F.L. Pogson (New York: Macmillan, 1910), 100.
60. Loy, "Gertrude Stein," [essay] in *The Lost Lunar Baedeker*, 289.
61. Loy, "Gertrude Stein," [essay] in *The Lost Lunar Baedeker*, 289.
62. Jonathan Cross, *The Stravinsky Legacy* (Cambridge: Cambridge University Press, 1998), 11.
63. Stein, *The Autobiography of Alice B. Toklas*, 150.
64. Stein, *The Autobiography of Alice B. Toklas*, 148.
65. Loy, "Stravinksi's Flute," in *The Last Lunar Baedeker*, 219. This poem was first published in the 1958 *Lunar Baedeker & Time-Tables* volume.
66. Loy, "Modern Poetry," in *The Lost Lunar Baedeker*, 160.

Musical and Ideological Synthesis in James Weldon Johnson's Autobiography of an Ex-Colored Man

1. James Weldon Johnson, *The Autobiography of an Ex-Colored Man*, 1912 (New York: Penguin, 1990):32.
2. Nathan Irvin Huggins, *Harlem Renaissance* (New York: Oxford, 1971):145.
3. Johnson, *The Autobiography*, 58.
4. Ibid 139.
5. Ibid 154.
6. Ibid 154.
7. Huggins, Harlem Renaissance, 145.
8. Eugene Levy, *James Weldon Johnson: Black Leader, Black Voice* (Chicago: University of Chicago Press, 1973):131.
9. Ibid 127.
10. Although Johnson, in *Along the Way*, claims that most of the reviewers "accepted [the novel] as a human document" (238), the available evidence indicates otherwise. *Muncey's Magazine* wrote: "It has indisputable veracity, even if it is imagined rather than recollected." Rev. of *Autobiography of an Ex-Colored Man*, by James Weldon Johnson, *Muncey's Magazine* 49 (1913): 798. *The New York Times* wrote that "whether or not it is accpted on its face value, there remains the very interesting fact that it does make an astute, dispassionate study of the race problem in the United States from the standpoint of a man who has lived on both sides of it." Rev. of *Autobiography of an Ex-Colored Man*, by James Welson Johnson, *The New York Times* 26 May 1913: BR 319. And Jessie Faucet in *The Crisis* wrote that the story "suggests a work of fiction founded on hard fact." Rev. of *Autobiography of an Ex-Colored Man*, by James Weldon Johnson, *The Crisis* 5 (1912-13):38.
11. Levy, *James Weldon Johnson: Black Leader, Black Voice*, 128.
12. Charles Willis Thompson, "The Negro Question," Rev. of Autobiography of an Ex-Colored Man, *The New York Times*, 16 October 1927, sec. BR, p.16.
13. Johnson, *The Autobiography*, 32.

14. James Weldon Johnson, *The Book of American Negro Poetry* (New York: Harcourt, Brace, and Company, 1922), vii.
15. Johnson, *The Autobiography*, 4-5.
16. Ibid, 5
17. Ibid, 19-20.
18, Ibid, 35.
19. Ibid, 72.
20. Ibid, 63.
21. Ibid, 133.
22. Kevin Kelly Gains, *Uplifting the Race: Black Leadership, Politics, and Culture in the Twentieth Century* (Chapel Hill: University of North Carolina Press, 1996):2.
23. Johnson, *The Autobiography*, 3-4.
24. Steven C. Tracy, *Langston Hughes and the Blues* (Chicago: University of Illinois press, 2001):17.
25. Ibid, 20.
26. Gains, *Uplifting the Race*, 3.
27. Johnson, *The Autobiography*, 40.
28. Ibid, 123.
29. Ibid, 126.
30. Ibid, 81.
31. Ibid, 85.
32. Frederick T. Griffiths, "Copy Wright: What Is an (Invisble) Author?" *New Literary History* 33 (2002):332.
33. Edward Berlin, in his biography of Scott Joplin, notes for instance Joplin's use of the "augmented sixth" chord which is strikingly characteristic of European classical music. See Edward A. Berlin, King of Ragtime: Scott Joplin and His Era (New York: Oxford University Press, 1994):26.
34. Robert H. Cataliotti, *The Music In African American Fiction* (New York: Garland Publishing, 1995): 64.
35. Ibid, 65.
36. Johnson, *Poetry*, viii.
37. Ibid, xv.
38. Johnson, *The Autobiography*, 63.
39. Johnson, *Poetry,* 74.
40. Dickson D. Bruce, "The Two Worlds of James Weldon Johnson," in *Black American Writing From the Nadir: The Evolution of a Literary Tradition, 1877-1915* (Baton Rouge: Louisiana State University Press, 1989):237.
41. Johnson, *Poetry*, 91.
42. Bruce, *Black American Writing from the Nadir*, 237.
43. Levy, *James Weldon Johnson: Black Leader, Black Voice*, 87.
44. Ibid, 314.
45. Ibid, 301.
46. Ibid, 146.
47. Bruce, *Black American Writing from the Nadir*, 251.

Opera, Maternal Influence and Gender in Ernest Hemingway's "The Ash Heel's Tendon"

1. Ernest Hemingway, *The Complete Short Stories of Ernest Hemingway: The Finca Vigía Edition*, (New York: Scribner's, 1987); Susan F. Beegel, ed., *Hemingway's Neglected Short Fiction: New Perspectives,* (Ann Arbor, Michigan: UMI Research P, 1989); Paul Smith, *A Reader's Guide to the Short Stories of Ernest Hemingway* (Boston: Hall, 1989); Carlos Baker, *Ernest Hemingway: A Life Story* (New York: Scribner's, 1969).
2. James Mellow, *Hemingway: A Life without Consequences* (Reading, Massachusetts: Addison-Wesley, 1992), 92.
3. Michael Reynolds, *The Young Hemingway* (New York: Basil Blackwell, 1986), 91-92.
4. Ernest Hemingway, "The Ash Heel's Tendon—A Story," in Peter Griffin, *Along with Youth: Hemingway, The Early Years* (New York: Oxford U P, 1985), 174. Other references to this work will be in parentheses in the text.
5. Karl Kohrs, ed., *The New Milton Cross' Complete Stories of the Great Operas*, rev. and enlarged ed. (Garden City, New York: Doubleday, 1955), 435-38.
6. Henry S. Villard and James Nagel, *Hemingway in Love and War: The Lost Diary of Agnes von Kurowsky* (New York: Hyperion, 1989), 163.
7. Marcelline Hemingway Sanford, *At the Hemingways: With Fifty Years of Correspondence between Ernest and Marcelline Hemingway*, Centennial edition (Moscow, Idaho: University of Idaho P, 1999), 58.
8. Mellow, *Hemingway*, 9.
9. Baker, *Life Story*, 2.
10. Michael S. Reynolds, "High Culture and Low: Oak Park before the Great War," in *Ernest Hemingway: The Oak Park Legacy*, ed. James Nagel (Tuscaloosa: U of Alabama P, 1996), 28.
11. Reynolds, *Young Hemingway*, 106.
12. Reynolds, "High Culture and Low," 127.
13. Reynolds, "High Culture and Low," 129-30.
14. Baker, *Life Story*, 9.
15. Sanford, *At the Hemingways*, 125.
16. Sanford, *At the Hemingways*, 125-26.
17. Kenneth S. Lynn, *Hemingway*, (New York: Simon & Schuster, 1987), 38.
18. Sanford, *At the Hemingways*, 124.
19. Sanford, *At the Hemingways*, 154.
20. Lynn, *Hemingway*, 24.
21. Reynolds, "High Culture" 18.
22. Baker, *Life Story*, 19.
23. Baker, *Life Story*, 23-24.
24. Quoted in Villard and Nagel, *In Love and War*, 193-94.
25. Sanford, *At the Hemingways*, 288.
26. Sanford, *At the Hemingways*, 185-86.
27. Reynolds, *Young Hemingway*, 155.

28. Reynolds, *Young Hemingway*, 150.
29. Gioia Diliberto, *Hadley* (New York: Ticknor & Fields, 1992), xiv, 26.
30. Diliberto, *Hadley*, 63, 171, 260.
31. Diliberto, *Hadley*, 107.
32. Hilary Justice, "Alias Grace: Music and the Feminine Aesthetic in Hemingway's Early Style," in *Hemingway and Women: Female Critics and the Female Voice*, ed. Lawence R. Broer and Gloria Holland (Tuscaloosa: University of Alabama Press, 2002), 222.
33. Sanford, *At the Hemingways*, 202-03.
34. Lynn, *Hemingway*, 550.
35. C. Howatson, ed., *Oxford Companion to Classical Literature*, 2nd ed. (New York: Oxford U P, 1989), s.v. "Achilles."
36. Hilary Justice, "The Lion, the Leopard, and the Bear," *Hemingway Review* 19.1 (Fall 1999): 39-42.
37. Wayne Koestenbaum, *The Queen's Throat: Opera, Homosexuality, and the Mystery of Desire* (New York: Poseidon Press, 1993), 66.
38. Koestenbaum, *Queen's Throat,* 183-84.
39. Koestenbaum, *Queen's Throat*, 199.
40. Koestenbaum, *Queen's Throat*, 28.
41. Koestenbaum, *Queen's Throat*, 33.
42. Koestenbaum, *Queen's Throat*, 221.
43. Koestenbaum, *Queen's Throat,* 156.
44. Howatson, "Achilles," 4.
45. Lynn, *Hemingway*, 38-42.
46. Edith Hamilton, *Mythology* (New York: New American Library, 1969), 182.

Music: Wallace Stevens' Supreme Fiction

1. Wallace Stevens, *Collected Poetry and Prose* (New York: Library of America, 1997), 662.
2. Eric Sellin, Valéry, Stevens, and the Cartesian Dilemma (Brockport: Dept. of Foreign Languages, State University College of New York, 1975)
3. Stevens, 665.
4. Ibid., 786.
5. George Santayana, "Music." *The Life of Reason* (New York: Prometheus Books, 1998), 318.
6. Stevens, 664.
7. Ibid., 786.
8. Ibid., 662.
9. Santayana, 316.
10. Stevens, 645.
11. Walter Pater, *The Renaissance: Studies in Art and Poetry* (Berkeley: U of California P, 1980), 188.
12. Stevens, 782.
13. Santayana, 319.

14. Michael Faherty, "Kandinsky at the Klavier: Stevens and the Musical Theory of Wasssily Kandinsky," *The Wallace Stevens Journal* 16, ii (Fall 1992): 153.
15. Ibid., 153.
16. Ibid., 154.
17. Stevens, 72.
18. Howard Needler, "On the Aesthetics of 'Peter Quince at the Clavier,'" *WS Journal* 18, i (Spring 1994): 52.
19. Kinereth Meyer and Sharon Baris, "Reading the Score of 'Peter Quince at the Clavier': Stevens, Music, and the Visual Arts," *WS Journal* 12, i (Spring 1988): 60.
20. Stevens, 72.
21. Ibid., 73.
22. Needler, 59.
23. Stevens, 74.
24. Needler, 59.
25. William Doreski, "Fictive Music: The Iridescent Notes of Wallace Stevens," *WS Journal* 20, I (Spring 1996): 58.
26. Wallace Stevens, *Letters of Wallace Stevens* (New York: Alfred A. Knopf, 1966), 251.
27. Stevens, *CPP*, 76.
28. Ibid., 75.
29. Ibid., 75.
30. Ibid., 58-59.
31. Faherty, 153.
32. Doreski, 52.
33. Stevens, *CPP*, 70-71.
34. Ibid., 71.
35. Ibid., 71.
36. Ibid., 105.
37. Barbara Holmes, *The Decomposer's Art: Ideas of Music in the Poetry of Wallace Stevens* (New York: Peter Lang, 1990), 65.
38. Stevens, *CPP*, 106.
39. Ibid., 662.
40. Holmes, 80.
41. Doreski, 62.
42. Stevens, *CPP*, 645.

Proust's Unstable Metaphors of Divinity: A Theology of Musical Aesthetics

1. Carl Dalhaus, *The Idea of Absolute Music* (Chicago: University of Chicago Press, 1989) 101.
2. Marcel Proust, *Remembrance of Things Past*, Vol. I-III (New York: Vintage Books, 1981) III. 899.
3. Samuel Beckett, *Proust* (New York: Grove Press, 1931) 71.

4. The two gods are demonstrated in the changing nature of Jacques Derrida's identification of God. Although he denies a true shift in his depiction of God, others have located in Derrida's early works a god of closure and in his later works a god that actually denies closure, one who encourages an opening up to the impossible/possible to come. His God of *Grammatology* is a logocentric God of the "book" who guarantees absolute knowledge. Derrida's God in later, however, is a God of secrets, interruption and instability. It is a God who is not "transcendent," but is the "name of a possibility" (The *Gift of Death* 108) and "absolute interruption" (*Religion* 64).
5. As art critic Robert Hughes puts it, "the view from the train was not the view from the horse. It compressed more motifs into the same time. Conversely, it left less time in which to dwell on any one thing." (12)
6. See Nattiez's *Proust as Musician*, 41-77, for a similar tracing of artistic and musical perception in the novel.
7. Dalhaus, 88.
8. Dalhaus, 86.
9. Dalhaus, 91-92.
10. George Painter, *Marcel Proust: A Biography* (New York: Random House, 1989) 246.
11. Although, as Eric Prieto correctly says, pointing to Wagner's *leitmotif* as a musical structure translated to literature is deceiving since it is essentially a literary device to begin with (16).
12. Eduard Hanslick, *The Beautiful in Music* (New York: Bobs-Merrill, 1957) 20.
13. The relationship of Schopenhauer to Proust has been noted as far back as Samuel Beckett's *Proust*, and is the subject of a whole chapter in Jean-Jacques Nattiez's *Proust as Musician.*
14. Dalhaus, 8-9. Although this debate was initially German, by the late 19th Century it had also entered French consciousness, and was influencing how they thought and wrote about music.
15. Dalhaus, 78.
16. Dalhaus, 80.
17. Dalhaus, 102.
18. Soren Kierkegaard. *Either/Or*. (New York: Harper and Row, 1986) 56.
19. Dalhaus, 115.
20. Beckett, 71.
21. Arnold Schoenberg. *Style and Idea: Selected Writings* (University of Chicago, 1975): 215.
22. Dahlhaus, 26.
23. Dalhaus, 31.
24. Leonard Meyer. *Emotion and Meaning in Music* (Chicago: University of Chicago, 1967) 33.
25. Meyer, 35.
26. Dahlhaus, 74.
27. Dahlhaus, 131.
28. Roland Barthes, *The Pleasure of the Text* (New York: Hill and Wang, 1975) 11.
29. Berthold Hoeckner, *Programming the Absolute: Nineteenth Century German Music and the Hermeneutics of the Moment* (Princeton: Princeton University Press, 2001) 3.

30. Swann, on the very edge of a transcendent experience, realizes that the "pleasure which the music gave him… was in fact akin at such moments to the pleasure which he would have derived from experimenting with perfumes, from entering into contact with a world for which we men were not made" (I.259).
31. Gilles, Deleuze. *Proust and Signs* (New York: George Braziller, 1972) 83.
32. Deleuze, 42.
33. Deleuze, 45.
34. Leo Treitler, "Language and the Interpretation of Music," *Music and Meaning* (Ithaca: Cornell University Press, 1997) 23-56.
35. Deleuze, 47.

Silent Music in James Joyce's Sirens

[1] James Joyce, *Ulysses*, edited by Declan Kilberd, Penguin, (London 1992):330.
2 Jules Law, 'Political Sirens', in K.J. Devlin and M.Reizbaun, ed., *Ulysses: An Engendered Perspective*, 150.
3. Ibid
4. *Ulysses* 329.
5. *Ulysses* 95.
6. *Ulysses* 330.
7. James Joyce, *Finnegan's Wake*, edited by Seamus Deane, Penguin, London, 628.
8. *Ulysses* 331.
9. *Ulysses* 87.
10. *Ulysses* 71.
11. *Ulysses* 368.
12. *Ulysses* 374.
13. *Ulysses* 336.
14. Bettina Klein, 'Traces of Homer: Between Sources and Models in Joyce's "Aeolus" and "Sirens", in Frances Ruggeri, ed., *Classic Joyce- Joyce Studies in Italy*, Vol.6, Bulozi, Roma, 1999, p.276.
15. *Dubliners* 211.
16. *Ulysses* 367.
17. *Ulysses* 357.
18. *Ulysses* 361.
19. Allan Hepburn, 'Ulysses, Opera. Loss,' in *JQQ*, vol.38, 1&2, 2000-2001, p.67.
20. Ibid p.67.
21. *Ulysses* 352.
22. *Ulysses* 362-63.
23. *Ulysses* 366.
24. Richard Ellmann, *The Consciousness of Joyce*, London: Faber and Faber, 1977.
25. Emmanuel Swedenborg, *Heaven and Hell*, Swedenborg Foundation, New York, p.84.
26. Ulysses 359.
27. James Joyce, Letters I, edited by Stuart Gilbert, London: Faber and Faber, I, 1957, p.128-29.
28. Richard Ellmann, Ulysses on the Liffrey, p.104.

29. A. Walton Litz, The Art of Joyce, London: Oxford University Press, 1961, p.70.
30. Ibid 73.
31. See Declan Kiberd, 'Theatre as Opera: The Gigli Concert' in Eamonn Jordan, ed. Theatre Stuff, Carlsfort Press, Dublin 2000, p.145.
32. Hepburn p. 64.
33. *Ulysses 3*54.
34. Hepburn p.63.
35. *Ulysses* 359.
36. *Ulysses* 48.
37. *Ulysses* 359.
38. John Senior, *The Way Down and Out*, New York: Greenwood Press, 1968, p.29.
39. Sheldon Brivic, 'The Mind Factory: Kabbalah in Finnegan's Wake' in *James Joyce Quarterly*, 21, 1: 1983, p.13.
40. *Ulysses* 359.
41. Gershom Sholem, *On the Kabbalah and its Symbolism*, New York: Schocken Books, 1965, p..I.
42. J.I. Cope, *Joyce's Cities*, Baltimore: Johns Hopkins University Press, p.70-81.
43. Sheldon Brivic, 'The Mind Factory: Kabbalah in Finegan's Wake", p.7.
44. Ibid, p.28.
45. James S. Atherton, *The Books at the Wake*, New York: Paul P. Appel Publisher, 1974, p.46.
46. Ibid p.47.
47. Ibid p.44.
48. Gershom Scholem, *On the Kabbalah and its Symbolism*, p. 56.
49. *Ulysses* 806.
50. J.I. Cope, 'Sirens' in Hart & Hayman, *James Joyce's Ulysses*, pp.236-37.
51. Ulysses 46. See also next chapter.
52. Gershom Scholem, p.35.
53. Ulysses p.274.
54. The third sephiroth also called the upper mother, is a demiurgic potency, an aspect of God, an almost feminine independent element within him.
55. See Gershom Scholem p.105.
56. For the importance of the sephiroth in the Wake, see Sheldon Brivic, "The Mind Factory: Kabbalah in Finnegan's Wake" pp.13-19; Roland McHugh, Annotatins to "Finnegan's Wake", New York: Harcourt, Brace, 1944, pp.171.
57. *Ulysses* 333.
58. *Ulysses* 369.
59. Carolyn G. Heilbrun, Towards Androgyny: Aspects of Male and Female in Literature, p.95.

T.S. Eliot's Ubiquitous Music

1. Alfred Appel, Jr. *Jazz Modernism: From Ellington and Armstrong to Matisse and Joyce*. (New York: Alfred A. Knopf, 2002) 13-14. Subsequent references to this edition will appear in the text.

2. David Chinitz, *T.S. Eliot and the Cultural Divide*. (Chicago: University of Chicago Press, 2003) 40.
3. For a classic example of a very different kind of involuntary listening, see Samuel Taylor Coleridge's "The Rime of the Ancient Mariner."
4. Lyndall Gordon, *T.S. Eliot: An Imperfect Life*. (New York: W.W. Norton and Company, 1998) 7.
5. David A. Jansen and Gene Jones. *That American Rag: The Story of Ragtime from Coast to Coast.* (New York: Schirmer Books, 2000) 1,5.
6. T.S. Eliot, Inventions of the March Hare: Poems 1909-1917 (New York: Harcourt Brace and Company, 1996) 64. Subsequent references to this edition appear in the text.
7. Robert Jourdain, *Music, the Brain, and Ecstacy: How Music Captures Our Imaginations*. (New York: William Morrow and Company, 1997) 32. Subsequent references to this edition will appear in the text.
8. Robert Crawford. *The Savage and the City in the Work of T.S. Eliot.* (Oxford: Clarendon Press, 1987) 53.
9. A.D. Moody, *Thomas Stearns Eliot: Poet*. (Cambridge: Cambridge University Press, 1979) 26.
10. T.S. Eliot, *The Waste Land and Other Poems*. (New York: Penguin Books, 1998) 11. Subsequent references to this edition appear in the text.
11. Simon Frith. "Towards an Aesthetic of Popular Music." *Music and Society: The Politics of Composition, Performance and Reception.* (Cambridge: Cambridge University Press, 1987) 143.
12. Reebee Garofalo, *Rocking Out: Popular Music in the USA*. (Boston: Allyn and Bacon, 1997) 22.
13. William Howland Kenny, *Recorded Music in American Life: The Phonograph and Popular Memory, 1890-1945*. (Oxford: Oxford University Press, 1999) xii.
14. John Dos Passos, *Manhatten Transfer* (New York: Mariner Books, 2000) 166.
15. Walter Benjamin, "The Work of Art in the Age of Mechanical Reproduction." *Illuminations*. (New York: Schocken Books, 1968) 221. Subsequent references will appear in the text.
16. John T. Mayer, "The Waste Land and Eliot's Poetry Notebook." *T.S. Eliot: The Modernist in History*. (Cambridge: Cambridge University Press, 1991) 71.
17. T.S. Eliot, *The Waste Land*. (New York: W.W. Norton and Company, 2001) 9. Subsequent references to this edition appear in the text.
18. Friedrich A. Kittler, *Gramaphone, Film, Typewriter* (Stanford: Stanford University Press, 1999) 36. Subsequent references to this edition appear in the text.
19. Martin Schofield, *T.S. Eliot: The Poems*. (Cambridge: Cambridge University Press, 1988) 117.
20. Calvin Bedient, *He Do the Police In Different Voices: The Wasteland and Its Protagonist* (Chicago: University of Chicago Press, 1986) 138. Subsequent references to this edition appear in the text.
21. T.S. Eliot, *The Waste Land: A Facsimile and Transcript of the Orginal Drafts Including the Annotations of Ezra Pound.* (New York: Harcourt Brace Jovanovich, 1971) 5.

22. Michael North, *The Dialect of Modernism: Race, Language, and Twentieth Century Literature*. (Oxford: Oxford University Press, 1994) 87.
23. "The Sound Laser." *Esquire*. (December 2003): 165.

The Beatles as Modernists

1. Mann's allusion to Mahler coheres rather appropriately with the Beatles' sustained textual analyses of nostalgia. As Michalis Lapidakis observes, Mahler's modernism connotes a certain "quality of nostalgia that provides his music with [its] characteristic tragic tone" and its "paradigmatic manifestation of musical pluralism."
2. In one of the more incredible arguments regarding the Beatles' alleged postmodernity, Julia Stephens reads "the singing of 'Yellow Submarine' (the song itself being a fairly impenetrable collage) as a rudimentary postmodern moment, signaling the demise of a certain kind of political memory where, to use Jameson's words: 'the past as referent finds itself gradually bracketed, and then effaced altogether.'" Her analysis belies, of course, the unabashed sincerity of the recording and its songwriters' genuine belief in an immutable past. Henry W. Sullivan illustrates the Beatles' ostensible postmodernism with even broader strokes, describing all of their albums as veritable "postmodern classics."
3. Although *Let It Be* was the final studio album released by the Beatles, it was actually recorded before *Abbey Road*, which was released in September 1969.
4. Zanes further asserts that "there is a very real connection between a rock cultural desire for authenticity and rock culture's fertility as a soil for traditional values, including romantic notions of artistic genius, gender norms, a nostalgic longing that is often aimed at a mythic past (a past not unrelated to the traditional family values espoused in mainstream political rhetorics), and so forth" (67). Even more significantly, Zanes argues against the intelligentsia's knee-jerk reaction to nostalgia as a balm for the masses: "I believe that denigrating nostalgic tendencies without assessing the character of those nostalgias is a mistake, primarily because nostalgia might be the most powerful political tool of our time, one worth considering as potentially oppositional rather than simply conservative" (69).
5. "Yes It Is" clearly exists as one of the Beatles' more mature pre-1966 compositions about nostalgia's potency. Alan W. Pollack praises the song for the "manner in which the tyrannical, debilitating power of . . . memory is contrasted with the simple, mundane objects and sensations of life which are capable of triggering such hot flashes."
6. Ironically, the French national anthem's lyrics—while certainly nostalgic in their own right—revel in bloody images of war and carnage: "*Entendez-vous, dans la compagnes / Mugir ces farouches soldats? / Ils viennent jusque dans nos bras / Egorger vos fils, vos compagnes* [Do you hear in the countryside / The roar of these savage soldiers? / They come right into our arms / To cut the throats of your sons, your country]." Rather fittingly, the anthem was originally entitled "*Chant de guerre de l'armeé du Rhin* [War Song of the Army of the Rhine]," which certainly connotes the song's militaristic roots. Interestingly, Pollack contends that Martin's arrangement "intentionally misquoted" the anthem in an effort both to reference "La Marseillaise" and to subvert its power as an enduring cultural cliché.

7. "In My Life" represents one of the band's most complicated instances of writerly dispute. As Lennon remembers, "It was, I think, my first real major piece of work. Up till then it had all been sort of glib and throwaway. And that was the first time I consciously put my literary part of myself into the lyric." The testimony would seem to be in favor of Lennon, who recalls that "the whole lyrics were already written before Paul even heard it. In 'In My Life,'" he adds, "[Paul's] contribution melodically was the harmony and the middle-eight itself" (*All We Are Saying* 178-79, 193, 153). Conversely, McCartney remembers a writing session in which Lennon had already completed the song's opening stanzas: "But as I recall, he didn't have a tune to it." McCartney supposedly devoted half an hour to composing the song's musical structure in its entirety: "I recall writing the whole melody. And it actually does sound very like me, if you analyze it. I was obviously working to lyrics. The melody's structure is very me" (qtd. in Miles 277).
8. With the exception of their impromptu rooftop performance in London on 30 January 1969, the Beatles held their last concert—a 33-minute affair at San Francisco's Candlestick Park—on 29 August 1966. After more than 1,400 appearances since the late 1950s, they were understandably exhausted from the grueling life of a working rock-and-roll band. At the conclusion of the band's rooftop performance, Lennon famously remarks that "I'd like to say 'thank you' on behalf of the group and ourselves, and I hope we passed the audition!" In addition to underscoring the Beatles' self-consciousness about the portentous events of 1969, Lennon's comment demonstrates their larger understanding of life's inherently fleeting nature.
9. McCartney's nostalgic contentment in "Mother Nature's Son" is brought into bold relief on the *Grey Album* (2003), DJ Danger Mouse's controversial mergence of the Beatles' *White Album* with Jay-Z's hip-hop *Black Album* (2003). In spite of its notorious (and, quite frankly, illegal) origins, Danger Mouse's revisioning of "Mother Nature's Son" makes for one of the *Grey Album*'s finest tracks. By combining McCartney's sanguine acoustic guitar in "Mother Nature's Son" with Jay-Z's heartbreaking lyrics in "December 4th" about growing up in a world fraught with poverty and drugs, Danger Mouse succeeds in brilliantly contrasting McCartney's idyllic childhood memories with Jay-Z's difficult youth—especially in terms of the hip-hop star's disquieting relationship with his mother, Gloria Carter, whose strained memories are featured in a moving pair of narrative interludes. Danger Mouse's coalescence of "Mother Nature's Son" and "December 4th" posits an implicit commentary about the starkly divergent sociohistorical experiences among various segments of white and black culture, as well as a meaningful analysis of the ways in which we think and feel about the past.
10. Interestingly, in "Revolution 1," Lennon teeters between revolutionary and antirevolutionary stances: "I put in both because I wasn't sure," he later remarked (qtd. in *Anthology* 298). In the more up-tempo, raucous version of the song (entitled simply "Revolution" and released as the B-side of "Hey Jude"), Lennon abandons his militant extremism, thus embracing the peace movement's pacifist outlook.
11. All four Beatles assembled for the last time on 22 August 1969 for a photo session at Lennon's Titenhurst Park mansion.
12. In recent years, works of popular music that evince symphonic or classical aspirations like the Beatles' *Abbey Road* medley have come to be referred to as "poperas."

13. Interestingly, Fredric Jameson interprets the Beatles and the Rolling Stones as the "high-modernist moment" of punk and new wave rock. In the same breath, he locates the Beatles somewhere just beyond modernism's steady decline, yet nevertheless appears to acknowledge their incongruity with postmodernism's "inverted millenarianism" (1).
14. I am indebted to Sheila Hardie for this translation. See <www.proz.com> for additional details.